Boundary Spanning

Boundary Spanning

An Ecological Reinterpretation
of Social Work Practice
in Health and Mental Health Systems

Toba Schwaber Kerson

COLUMBIA UNIVERSITY PRESS
New York

Columbia University Press
Publishers Since 1893
New York   Chichester, West Sussex
Copyright © 2002 Columbia University Press
All rights reserved
Library of Congress Cataloging-in-Publication Data

Kerson, Toba Schwaber.
    Boundary spanning: an ecological reinterpretation of social
work practice in health and mental health systems / Toba
Schwaber Kerson.
        p. cm.
    Includes bibliographical references and index.
    ISBN 0-231-11036-7 (cloth : alk. paper)
        1. Medical social work. 2. Psychiatric social work. I. Title.

HV687 .K47 2002
362.1'0425—dc21

                                                    2001037128
∞
Columbia University Press books are printed on permanent
and durable acid-free paper.
Printed in the United States of America
c 10 9 8 7 6 5 4 3 2 1

Contents

Figures

Tables

Preface

The purpose of *Boundary Spanning: An Ecological Reinterpretation* of *Social Work Practice in Health and Mental Health Systems* is to provide a framework and sufficient information to enable social workers to work efficaciously for and with people with health and mental health problems. In this book, physical and mental health are viewed as parts of a global definition of health that is consonant with a contemporary understanding of the etiology and symptomatology of illness (Mordacci and Sobel 1998). The traditionally separate classifications of illnesses as mental or physical cannot be sustained in view of present-day knowledge (Gur et al. 2000). Many illnesses that are considered mental illnesses, such as schizophrenia and serious depression, have critical biological dimensions (Keefe and Harvey 1994), and many that are classified as physical illnesses, such as multiple sclerosis, certain kinds of cancer, and stroke, can effect cognitive ability, mood, and affect. In the fourth edition of its *Diagnostic and Statistical Manual of Mental Disorders,* the American Psychiatric Association (1994) includes criteria for mental disorders associated with a general medical condition (Munson 2000), and a growing body of work focuses on psychological problems that mask medical disorders (Morrison 1997).

The World Health Organization (WHO) (2001) defines health as "a state of complete physical, mental, and social well-being and not merely the absence of disease or infirmity." Among the specific health problems that

WHO wishes to prevent and control are vaccine-preventable diseases, sexually transmitted diseases, new and reemerging infectious diseases, and mental health problems. Because societal responses often lag behind the growth of scientific knowledge, funding sources and systems of care have been slow to act on global definitions of health. Thus funding sources and systems for the care of physical and mental health problems continue to be separate, in spite of scientific knowledge that would move them in the direction of a more global definition.

Boundary Spanning begins by exploring the elements of context that profoundly shape social work practice: (1) a clearly articulated and dynamic ecological perspective, (2) some important forces and themes in the history of the field, (3) explanations of the ethical and legal issues that have shaped and continue to shape the work, and (4) an understanding of the organizations and systems in which health care and mental health care are provided. Contextual understanding empowers the practitioner in at least two ways. First, it provides a frame for understanding the present and planning for the future. Second, it demonstrates that little in life is immutable and that change occurs over time. Understanding history and context allows social workers to remain optimistic for their clients, their programs, their communities, their profession, and even themselves.

Along with such knowledge and understanding, social workers in health and mental health require tools to intervene on several levels of practice to help their constituencies manage problems (Kerson 1997). Critical here is the relationship between social workers and clients/programs/communities that supports and enhances the work. Using their relationship skills, social workers assess need and capacity. They utilize the planning dimensions of intervention, specific forms of planning, contracting, setting goals and objectives, strategizing, and teamwork. They intervene directly, choosing among a panoply of skills, including case management; brief, solution-focused work; and group work. In all cases, social workers evaluate their work.

This work is based on the following assumptions about contemporary social work practice in health and mental health care. Health care has two fundamental objectives: to restore people to the best level of functioning and well-being that they can possibly achieve and to prevent disability. "Preventing disability is an outcomes orientation. Functioning, what people are able to do and how they feel, directly leads us to the consumer or patient to assess these variants" (Ware 1997:45). To a great degree, practice is shaped by context (Kerson 1997). Professional, systems, and funding boundaries are in flux (Alter and Hage 1993). Systems are increasingly complex and multifaceted, with new forms of ownership (O'Brien 1991). Health care is being delivered through nontraditional funding streams, structures, and organizations. Such changes in the delivery and funding of health care mean that social workers must increase their understanding of and ability to work in complex organizations and systems in order to help their clients. Effective social work practice requires increased flexibility of role and place within and between systems with the ability to work in social work and multidisciplinary teams (Abramson 1993). The relationship between the social worker and the client/program/community system remains the primary vehicle for enhancing the work of the client. To best advance the work, social workers must command a wide array of assessment skills, intervention strategies, and evaluation techniques, including outcome measures. Social work interventions influence clients' abilities to reach their objectives. In these times, it is essential that social workers continue to be critical players in health care teams and that they be able to articulate their contributions.

THE CONTRIBUTIONS OF *BOUNDARY SPANNING*

Boundary Spanning makes several contributions to the literature. First, it provides information and tools that enable social work practitioners in health and mental health care to help clients/consumers, programs, organizations, and communities. Second, it does not separate health from mental health but sees both categories as artificially separated, constructed parts of a more realistically understood whole. Third, it draws the notion of health setting very broadly to include all health-related social work activity. Thus health settings are hospitals and home care agencies, as well as schools, family agencies, day care centers, community outreach services, and state offices for occupational and environmental safety. Fourth, this book includes business management theory and research as salient and necessary dimensions of the social work knowledge base. And finally, it incorporates a range of mapping devices, or graphic representations, that are drawn from business and organizational development as well as social work. These mapping devices are meant to inform assessment, strategy, intervention, and evaluation activities.

Given the nature of social work practice in health and mental health care, many of the topics in this book resemble those in other practice books. The purpose of any such book is to lay out a set of assumptions and then proceed to describe how to assess and intervene to help client systems reach their goals and, finally, how to evaluate the effectiveness of interventions. This book differs from other practice books in a number of significant ways. First, to enable social workers to work with varied client systems, this book draws from a broad range of social work literature, including clinical, community, organization, planning, and advocacy, as well as social science, medicine, administration, business, management, and organizational dynamics.

Second, this book uses case examples in uncommon ways. Early in each chapter readers will find a long example, a rich slice of practice that should resound and reverberate and add meaning and relevance to the ideas and directions presented in the chapter. Even those chapters directed toward understanding laws or systems have examples that demonstrate their relevance to practice. Although details have been altered to protect confidentiality, all the examples are drawn from actual experiences. In fact, I began work on this book by asking practitioners to contribute interesting, perplexing examples from their work. Because the stories are taken from real life, and because social work practice is difficult, the examples are meant to foster thoughtful discussion about interventions, ethical behavior, and many issues of diversity, including racial, gender, sexual orientation, religious, and class differences. Each chapter includes at least one long example and many shorter ones that encourage critical thinking.

Third, an overarching focus of this book is enhancement of the social worker's abilities to think critically and make decisions (Kerson 1997; Murdach 1995). Critical thinking involves skillful judgment in relation to truth and merit. Often, old ideas, values, and beliefs that one brings to a situation act as barriers to critical thinking. Such barriers are then sustained or eroded in the process of social interaction and feedback (Nurius, Kemp, and Gibson 1999).

Self-awareness—understanding the values, prejudices, and judgments that one brings to one's work—plays a major part in dismantling barriers to critical thinking. Self-understanding is a process social workers attend to for all their professional lives. The ways one acts when feeling stress, when dealing with populations different from one's own, or when encountering unpredictable outcomes are usually learned very early and often remain unquestioned. Even awareness of how one was taught by one's family to communicate about illness with family members and strangers is a critical factor in self-understanding. One's belief systems about the causes of illness and symptoms have to be explored and understood. It is helpful to think of the misconceptions that one's grandparents or great-grandparents held about the causes of illnesses such as epilepsy and tuberculosis. It is easy to laugh about their ignorance until one realizes how recently society was ignorant about the ways people could "catch" AIDS. When those of us who are in our fifties and sixties went to graduate school in the 1960s, we were taught that there were schizophrenogenic mothers, who, with other significant stressors, could cause schizophrenia in their children. The present-day understanding of schizophrenia has no such explanation, but such information, learned as the dominant explanatory paradigm, affects self-understanding, critical thinking, and decision-making abilities.

A setting that supports learning and empowerment allows all participants in the work to raise questions about what are considered objective facts in a situation, as well as the motives or reasons that support the facts (Argyris 1994). Dynamic social workers consider all possible options in all phases of the work, evaluate the options, and work actively with the client, program, or community to make practice decisions and enhance the work. This requires that the social worker be open and able to intelligently process information. Helping to expand options requires depth and breadth of knowledge, the ability to intervene in multiple ways, and the ability to help determine priorities and make decisions with vision and optimism. To do so requires relating goals to context, examining options in that light, strategizing, and being able to evaluate what has occurred.

Fourth, this book differs from other practice books in its use of graphic representations, or mapping devices, drawn from social work and business management to help students visualize their work with greater scope and over time, including genograms, ecomaps, linkage and network maps, organizational charts, timelines, strategic planning maps, balanced and personal scorecards, organigraphs, and driving force maps. Mapping devices are iterative, visual tools that can be used to understand many phenomena that are important to social workers in health and mental health care. In these devices, edges and boundaries remain both the key and the problem because they are artificial. The lines, circles, and arrows help organize one's thinking and foster some feeling of control, but in reality the divisions suggested are mutable, blurred, and transfusable. As with other dimensions of this book, these heuristic devices are taken from social work, organizational dynamics, business management, and strategic planning (Burkhart and Reuss 1993; McGoldrick and Gerson 1985; Meyer 1993; Mintzberg and Quinn 1991).

> Although mapping is more a learned art than a rigid methodology, the (work) group's task is the same as that of any scientist attempting to develop a theory or model to make sense of complex phenomena. Many scientists work inductively by carefully observing phenomena and then questioning why something appears one way in certain circumstances and a very different way in others. The scientist will develop an explanatory theory about his or her observations and then will test the model in a variety of different circumstances to strengthen or disprove the hypothesis. (Christensen 1997:144)

Such devices are helpful in several ways. First, visualizing what are often complex sets of relationships and activities gives viewers a broader scope, and that scope allows viewers to deepen their understanding and to choose points and methods of intervention. Second, mapping devices allow viewers to see elements tightly enough to give them some sense of control and can free them from the tyranny of measurement and numbers. In this regard, mapping devices can help social workers to concentrate on conceptual work, and then to collect data necessary to the analysis (Christensen 1997). A third benefit is that mapping devices require that assumptions be made explicit through diagrams, thus enabling team members to achieve consensus more easily. They facilitate reaching agreement or contracting about how to view systems in context. Additionally, they provide ways to intensify moments in helping relationships by creating a concrete focus of attention. In sum, such devices help social workers to assess, plan, make concrete, monitor, and compare.

When well devised, these graphic representations follow the design strategy of the smallest effective difference: make all visual distinctions as subtle as possible, though still clear and effective (Tufte 1997:73). Using mapping devices allows multiple parallel images to become transparent, powerful methods of enforcing visual comparison. "Parallelism connects visual elements. Connections are built among images by position, orientation, overlap, synchronization, and similarities in content" (Tufte 1997:82). In addition, legends on maps, labels, and codes, as well as captions are, in part, representations of the image itself, occurring in parallel with the image.

For example, figures P.1 and P.2 have been used at very different times

FIGURE P.1. Model of case coordination (Richmond 1901).

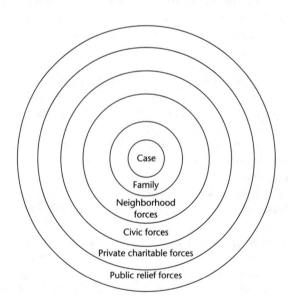

FIGURE P.2. Systems and target problems (Garbarino 1982, in Tolson, Reid, and Garvin 1994).

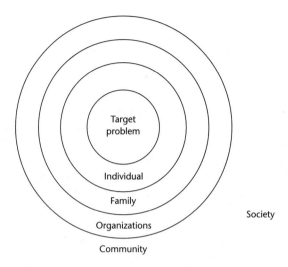

in the history of the profession to help social workers visualize the work. They are introduced here for three reasons: (1) to demonstrate that many social workers have been grappling with an ecological perspective and trying to understand and explain the relationship between factors in the environment and the life of the individual since the very beginnings of the profession; (2) to demonstrate that these environmental factors have been quite consistent over many years; and (3) to demonstrate that even these simple graphic representations help the viewer to see and begin to understand grand, complicated concepts and what is known about the relationships among those concepts.

Figure P.1 shows Mary Richmond's model of case coordination, in which the case is in the center and the five concentric circles illustrate ever-larger levels of forces impinging on the case. In figure P.2, the mapping device is so similar to the one shown in figure P.1 that the two can be seen in parallel and compared, although they were devised almost a century apart.

What Richmond (1901) calls the case, Garbarino (1982) calls the target problem. What Richmond calls forces, Garbarino refers to as systems. In this way, Garbarino, as well as Tolson, Reid, and Garvin (1994), reflect the influence of ecological systems theory. With the benefit of ecological systems theory, the creators of figure P.2 refer to systems, whereas Richmond referred to forces. Their systems, also illustrated through ever-larger concentric circles, are family, organization, and community. Outside the circles sits society, which has no boundaries. The health and mental health systems addressed in this book would be located in Richmond's circles of private charitable and public relief forces and in Garbarino's organizations and community circles. The attention given to these foci in chapters 3 and 4 reflects the importance of the understanding of organizations and their mandates in this ecological reinterpretation.

As Tolson, Reid, and Garvin (1994:6) suggest, "The fundamental assumption in ecological systems theory is that systems are mutually interacting and the nature of this interaction at least partially explains a variety of phenomena, including the existence of problems, the nature of behavior, and the course of human development. The diagram is similar to those commonly used to analyze human situations within this perspective. Typically, the individual is nested in the center of the concentric circles, however, rather than the problem. [Tolson, Reid, and Garvin] have placed the problem at the center because it is the target of change in [their] approach to practice."

Such techniques are used to (1) locate and follow the social worker in his or her working system, (2) locate and follow the client system, (3) visualize the networks of services for client systems, (4) provide timelines with clear tasks and responsibilities, (5) understand organizations and systems, and (6) engage in strategic planning. Mapping devices are used throughout this book to help the reader understand organizations and systems, plan and strategize, assess clients and communities, intervene appropriately, and, evaluate the work.

Finally, this book refocuses the ecological perspective, highlighting the legal and ethical dimensions of practice as well as the need for social workers in health and mental health to become expert in organizational systems and principles of management. Because of many changes in the context of social work practice, social workers must learn to advocate effectively for their clients no matter what level of intervention or modality they practice. Increased attention to legal and ethical dimensions of practice and to understanding organizations will inform social workers as advocates. This ecological reinterpretation can be best understood as a boundary-spanning approach to social work practice. It spans the boundaries of health and mental health, knowledge bases of social work, social science, science and medicine, law, and business management. In addition, it spans practice with individuals, families and groups, case management, program management, and community work. Boundary spanning allows social workers to understand and intervene with and for clients/patients/consumers in all the dimensions of context that affect their work in reaching their goals.

ACKNOWLEDGMENTS

This book would be flat and dry without the practice examples used throughout each chapter. They set the tone for the book and were collected primarily before the book was written. The following expert practitioners contributed practice examples. I hope that I have not forgotten anyone. Special thanks go to Sherri Alper, Susan Balis, Rosemary Barbera, Joretha Bourjolly, Yvette Bradford, Thomas Cain, Joanne Chimchirian, Linda Conroy, Genevieve Coyle, Frank Daloisio, Susan Dawson, Elisabeth Doolan, Marilyn Drukin, Wendy Emerson, Karen Erlichman, Darlene Furey, Randi Gallo, Danielle Hammer, Lyne Harmon, Nancy Harper, Winifred Hope, Melissa Huber, Lisa Janoff, Celeste Johnson, Cathy May Kalinowski, Angela Keane, Jennifer Keller, Aura Kuperberg, Jenifer Lamken, Linda Millison, Christine Moody, Mary O'Neill, Lisa Pearson, Rebecca Polss, Karen Raven, Joseph Rivers III, Nancy Rocereto, Rhonda Rhone, Kathleen Rounds, Bernadette Ryan, Pat Schang, Wendy Schmid, Carol Shapiro, Kim Sheehan, Leta Shubin, Susan Spencer, Deborah Steinman, Jan Taksa, Joan Tannebaum, Carolyn Weiss, Joan O. Weiss, Naomi Wilansky, Lucy Woodman, Jane Wright, Bonnie Zettick, and Sylvia Ziserman.

I would also like to acknowledge my debt to Carel Germain. Her willingness to take on the ecological perspective and to work with it for so long with many other fine social work educators was an enormous contribution to all of us who follow. Germain was a remarkably generous colleague who was willing to spend time reviewing materials and acting as an advocate in large, highly bureaucratized organizations where many are faceless. Although I never met her, I was one of the many younger academics who benefited from those selfless actions. So whatever good place this finds her in, I thank her for her contributions to my work in general and this book in particular.

This manuscript would have been part of my life every day for even more years if I had not had the extraordinary good fortune to have Judith L. M. McCoyd join me as chief research assistant and coauthor of chapter 5, "The Power of the Relationship Between the Social Worker and the Client System." I envision for her an extraordinary and delightful career in the academy and look forward to watching her ascendancy. She is a star.

Special thanks go as well to Ruth W. Mayden, dean of the Graduate School of Social Work and Social Research at Bryn Mawr College, who has helped my scholarly efforts as she could and has never said to me, "When is that book going to be finished?" Finally, just one more time, I thank Larry, who loves a lot, and Jennie, who sparkles plenty, for their continued support.

Boundary Spanning

Introduction: Boundaries and Barriers

A boundary (a line, a point, or a plane) indicates or fixes a limit, an edge, an extent, or a barrier. To span is to form an arch over, to extend over or across. Thus a boundary-spanning approach to health-related social work extends over previously drawn barriers in order to afford social workers a greater scope of understanding, greater latitude in interventions, and greater access to organizations and systems. This book was written because I believe that boundary spanning in all these areas is critical to social workers' abilities to help their clients/patients/ consumers to reach their goals.

During its century of experience, social work practice in health and mental health has defined itself by or has been defined by many boundaries. At times, the borders have been drawn for the participants; at other times, the limits have been formulated by the participants themselves. Such parameters have sometimes interfered with social workers' ability to understand or intervene in the most helpful ways. Over time, even when social workers have drawn the boundaries themselves, they have found the parameters too restrictive. In response, social workers have had to find means to break down barriers, to do the practice equivalent of locating stronger or broader scopes, opening gates, knocking down walls, or pressing for more latitude. This ecological reinterpretation addresses and redefines several extant boundaries, and this reinterpretation asserts that boundaries have to be spanned in ways that are less limiting.

The first boundary that must be spanned is the one that separates health care from mental health care. New knowledge about the etiology, symptomatology, and treatment of a range of illnesses indicates that the dichotomy between physical health and mental health is false. While scientific and medical knowledge do not support this split, social responses, including administrative structures and funding streams, continue as if physical health and mental health were separate entities.

The second boundary area that must be redefined is the setting of health-related social work, which really began out on the streets in public health enterprises. Then it moved primarily within the walls of university-affiliated teaching hospitals and, in those early days, was allowed to work only with indigent patients. As psychiatry and psychoanalysis developed, social work established new boundaries in terms of setting and discipline, with psychiatric social work splitting off from medical social work. There was a time following that split when social workers set and allowed to be set for them parameters related to the levels of consciousness on which they could work. While psychiatrists could work on all levels, social workers could work only on the conscious and preconscious levels, never the unconscious level. At that time, many social workers worked one-on-one with their clients in fifty-minute increments, thus again setting tight parameters for their work.

A third boundary area exists between levels of practice or practice modalities. For many years, boundaries were drawn between modalities, with social workers calling themselves caseworkers, group workers, or community organizers. There were courses in schools of social work called "Group Work for Caseworkers" and "Community Organizing for Group Workers," but even within such courses, the lines were clear. They could sometimes be stepped over, but the primary definition of the work was the tightly drawn modality. Now boundaries are drawn between those who are direct practitioners, those who do program development, and those who work in the policy arena. Those are equally limiting barriers that must be spanned.

Other boundaries were drawn through determining what kinds of knowledge bases could inform social work in health and mental health. The field has embraced, rejected, or debated various aspects of psychology, biology, sociology, economics, and political science, but sometimes has difficulty absorbing important knowledge that comes from sources not thought to reflect social work's value base. In the past, feuds erupted about the knowledge base for social work, such as that between the diagnostic and functional schools, or various schools of community action or group work. In the current managed care environment, the field has been loath to embrace the aspects of business management that might be very helpful to the social work enterprise. Many of these debates continue.

This book presents many opportunities and venues for health-related social workers to span the boundaries that limit their work. For example, understanding the legislation that protects and entitles particular client/patient/consumer populations will enable social workers to help clients use all the entitlements and protections available to them through state and federal government as well as the courts. More boundary-spanning opportunities are afforded by exploring and becoming comfortable with a range of ethical issues that are part of the work; using similar relationship skills for working with clients, colleagues, and those from all related systems; implementing a broad range of assessment techniques that involve decisions about the capacities of individuals, programs, organizations, and communities; understanding the nature and functions of organizations and systems using material developed in organizational and business management contexts; being able to work in several modalities; and knowing and applying several kinds and levels of evaluation. Included in each of these areas are mapping devices drawn from social work and business that enable social workers to clarify relationships between systems and inform action. Boundary-spanning practice examples gathered from experienced and expert practitioners shape the book. Chapters and sections of chapters begin with examples that were elicited before the book was written. All told, the purpose of the *Boundary Spanning* is to enable social workers to span outmoded barriers to work as deeply and broadly as possible to help their clients reach their goals.

THE CONTENT AND STRUCTURE OF THE BOOK

Boundary Spanning assumes that to fulfill the purpose of social work, social workers must have a depth and range of knowledge that enables them to work using an ecological perspective. The content and structure of this book support that assumption. To practice in this way means that social workers must understand the forces that have shaped the profession and the laws and ethical issues that are important to the profession. In addition, social workers must possess the ability to understand systems and organizations; a deep understanding of themselves; excellent relationship skills; the ability to plan, contract, and strategize on many levels; a capacity to intervene as advocates, using case management, group, and brief work skills; and the ability to evaluate their work and their clients' progress.

Content of Individual Chapters

Chapter 2 reviews and revalues the ecological perspective for social work practice and discusses the forces that have shaped contemporary social work practice in health and mental health care. Also included is a brief history of social work practice in health and mental health care, as well as a description of the impact of specific federal policies related to health and mental health care.

Chapter 3 reviews the meaning and purpose of law and ethics and describes many of the federal laws and legal issues that affect social work's clients and communities. Both laws and ethics are discussed in relation to the dynamics and consequences of social and economic injustice, including all forms of human oppression and discrimination. Chapter 3 also reviews the place, meaning, and importance of professional codes of ethics, with special emphasis on the National Association of Social Workers *Code of Ethics*. Related to these codes is a discussion of respect for and acceptance of the unique characteristics of diverse populations. Concepts, literature, and examples related to ethical dilemmas are included. Examples of ethical decisions in which social workers might be involved include allocating limited health care resources, beginning or ending aggressive treatment, return to home or nursing home, and clashes between patient, family, and institutional interests.

Specific concepts such as self-determination, social justice, personal values, the dignity and worth of all people, competence, and social workers' responsibility for their own ethical conduct and the quality of their practice are reviewed. The importance of understanding the law in relation to a particular clientele is presented, including laws that "entitle" and laws that "restrict." Among the legal issues presented are guardianship, advance directives, durable power of attorney, confidentiality/privacy, authority to practice, licensure, and informed consent. Although this chapter may seem complex, and may be better understood when students have more experience and knowledge, it carries dimensions of context that must be understood on some level before beginning any practice. Many of the concepts introduced in this chapter are used in the chapters that follow.

I recommend that chapters 2 and 3 be reread when the reader has finished the book. This second reading will bring the reader back to the context of practice and the circularity of this ecological interpretation, and it will allow for a deeper understanding in the context of greater experience and knowledge.

Chapter 4 enables the reader to understand organizations, and linkages and communication between organizations. This knowledge allows social workers to move more freely, build professional and interdisciplinary networks, understand patterns of authority and responsibility, and make organizations more responsive to direct and indirect client systems. It reflects an ecological perspective because it assumes a constant interplay between the individual and the environment. Covered here are issues related to location, access, authority, and change. Issues and dynamics such as interdisciplinary turf conflicts, racial bias and harassment, and ethnic and racial differences are discussed. Discussions of teamwork and of interdisciplinary, intra-, and interagency work are also included in this chapter. Social workers' roles in diverse settings such as hospitals, rehabilitation programs, neighborhood health centers, mental health centers, prisons, long-term care settings, schools, and self-help groups are examined.

An overarching theme is that, although the settings where the work occurs may change, the critical importance of the work and the very high levels of knowledge and skill that social work requires will not. For example, because ill people are now hospitalized for as short a time as possible, work that used to occur in a hospital setting may now have to take place in a rehabilitation center, a nursing home, a senior center, or the client's home. The chapter draws from social work administration, community and organizational development, and business literature.

The basic premise of chapter 5 is the essential utility of relationship as a conduit for effecting change for the client system in direct and indirect practice. Although both the context and strategies of the social worker in health care have become more extensive over the decades, the importance of the relationship between social worker and client system remains constant. No matter how large the unit of attention—whether it is a community, a large organization, a family, or an individual—the accomplishment of goals depends on the social worker's relationship abilities with individuals as clients or with individuals who represent larger client systems or health care organizations. Communication skills remain critical. The ability of social workers to understand the psychological nuances of relationship and to carry themselves differently in the relationship depending on the needs of the client system and the goals of the service are critical to this endeavor. Therefore, traditional social work concepts such as self-awareness, conscious-use-of-self, helping alliance, and the overall capacity to develop and sustain relationships are explored. The chapter describes the overarching tasks of the relationship: acting as a conduit or catalyst for helping the client to reach goals, carrying hope, lending a vision, and intervening in varied ways depending on the capacities and needs of the client system, the needs of other systems with whom social workers may be working, and the tasks necessary to meet needs and objectives. The notion of boundary spanning is essential to social workers' building and maintaining such relationships.

Chapter 6 involves making judgments about capacities, needs, and goals. Direct and indirect practice concerns gathering information, making judgments and decisions, and acting on those judgments. The relationship of assessment to the development of goals, objectives, and outcome measures is discussed, underscoring the increasing importance of outcome measures for evaluation and continued support of individual client systems and programs. Every attempt is made in this and the following chapters for practice to be empirically based, that is, closely linked to the products and processes of research. Also underscored is the importance of differentiating between short- and long-term goals so that social worker and client systems are aware of the relationships between their activity, the goals they are working to reach together, and the goals the client system will continue to address over time.

Chapter 6 answers the following questions related to assessment:

1. Who makes up the client system? Am I being sensitive to, and understanding of, the ethnicity, race, religion, gender, sexual orientation, and age within the client system? Am I knowledgeable about the ethical issues involved in care for this client?
2. What are the ecological boundaries that must be drawn to make sense of the situation? What are the probable parameters based on access, proximity, entitlement, and need that help the social worker to draw ecological boundaries?
3. What range of services should be viewed as possible in this situation, especially in relation to the needs and capacities of the client system?
4. What are the goals of the client seeking help? Are they realistic in the face of capacities and access?
5. Are objectives drawn ahead of time by an organization, law, or funding source?
6. What tools are available for assessment? Examples of tools such as Mini Mental Status exams, Activities of Daily Living scales, Functional Status, and Community Assessments are provided, and their appropriate uses are discussed.
7. Is the bio-psycho-social assessment sufficient to help client systems to develop strategies to reach their goals?

Chapter 7 describes and examines the planning process; determination of goals and objectives; uses and varieties of contracts in social work practice in health and mental health; the place, uses, and importance of strategizing; and the overarching importance of teamwork in all of social work practice. Typically, strategies are an amalgam of professional, family and other social supports, governmental, voluntary, self-help, relational, informational, and in-kind interventions. These may not occur at the same time or be carried out by one social worker, but the social worker is part of a large network of helpers moving in and out of work with the client system over time. Particular attention is paid to the relationship between self-help and professional help, as well as to interdisciplinary teamwork.

Chapter 8 covers social work practice interventions. In this chapter, advocacy is seen as an intervention in its own right, as well as part of all other interventions. Universal strategy issues are examined: the place of relationship techniques in all interventions, problem solving, the ability to partialize (to break problems down into their component parts), giving advice, the place of insight-interpretation-reflection, the use of questions designed to refocus the work (Are we working? What are we working on?), issues of timing (including sources of time constraints), court orders, funding sources, and varied models of intervention. Group strategies are also discussed as tools for work with individuals, families, organizations, and communities, in relating to other social workers, to interdisciplinary teams, and even in adversarial situations. Thus group techniques from problem solving, psychotherapy, and community work are presented. In the same way, skills for developing and implementing policy are discussed in ways that demonstrate that social workers can formulate and implement policies and be actively involved in policy debates. The usual boundaries are spanned in order to extend the panoply of interventions available to all health-related social workers.

Chapter 9 describes the relationship of the establishment of realistic goals and objectives to concrete measures of outcome to evaluate direct and indirect practice. Much of the discussion will relate back to chapter 6, in which the determination of goals and objectives is discussed, and to chapter 7, which covered planning and contracting. Quality assurance and evaluation of the social worker, as well as evaluation of particular work with individuals, families, organizations, and communities, are described. In differential discussion, at the end of work with each client system, social workers review all the decisions they made to structure work with the client system, and then they predict what they might alter the next time they work with a similar client system. Examples of differential discussion will help social workers to use techniques to refine and advance their practice and to generalize their learning. This chapter concludes with reference to the ecological interpretation of social work practice in health care systems, which helps the social worker to proceed responsively, flexibly, professionally, and efficiently to help client systems to enhance their well-being.

Mapping Devices and Practice Examples

A range of graphic representations and mapping devices are used throughout this book. Like other kinds of maps, they are meant to show social workers and clients where they are in a situation or in the work process, and to indicate direction for work. Turning something complex and overwhelming into a flat image on one page provides a sense of mastery and control, so long as the image can suggest movement and direction. Using such graphic representations in varied ways allows social workers to span boundaries of time, place, and system in planning, monitoring, and evaluating their work.

Included in each chapter are rich practice examples derived from actual social work settings. In these examples, the names of organizations, programs, clients, consumers, and communities are disguised. Most of the examples were gathered when I first began work on the book, because I wanted the content of the book to be developed from the experiences of real social workers. I sent letters to almost one hundred colleagues, many of whom are former students and all of whom I consider to be superb social workers in health and mental health care. Each social worker was asked to provide a practice example involving (1) relationships with two or more systems, (2) managed care, (3) the crossing of funding and/or policy boundaries, (4) an ethical or another dilemma, (5) an innovative assessment, (6) creative or unusual intervention strategies, (7) creative definition or social work roles, title, department, affiliation, or function, or (8) another dimension that is important for learning to be a social worker. The simple form that followed asked for

- The presenting problem, concern, or need
- Means of and tools used for assessment (attach graphic and mapping devices)
- Strategies and interventions (attach charts, pathways, timelines, or strategic plans)
- Conclusions

As I had hoped, the examples that social workers sent brightened and sharpened the content of the book. First, I sent forms to some social workers who I knew had redefined or stretched the boundaries of health-related activity. Several of those people sent me an example of the closest they came to "classical" social casework because they themselves did not classify what they were doing as social work. For example, one social worker whom I contacted organizes fund-raising events for self-help groups focused on a particular illness. I consider that all her activity (even organizing banquets) is "on behalf of" her population, and it is all health related. Another social worker I contacted scouts opportunities for new programming and new facilities in cities other than her own. Another manages all the step-down units in her hospital, and another runs a rehabilitation facility for substance abuse. All these activities are health related and are done on behalf of the social workers' clientele.

I learned that social workers can be an extraordinarily persistent and patient lot. Many of the programs they describe were created over a long period while they were doing many other kinds of work in an organization. They had a vision and they held onto it, nurtured and tended to it until it came to fruition. In this same vein, although managed care and the increasing attention to finances and financial constraints are extraordinarily frustrating and individual clients and consumers are moved too quickly through systems of care, social workers are maintaining their optimism and vision for their clients, programs, and organizations.

CONCLUSIONS

As in all practice books, these chapters appear to suggest that learning is linear; that is, social workers use relationships to assess, then strategize, then intervene, then evaluate, all within a context that comprises history, laws, values, ethics, and organizational constraints. In fact, little learning or intervention is linear, and context is not made up of smaller and smaller concentric circles in which the social worker and client sit. Each element flows into all the others, and learning and intervening are both circular and continuous activities.

Overall, this book combines management and more traditional social work information with a series of mapping devices, calls for social workers to be advocates and case managers, and requires excellent relationship skills and decision-making abilities. The approach is ethical, flexible, and practical. Every part of the work is related to meeting the needs of clients, consumers, programs, and communities. The work answers these questions: What do clients need from me? What can they expect from me and from my profession here in my organization and in the larger systems to which they and I must relate? The work honors the past, is responsive to the present, and helps the social worker to proceed sensitively, professionally, and efficiently to help clients, consumers, programs, and communities enhance their well-being.

No approach to practice that has been developed so far is without serious flaws, and this reinterpretation is no exception. However, this approach does address problems in most approaches to social work practice. First, it widens the lens of the social worker to incorporate a great deal of context that is necessary to help clients. Second, even on this broad and complex level of context, it encourages and enables social workers to act in powerful ways. It suggests that social workers must obtain and keep sufficient authority to do their work by becoming experts in relation to specific populations. It exhorts social workers to understand the needs and capacities of clients/consumers, programs, and communities, to understand the rich and complex systems in which the work occurs, and then to take their place and move the work forward.

Developing an
Ecological Perspective

Every discussion of an ecological perspective for social work practice requires that questions of context and culture be considered. Culture can be defined as the customary and shared values, beliefs, attitudes, goals, practices, social forms, and material traits of a racial, religious, ethnic, or social group. Each human society has its own particular culture or sociocultural system, which overlaps to some extent with other systems. The attitudes, values, ideals, beliefs, and behaviors of all individuals are greatly influenced by the cultures in which they live. Individuals in our complex society live, work, and move among several different cultures. Such cultures include race, ethnicity, gender, sexual orientation, and social class.

CONTEXT AND CULTURE

According to philosopher Ben-Ami Scharfstein (1989:xi), "The need to understand everything in context makes it impossible to arrive at a fully objective solution of the intellectual problems created by the differences between cultures: the solutions proposed are necessarily inadequate. . . . It is the inexhaustibility of contextual differences that makes it so difficult for the members of one culture to appreciate the position of those of another." Members of different cultures see one another differently. In some ways, the image of each is projected by the imagination of the other, and therefore is distorted. While it is difficult and perhaps painful to enter and understand a culture very different from one's own, it is also important and rewarding (Scharfstein 1989). It is difficult to understand all the important differences, to treat each person as if he or she is unique, and to be able to generalize sufficiently to work. While honoring the uniqueness of every client/patient/consumer, social workers must also be able to group people in systems of assessment, intervention, and evaluation. In that way, social workers can be of maximum benefit to each client/patient/consumer and can then generalize knowledge and skills to work with others who resemble that unique client. This process, too, is part of critical thinking and decision making.

Multicultural issues are important to the contextual and relationship dimensions of practice, the understanding of values, policies, systems, relationships, and disease processes. Some statistics convey this message resoundingly. By the year 2020, 50 percent of all school-age children will be non-Caucasian. This will be a 25 to 40 percent composition in some schools. African Americans are the majority population in fifty-three major American cities (Castex 1996). By the year 2015, Hispanic Americans will outnumber African Americans, and by 2050, non-Caucasians will outnumber Caucasians in the United States. Even referring to all Spanish-speaking populations as Hispanics is simplistic and unhelpful, because Hispanics come from twenty-six nations whose cultural traits vary greatly (Castex 1996:524).

Opportunities for social programs and clinical social work services for the elderly were expanded through federal legislation in the 1960s and early 1970s (Cox and Parsons 1994; Gelfand and Bechill 1991; Hooyman and Kiyak 1993; Rowland and Lyons 1996). All the legislation supports services that enhance independence and, as a consequence, prevent or delay institutionalization. Women use more services than men do, those who live alone use more services than those who do not, and use tends to increase with age and functional limitation. More than 9 million noninstitutionalized elderly persons live alone; approximately 2.5 million elderly minority members have incomes less than twice the poverty level; almost 6 million noninstitutionalized elderly persons have physical impairments; about 3.5 million have Alzheimer's disease, and almost 1 million elderly people are abused (Zuniga 1995).

Effective social work must be cross-generational as well as culturally competent (Grant and Haynes 1996). We know now that elderly people should participate fully in all types of services because they are capable of adaptation and change (Achenbaum 1983; Dunkle 1984; Hartz and Splain 1997). We also know that generations within the same culture may respond differently to similar stresses (Kao and Lam 1997; Lee 1997). For instance, in some ethnic groups, elders may utilize traditional systems of medical care, while younger generations may spurn such systems for the dominant system (Panos and Panos 2000).

Examples of what happens when practitioners are unaware of cultural factors are rarely found in the literature. Following are three examples of well-intentioned but ignorant interactions with clients.

A social worker in an OB-GYN clinic greeted a Cambodian woman and her infant daughter by patting the child on her head. The mother became visibly upset, and the translator was unable to explain why. Later, when the social worker repeated her story to another interpreter, the interpreter explained that in the Cambodian culture it is thought that touching a child's head, a sign of affection in mainstream American culture, is thought to remove the child's soul.

In a community where heavy beer drinking was the norm, a young social worker assigned to a hospital emergency room was told to ask every patient about alcohol intake, regardless of the medical problem listed on the referral. For religious reasons, the social worker's family did not drink. When she asked a patient who had come to the emergency room for treatment of an arm injury how much he drank, he said he probably drank about a case of beer over a weekend. The social worker replied, "Don't you think you are an alcoholic?" At that point, untreated for his injury, the patient left the emergency room.

A social worker in a community mental health center was asked by a psychiatrist to talk to a patient who he said was schizophrenic. All that the psychiatrist could find out from the patient about her home life was that she "listened to a web," and although he thought she should be hospitalized, he was unclear about her home situation. The social worker found the patient to be a very depressed young woman with a flat affect who lived with her parents, had completed high school, and had been unable to find a job. When the social worker asked what she did all day, the patient said that she listened to the WEBB, which the social worker knew was a radio station that was very popular in this patient's community. The social worker doubted that the psychiatrist had ever heard of the station.

Being culturally sensitive will not be enough; we must be competent in cross-cultural work. Cultural competence, the ability to integrate cultural sensitivity and knowledge and skill in the process of helping, must be the goal of every social worker in health and mental health care (Proctor and Davis 1994; Weaver 1999). Like relationship skills, cultural competence can never be fully attained and remains a goal for one's lifetime. Green's

(1998) human services model for becoming culturally competent is helpful in this regard. He suggests that the first step is to identify what is salient in the cultures of the social worker and the individuals and communities that can be applied to the problems that must be addressed. The second step includes self-assessment, since "no one can really understand the differences in others without confronting directly one's own limits and capabilities" (Green 1998:37).

Scharfstein (1989:53) writes that "presumably, anyone living within an embracing context, such as that of a culture, is immersed in it so deeply that a clear notion of what it would be like to be out of it can hardly arise in one's mind; but the stronger the sense of the foreign, which lies outside, the stronger the likelihood that the foreign already exists within—at least in the form of an unexpressed attraction outward. An explicit presentation of the contextual differences between different cultures is an implicit appeal to go beyond any and all of them." So knowledge that one does not understand cultures that are different from one's own and the desire to understand are important first steps in this lifelong learning process.

AN ECOLOGICAL REINTERPRETATION

The ecological perspective suggests that clients, projects, programs, communities, and all the salient aspects of environment are parts of an interacting whole. In order to know why, when, and how to intervene, social workers must understand context, the interrelated conditions in which the client, project, program, or community exist. The term *perspective* conveys depth and distance, as it does in art, lending added dimensions to understanding. The term *ecological* comes from ecology, the division of biology that studies the relationships between organisms and all the parts of their environment that affect them and that they affect in any way. Ecology views people and their environments as interdependent. Individual components and aspects are separated for study in order to develop strategies for altering the relationships, but all units, dimensions, and aspects must be viewed together to be truly understood. Thus an ecological perspective assumes a specific worldview and view of the individual from which all means of assessment, strategy building, and tools for intervention are drawn.

This framework is neither a model nor a theory but a perspective that is a useful way of thinking about practice (Meyer 1988). A framework is a structure designed to enclose or support a written work or system of ideas; whereas a model is a description or representation of a structure that shows the proportions and arrangements of its component parts; and a theory is "a scheme or system of ideas or statements held as an explanation or account for a group of facts or phenomena; a hypothesis that has been confirmed or established by observation or experiment and is propounded or accepted as accounting for the known facts; a statement of what are held to be the laws, principles or causes of something known or observed" (*Oxford English Dictionary* 1971:278).

An ecological perspective presupposes the necessity of thinking systematically and necessarily disallows linearity. Thus one cannot think in terms of one cause and one effect. It also presupposes that all systems have boundaries but that the boundaries are almost all permeable. In the case of social entities, that is, families, groups, organizations, or communities, boundaries can be redrawn or recast to work most effectively for the client. An ecological perspective is all about relationships, especially the relationship between people and their environments. It is particularly suited to social work practice because it is all-encompassing and solves the perpetual social work dilemma of how to address the person and environment in a way that subsumes both.

Richmond's model of case coordination (see figure P.1 in the preface) demonstrates the focus on person-in-environment that has long been an issue for social work. Minahan (1981:6) says that "the purpose of social work is to promote or restore a mutually beneficial interaction between individuals and society in order to improve the quality of life for everyone." In 1994, through a grant from the National Association of Social Workers (NASW), Karls and Wandrei (1994) developed the person-in-environment system (PIE) for describing, classifying, and coding adult social functioning problems, which is a fine contemporary effort to make an ecological perspective practical and systematic.

One social worker who devoted herself to the explication of an ecological perspective was Carel Germain (1979, 1984). First alone and then with colleague and collaborator Alex Gitterman (1991), she developed the ecological approach, expanding definitions, interpretations, concepts, and strategies. Wakefield (1996a, 1996b), MacNair (1996), Gitterman and Shulman (1994), Allen-Meares and Lane (1987), Meyer (1983, 1988), Siporin (1980), and others have also made important contributions to this approach. Much of the following discussion is drawn from their work.

General System Theory

Work on an ecological perspective for social work practice was clearly shaped by an understanding of general system theory (Bertalanffy 1974). The general systems paradigm provided social work with "a way of thinking and a means of organizing our perceptions of relatedness and dynamic processes" (Ell and Northen 1990:2). General system theory has been described as a direction or program in the contemporary philosophy of science, an overarching framework, an abstract metatheory, or a model of relationships between objects rather than a theory.

Some of the earliest work in the area was an extension of organismic biology. The framework purports that any systems—be they biological, social, or psychological—operate according to the same fundamental principles. All systems, for example, are open to influencing activity, are adaptive, incorporate notions of communication and control, have smaller organized activity flows that serve larger activity flows, and define the individual actor through the functional linking of subordinate parts to the operating whole. Systems are organized wholes consisting of elements that are related in varying nonlinear, mutual, or unidirectional and intermittent causal relationships. They are capable of primary and reactive change and evolution, and they maintain differentiation through continuous input from and output to their environment. Thus systems are made up of complexes of interacting components or subsystems. Therefore, action flows within each system and outside of it, linking it to other systems and influencing that system. Systems thinking represents a major paradigm shift, not only in social work and all the social sciences but in diverse fields such as ecology, biology, management, and physics (Kuhn 1970).

General System Theory and an Ecological Perspective. In biological terms, ecology deals with the relations between organisms and their environment. In sociological parlance, ecology is the branch concerned with the spacing of people and institutions and the resultant interdependency. Ecologists study adaptation to changes in the environment. Thus studies of the relationship of structural, physical, and social stress to illness, life event research, and studies of social support and health are all part of an ecological understanding of the relationship of the individual to the environment. "An ecosystemic perspective enlarges the unit of attention to include the individual, social institutions, culture, and the interactions and transactions among systems and within specific systems" (Ell and Northen 1990:10).

Allen-Meares and Lane (1987) reviewed the theoretical assumptions, practice principles, and research methods of four approaches to human behavior and from them identified the general characteristics of an ecosystems perspective. With some little modification, their list of characteristics holds true for the biological, social, and behavioral sciences:

1. The whole consists of continuous interlocking relationships.
2. Person, behavior, and environment are mutually interdependent.
3. Systems concepts can be used to investigate those interrelationships.
4. Behavior is specific to situation.
5. Means of study should be naturalistic, direct observation of the intact undisturbed system.

6. The relationships of dimensions of the ecosystem are patterned and abide by specific rules.
7. Behavior is the result of a mediated process between all dimensions.
8. A task of science is to develop taxonomies of environments, behaviors, and behavior-environment linkages and to determine their distribution. (Allen-Meares and Lane 1987:518)

In summary, to think in terms of behavioral science or any other single discipline such as sociology or biology is much more limited than thinking in the systems terms that an ecological perspective stipulates.

> Once the model of ecology becomes the lattice-work upon which such realignment of knowledge is hung, it is no longer possible to limit oneself to the behavioral sciences alone. The physical sciences, the biological sciences, in fact, all of science must be included. Since the people who have been most concerned with constructing a model for a unified science and with the ingredients of the human ecological field have been the general systems theorists, the approach used by behavioral scientists who follow this trend is rapidly acquiring the label of the "system approach," although a more appropriate label might be the "ecological systems approach." (Auerswald 1968:203)

Therefore the ecological perspective is overarching throughout this book because it allows for an understanding of practice in context that is closer to real life, richer, and more pragmatic than any other perspective.

General System Theory and Models of Business Management. In much the same way that an ecological perspective in social work is drawn from general systems theory and ecology, many frameworks and models of business management are derived from those same sources. These frameworks have much to offer to social work practice. With the exception of certain public health reforms, no new knowledge has contributed more to productivity and profitability in this century than developments in systems, people, and information management (Drucker 1974, 1999). Specifically business management frameworks provide pragmatic, clear ways for people to make sense of the structure, organization, and processes of systems. Because they are action-oriented and empowering, focused on the mission and goals of systems and the relationship of the work of all participants to the system, such frameworks undergird social workers' abilities to negotiate systems and advocate effectively for clients.

The ability to work within and manage these systems in highly productive, goal-oriented ways is critical for social work. Such information has always been salient for social work practice, but the current environment in health and mental health care makes critical social workers' ability to understand organizations as systems, to speak the language and to maneuver in ways that help clients reach their goals (Levinson 1992). In particular, the work of Peter Senge, Chris Argyris, John Kotter, Henry Mintzberg, and Peter Drucker inform this book. Each of these people explores different dimensions of management that contribute to social workers' understanding of systems and to their ability to practice in increasingly complex environments. For example, Drucker's "management by objectives," Senge's "learning organizations," and Kotter's particular understanding of leadership enrich social workers' understanding of systems, ecology, and an ecological perspective (Bailey and Grochau 1993).

Drucker explains that every system that is more complicated than the simplest mechanical assemblage of inanimate matter contains multiple axes. Thus the body of every animal has many systems, including a skeletal-muscular system, several nervous systems, an ingestive/digestive/ eliminating system, a respiratory system, sensory systems, and a reproductive system. While each system is to some degree autonomous, all interact, and each is an axis of organization. Organizations are not, and should not be, as complicated as biological organisms. Still, business and public service organizations must be constructed with several axes, including one for making decisions and distributing authority and information, as well as one for understanding the logic of the task and the dynamics of knowledge. In addition, individuals must have positions within these organizations so that they can understand and manage a number of axes related to tasks and assignments, decision responsibility, information, and relationships (Drucker 1974:527).

Systems thinking is guided by two central principles. First, "structure influences behavior," which means that the ability to influence reality comes from recognizing structures that are controlling behavior and events. The second principle, "policy resistance," refers to the tendency of complex systems to resist efforts to change their behavior. Therefore efforts to manipulate behavior will generally improve matters only in the short run and often lead to more problems in the long run (Senge 1990:373–74). Such thinking uses systems archetypes to observe and fathom underlying structures in complex situations. For example, a mastery of systems thinking leads one to understand family problems or organization problems as emanating from underlying structures rather than from individual mistakes or negative intentions. Systems thinking leads to seeing "wholes" instead of "parts" and experiencing the interconnectedness of life. Thus systems theory contributes to the understanding of organizations and management that has been developed in business, and social workers in health and mental health need this knowledge in order to be effective with and for their clients.

The Beginnings of the Ecological Perspective

Adopting an ecological perspective has been the most popular effort to find a generic theory for social work over the last two decades: "Contemporary concerns about generic theory can be traced to reinvigorated attempts to define social work's purpose after the formation in 1955 of the National Association of Social Workers" (Wakefield 1996b:186). Specialty areas such as medical social work, psychiatric social work, and group work amalgamated at that time because each was having difficulty locating enough people who wished to be social workers. They hoped that by uniting they would become a significant force and thus recruit new members to the profession more effectively.

Some questioned whether the specialty areas had enough in common to keep everyone together and whether they could maintain enough of their separate identities to sustain the expertise they had developed. A common purpose had to be conceptualized that would speak to group workers, community organizers, and psychiatric and medical social workers. Harriet Bartlett, chair of the committee formed for that purpose in the "salad days" of the NASW, wrote a working definition of the profession. Bartlett (1958:6) proposed that social work be defined as a combination of purpose, values, knowledge, sanction, and methods. The working definition stated that the practice of social work had as its purposes

> (1) to assist individuals and groups to identify and resolve or minimize problems arising out of disequilibrium between themselves and their environment, (2) to identify potential areas of disequilibrium between individuals or groups and the environment in order to prevent the occurrence of disequilibrium, and (3) in addition to these curative and preventive aims, to seek out, identify, and strengthen the maximum potential in individuals, groups, and communities.

Later, Bartlett (1970:130) defined the purpose of social work as creating a "balance between demands of the social environment and people in coping efforts." Like a good parent, she continued to try to ascertain concepts that encompassed and embraced all parties and that avoided favoritism. To this day, scholars continue to use ecological concepts to define the purpose of social work in ways that incorporate all domains.

For example, in a special centennial issue of *Social Work*, editor-in-chief Stanley Witkin (1999:297) wrote that social work is defined by its contextual and relational framework. As their guiding vision, "social workers advocate for a just and civil society that supports these values and promotes the fulfillment of basic human needs, the fair distribution of resources, equal opportunity, and respect for all people." Concern with the explication of purpose and function has been with social work since its inception. In his report, Flexner (1915:584) said that social work's mission or cause was the "persistent and deliberate effort to improve the living or working conditions in the community or to relieve, diminish or prevent distress."

Overall, an ecological point of view alters the vantage point of the professional by focusing on interfaces between parts and dimensions of the whole, as well as communication processes between dimensions. With an ecological point of view, one first analyzes the structure of the field using the common language and concepts of general system theory to identify the systems and subsystems involved. Next, one traces the communications within and between systems in order to understand relationships and structure, sources, pathways, content, and functions of messages (Auerswald 1968:204).

The Contributions of an Ecological Perspective

I believe that the ecological perspective is comfortable for many social workers, especially social work scholars, because it best accounts for the overarching values of the profession. It is, in fact, the value system of social work that unites all domains, methods, and specializations. The ecological perspective informs this work in two major ways: as a metaconstruct and as a metaphor. First, as a metaconstruct, it offers an all-inclusive framework for social work. As theorist Max Siporin (1980:525) noted,

> Ecological systems theory is such a general meta-theory, one that provides for the many, and at times contradictory, purposes and activities of social workers. It constitutes an essential element of the generic core of social work knowledge, of its common person-in-situation and dialectical perspective, and of its basic helping approach. It supports the social work assessment and interventive focus.

For practitioners, the perspective works best as a metaphor for thinking about all the elements as well as the whole of social work practice:

> The perspective offers a series of related concepts that are useful for allowing social workers from many areas to think about practice. The concepts are (1) person/environment fit, (2) reciprocal transactions between people and environments support or inhibit the ability to adapt, (3) circular causal relationships are ones in which systems

interact with and affect each other, (4) systems can be open to many degrees or closed to outside interaction, (5) systems are linked hierarchically, (6) systems can possess states of equilibrium or disequilibrium, and (7) people and environments must be viewed as a unitary system within a particular cultural and historical context. (Germain and Gitterman 1995:816)

Gitterman and Germain's (1995:818) concepts, refined from Germain's early thoughts about the subject, are (1) person–environment fit, (2) adaptations, (3) life stressors, (4) stress, (5) coping measures, (6) relatedness, (7) competence, (8) self-esteem, (9) self-direction, and (10) habitat and niche. *Person–environment fit* is the actual fit between an individual's or a collective group's needs, rights, goals, and capacities and the qualities and operations of the physical and social environments within particular cultural and historical contexts. *Adaptations* are continuous, change-oriented, cognitive, sensory-perceptual, and behavioral processes people use to sustain or raise the level of fit between themselves and their environment. *Life stressors* are generated by critical life issues that people perceive as exceeding their personal and environmental resources. *Stress* is the internal response to a life stressor and is characterized by troubled emotional or physiological states or both. *Coping measures* are special behaviors, often novel, devised to meet the demands posed by the life stressor. *Relatedness* refers to attachments, friendships, positive kin relationships, and a sense of belonging to a supportive social network. *Competence* assumes that all organisms are innately motivated to affect their environment in order to survive. *Self-esteem* is the most important part of self-concept; it represents the extent to which one feels competent, respected, and worthy. *Self-direction* is the capacity to take some degree of control over one's life and to accept responsibility for one's decisions and actions while simultaneously respecting the rights and needs of others. *Habitat and niche* further delineate the nature of physical and social environments. While Germain and Gitterman see *habitat and niche* as particularly helpful ideas in work with communities, this reinterpretation sees them as critical to all social work practice.

Additional concepts that enrich an ecological perspective are (1) coercive power, (2) exploitative power, (3) life course, and three notions of time: (4) individual time, (5) historical time, and (6) social time. *Coercive power* is the withholding of power from vulnerable groups on the basis of the group's personal or cultural characteristics. *Exploitative power* leads to technological pollution of air, food, water, soils, and oceans and the increasing pressure of toxic chemical and hazardous wastes in dwellings, schools, workplaces, and communities. *Life course* conceives biopsychosocial development as consisting of more uniform, indeterminate pathways of development from birth to old age within diverse environments, cultures, and historical eras. Of the three notions of time, *individual time* refers to the continuity and meaning of individual life experience over the life course, *historical time* refers to the impact of historical and social change on the developmental pathways of a birth cohort, and *social time* refers to the timing of individual and family transitions and life events as influenced by changing biological, economic, social, demographic, and cultural factors (Germain and Gitterman 1995:817–21).

Life-Modeled Practice. As their work with the ecological perspective progressed, Germain and Gitterman (1996) developed what they referred to as a practice modality derived from ecological concepts that integrated work with individuals, families, groups, organizations, community practice, and participation in political advocacy (Gitterman and Shulman 1994). This approach is patterned on life processes directed to people's strengths, modification of the environment to promote and sustain well-being, and raising the level of person–environment fit. "As an evolving practice modality, the life model continues to be open to newly-developed ideas and knowledge, newly-articulated skills, emerging professional issues, and ever-changing social and cultural forces" (Germain and Gitterman 1995:822). This is the life model's greatest strength and its most profound weakness. It can incorporate everything that is learned and can be added to the social work knowledge base, but its "all-encompassing" nature means that it ultimately does not help the social worker to know where, when, and how to intervene.

Concerns About an Ecological Perspective. The fit between an ecological perspective and the whole of social work is questioned regularly. In one example of such healthy and important skepticism, Wakefield (1996a) asks, "Does social work need the eco-system perspective?" He argues that the perspective is not clinically useful first because it is not domain-specific and second because it is not conceptually useful. I have difficulty with the relevance of Wakefield's first argument because insistence on being domain-specific has been so destructive to the profession. An ecological perspective has been an answer for those who find an overarching comprehensive perspective helpful.

Wakefield (1996a:3, 5) is correct in saying, "There exists no empirical literature on the perspective." And "any set of ideas, however different, can be put together under one overarching concept if the concept is abstract enough. However, higher-level abstractions are unlikely to yield insight relevant to practice." I also agree, to some extent, with this statement:

So the issue raised by the ecological perspective is not whether clinicians should ignore social factors—they cannot afford to do so

because such factors heavily influence the client's measuring system—but whether it is essential for the clinical practitioner to directly assess environmental systems, even where it is known that
nothing can be done about such larger systems in the context of
clinical practice. (Wakefield 1996a:17)

However, I very much disagree with the last part of this quotation. Remaining hopeful, idealistic, and even visionary about changing larger systems is
part of the social work value system. Work in an ecological perspective contains fallacies regarding discussions of coherence, generic applicability, and
comprehensiveness, but the perspective does not have to solve these problems to be helpful to the profession. Finally, I disagree with Wakefield's
(1996b:198) notion that "the eco-system perspective loses the specialness
of the person in social work." Honoring individuals and addressing their
problems and goals remain central in any ecological work. In fact, I would
argue that while the ecological perspective maintains the focus on the individual, it does not easily support a shift in focus to other dimensions of
the environments or to client populations rather than individuals. This ability to shift focus from individual client units—individuals, families, or small
groups—to organizations, communities, or populations is difficult using an
ecological perspective or any other perspective or theory thus far developed
for social work practice (Tolson, Reid, and Garvin 1994:6).

Tolson et al. (1994:10) attempt to solve this problem by first identifying
the primary system with which social workers will conduct most of their
work in resolving target problems. According to them, the one firm rule for
the primary system is that it be willing to accept help. Usually the primary
system either (1) has an internal problem that is capable of being resolved
internally and either requests or agrees to accept help, (2) has an external
problem, either requests or agrees to accept help to resolve it, and alleviation
of the problem is expected to be possible through the combined resources
of the system and the social worker, or (3) change in the system is necessary
to solve the problem of another system, and the system agrees to help. At
times, the primary system may have to change in order to resolve problems.
Also, collaterals and members of other systems may have to be involved in
order for problems to be resolved.

System selection depends on four variables: problem identifier, problem location, location of necessary changes, and problem solver location
(Tolson et al. 1994:8). The problem identifier is the system that identifies
the problem, and it is thought that identifying a problem indicates accessibility and motivation for working toward the solutions to that problem.
Locations are determined through explanations of problem causes. Problem location refers to where the change will be seen. Next, the system in
which change must occur in order for the problem to be alleviated must

be decided. Then, the system that is best able to make the change is determined.

For example, Joey Romstadt, 17 years old, had been facially disfigured in an automobile accident, and he was very depressed because he thought he looked like a freak. Joey's general practitioner referred him to a community mental health center to be treated for depression by Ruth Weiss, a social worker. The cause here is clear, and the change that had to occur was in Joey. Part of the background information that the social worker gathered from Joey was that he was insured through his father, who was divorced from his mother and lived in another state. Rather than focus solely on helping Joey become used to his damaged face, Weiss asked if she could review the father's insurance policy. Although the cause was clear and the location where the change had to take place was also clear, the social worker had not decided about the system in which changes had to occur in order to alleviate the problem. Close reading of the insurance policy yielded information that said if disfigurement was a result of an accident or illness the insurance plan would cover surgery to alter the condition. A series of surgeries made the young man's appearance unremarkable, his depression lifted, and he was discharged. Thus although the problem identifier and the problem location remained the same, the location of necessary changes and the problem solver location were altered as a result of the social worker's understanding practice in context. Thus it was important to gather more information to identify the locations that would best meet the client's goals.

A truly generic perspective should allow a shift in system focus and modality to meet clients' needs. The generalist approach has been referred to as a perspective by others (Gordon 1969). For example, according to Schatz, Jenkins, and Sheafor (1990:219), "The generalist social worker (has) the tools to work in various settings with a variety of client groups, addressing a range of personal and social problems and using skills to intervene at practice levels ranging from the individual to the community." Articulated principles for this approach include (1) incorporation of the generic foundation for social work and use of multilevel problem-solving methodology, (2) a multiple, theoretical orientation including an ecological systems model that recognizes an interrelatedness of human problems, life situations, and social conditions, (3) a knowledge, value, and skill base that is transferable between and among diverse contexts, locations, and problems, (4) an open assessment unconstricted by any particular theoretical or interventive approach, and (5) selection of strategies or roles for intervention that are made on the basis of the problem, goals, and situation of attention and the size of the systems involved (Group for the Study of Generalist and Advanced Generalist Social Work, in Schatz et al. 1990:223). For example, sometimes it is more helpful for social workers to pay most attention to life stressors and delivery systems as dimensions of the environment that concern groups or populations of clients.

In a study of adolescent mental health and urban families, Stern, Smith, and Jang (1999:22–23) argue that prevention and intervention strategies must be more responsive to families' contextual realities rather than being based solely on traditional clinical theories. "Viewing disturbed mood as a response to social context rather than as parent psychopathology points to interventions that help families cope with adversity." At those times, the organization or delivery system becomes the unit of attention. That vantage point does not seem to be a good fit with an ecological perspective as it has been drawn for social work. However, it fits well with the systems perspective drawn by the business management scholars whose work is incorporated in this book. It also supports emphasizing the legal and ethical dimensions and organizational understanding as critical for contemporary practice in health and mental health. This is a good example of an ecological reinterpretation.

There are three problems: (1) the necessity of mastering several interventional modalities, (2) the necessity of understanding notions of "practice in context," and (3) being paid to intervene in ways that are limited by funding sources. One worries that it is impossible to master a large range of modalities and that social workers will become "jacks of all trades, masters of none." Also, the generalist approach seems to ignore the knowledge necessary to practice effectively in context, and the fact that social workers are often paid to work with one interventional method when they think that solutions require a multimodality approach. Again, an ecological perspective seems to work best for practice because it requires a rich understanding of many dimensions of context. Not only are social workers most often educated to intervene at one specific system level and sometimes using only one particular modality, but they are also very often paid to work on only one level, and that level is related to where society places the responsibility for problems. In the examples that have been cited here, teenagers with mood disorders had been treated for the disorders without any intervention occurring at the system levels that could alter the problems, and a young man had been referred for psychotherapy when there was a more effective and concrete solution at a different system level.

The Advantages of an Ecological Perspective. In his discussion of ecological systems theory in social work, Siporin (1980:512, 516–18) points to the significant contributions of an ecological model for social work practice:

1. It contributes to a larger, more unitary and comprehensive unit of attention, a holistic and dynamic understanding of people and all dimensions of environment.
2. It demands multiple perspectives, ways of thinking about dimensions, aspects, parts, and wholes.
3. It supports a theoretically and pragmatically eclectic approach.
4. It is useful in assessment and helps one to understand systemic fit.
5. It is useful in planning interventions, especially in terms of identifying actions needed to alter systemic relationships to address fit.
6. It encompasses a varied assessment and intervention repertoire and is therefore multifactual.
7. It helps to monitor multidimensional systems outcomes of interventions.

The ecological perspective is helpful because it spans boundaries, refusing to allow social workers to limit problem definitions, supports, or solutions. The focus on interaction prevents social workers from locating blame or responsibility within an element of a problem. It corrects a series of limitations and biases, such as placing problems and solutions in small domains (Wakefield 1996a:21). In fact, it negates the need to understand motivation, to explain why someone did something. Because an understanding and acceptance of an ecological perspective belies a stance in a particular and more traditional behavioral science or psychology, it helps the social worker avoid the need to ascribe motivation, which rarely helps to solve problems. "Instead of valuing predictions based on simplistic cause, ecological thinking embraces indeterminacy in complex human phenomena" (Germain and Gitterman 1995:817). Also, as Meyer (1983:31) said, "Serving merely as a perspective (a lens) for looking at phenomena, it provides no prescription for intervention. It extends one's view of case situations; it does not tell what to do or how to define problems." Thus an ecological perspective serves the following purposes:

1. It helps social workers to avoid linear, unidimensional, and single-motive thinking.
2. It speaks to the social work value system.
3. It includes multiple social work endeavors and all possible levels and kinds of information the social worker needs for understanding.

But an ecological perspective is not a true theory and does not help to define levels and kinds of action.

That does not justify the ecological perspective's place as the overarching theory for social work practice that can replace domain-specific theory.

Over time, the ecological perspective may be found to have been a transitory solution that suits the values of the profession and the needs of many teachers of social work practice, such as myself. Exploring and analyzing the perspective causes one to appreciate its contributions. Having reviewed much of the writing on the subject, I think that those who have attended to it would agree about the helpfulness of many of its concepts but disagree about the extent of its contribution and its flaws. In time, when we have more effective paradigms, we may forsake it (Kuhn 1970). At least, it does allow social workers to span boundaries that may interfere with their best ability to help clients/consumers/communities to reach their goals.

Certain questions remain. For example, what dimensions must be studied and understood in order to have social workers intervene most effectively and efficiently? Also, even when social workers are sure they have included all the salient dimensions, how do they choose which dimensions to concentrate on for maximum effectiveness? It is most helpful to keep goals and objectives clear and agreed-upon and to maintain a partnership with the individuals, groups, and communities with whom, and on whose behalf, one is working. "Ecological thinking suggests that we should be less concerned with causes than with consequences, and that we should concentrate on helping change maladaptive relationships between people and their environments. We should ask the questions: 'What is going on?' rather than 'Why is it going on?' and 'How can the "What" be changed?' rather than the 'Who'?" (Germain and Gitterman 1996:7–8).

EXPERTISE IN RELATION TO
SPECIFIC POPULATIONS

An ecological perspective in which social workers are systems savvy and facile with enough modalities to be able to practice across systems provides social workers with great breadth. However, being a professional social worker in health and mental health care also requires expertise in relation to a specific population, such as the elderly, the seriously mentally ill, those with AIDS or other chronic illnesses, or those with developmental disabilities. This level of expertise means understanding the natural history of the illnesses and conditions to which that population is subject; the available medical and social interventions; all the laws and policies that affect the population; any special genetic, ethnic, or cultural proclivities; and the effects of the conditions on the population and family members, particularly in relation to development, independence, and social roles.

This level of expertise is beyond the scope of this book, but it is as vital as any information provided here. Illustrations of this kind of expertise are found in the examples provided throughout the book. Each of the expert social work practitioners who furnished the examples is a generalist in terms of being able to intervene in multiple ways in relation to work with individuals, families, programs, or organizations but is a specialist in relation to a clearly defined population. Defining oneself in this way allows for the broadest synthesis of the range and depth of knowledge required for excellent social work in health and mental health care, and it sharpens one's focus and thus one's ability. Most helpful in the pursuit of this kind of population-based knowledge building are the professional social work groups that are devoted to specific populations or health problems and the many self-help groups that have been formed to advocate for and support specific populations or health problems. Examples of professional groups include the National Association of Oncology Social Workers and the National Association of Perinatal Social Workers, as well as specific sections of the NASW and the Council on Social Work Education. Examples of self-help groups include the National Alliance for the Mentally Ill, the Epilepsy Foundation of America, and the Alzheimer's Disease and Related Disorders Association. Just as a combination of professional and self-help is useful for people managing all kinds of problems, this combined approach lends depth to social workers' understanding of problems, ability to advocate, and capacity to intervene.

A BRIEF HISTORY OF SOCIAL WORK PRACTICE IN HEALTH AND MENTAL HEALTH CARE IN THE UNITED STATES

An understanding of history is necessary to situate the work in the political and cultural contexts that have shaped its forms and meanings (Scholes 1998). Mary Richmond (1907), who first formulated direct social work practice, discussed the forces that shaped care in the United States at the turn of the twentieth century; we can now describe the forces shaping health and mental health care at the turn of the twenty-first. It is important that social workers understand that the profession has weathered and advanced through times of comparable turbulence, and the result of such weathering has been new knowledge and strength (Kerson 1981; Mackelprang and Salsgiver 1996).

Just over 100 years old, health-related social work has a grand and interesting history. As has occurred many times in the past, the field is being transformed as a result of radical policy and funding shifts in the national health care arena. The most diverting shift of all is the physical relocation of social workers in health care away from acute care institutions whose identities were closely linked with universities or communities or both. Both identifications were sources of prestige and power. Because the same institutions will continue to control funding, some part of that identification will continue, but it will be at a distance. However, the history of social work practice in health and mental health care is much richer than its identification with acute care university-affiliated hospitals.

A long backward glance shows many themes that remain important to social work practice in health and mental health care. Three such themes are important to understanding how this book is structured. The first is a recurrent emphasis on public health, case management, and advocacy; the second is the relationship of social work to technological solutions to the problems of disease and trauma (Abramson 1991; Kerson 1981, 1997); and the third is the social work profession's definition of a health care setting (Menefee 1997). An understanding of these themes demonstrates that acute care hospitals have been important, because it was in those settings that social work could accomplish the tasks we had set for ourselves. Because those were the strongest health care institutions, they were where we could count on getting paid. Also, it was in such institutions that the populations with whom we wanted to work could be found. Finally, these institutions were training centers for many kinds of health and mental health personnel, and social work could establish effective field placements as well.

Social work in health care began in the late nineteenth century in the United States. In many ways, social work assumed many of the functions that had been previously carried out by family members and religious organizations. "The power of the church had declined and families were unwilling or unable to care for the old, the sick or financially needy relatives as they had in the past" (Kerson 1981:40). In reviewing the history, it is important to remember that social work began as a private, voluntary undertaking that was part of the philanthropic movements reflecting a residual view of social welfare. That is, social work at that time viewed people's problems as their own failings rather than as a failure of society. Also, social work in health and mental health began as parts of a collection of specialties that were that generally viewed as ancillary to other professions in several organizational contexts. Thus hospital social workers provided auxiliary services for physicians in acute care hospitals, and psychiatric social workers later worked in the same way in relation to psychiatrists in mental hospitals. In addition, until after World War II, social workers were almost always women. Over time, the roles and tasks of social workers have changed considerably, but we continue to care primarily for the poor and disenfranchised; we are still predominately women, and we continue to be defined most often by the organizational setting in which we work.

Early instances of what we would call social work in health care began as several visionaries saw relationships between health, education about health matters, and living conditions (Lubove 1975). In the 1850s when physician Elizabeth Blackwell, who established the New York Infirmary for Women and Children, visited patients at home, she hired another woman to train mothers in housekeeping and child care. In the 1880s, physician Annie S. Daniel involved the New York Infirmary in pioneering work in which medical care was related to teaching hygiene and improving living and working conditions.

Initially, social workers were helpers of ward patients in university-affiliated hospitals, dependent on physicians' largesse and definition of roles. Richard Cabot, a doctor at the Massachusetts General Hospital, established the first hospital social work department, locating the social workers in a curtained-off corner of a hallway (*First Annual Report of Social Work* 1906). In 1902, Charles P. Emerson (1910:1), a doctor at the Johns Hopkins Hospital in Baltimore, decided that knowledge of the patient's social environment would enhance medical students' understanding of medical conditions. Medical students "might learn how the poor man lives, works and thinks; what his problems are; what burdens he must bear. They learn the intimate relationship between the ills of the body and home environment." To educate medical students in this way, Emerson called on the Baltimore Charity Organization Society (Cannon 1913:14). This example is noteworthy because the teaching of medical students continues to be an important and prestigious task for social workers in health care.

Teamwork between nurses and social workers was encouraged. Many of the early social workers in health care were nurses. In 1920, a survey of hospital social work departments revealed that 193 out of 350 salaried workers had nursing experience, and of 61 head social workers, 36 were nurses. Increasingly, social workers wanted more autonomy and equality than nurses were allowed. For many years and in many situations, social workers and nurses have seen each other as both allies and competitors. Today this is especially true in areas such as case management, which both nursing and social work claim as their own. Because the skills and knowledge bases they bring to case management are so different, social workers and nurses provide the best case management when they work together in teams (Hammer and Kerson 1998).

Generally, before 1900, social workers, functioning as friendly visitors, helped society to judge who was worthy of assistance, who was capable of reform, and who was not. Facts were presented to a case committee of wealthy board members, and if the committee decided that the case was worthy and that the situation could be improved, the worker began to manipulate, treat, and reform the client (Cowin 1970). As social problems were identified, specific programs or agencies were developed, and by 1900 specialization had become a regular part of social work. By the early 1900s, more questions were raised about the nature of the poor. Social workers thought that causes had to be explicated before solutions could be found. They began to gather copious facts to locate the cause of the problem, name its solution, and provide proper advice. If advice, in the form of "sweet coercion," was not taken, the case was closed because the individual or family would not cooperate (Briar and Miller 1971:4). By 1910, the process of gathering facts began to be professionalized, and the first schools of social work were founded. In 1917, Mary Richmond, considered to be the mother of social casework, wrote *Social Diagnosis,* in which she described the social worker as an expert collector and interpreter of social evidence (Richmond 1917). Social diagnosis was "the attempt to make as exact a definition as possible of the situation and personality of a human being in some social need—of his situation and personality, that is, in relation to the other human beings upon whom he in any way depends or who depend upon him, and in relation to social institutions of his community" (Richmond 1917:357). According to Richmond, casework consisted of "those processes which develop personality through adjustments consciously affected, individual by individual, between men and their social environment" (Richmond 1922:8). These were some of the first attempts to describe the elements that were common to casework regardless of institutional or agency setting.

World War I affected social institutions and professions throughout the United States, including social work. The Red Cross organized its Home Service Bureau, and casework found a way to work "above the poverty line" (Robinson 1930:48–49). Many social workers were attached to neuropsychiatric hospitals, and in 1919 Mary Jarrett presented a paper at the National Conference of Social Work demonstrating social work's rapt devotion to psychiatry. From 1918 until 1926, psychiatric social workers and medical social workers were all part of one group. In 1926, the psychiatric social workers left to form their own group. It is ironic that the two groups worked together when medicine and psychiatry were considered separate fields and that they split when psychosomatic studies were bringing the two fields together and when social work educators were emphasizing the generic elements in the social work process. This was a period, though, when the health-related social workers were still called "hospital social workers," and that title limited identification and membership.

By the end of the 1920s, five areas of social work practice—family, child welfare, medical, psychiatric, and school social work—believed that their methods and settings were sufficiently different to warrant specialization. However, those participating in the landmark Milford Conference wrote, "the problems of social casework and the equipment of the social caseworker are fundamentally the same for all fields. . . . Generic social casework is the common field to which the specific forms of social casework are merely incidental" (*Social Casework* 1929:11). The base had moved from the socioeconomic to psychological and human behavior. Those participating in the conference supported the following assumptions:

1. All behavior is purposeful and determined.
2. Many determinants of behavior are unconscious.
3. It is not the social order so much that determines behavior but how the specific individual reacts to the social order.
4. Casework's job is the treatment of these individual reactions.
5. Such reactions are a function of the early life experiences of the client—specifically his sexual instincts and infantile experiences.
6. Casework will ultimately expose these early conflicts.
7. The formula of study, diagnosis, and treatment remains.

Informants from that era said, "We were eating up psychiatry," "a whole new world had opened up with an answer to every question," and "social workers got themselves out of doing many tangible things" (Kerson 1981:43). The provision of concrete services was spurned and avoided. Pecking orders developed within the profession, with those who focused on the psychological and on the interior life elevating themselves above those who concerned themselves with social, economic, and physical health dimensions of life.

Further rifts were caused when the profession embraced two divergent schools of thought for understanding and teaching direct practice. Both the diagnostic school (whose belief system was Freudian theory) and the functional school (whose system was Rankian) insisted that their theoretical orientation was the only one that could educate social workers effectively (Roberts and Nee 1970; Turner 1979). It was said that the diagnostic school, which over time evolved into the psychosocial approach, was a system theory approach to social work. The major system to which diagnosis and treatment were addressed was the person-in-situation gestalt, or configuration (Hollis 1970). According to the diagnostic school, treatment was differentiated according to the client's need and was "conceptualized as a blend of processes directed as diagnostically indicated towards modification in the person or his social or interpersonal environment or both, and of the exchanges between them" (Hollis 1970:36–37).

The functional approach differed from the diagnostic approach in its understanding of three areas: (1) the nature of man, (2) the purpose of social work, and (3) the concept of process (Smalley 1970). First, while the diagnostic school worked from a psychology of illness, in which the social worker was responsible for diagnosing and treating a pathological condition with the center for change residing in the social worker, the functional school worked from a psychology of growth, with the center for change residing in the client and with the social worker "engaging in a relationship process which released the client's own power for choice and growth" (Smalley 1970:79). In relation to the purpose of social work, whereas the diagnostic school saw the purpose of the social work agency as secondary to, detached from, or even in opposition to the purpose of the social worker, the functional school saw the purpose and function of the agency as giving focus, direction, definition, and support to the social worker's practice. Finally, in relation to the understanding of process, the functional school saw direct practice as "a helping process through which an agency's service was made available" (Smalley 1970:80). The functional approach also had specific views regarding the use of time phases in the process, and structuring the relationship according to function and process to further the effectiveness of the work.

In 1937, Jessie Taft, one of the founders of the functional school, wrote that social work had become confused by its inability to find its place between psychotherapy and public relief:

> There is a universal tendency in all human development to progress by extreme swings from object to subject, from the external, the physical and the social, to the internal, the psychological and the individualistic. . . . At one moment we place all truth in the outside world where we try to analyze the object as a separate entity; again we turn upon the self, the doer, and study him in all his subjectivity. Either concentration destroys or ignores the reality that lies only in the living relationship between the two. (Taft 1937:1)

That these arguments continued throughout the Great Depression makes them seem insular and outlandish in retrospect. Private agencies, which employed most of those who had been educated as social workers, could not handle the tremendously accelerated demand for assistance during and after the Great Depression (Trolander 1973). More and more of the relief and counseling functions of social workers had to be handled by public agencies, and social workers had to work with problems that were reality-oriented and, hopefully, short-term. Because social work offered the possibility of secure employment, men entered the field in larger numbers and began to expand and refine social group work and community work. Thus social work was becoming polarized between the public and the private, the social order and the inner world.

In the 1940s, social work embraced Anna Freud's (1946) newly published *Ego and the Mechanisms of Defense*. With its focus on the ego, Freud's thesis allowed social workers to work in social and psychological dimensions and indicated that clients were to participate actively in their treatment. They were to be assessed in terms of strengths and weaknesses rather than psychopathology.

The division between public and private agencies continued beyond World War II, but social workers began to see work with involuntary clients as a legitimate endeavor. Aggressive or authoritative casework, and reaching the unreached or hard-to-reach were rubrics under which involuntary clients were validated for social work's services (Briar and Miller 1971). New techniques developed for work with groups and crisis intervention helped social workers to develop expertise in working with involuntary clients.

During this same period, through a shift of attention from mission to function, social workers increased their identification with their work settings. Function was defined as "an organized effort incorporated into the machinery of community life in the discharge of which the acquiescence at least and ultimately the support of the entire community is assumed" (Lee 1929:4–5). However, organizational goals were and are often in conflict with the mission of social work (Tolson 1988:14) to the point that "the unavoidable vagueness inherent in the breadth of the goals, together with the resulting wide variation inherent in what social workers actually do, has given rise to serious doubts among some segments of the profession about the identity of social work" (Briar 1977:1530). "The supremacy of function over cause has led to the primacy of organizational as opposed to professional goals, the capitulation to serving those who pay the bills over those who need the service, and the dilution of the profession" (Tolson 1988:15). The power of those who pay the bills, including insurers and businesses who pay insurance premiums for their workers, continues to be an issue for all health care providers. As Ware notes, "a troubling kind of thinking occurs when employers and other payers are determined to reorganize health care no matter what the government does. The currency of great importance to this constituency is the effect of health status, disease, and treatment on worker productivity" (Ware 1997:58).

Now most people with illnesses are never admitted to the hospital, or hospital stays are too brief for social work to do more than "best possible" discharge planning. Also, hospitals that survive current cost-cutting measures will exist as small parts of huge, complex systems that manage a range of health services. People continue to be hospitalized infrequently and for very short periods. Thus this comfortable and relatively predictable location will be a less common and probably less important location for social workers in health care. Instead, social workers will work in a range of health-related situations.

PUBLIC HEALTH, CASE MANAGEMENT, AND ADVOCACY

Social work in health care clearly began as a public health effort (Kerson 1981). Public health is primarily concerned with health promotion and the prevention of disease and disability (Garrett 2000). In these endeavors, organized community efforts are directed toward the protection and improvement of community health. Throughout the history of social work practice in health and mental health systems, social workers have worked in this arena as advocates and case managers. Succinctly put, advocacy is the act or process of supporting a cause. Advocacy includes (1) case advocacy, in which a social worker helps a client to meet a specific need, and (2) cause or class advocacy, in which similar unmet needs are grouped and organized into advocacy activity by a group of people (an agency, a section of an organization, or a combination of professionals and community people) (Erickson, Moynihan, and Williams 1991). The job of the case manager is to work with clients to identify the type of help needed, to identify and overcome barriers to using that help effectively, to provide direct service to overcome those barriers, to connect the client with potential helpers, and to provide indirect coordinating services to maintain these connections until the problems are resolved (Ballew and Mink 1996).

The earliest instances of public health social work occurred in 1898, when Henry Dwight Chapin, a New York doctor, organized volunteers to help mothers care for their babies by providing milk, education, and support. During the same year, the Ladies Auxiliary of the New York Lying-In Hospital hired an agent to visit dispensary patients at home during their confinements (Chapin 1918). Much later the social workers fought for permission to work with those who were sick but not poor. In Boston in 1907 social workers were hired to work in communities to address the low living standards, poor diets, and lack of education that were contributing to infant eye conditions that caused blindness. By new law, these infections had to be reported to the health department, which in turn sent the social workers to address the problems that gave rise to the blindness.

Increasingly, social workers were drawn out of hospitals. In 1934, the name of the American Association of Hospital Social Workers was changed to the American Association of Medical Social Workers. Hospital social workers would function intramurally, but medical social workers could address the social components of illness wherever such problems were managed. As now, the work became less based on location. Just after World War II, the demand for social workers in health and mental health increased dramatically. In response, several condition- or population-specific organizations, such as the National Tuberculosis Association and the Veterans Administration, funded graduate education for social workers.

It has been said that "casework with a patient with a serious aftermath to polio [was] frequently medical social work in microcosm" ("Medical Social Work" 1952:105). Polio was the greatest epidemic disease from the early 1950s until the 1980s (Garrett 2000). An editorial comment in *Medical Social Work* ("Editorial Comment" 1952:121) summarized the experience of medical social work in poliomyelitis. The last of five severe polio epidemics in the United States, the 1952 epidemic had a case rate of 36.9 per 100,000 population and a death rate of 2.0. Little was understood about the disease or how to combat it. However, it presented great opportunities for medical social work because it primarily affected children and young adults; it was severely crippling; the acute phase created many anxieties for the patient, the family, and the community; and the long convalescence raised many questions beyond physical status. Beyond the physical needs, there were social, emotional, and vocational needs that, if unmet, could nullify effective medical treatment.

In 1954, Jonas Salk developed the hypodermic poliomyelitis vaccine that prevented the illness in anyone who was vaccinated. Ironically, as Harriett Bartlett, doyenne of social work in health care said, "The very conquest of polio was bad for us [meaning medical social workers] because we had gotten $80,000 a year or more [for training social workers to work with polio patients] and we no longer had that source. We tried to get it from other places and could not" (quoted in Kerson 1978a:198). Because the social implications of this terrifying and devastating scourge were integral to medical diagnosis and treatment, the psychosocial helpers were of paramount importance. Other early examples include work in the influenza epidemic of 1918 and work with those who had syphilis and tuberculosis (Kerson 1978a). Such work always combines skills in case management and advocacy in working for the health of the public.

Present-day work in the areas of well baby care; early and periodic screening, diagnosis, and treatment; outreach services to those with drug and alcohol addictions and to the homeless; neighborhood work designed to control the spread of AIDS, tuberculosis, and other communicable diseases; outreach and case management services for those with persistent mental illness and for the frail elderly continues the tradition of health promotion (Bracht 1990). An example of contemporary public health advocacy is work done on behalf of Native American uranium miners, mill workers, and their families, who were not informed that radiation causes health problems. A primary goal of the work is to obtain compensation through the Radiation Exposure Compensation Act (Dawson, Charley, and Harrison 1997). Examples of contemporary case management in health and mental health are the intensive case management programs available for children and adults across the country (Donovan, Blanchard, and Kerson 1997; Frankel, Harmon, and Kerson 1997; Michelsen and Kerson 1997; Weiss and Kerson 1997).

THE EFFECTS OF TECHNOLOGICAL ADVANCES

As has been suggested, the relationship of social work to health and mental health care is complex and paradoxical. While social workers have continued to be helpful in areas of highly technical intervention, such as renal dialysis and transplant, acute psychiatric units, and newborn intensive care nurseries, and medical practitioners in those areas understand and value the contributions of social work, the majority of social work practice in health and mental health care occurs where there is no available cure or highly effective treatment (Kerson 1997).

One interesting example of the effects of medical advances is social work's early work with syphilis patients, when the treatment took many months. The most important social work function in this area was to "secure patients at the beginning of their infections and hold them under treatment until danger from them as active carriers passed" (Cressman 1944:446). Goals were accomplished through personal interviews and home visits (Kerson 1981). To explain this function, one social worker wrote,

> The syphilitic patient requires constant encouragement and reassurance. Interpretation on the part of the social worker to the doctor and to the family is very essential. In social study and treatment of those families, it is important to remember that there is often the danger of syphilophobia or anxiety neurosis developing in one of the members of the family who has neurotic tendencies. (Lewis 1944)

The use of penicillin for the treatment of syphilis seriously curtailed social work's role. It is perhaps uncomfortable and definitely ironic to contemplate how much social work practice in health and mental health will be altered by cures for or vaccines against AIDS, dementia, schizophrenia, and a range of developmental disabilities. The ways the work will be transformed by today's information and genetic revolutions are probably too profound to be articulated at this time (Ludmerer 1999). History has shown, however, that there is much work for health-related social workers when medical solutions are ineffective or leave great social and psychological problems in their wake.

Technological advancement has had a very interesting effect on social work practice in the care of the seriously mentally ill (Idle 2000; Johnstone 1999; Kaplan and Sadock 1995; Nicholi 1999). Antipsychotic medications have allowed many people with serious mental illness to live in the community. Many antipsychotics combine efficacy with side effects that can affect each system of the body and range from jaundice and photosensitivity to potentially fatal conditions (Arana 2000; Keks, Mazumdar, and Steele 2000). Such antipsychotics require close medical follow-up and regular blood monitoring (Miller 2000). Both the side effects and the nature of such illnesses increases patients' inability or unwillingness to comply with medical regimens. Thus, as a result of these medical advancements, work for social workers has not lessened but changed.

Social workers help clients and consumers to stay with their medical regimens and help them to monitor side effects. These medications are not a panacea. It has been argued that the lack of successful medical regimens has kept some of those who are seriously mentally ill from being able to live in the community, but often such patients are hospitalized for the shortest time it takes to be effectively medicated. Many of these clients leave the hospital and stop taking their medications because of problems in the system, the nature of their illness, or unpleasant side effects. Payers argue that chronically mentally ill persons do not have to live in protected settings because they have access to more effective antipsychotics. While many of these medications are effective, and many people are being helped, seeing these medications as the sole treatment a patient requires and can receive worsens the problems and ultimately blames the patient for those problems. Again, advocacy roles are key for effective social work practice.

SHIFTS IN HEALTH CARE SETTINGS

Boundaries are shifting and permeable. Notions of inpatient and outpatient, preventive and curative, public and private, not-for-profit and for-profit, acute and chronic, traditional and alternative, physical and mental are mutable and unimportant, except that they may affect funding sources. A health care setting is a location in which people are in the business of preventing or managing illness (either physical, mental, or both). To work in such settings, social workers must understand (1) the natural history of illnesses or conditions (what would occur if the illness or conditions were not treated), (2) the treatments for those illnesses, (3) the impact of the policies that affect service, (4) the impact of particular organizational structures and cultures, (5) the ways their organization fits with others in elaborate systems, and (6) ways to keep abreast of changes in order to heighten their effectiveness. Thus it hinders the profession to define itself in terms of location.

Initially, social work practitioners in health care were referred to as hospital social workers, but because this title was felt to be constricting and unreflective of the work, practitioners became known as medical social workers. Along the way, psychiatric social work developed and wanted an identity and title separate from medical social work. Then there was clinical social work and social work in health care, which the British now call health-related social work. A historical view again proves helpful. In 1926, Elsie Wulkop began her book *The Social Worker in a Hospital Ward* with the sentence "The work described in this book was carried out at the Massachusetts General Hospital, a private hospital, receiving no aid from city or State, and serving patients from all over New England and even from Canada." In 1944, Edith Cressman wrote, "In recent years, medical social work has developed rapidly outside of hospitals, and at the same time, it is participating in programs growing out of the war and in preparation for the post-war era. Caseworkers are being drawn from the area of clinical medicine, and standards are jeopardized by the lack of relatively clear and fixed medical social work function in many of those emergency settings." Times, funding sources, mandates, knowledge about health and illness, and definitions of appropriate settings for social workers in health and mental health care are all in flux.

Following are brief examples of new or rediscovered health care settings. A social worker was hired by a group of relatives of chronically mentally ill adults to advocate for them, monitor case management, do educational programs, and expand their own program. In relation to self-help and advocacy work, social workers work for societies and foundations related to specific illnesses to run support groups, provide information and referral, and manage special events. Social workers work in early periodic screening, diagnosis, and treatment programs run through child welfare departments. Social workers provide a range of services for the elderly, both well and frail, which involve patients with Alzheimer's disease, stroke, or other chronic illnesses (Michelsen 1994). They provide services at schools, day care facilities, and camps for those who are developmentally disabled. Sometimes through direct employment and other times through contracted work, social workers are involved in employee assistance programs that range from helping those with substance abuse problems to problems with frail elderly parents. Social workers work in home care situations ranging from support for children living on ventilators to working with adults who require one or two visits to secure support services. Social workers provide AIDS outreach services, as well as services required by those with AIDS across a continuum of care. They provide services to maternal and child health programs located in public health settings. Social workers work in college community outreach programs to help establish health centers with social work as one of the primary services. This is only a sampling of the breadth of social work in health and mental health care settings.

An area project on occupational safety and health involves a nonprofit coalition of unions, health and legal professionals, and others concerned with occupational safety and health issues. A social worker works on a program that provides education, information and referral, and health intervention to prevent the onset of diseases that are common in persons with asbestos-related disease. She provides outreach in the form of a quarterly newsletter and self-help groups for asbestosis victims and their families. She is the primary coordinator of the asbestos illness prevention program (Mama and Kerson 1994). In a nursing home, a social worker helped modify and simplify the environment of a woman with Alzheimer's disease in ways that gave her more control and made her and her family much more comfortable (Mercer 1996; Mercer, Robinson, and Kerson 1997).

In a home for severely handicapped children and young adults, a social worker worked with a young woman who had severe cerebral palsy, was unable to speak or walk, had an IQ between 40 and 55, and had such angry outbursts that no one in the institution could stand her. Through forms of positive behavior modification, she helped the young woman to manage herself, to be a more accepted member of the community, and to move to a new facility with residents who functioned at a higher level than those at the former location (O'Neill 1997). Social workers work with members of the military to keep them fit to serve after having been exposed to traumatic stress (Martin 1997). A social worker runs a fly-fishing camp for breast cancer survivors. Social workers advocate for those who have occupationally or environmentally related illnesses (Dawson et al. 1997). Social workers now carry myriad responsibilities in life-care communities. All the above can be considered health care settings, because a health care setting is a location where people are in the business of preventing or managing illness (either physical, mental, or both). Thus the evolving place of contemporary social work in health care reflects (1) the changing emphasis on systems of care, (2) the breakdown of the boundaries between physical health and mental health, (3) the revision of notions of inpatient and outpatient care, and (4) the need for the practitioner to be a generalist in terms of intervention strategies, that is, to be able to intervene on many levels (individual, family, group, organization, advocacy, and community), and (5) the need for practitioners to be experts regarding specific populations.

THE IMPACT OF MANAGED CARE

We are in the midst of a managed care revolution. Social workers have to find ways to advocate for clients within health care delivery systems, within multiple payment structures, and perhaps within the courts. As managed care companies increasingly assume responsibility for payments to providers of health and mental health care for the most fragile and dependent populations in our society, the advocacy function of social work grows.

Managed care involves providing some form of social or health care for a specified population in ways that incorporate quality, continuity, and fiscal responsibility. A Congressional Budget Office report defines managed care as including interventions in health care financing and delivery. Major dimensions include cost-funding prospectively or retrospectively; reviewing and intervening in decisions about services to be provided; limiting or influencing patients' choice of providers; and negotiating payment terms with providers (Langwell and Menke 1991:37). Additionally, managed care can be defined as "any measure, that from the purchaser's perspective, favorably affects the price of services, the site at which services are delivered or received, and/or their utilization" or "an arrangement or system in which there are financial, administrative, organizational and monitoring constructs whose end is to minimize resource allocation and maximize efficiency and quality" (Croze 1995:334). Managed competition, which has been one dimension of the discussion regarding managed care, is "a purchasing strategy to obtain maximum value for money for employers and consumers. It uses rules for competition, derived from rational microeconomic principles to reward with more subscribers and revenue those health plans that do the best job of improving quality, cutting cost, and satisfying patients" (Enthoven 1993:29). At this time, managed competition has not been widely adopted (Marquis and Long 1999).

The earliest example of managed care in the United States was Washington's Western Clinic, which in 1910 contracted with lumber mills to provide care to their employees for fifty cents per month per person. In some early examples (beginning with Kaiser Permanente in California in 1939 and the Health Insurance Plan of Greater New York in the 1940s), managed care was highly successful. For many years, HMOs were touted as the solution to managing health care in the United States. Since the "golden years" of HMOs, many societal transformations have caused what was seen as the ideal solution by almost everyone with a role in health care to be seen as withholding, insensitive, and unethical. For example, medical technology for assessment and intervention has proliferated and become more expensive. The population has aged, and technological intervention has kept alive many ill and disabled people whose conditions would have caused them to die had they lived in earlier eras. Health insurance (especially indemnity insurance like Blue Cross/Blue Shield) has become prohibitively expensive for employers, who traditionally have paid for health insurance for their workers. Enrollment shifts from traditional indemnity plans to managed care plans largely reflect employers' choices about the types of plans to offer rather than voluntary choices among multiple options by employers (Marquis and Long 1999:85).

As the government has increasingly shouldered the expense of insuring many of the unemployed segments of society and employers look desperately for ways to reduce health insurance costs, controlling and/or capping the costs of health insurance and health care has overtaken other issues in health care. In fact, it often seems the primary issue (Levit, Lazenby, Braden, and the National Health Accounts Team 1998; Stiller, Won, Donham, Long, and Stewart 1996). Managed care, with its emphasis on fiscal accountability, is the present, but not the final, solution to controlling and/or capping health care spending. As numbers of for-profit businesses have become involved with managed care, an imbalance has been created, and fiscal concerns appear to far outweigh concerns with quality and continuity. As employers switch to lower-bidding plans and Medicaid managed care plans sometimes falter or collapse, barriers are raised to specialized and acute care. Access to preventive and primary care does not seem to be increasing, and providers are become more disheartened. There seems to be less attention given to quality or continuity, except for their being big sticks with which to whip providers. More than in any other dimension of health care, this is where the health care revolution is being felt (Davidson, Davidson, and Keigher 1999). As health care is controlled by larger and larger systems, corporations, and bureaucracies and is increasingly market driven, the loci for decision making move further and further from patients and providers.

Behavioral Managed Health Care

Nowhere is this revolution felt more profoundly by social workers than in mental health care, where social workers provide the majority of psychotherapy (Stroul, Pires, Armstrong, and Meyers 1998). Overall, there has been a great drop in insurance payments for psychiatric care. Benefits for the treatment of psychiatric disorders fell by 54 percent between 1988 and 1997. As part of this trend, managed care companies and other kinds of insurers routinely refuse to pay for even the brief forms of psychotherapy that they claim to find acceptable. Neither will they pay social workers to provide community support to those with serious mental illness (Hughes 1999). Many mental illnesses cannot be managed using short-term or brief forms of treatment. In order to fund mental health services, insurers want proof of efficacy and cost-effectiveness (Spiegel 1999). Whether this transformed service should continue to be called psychotherapy is debatable, but in its current guise, its primary payer is managed behavioral health care (Edward 1999; Wineburgh 1998).

Behavioral health care can be offered as a carve-in (using inside staff and facilities) or a carve-out (using contracted local providers) by Medicaid and Medicare managed care providers (Colenda, Banazak, and Mickus 1998). Rather than develop behavioral health programs, large insurance companies have bought companies that deliver those services. For example, MCC/Cigna is a national managed behavioral health care company that was bought by Cigna with a network of providers and clinics throughout the United States that covers more than 5 million lives. Value Behavioral Health, a behavioral health company that has remained independent of insurance companies, covers about 15 million lives (Geller 1996). Managed behavioral health is promoted as providing early detection of mental illness, providing high-quality, cost-effective continuity of care through a broad range of services, and reducing cost shifting to individuals. Little of the programming takes into account the complexity of mental illness and substance abuse, the disagreements about diagnosis and treatment, the lack of clear outcome criteria, the need for confidentiality, the range of mental health professionals attesting to their ability to manage these problems, and the social stigma attached to mental illness (Wineburgh 1998).

Forms of Managed Care

A brief description of four basic models of managed care demonstrates important differences in the relationships between health care plans and providers. These are all network-based provider organizations that "differ in the amount of financial risk they assume, the way they share risk with providers, the restrictiveness of their provider policies, and the level of out-of-pocket costs the beneficiary may carry" (Gage 1998). In a staff model HMO, the plan employs its providers. In a group model HMO, the plan contracts for the exclusive services of large physician group practices, most of whose patients belong to the HMO. In a network model HMO, the plan contracts with large groups of practitioners in a nonexclusive relationship. In an independent practice association using an intermediary, the HMO contracts with individual or small group providers. In the last several years, with consumers demanding more choice, insurers have offered more expensive options that have allowed their enrollees to see providers who were out-of-network, that is, outside the list of providers with whom the plan has contracted. This kind of option (which demonstrates how ideal and mutable the four models are) is called a mixed category with an out-of-network option. More forms are evolving.

Choices Related to Managed Care

Choice is one of the issues most often discussed with regard to managed care. Companies choose the health plans in which their employees may enroll. Plan managers choose providers and make decisions regarding access to and limits on specialists, diagnostic tests, and interventions. Individuals choose among the health plans made available by their employers.

Those on Medicaid may choose between Medicaid providers. Those primarily insured through Medicare choose what kinds of medigap insurance to add (if any) or whether to choose a Medicare managed care plan (Kuttner 1999). However, every one of these choices proves limiting.

> On balance, the emergence of managed care has probably reduced the range of choice in health care by individuals. Nonetheless, the rationale behind the transformation of the financing and delivery of health care is the belief that individuals, if forced to bear the financial consequences of choosing higher-cost health plans, will make choices that promote competition among risk bearers and health care providers, and that increased competition will ultimately bring about an improved balance of social costs and social benefits from health care. (Aaron 2000:38)

The Development of Antagonistic Relationships

Many dimensions of managed care have contributed to antagonistic relationships between various players. Managed care has been characterized as a battleground with payers and providers battling about enrollees, money, and control of care (Iglehart 1999b; Vitberg 1996). "The relationships of the insured to their insurers and of health care providers to their payers have changed more in the past five years than they did cumulatively since health insurance became commonplace in the 1950's" (Aaron 2000:38). "Plans shift their financial risks to the physicians and medical groups with whom they contract through capitation or withholding. In capitation, providers are paid a fixed payment to provide all of the care that the enrollee may need. In withholding, physicians are given financial incentive to limit referrals to specialists, tests and hospitals" (Grumbach 1999:2008).

Medicaid and Medicare Managed Care

Employers and federal and state governments have encouraged or compelled consumers to join managed care plans in order to control costs. Payers and consumers have turned to managed care as a way of paying lower premiums and lower rates of cost sharing (Gage 1998). "In 1994, the Medicare and Medicaid programs alone accounted for nearly one-third of all health care spending in the United States and more than 17% of all spending by the federal government. Spending for Medicare continues to increase at a rate of 10% per year" (Epstein and Aldredge 2000:17–18). As the baby boomers enter the Medicare group, the cost will increase even more dramatically.

Medicaid is the largest health insurer in the country, covering medical services and long-term care for some 41.3 million people, most of whom are outside the employment-based insurance system. All states except Alaska provide for their Medicaid populations using managed care. "The proportion of Medicaid beneficiaries enrolled in managed-care plans increased from 9.5% (2.7 million people) in 1991 to 48% (15.3 million) in 1997" (Iglehart 1999a:407). The states contract in three ways: (1) they hire primary physicians who act as gatekeepers, (2) they contract with clinics or group practices that provide services but do not assume all financial risk, or (3) they enroll beneficiaries in HMOs that assume all financial risk and provide all services. When HMOs are willing to assume all financial risk, the states choose that approach.

The Urban Institute reports that, thus far, Medicaid managed care is more of a skirmish than a revolution because there has been limited success either in expanding access to mainstream providers or in saving money (Iglehart 1999a). Generally Medicaid managed care is limited to children and young adults. In fact, "eighty five to ninety percent of Medicaid managed care enrollees are women of childbearing age and children, who together account for 69% of Medicaid recipients, but only 26% of program costs" (Deal and Shiono 1998, p. 93). Potential savings have been limited because few states have extended enrollment to more expensive elderly and disabled enrollees (Iglehart 1999a).

Also, in state negotiations with HMOs, already low Medicaid reimbursements make it difficult for states to lower capitation levels or for HMOs to demand further discounts. Therefore, the result of low capitation fees and protections for providers has found HMOs unwilling to contract with states. Many commercial HMOs that contracted with individual states when the states first allowed such contracts have withdrawn from the program. In areas where managed care plans exist, increased competition among managed care plans has threatened and continues to threaten the fiscal stability of traditional Medicaid providers, including low-income neighborhood hospitals, community health centers, and physician offices (Sparer 1996). Patients, too, are frustrated and dissatisfied with service. For example, results of a study of Tenn-Care, a compulsory Medicaid managed care program initiated in Tennessee in 1994, reported long waiting periods, out-of-town specialist care, problems with medications, and general system confusion (Rocha and Kabalka 1999).

In 1997 Medicare insured 39 million people (34 million over age 65 and 5 million disabled younger people, and almost 3 hundred thousand with end-stage renal disease) and spent $214.6 billion to diagnose and treat acute illness. The number of Americans age 65 or older is projected to be 68 million in 2040, and enrollment in Medicare is expected to be 22 percent of the population by 2030 (Marmor and Oberlander 1998). Like Social Security, the program is funded by having the contributions of presently working people cover the costs of medical care for those who are no longer part of the workforce. As costs and numbers of participants increase, the government must find ways to control expenditures.

Medicare has had a managed care option since its inception. Few managed care plans participated until 1985, when the Tax Equity and Fiscal Responsibility Act allowed Medicare to pay plans 95 percent of the average local cost per beneficiary and allowed the plans to keep the difference between their payments and their allowable costs (Gage 1998). The government pays HMOs a capitated amount per month (a preset amount per person regardless of service use), and in turn the HMO is responsible for all costs a patient can incur that are part of standard Medicare coverage. HMOs lower costs by eliminating unnecessary services, reducing payments to providers, using a less expensive mix of services, and enrolling consumers who tend to be healthier than average and therefore require less care. At this time, managed care programs are not lowering costs for Medicare, and plans, providers, and consumers describe many problems with the program.

The Balanced Budget Act of 1997 changed Medicare from an insurer working directly with providers to deliver services to a payer promoting an array of private health insurance plans, including but not limited to traditional Medicare and managed care plans. Through Medicare + Choice, Medicare is responsible for managing the process by which beneficiaries choose from among the plans and finances services by paying plans a capitation fee for each beneficiary. The purpose is to increase choice and curb spending by having plans compete for business (Gage 1998:15). In addition, Medicare is sponsoring demonstration grants that will test new forms, such as social health maintenance organizations, which will pool capitated payments from several sources to provide short- and long-term care. Also, payments for Medicare managed care have varied greatly by state, and Congress is working to redistribute payments more equitably. As Congress works to curb spending and increase equity, Medicare becomes more complex and difficult to understand. Thus it is increasingly important for both beneficiaries and professionals to understand the choices and trade-offs (Gazmararian 1999).

In 1998 and 1999, almost 750,000 people were dropped from Medicare HMOs because the HMOs considered payments too low, financial risks too great, and regulatory strictures too burdensome (Iglehart 1999b). On July 1, 1999, almost one hundred managed care plans said that they would withdraw from Medicare or reduce the number of geographic areas in which they would enroll Medicare participants. As a result, in 2000, based on a blend of national and local fee-for-service costs, rates rose by at least 2 percent in 63 percent of United States counties (for 18 percent of the population). Medicare managed care plans will continue to evolve to meet access, programmatic, and fiscal needs of all stakeholders. Particularly, they will have to address needs of the elderly with chronic illnesses and the costs of prescription drugs.

Managed Care and Advocacy

"The advent of large-scale managed care organizations presents the challenge to persist as advocates despite new limitations and hazards" (Sunley 1997:93). As the social work value system demands, social workers must remain positive and hopeful for ourselves and our clients in what is being called the managed care environment. Because it appears to be the most likely way to contain costs and monitor services, managed care in various forms will be part of health care and social services in the United States for the foreseeable future. As with other alterations in society, the most dependent and vulnerable populations, often those with whom social work practitioners work most closely, will continue to be most affected by the restrictions of managed care.

Managed care is the current answer to concerns about cost containment. As in the cases of other less-than-perfect solutions that preceded managed care and those that will follow, social workers will abide by their ethics and values and optimize their work with clients. There are opportunities for significant, positive change to be derived from managed care. Necessary reforms include more effective incorporation of safety-net providers into managed care networks, better adjustment of reimbursement for case mix, greater sensitivity to cultural and linguistic differences, greater support for trauma and burn centers and neonatal intensive care units, and more public functions (Andrulis and Carrier 1999:187). As has been true since the beginnings of social work practice, astuteness regarding laws (especially those related to entitlements) and regarding the workings of organizations and systems will help social workers to help their clients to negotiate the managed care environment (Epstein and Aldredge 2000; Galambos 1999; Strom-Gottfried 1998; Wernet 1999). As always, social workers will find the ways.

PREDICTIONS FOR THE FUTURE

Twenty-first-century social work practice in health care will be different at least in relation to location, territory, financing, knowledge requirements, the means for assessment, strategies of intervention, and the use of outcome measures. The following are the primary factors affecting the health care arena and social work in health care at the turn of the twenty-first century: (1) growing numbers of elderly people; (2) the determination of government and business to control and limit spending for health care, and (3) new, powerful, and more expensive technology for the assessment and treatment of illness, enabling people to live longer and require greater intervention (Koop 1993). Managed care will play an increasingly important part in the delivery of health care services because it seems to be the only way businesses and federal and state governments can cap spending (Corcoran and Vandiver 1996). In this regard, those who deliver care will have less latitude for determining the nature of care and therefore will require highly efficient and effective means for intervention to work successfully within managed care schema. If the trend continues, all levels of government will provide less direct care but will increase oversight. Technological interventions, including drugs and testing and interventional medical devices, will become increasingly expensive. Because health care is so expensive, businesses that fund insurance policies as well as all forms of insurance will find ways to enhance health, and there will be increased attention to the prevention of disability.

To practice most effectively, social workers in health and mental health care will require an ecological perspective that allows them to maintain a high level of knowledge and skill to be able to adapt to changes in technology, social policy, and health care delivery. Spanning boundaries will enable social workers to be less dependent on particular settings and more knowledgeable, adaptable, and flexible in their quest to be of greatest help to their clientele.

Legal and Ethical Issues

Laws and ethics are major components of the context of social work practice, shaping what we do, with whom we do it, and how we work. They are also our most powerful tools in our advocacy efforts for clients. Bertelli (1998:3) argues persuasively that social workers may have a role in providing routine legal services, especially in light of the drastic cuts in legal services for the poor. He notes that social workers in settlement houses and community centers "are well-positioned to assist poor persons with simple legal problems." He cautions against practicing "unauthorized law," particularly urging referral to an attorney for any criminal cases. He encourages a "basic package of legal skills" for all social workers, including "(1) working communication skills with regard to legal resources; (2) the ability to see a problem through a legal lens; (3) a working knowledge of client communication techniques" and awareness of legal aid resources (Bertelli 1998:11). Even if not called on to act directly with the client in overtly legal contexts, the social worker must be aware of the societal legal context.

A law is a binding custom or community practice that is prescribed and formally recognized. Laws are the most explicit dimensions of the codes that govern society's behavior. The judicial system and ultimately the policing power of the state enforce the laws of the community. Laws inform, provide latitude to, and constrain social work practice. They protect rights and entitlements and restrain and define behavior. The law, the whole body of such rules, customs, and practices, is a society's most forceful way of making a code of behavior explicit and rational.

Legislators pass statutes and make law; judges decide cases and issue opinions through the courts, in effect, using administrative discretion and the power legally delegated to them to interpret law. Administrators, who may be judges, interact most with social workers and clients. "Using their discretion, administrators establish rules for the enforcement of child abuse statutes, and determining removals of children from the home, for the provision of patient rights and release of institutionalized mental patients, or for running a correctional facility, a hospital or a school" (Dickson 1995:10).

There are four types of laws: constitutional, statutory, case, and administrative. With regard to constitutional law, the federal government and all states have constitutions containing the laws that establish the government and legal system and protect the basic rights of their populations. The first ten amendments of the federal constitution establish the basic rights of all citizens. Statutory law is legislation enacted by federal and state legislative bodies that covers many areas important in health and mental health care. It is this type of federal law that will be addressed in this chapter. In case law, a judge applies existing law to facts in a dispute brought before the court and decides which party should prevail:

> The disputes that come before the court may be as narrow as whether an individual child has been neglected or whether a particular zoning ordinance should apply to a group home for disabled citizens or as broad as whether all institutionalized developmentally disabled individuals throughout the country have a constitutional right to habilitation or whether the death penalty can be applied to juveniles convicted of certain crimes. (Dickson 1995:9)

Administrative law includes federal and state administrative codes, state agency policies and procedures, and local government regulations. Through administrative law, for example, Medicaid administrators have the power to regulate medical assistance programs.

Aligned with the legal dimensions of practice are the ethical and moral dimensions, codes of behavior that have been taught and internalized. For social work practice, the ethical and moral dimensions have to be understood on two levels: the personal one, which guides an individual to behave properly, and the professional one, which guides the behaviors of an entire occupational group. Ethics inform beliefs and behavior. Values are unprovable assumptions or tenets of faith that guide social work practice

(Compton and Galaway 1998:5). Often a personal moral code causes an individual to become a social worker.

Differences may be drawn between ethical and legal arenas in terms of how specifically behavior is codified. Ethics provide guiding sources of moral knowledge and judgment that govern all behavior, rather than providing concise statements of rules or norms of behavior that act as "action guides" (Reich 1995:xxviii). Laws are directed toward governing and, in fact, policing specific behavior. For example, ethically, it is wrong to hurt others. Legally, one who murders or assaults another can be charged with a crime, brought to trial using the force of the police, and if found guilty can be jailed or even executed for the crime. The law can be enforced by the full power of the state, whereas ethical behavior is governed by internalized principles and other less enforceable codes. Professional organizations can provide some midlevel enforcement via sanctions. Although both laws and ethical codes serve to guide and clarify action, many of the circumstances surrounding health and mental health problems are so complex, insoluble, or unpredictable that the correct ways to proceed are not clear. Dilemmas, predicaments, and impasses are a regular part of social work practice.

THE FIDUCIARY RELATIONSHIP

A fiduciary is a person to whom property or power is entrusted for the benefit of another. The word is derived from Roman law, in which it referred to the transfer of a right to a person who was then obligated to transfer or return that right at a certain future time and/or when some condition had been fulfilled. In a fiduciary relationship, one person acts primarily for the benefit of another in specific undertakings. Such a relationship exists when one member of the relationship relies on the judgment and advice of the other. All professional relationships are fiduciary ones. A fiduciary relationship comes from the trust that clients place in professionals (Kutchins 1991). In turn, when professionals agree to work with clients, their fiduciary responsibility obligates them to understand and never abuse the power they have been given by the clients and to act in their clients' best interests. The nature of that relationship requires that social workers discuss the services they can provide, the risks of injury, the probability of outcome, possible alternatives, careful referral, and planned termination. Above all, social workers must assure those whom they wish to help that they will engage in no exploitative behavior. The client relies on the social worker to act honorably. Fiduciary relationships are governed by law. "By evoking fiduciary obligations, clients can hold professionals to a higher standard of conduct than usually is required in malpractice cases and can shift a major portion of the burden of proof to professionals to demonstrate that they acted appropriately" (Kutchins 1991:110).

LAW

People infected with the human immunodeficiency virus (HIV) are stigmatized in ways that create barriers to health care as well as employment and housing, and they require legal protection. Although statutory regulations (the Americans with Disabilities Act of 1990) prohibit discrimination against HIV-positive individuals and have created avenues for resolving discriminatory practices, the need for legal advocacy and advocacy services remains compelling. This need is compounded by the fact that the populations currently most likely to be infected are socially vulnerable in other ways. They frequently have higher-than-average rates of poverty, homelessness, and bankruptcy or other debtor/creditor problems, and they have limited access to health care. They are gay and bisexual men; racial, ethnic, and cultural minorities; incarcerated men and women; individuals with substance abuse and/or mental health problems, and users of illegal intravenous drugs. Vulnerable youths must deal with issues such as undocumented immigration, rights of minors, medical insurance, quality of care, and parenting rights. The following practice case involves the Americans with Disabilities Act, Social Security Disability Insurance, Supplemental Security Income (SSI), the Fair Housing Amendment, the Rehabilitation Act, the Plan for Achieving Self-Support, and the Patient Self-Determination Act, as well as discussion of living wills and durable powers of attorney.

Alvin Johnson is a 45-year-old African American who has AIDS. Before he became too ill to work, Mr. Johnson had been employed for fifteen years as a display manager for a national chain of retail stores. He was infected about ten years ago through recreational intravenous drug use. He is presently in a committed relationship with Maria Olivera, a 35-year-old Hispanic woman who is also HIV-positive symptomatic. Mr. Johnson has no living relatives and, with the exception of Ms. Olivera, considers himself alone in the world. He was discovered to be HIV-positive in 1991, when he entered a drug rehabilitation program, and he has not used drugs since that time.

Since 1991, Alvin Johnson has received help from a local AIDS services organization, where his primary resource has been his social worker and case manager, Bette Dawson (figure 3.1). He developed full-blown AIDS in 1993 and soon became too ill to work. He was deeply distressed when his first application for Social Security Disability Insurance (SSDI) was returned with questions about his drug involvement. Because Ms. Dawson understands the

FIGURE 3.1. Ecomap for Alvin Johnson.

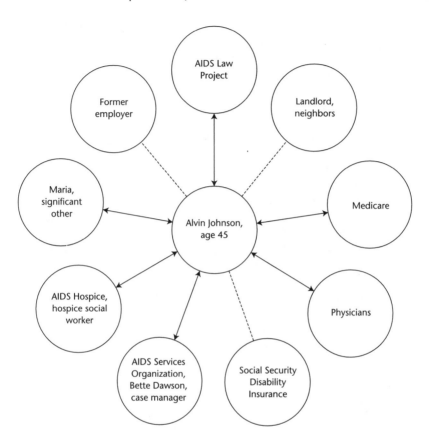

Social Security legislation, she persuaded Mr. Johnson to request reconsideration, clarified the necessary steps for a successful claim, and coordinated the work of his physician, the clinic through which he received services, and the local AIDS Law Project. Both Dawson and Johnson are convinced that the application was successful because Dawson included two additional letters in the reapplication: one from the drug rehabilitation center that Johnson had attended saying that he had been rehabilitated and another from his employer stating that each of his spot urine checks since rehabilitation had been negative. Mr. Johnson's SSDI benefits were approved eight months after his initial denial. Retroactive payments were made to the date that he could no longer work.

While Ms. Dawson and Mr. Johnson awaited the outcome of the reapplication, neighbors in Mr. Johnson's apartment building learned of his infection and told their landlord that they wanted him evicted. Ms. Dawson's understanding of the Fair Housing Amendments Act of 1988 and the Americans with Disabilities Act of 1990 helped her to convince the landlord that there was no basis for eviction. In addition, through an outreach effort targeting the community surrounding the apartment building, Ms. Dawson educated building residents, the landlord, and other community members about their lack of risk.

In 1995, Mr. Johnson's employer, who had been providing Mr. Johnson with medical insurance since he had become disabled, took advantage of a recently passed federal law that allowed businesses to move individuals on long-term disability from their medical insurance to Medicare. He was eligible for Medicare eighteen months after becoming eligible for disability payments, two years after leaving work. His employer also terminated his employment as a result of his long-term disability. Again, Ms. Dawson advocated for Mr. Johnson during his transition from the private insurance to Medicare. The transition was complicated and difficult because so many parties (the employer, the employer-provided medical insurer, the Social Security Administration for Medicare Parts A and B, Mr. Johnson's doctors, and his pharmacy) had to be consulted and included. Ms. Dawson and Mr. Johnson had to understand the legislation itself, the description of Medicare benefits, and the effects of the loss of Mr. Johnson's employer-provided medical benefits.

In 1996, the Contract with America Advancement Act of 1996 was signed into law. Because it eliminated drug addiction and alcoholism as a basis for disability in SSDI and SSI programs, this law affected current recipients for whom drug abuse or alcoholism was a "material factor" contributing to the determination of their disability. Ms. Dawson was concerned that Mr. Johnson's original application for SSDI listed drug addiction and rehabilitation as factors to be considered. Her understanding of the new law and written reminders of the employer and drug rehabilitation letters submitted earlier helped ensure that Mr. Johnson would continue to receive benefits.

In 1997, very ill with a number of opportunistic infections, Mr. Johnson was considered terminally ill, with a life expectancy of less than five months. Maria could not provide the kind of care and support that he required. Ms. Dawson explained that Mr. Johnson was now eligible for hospice services that would be covered by Medicare. Ms. Olivera asked Ms. Dawson to help her have Mr. Johnson admitted to the local AIDS Hospice so he could spend his final days in peace and so Ms. Olivera could continue to work to support herself. As a result of Mr. Johnson's admission to hospice, other issues arose.

Mr. Johnson and Ms. Olivera were informed about the Patient Self-Determination Act, which mandates that hospitals and other health care institutions discuss with patients their advance directives, the medical decisions they wish to have made on their behalf if they become unable to make them. Ms. Dawson and the hospice social worker helped Mr. Johnson to complete a living will and a durable power of attorney. One of the issues that arose was that Mr. Johnson and Ms. Olivera were not legally married and that therefore Ms. Olivera did not have legal authority to act for Mr. Johnson.

While Mr. Johnson was in hospice care, effective new combinations of medications allowed him to combat the opportunistic infections, increased his T-cell count, and lowered his viral load. Released from hospice care with more energy and vitality, Mr. Johnson is now considering returning to work, and again Ms. Dawson is his advocate. His former employer is not interested in employing him, but he is being considered by another chain of stores. If he is hired, he will be covered under that employer's group health insurance policy despite his preexisting condition, because that is the law for all large group policies. Ms. Dawson's understanding of Social Security's return-to-work policies is helping Mr. Johnson make the best decision possible. Issues such as a trial work period, extended period of eligibility, and the continuation of Medicare have all been explored. Also, her knowledge of the Plan for Achieving Self-Support (PASS) is important. The PASS program is available for individuals who receive either SSDI or SSI, or both. If a PASS plan is approved by the Social Security Administration, income or assets (referred to as "set-asides") can be saved each month to meet education, vocational training, or business start-up expenses.

The termination of Mr. Johnson's employment by his former employer and his possible return to work are creating additional challenges for him. Ms. Dawson's understanding of the Americans with Disabilities Act of 1990 and the Rehabilitation Act of 1973 is helping Mr. Johnson to define and reach his goals. In addition, Ms. Dawson is providing information about Mr. Johnson's ability to obtain medical insurance should he have to work on his own and not be able to participate in a group plan and his ability to receive long-term disability insurance once he returns to work, as well as his ability to secure life insurance.

Generally, the law has two functions: to protect and to entitle. Following is a discussion of federally mandated programs, laws, and legal issues that health-related social workers must understand, although it is impossible to include all federal legislation related to health care. Many legal issues relate to specific populations, situations, and individuals. It is essential that social workers understand the laws that affect their clientele so that they participate fully in the process of protection and entitlement. Social workers involved with specific populations should know the law that affects those populations. Most of the descriptions provided here are very brief. Some, such as those for the Americans with Disabilities Act and the discussion of informed consent, have been broadened to demonstrate the minimal depth of information social workers need about laws and legal issues that directly affect their client populations. More in-depth information regarding all these laws and issues can be found in libraries, online, and through help lines.

Social Security

Many programs in health and mental health care are mandated under the Social Security Amendments Act of 1965: Medicare, Medicaid, Social Security Disability Insurance, and Maternal and Child Health Services.

Medicare. Established by the Social Security Amendments Act of 1965, Medicare provides health insurance to people who are 65 years old or older, people who are disabled, and people with permanent kidney failure. Medicare has two parts: Hospital Insurance (Part A) and Medical Insurance (Part B). Part A provides coverage of inpatient hospital services, skilled nursing facilities, home health services, and hospice care. Medicare Part B helps pay for the cost of physician services, outpatient hospital services, medical equipment and supplies, and other health services and supplies. Qualified individuals can enroll in Medicare by completing an application form at their local Social Security Administration office.

Elderly people who are eligible for Medicaid can receive both Medicaid and Medicare. In these cases, Medicaid can act as a supplement to the services covered under Medicare. If an individual has both Medicare and Medicaid and uses a service that is covered by both forms of insurance, Medicare is the first source of payment.

Medicaid. Enacted through the same legislation that established Medicare, and financed jointly by federal and state governments, this program assists states in providing medical care for certain individuals and families with low incomes and limited resources. Beneficiaries include children, the aged, persons who are blind or otherwise disabled, and people who are eligible to receive federally assisted income maintenance payments. The federal government provides broad national guidelines, and each state establishes its own eligibility standards; determines the type, amount, duration, and scope of services; sets the rate of payment for services; and administers its own program. Therefore, Medicaid provisions vary from state to state, and within each state they vary over time. However, services that must be provided by all states include inpatient and outpatient hospital care visits with a physician, nurse midwife, or certified nurse practitioner; laboratory and X-ray services; nursing home care; home health care; Early and Periodic Screening, Diagnosis, and Treatment (EPSDT) for children under age 21; and family planning.

Social Security Disability Insurance. For the purpose of determining eligibility for Supplemental Security Income and Social Security Disability Insurance, a disability is defined as "the inability to engage in any substantial gainful activity by reason of any medically determinable physical or mental impairment that is expected to result in death or that has lasted or can be expected to last for a continuous period of at least 12 months" (Social Security Amendments Act of 1965, Title II). People with AIDS may also qualify when they must severely limit their work or when they can no longer work. Beneficiaries must also accept state rehabilitation services if the Social Security Administration decides that these services would be helpful. Beneficiaries can continue to receive benefits for up to nine months while they test their ability to work.

The Social Security Administration's Office of Employment Support Programs "has expanded ways to provide social security and supplemental security income beneficiaries who have a disability with increased access to rehabilitation and employment services to help them go to work" (Social Security Act of 1935). One of these initiatives, the Plan for Achieving Self-Support, was mentioned in the case example presented earlier in this chapter. The applicant develops a plan for education, business start-up, or other occupational training and is then allowed to set aside additional assets in order to save for and implement the plan. The primary determinant of whether a plan is accepted by the Social Security Administration is how likely the plan is to allow the beneficiary to become self-supporting (i.e., to no longer need SSI or SSDI). The Social Security Administration also has an initiative called Project RSVP, administered by Birch and Davis (1-888-606-RSVP), that connects beneficiaries to vocational rehabilitation services to allow them to develop occupational skills.

Maternal and Child Health Services. The Maternal and Child Health Services Block Grant, originally authorized in Title V of the Social Security Act, is the only federally funded authorized program devoted exclusively to maternal and child health. Title V created a coordinated system based on a partnership between the federal government and the states. One of its goals is to extend and improve available services in each state, especially in very poor rural areas. Funds are used for prenatal care, well baby clinics, school health services, immunization, public health nursing, nutrition services, and health education. Grants are issued each year according to the percentage of low-income children living in each state. For every four dollars the federal government contributes, the state must contribute three dollars in cash or in kind.

The goals of the Maternal and Child Health Services are to

- Reduce infant mortality and the incidence of handicapping conditions among children
- Increase the number of immunized children who have received health assessment and diagnostic and treatment services
- Provide access to comprehensive prenatal services, primary child care, comprehensive care for special needs children, and rehabilitation services for children with disabilities under 16 years old who are eligible for Supplemental Security Income
- Facilitate comprehensive, community-based, culturally competent coordinated care systems of services for special needs children and their families

Supplemental Security Income

Supplemental Security Income is a federal public assistance program that provides a minimum cash income to people who are below a designated poverty level who are old, blind, or otherwise disabled. Those who are blind or disabled must have medical verification that they are unable to engage in any substantial gainful activity. Their impairment is expected to result in death or is expected to last for at least a year. Funding comes from the federal treasury and is usually supplemented by state funds. It is administered primarily by the Social Security Administration, but its funds do not come from the funds earmarked for funding Old Age Survivors Disability Insurance. Eligibility is determined by a means test and is not related to previous work record. Federal maximum benefits are well below the poverty line; they vary according to state and the eligibility standards are outdated (Gilbert, Specht, and Terrell 1993).

Supplemental Security Income, Temporary Assistance for Needy Families, and Medicaid

In most states, those who are eligible for SSI are also eligible for Medicaid. One result of the new welfare law, Temporary Assistance for Needy Families, is that some children who have previously received SSI are no longer considered eligible for it. Under the new law, children under the age of 18 are considered disabled if they have a medically determinable physical or mental impairment that results in marked and severe functional limitations and that can be expected to result in death or has lasted or can be expected to last for a continuous period of at least twelve months. No one under age 18 who engages in substantial gainful activity can be considered disabled. Now, the Social Security Administration must discontinue the individualized functional assessment for children and eliminate the criteria of maladaptive behavior in the domain of personal/behavioral function in determining whether a child is disabled. Because many of those affected by the new law remain eligible for Medicaid, states must reevaluate any individual who loses SSI when that determination affects the individual's Medicaid eligibility.

It is also important to understand the relationship between the Temporary Assistance for Needy Families (section 103 of the new law) and Medicaid. Until 1996, many poor families became eligible for Medicaid through their eligibility for cash assistance programs such as Aid to Families with Dependent Children (AFDC), which was designed to provide welfare assistance for single-parent families. The Personal Responsibility and Work Opportunity Reconciliation Act of 1996 replaced AFDC with a block grant program called Temporary Assistance for Needy Families (TANF). To be sure that low-income families with children continue to be eligible for Medicaid, the new law states that families who would have qualified for Medicaid under AFDC are generally eligible for Medicaid now, whether or not they receive TANF, as long as they meet two eligibility requirements: First, family income and resources must meet the prereform AFDC standards (section 1931(b)(1)(I) of the Social Security Act). Second, a child must be living with a parent or other relative and deprived of parental support or care by the death, absence, incapacity, or unemployment of a parent (section 1931(b)(1)(A)(ii) of the Social Security Act). If a family loses Medicaid eligibility because of employment or receipt of support payments and has received Medicaid in three of the preceding six months, the family is eligible for a period of extended Medicaid benefits (sections 408(a)(11) and 1931(c) of the Social Security Act). States are permitted to deny Medicaid benefits to adults and heads of household who lose TANF benefits because they refuse to work. However, welfare reform law specifically exempts very poor pregnant women and children from this provision and mandates their continued Medicaid eligibility (section 1931(b)(3) of the Social Security Act). Also, Congress has allowed states flexibility to expand Medicaid to increase coverage of low-income families, including two-parent working families.

The State Children's Health Insurance Program

The State Children's Health Insurance Program (CHIP) was created to extend free or affordable health insurance to uninsured children in low-income families (Balanced Budget Act of 1997, Title XXI). To receive federal money authorized under CHIP, states must have approved plans that explicate how they will use the funds, including the proposed methods of delivery; utilization control systems; outreach activities; methods (including monitoring) used to assure the quality and appropriateness of care, particularly with respect to well baby care, well child care, immunizations provided under the plan, and assurance of access to covered services. Basic service categories are inpatient and outpatient hospital services, physicians' surgical and medical services, laboratory and X-ray services, well baby and well child care, including age-appropriate immunizations. Categories of additional services are coverage of prescription drugs, mental health, vision, and hearing services.

The Child Abuse Prevention and Treatment Act

The Child Abuse Prevention and Treatment Act of 1974 (CAPTA) requires that states' child abuse laws meet the federal definition of child abuse, that is, harming or threatening the health and welfare of a child. In the judgment of some state legislators, the federal definition labels too many people as child abusers. Some states receive no federal money to address child abuse because they will not alter their definition of abuse to match the federal government's. More restricted state definitions sometimes limit child welfare workers' abilities to ensure the welfare of their clients.

The Early and Periodic Screening, Diagnosis, and Treatment Program

The Early and Periodic Screening, Diagnosis, and Treatment (EPSDT) program is a federally mandated Medicaid program intended to be the key component in the Medicaid program's provision of health care to children. Family-centered care and family-professional collaboration form the keystone of this legislation. Families are eligible for services if they have a child below age 3 who has exhibited a developmental delay or has a diagnosed mental or physical condition that will result in development delay or disability. "The financing of medical care and early intervention services for infants and toddlers with special needs is of ongoing concern, given proposed changes in health care financing, the rapid growth of managed care, and the shift in financial responsibility from the federal government to state and local governments" (Rounds, Zipper, and Green 1997).

The EPSDT program assists jurisdictions in developing statewide systems of early intervention services for children ages birth to 3 years who have disabling conditions or who are at risk for developmental delay. The services provided under the program must include, at minimum, a comprehensive health and developmental history and a comprehensive physical examination, including hearing and vision checks, appropriate immunizations, laboratory tests, and health education. All children insured under Medicaid can receive EPSDT services that include regular checkups. Children can apply for Medicaid at their local Social Services office or Presumptive Eligibility site. Case managers for the program, assigned on the basis of zip codes, monitor children's health care and link children with providers for well or sick care, dental needs, vision checks, and eyeglasses.

Services covered under the EPSDT program include all mandatory and optional services a state is permitted to cover under Medicaid, even if the state has chosen not to offer that service to adults. For instance, if a provider shows that physical therapy is medically necessary for a child with a disability, physical therapy must be covered, even if the child lives in one of the ten states that do not pay for physical therapy for adults. State Medicaid programs may not include copayments or coinsurance for the majority of Medicaid beneficiaries eligible for EPSDT. Unlike most private plans, very few limitations exist on the amount and duration of Medicaid EPSDT benefits. State Medicaid programs may not limit EPSDT benefits in any way that would have the effect of denying necessary health care. For example, if a state limits covered hospital days for adults (some state limits are as low as sixteen days per year), it must make an exception for children, such as sick newborns, who need longer hospital care. In addition, states are required to conduct aggressive outreach and informing activities, to provide case management services and nonemergency transportation necessary to obtain primary and preventive care and treatment, and to coordinate EPSDT services with other children s programs.

The Individuals with Disabilities Education Act

The Individuals with Disabilities Education Act (IDEA) of 1986 is an amendment of the Education of the Handicapped Act that states that all children with disabilities have the right to an appropriate free public education. First known as the Education of Handicapped Children Act of 1975, IDEA is a keystone in laws for disabled children's education (Dickson 1995). The federal government provides financial assistance to the states to establish a "statewide, comprehensive, coordinated, multidisciplinary, interagency program of early intervention services for handicapped infants and toddlers and their families" (Individuals with Disabilities Education Act of 1986, section 671b[1]). To qualify for federal funds, states must have an established policy assuring that all children with disabilities will receive a free appropriate public education within the regular educational environment. Children with disabilities include those with mental retardation, hearing impairments (including deafness and speech or language impairments), visual impairments (including blindness), serious emotional disturbance, orthopedic impairments, autism, traumatic brain injury, or other health impairments or specific learning disabilities.

Each child with a disability is required to have a written individualized education program developed by a representative of the local education agency or intermediate education unit who can coordinate the child's overall program with the ways the school plans to meet the child's needs. Removal from the regular classroom can occur only if the disability is so severe that education is not satisfactory even with the use of supplemental aids and services.

The Developmental Disabilities Assistance and Bill of Rights

The Developmental Disabilities Assistance and Bill of Rights of 1990 renewed funds for basic state grant programs, the protection and advocacy system, university-affiliated programs, and projects of national significance. Its purpose is to advocate for public policy change and encourage acceptance to enable all people with developmental disabilities to receive the services, supports, and other assistance and opportunities necessary to enable such persons to achieve their maximum potential through increased independence, productivity, and integration into the community.

The Americans with Disabilities Act

The Americans with Disabilities Act (ADA) of 1990 is an important resource for those with physical and mental disabilities because it expands their rights, supports them as they become more fully participating members of society, and, most important, makes society responsible for accommodating the individual (Orlin 1995). According to Orlin (1995:233), "The ADA establishes that the nation's goals regarding individuals with disabilities are to ensure equality of opportunity, full participation, independent living, and economic self-sufficiency." Unlike the Federal Rehabilitation Act of 1973, which prohibits employment discrimination by federal contractors and grantees, it applies to all covered entities whether or not they receive federal funding. The ADA requires public accommodations and services, businesses, transportation and communications authorities to treat people as if their disabilities do not matter while simultaneously requiring special treatment of them (Feldblum 1991; Kopels 1995). Thus the ADA demands that society accommodate those with disabilities to the degree that will allow them to take their rightful places in society.

Disability is broadly defined as a physical or mental impairment that substantially limits one or more of the major life activities. This definition covers a wide range of medical conditions, such as tuberculosis, hepatitis, syphilis, mental retardation, diabetes, cerebral palsy, Down's syndrome, cystic fibrosis, muscular dystrophy, arthritis, heart disease, some specific learning disabilities such as dyslexia (Anderson, Kazmierski, and Cronin 1995), and emotional illness (Perlin 1994). Persons with AIDS are covered, although there is concern about specific protections (Studdert and Brennan 1997). The ADA also covers alcoholism.

> However, a person who is currently using illegal drugs is not considered disabled, but is covered once he or she has been successfully rehabilitated and is no longer using drugs (sec. 510). Similarly, a range of socially disapproved behavior disorders are excluded from protection,

such as most gender-identity disorders, pedophilia, exhibitionism, voyeurism, compulsive gambling, kleptomania, pyromania, and psychoactive drug-use disorders (sec. 511). (Gostin and Looney 1995:623)

The protections are extended to groups with a record of such impairment or who are regarded as having such impairment (section 3). Thus someone who has recovered from a disease such as cancer can still be considered disabled even if he or she has no actual disability. If people are regarded as disabled, but are not (for example, people who are perceived to have stigmatizing or disfiguring conditions such as HIV, leprosy, or severe burns), they, too, are protected under the law. The ADA also makes it unlawful to discriminate against those associated with people with disabilities (Orlin 1995). Thus people with disabled family members cannot be denied employment because they have to miss a lot of work in order to take care of their relatives with disabilities, and a sibling of a child with HIV cannot be refused admission to a school. In the same way, entities such as social service agencies or health care providers cannot be discriminated against because of their association with people with disabilities. For example, a medical clinic could not be evicted because it provided services to persons with AIDS, and a halfway house could not lose its lease because it provided services to people with chronic mental illness.

To be protected by the ADA, people with disabilities must meet the criteria for performance or eligibility for the specific benefit, service, or job they seek. Qualification can require that an individual does not pose a direct threat to the safety or health of others.

In order to determine, for example, that a person with mental illness poses a significant risk to others, evidence of specific dangerous behavior must be presented. In the context of infectious diseases such as tuberculosis, the Supreme Court laid down four criteria to determine significant risk: (1) the mode of transmission; (2) the duration of infectiousness, (3) the probability of the risk, and (4) the severity of harm (School Bd. of Nassau County [1987]). These criteria would apply to HIV as well. (Gostin and Looney 1995:624)

According to the ADA, employees who want accommodation carry the responsibility for disclosing their impairments, proving to their employers that they fall within the legal definition of disability by providing documentation and requesting protection under the law. If the requested changes cause "undue hardship" as defined by cost, extent, or disruption, employers are not obliged to make the accommodations. This is especially true if the accommodations would alter the nature of the business, if those requesting accommodation pose a direct threat to the health or safety of other employees, or if those who have made the request exhibit dangerous or offensive behavior. If employers do not comply, employees must file a charge or complaint with the Equal Employment Opportunity Commission.

For those who need medical treatment, facilities must be made accessible, equipment must be modified to make it useful, and jobs must be restructured for increased flexibility of scheduling. For those who are qualified except for infectious conditions, the organization may have to eliminate or reduce the risk of transmission. However, an employer cannot be forced to endure a hardship that would be disproportionately costly or would change the nature of the business (Chirikos 1991). For example, the Eighth Circuit Court of Appeals held that a school for people with mental retardation did not have to vaccinate employees to accommodate a student who was an active carrier of the hepatitis B virus (*Kohl* v. *Woodhaven Learning Center* [1989]).

Despite the enormous gains of the ADA enactment, impediments remain for the attainment of a normalized lifestyle for people with significant disabilities. Much more needs to be done in terms of education, training, and support (West 1991). One problem area is that the need for security in terms of income support (SSDI and SSI) and health care (Medicaid) creates a disincentive for people with disabilities to accept employment or exceed an earning level that would end their eligibility for those benefits (Martin, Conley, and Noble 1995). Some thoughtful coalescing of the goals of the ADA and income and health support would be helpful.

The Patient Self-Determination Act, Living Wills, and Advance Directives

The Patient Self-Determination Act took effect in December of 1991 after being adopted as part of the Omnibus Reconciliation Act of 1990. It was the first federal legislation concerned with decision making about medical intervention and end-of-life issues (Soskis and Kerson 1992:1). It requires that all health facilities that receive Medicare or Medicaid funding provide information to patients about their rights to accept or refuse medical treatment and their right to execute Advance Directives. When Advance Directives are in place, they are to be documented as part of the medical record and are not to be the basis of discrimination (Soskis and Kerson 1992:2). Advance Directives take several forms: (1) a documented discussion with one's physician explicating one's wishes about treatment in various medical situations; (2) a formal legal document called a Living Will that records desires about medical intervention limits in various medical situations; and (3) a Durable Power of Attorney, or Health Proxy, appointing someone to make medical decisions when people are in situations that would preclude clarity in their own decision making (Soskis and Kerson 1992:3). The function of a Durable Power of Attorney is to eliminate the need for guardianship or conservator proceedings in court should individuals become incapacitated or otherwise unable to manage their finances or make their own health decisions. It allows individuals to choose who has legal authority to act for them if they are not able to act for themselves within guidelines and limitations stipulated when they choose the attorney. The person who has been chosen can handle bills, taxes, and investments and also can make health care decisions. Individuals who have appointed such attorneys can revoke the power at any time as long as they are competent.

Social workers should become familiar with state laws regarding Advance Directives, as well as their own institution or organization's policies about documentation, education, and application. They also need to understand the "psychologically and culturally complex set of decisions" (Soskis and Kerson 1992:14), the clinical implications, and the effects on family relationships that these Advance Directives entail. Executing one's own Advance Directive allows one to get a sense of the issues that arise when addressing these decisions.

The Fair Housing Amendments Act

The architectural access portion of the law, which says that condominium associations and landlords can not turn away qualified buyers or renters who are disabled, took effect in 1991. New multifamily buildings containing four or more units must have specific access features in their ground floor units. When multifamily dwellings have elevators, these features must be present in all units. This law is considered a breakthrough because it challenges the prevailing "percentage mentality" that assumes that a percentage of housing equal to their percentage of representation in the community should provide access for the disabled. Universal basic access benefits everyone. Builders often ignore the law; however, groups have sued or issued complaints against noncompliant builders.

The Mental Health Parity Act

The Mental Health Parity Act of 1996 applies to any employer offering health insurance to more that fifty employees. It essentially requires that mental health care be provided for in the same ways that physical health care is reimbursed or covered. If there is no lifetime or annual cap on physical health expense reimbursement, then such a cap is not allowed on mental health care expenses. There is some amount of controversy about this act, as some taxpayer and small-business groups express concern that it will raise the costs of insurance coverage and make it possible that businesses and states will quit providing some benefits altogether. Nevertheless, groups as varied as the American Academy of Family Physicians and the National Mental Health Association support the Mental Health

Equitable Treatment Act, as does the National Association of Social Workers (NASW).

The Occupational Safety and Health Act

Passed in 1970 and amended in 1990 and 1998, the Occupational Safety and Health Act was developed "[t]o assure safe and healthful working conditions for working men and women; by authorizing enforcement of standards developed under the Act." It applies to employers "engaged in a business affecting commerce" who must provide employment that protects each of their employees from recognized hazards that cause or are likely to cause death or serious physical harm (Schroeder 1995). Since 1971, workplace fatalities have been reduced by half, but an average of seventeen workers still lose their lives on the job each day, and an average of fifty are seriously injured each week. Social workers in medical settings need to be sensitized to bring workplace accidents and/or unhealthful working conditions to the attention of the Occupational Safety and Health Administration, as well as to be familiar with Workers' Compensation application and administration issues.

LEGAL ISSUES

Among the legal issues that social workers must understand are informed consent, competence, confidentiality, duty to warn, and emancipated or mature minor status.

Informed Consent

To take an active part in a consent procedure, social workers must be sufficiently informed to understand not only what clients are being asked to consent to, but any available diagnostic and treatment alternatives. Knowledge of the natural history of the disease or condition is important in case clients refuse intervention altogether, and the social worker is required to inform clients of the ramifications of the decision to refuse treatment. Informed consent is also involved when asking clients for permission to obtain records from another agency or institution (Sheafor, Horejsi, and Horejsi 1988:204). "At a policy level, the emphasis on cost savings, profit, and expediency creates ethical dilemmas for social workers by compromising the informed consent process" (Manning 1997:228).

Informed consent means that one must fully understand the risks and benefits of a proposed treatment before one can be considered responsible for decisions based on that information and before one consents to said treatment. This is a legal requirement for treatment of any kind. A client must be given basic information about what has been proposed and must agree with the proposal before a provider can give service to the client

(Annas 1989). The process of ensuring that the client understands the reasons for, and nature of, any intervention enhances the professional relationship and advances the work (President's Commission 1982).

Informed consent is important in every social work relationship, but its importance is heightened in any dependent or involuntary circumstance. For example, in systems providing mental health services, social workers must understand the rights of patients in the use of psychotropic drugs, voluntary and involuntary commitment to psychiatric facilities, restraints, and aversive measures. In systems dedicated to helping children and adolescents, social workers must understand issues of consent, including those related to minors living with biological parents or in a foster care arrangement, treatment of emancipated or mature minors (those whom the courts view as adults for making specific kinds of decisions related to their care), substance abuse treatment, contraception and abortion, and treatment of sexually transmitted diseases. State and local authorities do not necessarily agree about the interpretation and application of standards for informed consent. Generally, six standards must be met for consent to be considered valid:

1. There must be an absence of coercion and undue influence.
2. The party involved must be able to give consent.
3. Clients must consent to specific procedures.
4. The forms of consent must be valid.
5. Parties must have the right to refuse or withdraw consent.
6. Client decisions must be based on adequate information. (Rozovsky 1984)

Because they are often in positions in which they exert some control over the lives of their clients, social workers have to be sensitive to this level of power. It is possible that clients will feel coerced even when social workers have no intention of coercion. In the same way, although professionals agree that only competent individuals can give informed consent, it is more difficult for them to agree about how to determine competence. The President's Commission for the Study of Ethical Problems in Medicine and Biomedical and Behavioral Research states that competency is determined by (1) the possession of a set of values and goals, (2) the ability to communicate and to understand information, and (3) the ability to reason and to deliberate about one's choices (President's Commission 1982). Neither competency nor incompetency should be assumed. Since consent should be related to specific activities or interventions, social workers should also avoid having clients sign blank or very general consent forms. Social workers also have to allow for the possibility that clients may refuse or withdraw consent. Under those circumstances, it is best for an organization to have the client sign a release form absolving staff of responsibility for the consequences of the action. Finally, the following topics, commonly called "elements of disclosure," should be covered in consent discussions: (1) the nature and purpose of the recommended service, treatment, or activity; (2) the advantages and disadvantages of the intervention; (3) substantial, probable, or significant risks to the clients; (4) possible effects on clients' families, jobs, or social life; (5) possible alternatives to the intervention; and (6) anticipated costs to be borne by clients and their relatives (Reamer 1987).

The principle of informed consent was established by Justice Benjamin Cardozo in *Schloendorff* v. *Society of New York Hospital* (1914): "Every human being of adult years and sound mind has a right to determine what shall be done with his own body." To do otherwise is to commit an assault upon the person. The underlying case had to do with a woman who consented to an "ether examination" but stated she would not consent to "an operation." Despite the woman's reiterating this to several nurses and physicians, the surgeon proceeded to surgically remove a tumor that he found. Following complications, the patient sued the surgeon on assault charges and won. The verdict was upheld on appeal.

The phrase "informed consent" first appeared in *Salgo* v. *Leland Stanford Jr. University Board of Trustees* (1957). In this case, the plaintiff, who became paraplegic after a diagnostic procedure for a circulatory problem, alleged that his physician had not properly disclosed inherent risks before performing the procedure. "The standards for disclosure in informed consent were expanded in 1972 as a result of *Canterbury* v. *Spence*. The expansion meant that there was a duty to warn of the dangers lurking in the proposed treatment as well as any potential risks that may influence decision making" (Dickson 1995:161). Although both of these examples have to do with medical procedures, the concept has been applied judicially, legislatively, and administratively to a many different kinds of client groups, including the mentally ill, retarded, developmentally disabled, children, prisoners and those on probation or parole, the elderly, persons with drug and/or alcohol problems, and research subjects.

> In agencies that provide mental health services, for example, social workers must be familiar with consent requirements related to voluntary and involuntary commitment and the rights of institutionalized and outpatient clients regarding the use of psychotropic drugs, restraints, aversive treatment measures, isolation, sterilization, and psychosurgery. . . . [For minors] consent issues arise related to abortion, counseling, contraception, treatment of sexually transmitted diseases, mental health services, treatment for substance abuse, and services for children in foster care. (Reamer 1987:425–26)

Competence

Generally, competence refers to the ability to perform a specific task. Mental competence means having the ability to understand the subject matter and the consequences of giving or withholding consent. In situations related to health care, competence is the capacity to make autonomous health care decisions, that is, to decide for oneself how one wishes to proceed. The legal system presumes that one is competent unless proven otherwise; however, in the clinical literature the term *competence* refers either to an individual's general capability or to an individual's specific capacity to make decisions. Competence is a context-dependent, decision-specific interpersonal process, rather than a fixed property of an individual that is applicable to all decisions (Wettstein 1995). In contrast, as Wettstein (1995:446) explains,

> incompetence has come to mean the loss in court of a person's legal right to function in some area. Such a narrow legal definition of competence or incompetence contrasts with the more common clinical use of incompetence according to which a person has a legal right to function but is unable to do so. Clinical and legal competence may not correspond. An elderly, demented person, for example, may have the legal right to drive a car or make his or her own health-care decisions but may no longer be substantially able to do so. Similarly, an adolescent may not be legally competent to consent to health care but may be clinically or functionally able to do so.

The issue of competence is especially critical in relation to psychiatric treatment. Individuals who are seriously depressed, psychotic, or demented often do not understand that they need treatment and may have difficulty understanding the risks and benefits of treatment. At times the refusal of treatment is linked to the symptoms of the illness itself, as in the delusion that medication may be poisonous. When people are deemed too ill to understand that they must be hospitalized for psychiatric reasons, they can be involuntarily hospitalized for a specific number of days or until certain symptoms are no longer present. However, involuntary treatment remains a controversial solution. Many states allow the forced medication of an involuntarily hospitalized patient only after a judicial hearing and court determination that, as a result of the mental illness, the patient is incompetent to refuse the medication (Weiner and Wettstein 1993). Commitment is a legal process and is generally civil rather than criminal. In this situation, an individual is determined to require hospitalization because of a mental condition, but that person does not consent to the hospitalization. It raises serious ethical concerns because it deprives people of their freedom for a period of time during which they are usually locked in a psychiatric facility (Culver 1995).

Confidentiality

Confidentiality means that what a health care professional is told by a patient or client is to be kept private and known only to the two participants in the relationship. Legal protection of confidentiality is uneven and sporadic (Winslade 1995). In the case of programs for the treatment of substance abuse and some other settings, the federal government has set special rules for the protection of confidentiality in order to encourage those who need treatment to seek it without concern that records will be disclosed to law enforcement agencies that might prosecute them for abuse. The creation of a health care information infrastructure that relies on computer technology to facilitate record keeping and transmission greatly threatens confidentiality (Brannigan 1992). At this time, legal policies do not adequately preserve people's rights to control their medical information, protect people from unwarranted disclosure of information, or guarantee secure complex medical information systems (Alpert 1993; Gostin et al. 1993).

Duty to Warn

In the case of *Tarasoff* v. *Regents of the University of California* (1974), the California Supreme Court ruled that when they are treating patients who may present a danger to others, psychotherapists have a duty to warn threatened victims in order to protect them from harm (Mangalmurti 1994). In this case, a patient obsessed with a woman who did not want a relationship with him talked to his therapist about revenge. He was thought to have a gun. The therapist attempted to have him evaluated for involuntary hospitalization, but the police refused to bring the patient for a mental status assessment. Angry with the therapist, the patient halted treatment and later killed the woman. Consequently, the woman's parents sued the therapist and the therapist's employer for failing to warn the woman and her family about the danger. The case was settled, but the reasonable protection rule was spelled out by the court. Although this may infringe on the patient's right to privacy, the court observed that protective privilege ends where public peril begins.

Social workers' duty to warn is more circumscribed. Kagle and Kopels (1994) describe social workers' duty under the law and outline standards of care for assessing and responding to threats of harm. They place the duty to protect third parties in the larger context of social workers' legal and ethical obligation to protect confidentiality (Kagle and Kopels 1994; Kopels and Kagle 1993). At least one study has shown that warning the intended victim had a minimal or positive effect on the psychotherapeutic relationship (Binder and McNeil 1996). Regarding AIDS, there has been discussion about the duty to warn a client's sexual partners when the client has AIDS and is withholding that information. Therapeutic, legal, and ethical dimensions of the situation are reviewed, and social workers are cautioned to balance their clients' rights to privacy with clients' sexual partners' possible harm (Reamer 1991; Schlossberger and Hecker 1996).

Emancipated or Mature Minor Status

Several states now recognize that certain minors can provide their own consent in relationships with professionals and institutions. Emancipated minors generally live on their own, are self-supporting, or are in the armed forces, whereas mature minors are recognized as understanding the nature and consequences of treatment in spite of their chronological age (Rozovsky 1984:240). States vary on whether they consider pregnant or parenting minors to be emancipated.

Patients' Rights

It is possible that by the time this book is published, a Patients' Bill of Rights will have been passed by both the Senate and the House of Representatives, because versions of a bill of rights for patients have been circulating in many parts of the federal government for several years (ASAP! 2001). Once passed on the federal level, such a bill would define patients' right to sue health insurance companies and plans for damages when a patient's care plan has denied or failed to provide proper care ("A Narrative Discussion" 2001; "A Right to Sue" 1999; "Managed Care" 1999). Traditionally health insurance regulation has been a state rather than a federal activity; however, the presence and actions of managed care have caused both state and federal governments to become concerned about patient protection. Oregon, Texas, New Jersey, and Maryland are considered to be among the more progressive states in this regard (Rovner 1999). Earlier specific issues had to do with the banning of "drive-through baby deliveries" and the lifting of gag rules in managed care contracts that forbade doctors from discussing diagnostic or treatment options that were not covered by a particular plan (Rovner 1999).

Without a federal bill providing for specific protection and responsibilities for health care plans, employer benefits, physicians, and consumers (patients), processes for resolving managed care disputes will continue to vary according to the payer—with individual state laws, the Employee Retirement Income Security Act (ERISA), Medicaid, and Medicare differing greatly. For example, Medicare + Choice (Medicare Part C), in which managed care plans are part of the coverage, includes regulations on appeals and grievance procedures. "The ERISA 'shield' currently prevents all 125,000,000 Americans with employer-sponsored coverage (self-insured or not) from collecting damages by suing their health plans if they suffer injury as a result of benefit denials" (Rovner 1999:22). Consumers may sue in federal court, but remedies are limited to the cost of denied service plus legal fees. In many state and federal policies, words such as *complaint, appeal,* and *grievance* are often used interchangeably with little agreement about definition (Karp and Wood 1998).

For managed care to be effective, it has to address conflicts in ways that are clear and fair to all participants. Questions regarding who has the right to sue under what conditions and questions related to process, time frame, who is responsible for the costs of external reviews or suits have to be explained in ways that all participants can understand. Most important is the protection of the elderly, the disabled, the poor, and other vulnerable segments of society.

ETHICS

Professional Ethics

Ethics is "the study of how to live, of how to achieve human excellence, which in turn encompasses everything in our lives, from our daily, personal activities to our professional behavior as social workers" (Rhodes 1992:40). The term "professional ethics" refers to a system of norms that govern the behavior of those who practice a specific profession. Most professional groups carry such ethical obligations as part of their work: (1) the obligation to make services available to the public, (2) the primacy of the client being served, (3) an acknowledged obligation to the social institutions that sanction or fund professional practice, and (4) an obligation to the profession (Bayles 1981). Here the question may be raised: What if there are conflicts between the four obligations? Sometimes the social worker is caught between the wishes of a physician or treatment team and the client. For example, there are times when a treatment team is determined that a patient follow a particular plan of action or receive a specific kind of treatment and that treatment may prolong or even save a patient's life, but the patient is adamant that he or she does not want the treatment. Nowhere is this conflict felt more keenly than in a prestigious and powerful teaching institution. For instance, a well-respected senior surgeon and his team are determined to perform surgery on a patient who does not want it (Kugelman 1992). There, "the interplay between patients' rights and professionals' responsibilities [is] carried out in a modern, highly technological health care setting" (Levine 1989:2). Also, many times, a client will want to continue to live in her own home while many professionals who are involved in her care may want her to live in what they see as a more protected environment.

Self-Determination

One value that undergirds all social work practice is self-determination, the right of clients to make their own decisions. This right is a fundamental and necessary principle for social work practice (Biestek 1957). As the NASW (1996) *Code of Ethics* states, "the social worker should make every effort to foster maximum self-determination on the part of clients." The value of self-determination is as present in community work as it is in direct practice. Fundamentally, the issues are the same: legality, consideration, and the right of all to be heard, to participate, and to contribute to the overall purpose of the community. "What matters is that people feel free to choose the plan that makes most sense to them: that they can find out for themselves what works and what does not" (Hancock 1997). Thus social workers (1) help clients to understand and articulate their problems, (2) apprise clients of all available resources, (3) help clients to mobilize their resources, and (4) create safe but challenging relationships in which clients can learn and be enriched. Social workers should never act in ways that violate or diminish the civil or legal rights of clients. Situations calling for special vigilance are ones in which social workers act on behalf of legally incompetent clients, or when another person has been legally authorized to act for a client.

Social workers are obligated to involve their clients in the helping process to the maximum of their clients' capacities (Hancock 1997). Self-determination can be limited by the client's incapacity for positive and constructive decision making, by the framework of civil and moral law, by the functions and roles of the agency or organization, or by those who are paying for services (Biestek 1957; Kerson 1997). At times, particularly in this era when managed care companies fund professional practice, the social workers' obligation to clients and their obligation to the payers differ and, in fact, may sometimes be distinctly at odds. Ultimately, social workers must place their obligation to clients first.

Rose (1995) has argued that practice is increasingly driven by function rather than values. For example, a social worker in a community hospital emergency room works closely with a local program whose purpose is to thwart domestic violence. A young woman was referred to her who had literally run from her house to the hospital after being severely beaten by her husband. With her was her 2-year-old son, who had been discharged two days before, after his asthma had been brought under control. The social worker called the Medicaid managed care provider, who refused to pay for another nebulizer for the little boy since the woman had been given one when her son was discharged from the hospital. When the social worker tried to explain the plight to the managed care representative, she suggested that the social worker call the woman's husband and have him bring the nebulizer to the hospital or the shelter where the woman was going.

At times like these, when there is great tumult in social services, social workers worry that the profession is being forced to "sell out" to the system and shortchange clients. Social work's constituencies are often the most dependent members of society. In fact, although many alternations to the law and to service provisions are intended to protect society and the individual, they often increase the vulnerability of some individuals. For example, in deinstitutionalization, changes in the law restricted the states' power and means to hold and treat mentally ill persons (Donovan, Blanchard, and Kerson 1997). This change sometimes makes it more difficult to help those with serious mental illness because their conditions prevent them from understanding that they could benefit from the treatment (Wasow 1997).

In the same way, the federal creation of Diagnosis-Related Groups altered the system of hospital and physician payment from the providers' estimation of cost to a formula based on the patient's diagnosis (Fein 1986). Although the stated purpose of the changes was to help sustain the system financially, social workers worried that their clients would be given less care than they needed and, indeed, could be denied access to care (Clemens 1995; Dobrof 1991; Hammer and Kerson 1997; Lockery, Dunkle, Kart, and Coulton 1994; Proctor and Morrow-Howell 1990). Certainly, "social admission" (admission to a hospital that was the safest place to house a person) could no longer occur.

> Awareness of the potential for ethical problems with agency policies followed by thinking through the possible impact on clients is necessary. Discussions with colleagues in similar circumstances can help identify potential ethical dilemmas. Ongoing dialogue with clients about their experience with agency practice shows caring about their perspective helps increase practitioner and client understanding of the meaning of that experience. The practitioner can then take action by identifying problems and giving feedback about professional and agency practices, funding mechanisms, and theoretical models that are not conducive to client self-determination. . . . The opportunity to act in "loyal opposition" to agency policy is available through joining advisory boards to managed care companies, participating in writing standards and policies about service delivery, and giving consistent feedback about practices that are unethical or harmful to clients. (Manning 1997:223)

Ethics and Managed Care

Now there is great concern within the profession that social work not "sell out" to managed care, just as previously there was concern around deinstitutionalization (Belcher 1988; Belcher and Toomey 1988; Segal 1995). "With managed care a dominating feature of much of the nation's health care system, social workers may sometimes think of themselves as stand-ins for the proverbial 90-pound weakling while a 300-pound bully calls all the shots" (Landers 1997b:3). Ethical issues in managed care relate to access, fairness, quality, accountability, learning and improvement, and entitlement. The ethical challenges in a managed care environment include those in direct practice, in administration, among colleagues, and in malpractice and liability risks (NASW 1999). Among the latter are risks involving informed consent, confidentiality, substandard care, client abandonment, appeal procedures, negligent referral, supervisor liability, and, finally, the ethical imperative for social work advocacy (Reamer 1998).

It is important for social workers to remember the following points in relation to capitation and behavioral health. Behavioral health is actually quite narrowly defined, and by itself it does not provide a wide array of human services options. Private sector rules do not apply in the public sector. In addition, the 15 percent to 25 percent profit margins that many behavioral health providers expect disadvantage public sector consumers. Finally, in order to be effective, service networks must be developed more comprehensively (NASW 1999).

The following example is actually a series of dilemmas for the parents of the patient, the treating institution, and each member of the interdisciplinary team.

<hr>

Leah (age 28) and John Kendall (age 33) are a Caucasian college-educated couple from a rural county outside of a large city in the northeastern United States. They had been working as teachers in Saudi Arabia when hydrocephalus was diagnosed in the baby that Leah was carrying. Commonly called "water on the brain," this condition is defined medically as an excess of cerebrospinal fluid inside the skull owing to an obstruction of normal cerebrospinal fluid circulation. The Saudi physician made the diagnosis with the use of ultrasound and assured the couple that the condition was simple and easily corrected with surgery.

As a result of this diagnosis, when Leah was almost eight months pregnant, the Kendalls moved back to their hometown, where they had a great deal of social support and which was not far from a renowned children's hospital. When they called the hospital and described the unborn baby's condition, the Kendalls were given an appointment with a neurosurgeon. Because the Kendalls were unemployed when they returned to the United States, they were able to obtain Medical Assistance so that the hospital could be paid for its services. At the hospital, the pediatric neurosurgeon diagnosed myelomeningocele, a protrusion of the meninges through a bony defect that forms a cyst covered with a thin, transparent membrane that may be granular and moist and is filled with cerebrospinal fluid. Meninges are the membranes that surround the brain and spinal cord. The location at which the defect occurs determines the extent of the disability, and in this case, the defect's location high on the baby's back meant the probability of serious motor, sensory, and cognitive impairment. Disabilities can include paralysis, hydrocephalus, musculoskeletal deformity, mental retardation, and bladder/bowel dysfunction.

The neurosurgeon explained the condition and its poor prognosis to the Kendalls and referred them to the hospital's spina bifida clinic. Spina bifida, which literally means split spine, takes several different forms, ranging in severity from a condition that rarely causes medical problems to one that can cause great disability. Infants and children with all forms of spina bifida, including myelomeningocele, are followed in this clinic. The Kendalls met with the spina bifida clinic's team nurse and social worker, who reviewed treatment and care options for the baby and helped the Kendalls process their feelings and consider each alternative. The Kendalls were told that the most important decision they had to make was whether or not the baby should be treated. Either way, the impairments created by the myelomeningocele could not be reversed. Rather, the decision to treat would mean that soon after the birth of the baby surgery would be performed to close the opening in the baby's back to prevent infection and to shunt spinal fluid to another part of the body for absorption to prevent it from accumulating inside the skull. The decision not to treat would mean that the baby would be kept comfortable but the spinal opening would remain open to possible infection, potentially causing death.

It is important to note here that this dilemma has been created through technological advancement. If the shunting procedure were not possible, the parents would have been told that there was no medical intervention but that the opening in the baby's back would be closed to prevent infection. If, on the other hand, there were treatments to reverse the impairments, or if the team had not learned over the years that many patients were left with grave deficits, there would also be no dilemma. Twenty years ago, the standard of care was that surgical techniques were available and that every infant was treated. During that time, if a social worker suggested to a distraught couple that they give themselves a couple of days to ponder the decision, the physician would likely become angry with her. Now, however, after seeing the degree of disability of many people with this condition, the physician may suggest forgoing treatment and, like the rest of the treatment team, may see no clear path.

The Kendalls wanted the treatment team to provide them with as much information as possible to help them decide whether to have the baby treated. They were especially worried about what the nature and extent of the child's

FIGURE 3.2. Ecomap for Sarah before the move to Arizona.

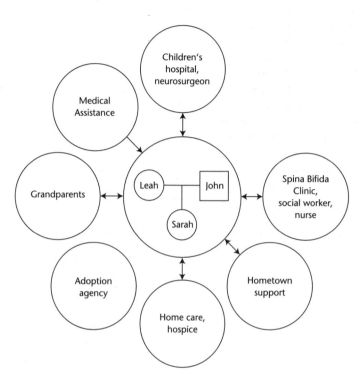

disabilities might be over time. They asked to see pictures of children and adults with myelomeningocele in order to more fully absorb the level of disability that they and their child would face.

The next question for the social worker was what pictures to show the Kendalls. The children who are followed in the spina bifida clinic range from those who are mildly retarded and ambulatory in leg braces to those who are severely retarded with very limited mobility. Seeing pictures of the most highly functioning patients might sway the parents to ask for surgical intervention, whereas seeing pictures of the most disabled patients might influence them to ask that their baby not be treated. The social worker decided to show them pictures of those who were braced but not most impaired.

The second decision the parents had to make was what living arrangements to make for the baby. In the past, and especially before surgical techniques were developed, babies with this condition were sent home with their parents, kept in the hospital (usually in a corner of the newborn intensive care unit), or sent to institutions (called homes) for long periods of time or until they died of infection. Now the alternatives that were described to the Kendalls were to take the baby home with them, place the baby in foster care, or place the baby for adoption. Information provided to the Kendalls included an appointment with the home care and hospice program in their area and an appointment with an adoption agency to explore that option.

Also of note is the Kendalls' very close relationship with their own parents. Mrs. Kendall's mother, who is chronically depressed, has longed for a grandchild for several years. Mr. Kendall's mother is a special education teacher, and Mr. Kendall grew up knowing many special needs children and appreciating his mother's deep commitment to those children. The grandparents all said they would support the couple no matter what decisions they made (figure 3.2).

The baby, who was named Sarah Elizabeth, had an uneventful delivery. The Kendalls decided to take her home without treatment and requested help from the local home care and hospice program for hospice services. This program had not previously provided hospice service to a child, and its nurses were appalled that the hospital was not treating a child with spina bifida. The clinic's social worker and nurse then had to educate the hospice team to enable them to work productively with the Kendalls. The most important point the hospice team had to understand was that there were no medical consequences to delaying surgical intervention. The hospice nurses' tasks were to monitor Sarah's head size to be sure it wasn't growing as the result of the release of spinal fluid into the head, to monitor the open meningocele, to take the baby's temperature to detect infection, and to emotionally support the parents. Clearly, the team's choice of hospice services meant that they thought that the baby would die.

When Sarah was 2 months old, her head began to enlarge, and she was not otherwise deteriorating physically, so the Kendalls decided to have the opening in her back closed and have a shunt inserted to prevent fluid from going to her head. The Kendalls, the treatment team, and the hospice nurses had to alter their outlook, mindset, and emotional stance from that of comforting the parents and supporting an infant who was expected to die to one of helping an extended family accept a child who is likely to be disabled to live as full, healthy, and rich a life as possible. In the hospital, the Kendalls appeared almost elated, pointing out to everyone who knew them how wonderfully their baby was doing.

The next month, the Kendalls moved to Arizona, a move they had planned even when they lived in Saudi Arabia. Mr. Kendall has found well-paying and satisfying employment, Sarah has been enrolled for early intervention services, and a spina bifida team is following her medically (figure 3.3). Sarah is now 5 months old. The social worker calls Mrs. Kendall to hear about Sarah's progress, and Mrs. Kendall says that she feels that the hospital respected the couple's wishes at the time, but she wishes that someone had said to her, "Look at what a strong and wonderful kid you have."

FIGURE 3.3. Ecomap for Sarah after the move to Arizona.

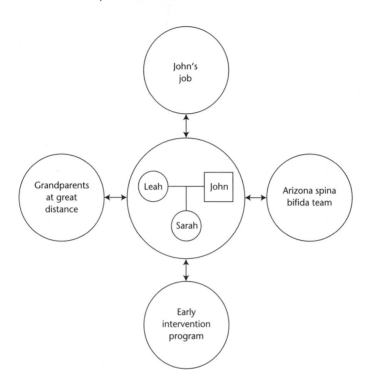

When Mrs. Kendall looks at her infant, she sees a responsive and happy baby whose overall development appears normal. When the spina bifida team looks at the same baby, they see the baby's future based on many years of experience with several hundred children born with spina bifida. Will she be able to walk with braces, will she begin to use a wheelchair when she reaches puberty as many children with this condition do, will she have the mental ability to care for herself, will she be able to enjoy some measure of independence? Only time will tell.

Codes of Ethics

A code of ethics can be described as the social conscience of a profession or association. Social conscience is a notion of what is right and good to promote in a culture plus the obligation to promote it (Towle 1969). "All social workers have a responsibility to assess the ethical implications of their decisions and to develop a framework for addressing the value dilemmas that arise in practice" (McGowan 1996:37). After all, "a value has small worth, except as it is moved . . . from believing into doing, from verbal affirmation into action" (Perlman 1976:381–82). To enrich social workers' understanding of ethics, Manning provides the notion of moral citizenship, the responsibility to determine right and good behavior as part of the rights and privileges social workers have as members of a community that includes clients, colleagues, agencies, and society. Moral citizenship is congruent with ethics—how people determine what they ought to do (Manning 1997:224). It is also transformational in that it sets out to alter structures to reflect social work's purposes and values and can guide co-workers toward higher moral behavior as well. This notion is similar to the dimensions of "head, heart, and hand" with which Towle (1969:14) says that social work practices as the conscience of the community.

The NASW's (1996) *Code of Ethics* reflects the profession's value base, mission, goals, and priorities. The primary mission of the social work profession is to enhance human well-being and to help meet the basic human needs of all people, with particular attention to the needs and empowerment of people who are vulnerable, oppressed, or living in poverty. A historic and defining feature of social work is the profession's focus on individual well-being in a social context and the well-being of society. Fundamental to social work is the attention to the environmental forces that create, contribute to, and address problems in living. Commitment to clients is first among the ethical standards listed in the NASW's *Code of Ethics*. Following close behind is client self-determination. The profession is admonished not to accept employment in an organization when commitments made to the employer do not appear to be in the best interests of the client (Landers 1997a; Wells and Masch 1991).

Cultural competence and social diversity are part of the *Code of Ethics*. The code states that social workers should understand culture and its function in human behavior and society, recognizing the strengths that exist in all cultures. They should become educated about and try to understand the nature of social diversity and oppression with respect to race, ethnicity, national origin, color, sex, sexual orientation, age, marital status, political belief, religion, and mental or physical disability. Social justice is part of the code as well. Social workers have a duty to advocate for social justice, including living conditions that support basic human needs. No matter what their work, all social workers should promote values and institutions that fit with the realization of social, political, and economic justice.

Guidelines for Conduct. The NASW *Code of Ethics* provides guidelines for conduct by specifying principles of behavior in relation to social work's ethical responsibility to clients, commitment to clients, client self-determination, informed consent, competence, and confidentiality. These core values support serving a diverse population; providing assistance to those in need; achieving medical, economic, political, and legal equality; respecting and caring for clients in ways that reflect their worth and dignity; building alliances and strengthening relationships; establishing trust with clients; and practicing according to NASW standards.

The code bases six broad principles on social work's core values of service, social justice, the dignity and worth of the person, the importance of human relationships, integrity, and competence (NASW 1996:5–6). The related principles call social workers to (1) help people in need and to address social problems, (2) challenge social injustice, (3) respect the inherent dignity and worth of the person, (4) recognize the central importance of human relationships, (5) behave in a trustworthy manner, and (6) practice within their areas of competence and develop and enhance their professional expertise. Ethical standards are related to clients, colleagues, settings, fellow social work professionals, the profession, and the broader society.

Several other codes of ethics have been developed by specific groups of social workers. These codes focus on either a specific population of social work professionals, such as the National Association of Black Social Workers, the Association of Jewish Communal Social Workers, or the National Association of Christian Social Workers, or client populations, such as the National Association of Perinatal Social Workers.

Ethical Decision Making. Ethical decision making has been defined as "a pattern of moral reasoning [through which] one determines what one should do in a particular situation by reference to certain general principles or rules which one takes as premises from which to deduce a particular conclusion" (Frankena 1973:2). Two approaches to ethical decision making are to adhere to basic ethical principles and to attend to the decision making process (Abramson 1990). The President's Commission for the Study of Ethical Problems in Medicine and Biomedicine and Behavioral Research (1983) described the following as most important:

1. The well-being of people should be promoted.
2. People's value preferences and choices should be respected.
3. People should be treated equitably.

These principles suggest that when people lack the capacity to make decisions for themselves their interests should be protected according to the standards that reasonable people would use in similar situations in measuring possible costs and benefits. A process that includes all relevant and salient facts and responses; eliminates conflicts of interest; and is as dispassionate, calm, and reflective as possible in matters of morality that affect definition of family, life, and death comes as close as possible to reaching the best decision (Abramson 1990:11).

Frameworks for Addressing Ethical Problems. In social work, several frameworks are available through which to identify, clarify, and analyze ethical problems. Abramson (1989) studies the complex relationship between client autonomy and worker paternalism (Abramson and Black 1985). Reamer (1990, 1995) examines systems of ethical decision making that are useful for resolving issues in the social work profession. Rhodes (1986) explicates the conflicting ethical and political assumptions that underlie professional decision making.

Bioethics. The term *bioethics* can be defined as "the systematic study of the moral dimensions—including moral vision, decisions, conduct, and policies—of the life sciences and health care, employing a variety of ethical methodologies in an interdisciplinary setting" (Reich 1995:xxi). The moral issues that are contemplated in bioethics concern the individual and society's moral vision and aspirations, how individuals should act in specific situations, and how people can live harmoniously (Reich 1995). As this field has evolved it has reached far beyond biomedical ethics to encompass health-related and science-related issues in public and environmental health, considering not only the medical but the social dimensions of health and the life sciences. Moral choices in the community setting, in fact, involve many more lives than moral choices in clinical settings. Thus in bioethics environmental and clinical concerns are seen as parts of a greater whole. For example,

> The choice to introduce pollutants into the environment is the choice to cause deadly diseases. Thus, to attend only to the moral problems associated with treating the disease (e.g. forgoing ventilator support for persons with terminal lung disease) and to neglect the moral problems raised by the social, environmental, and economic causes of the disease (e.g. tobacco and other environmental pollutants) distorts the moral enterprise regarding health. (Reich 1995:xxii)

Ethical Issues Raised by Technological Advances. Many of the ethical issues that face social work and other health-related professions at this time have been created by the technological advances of our age. In our society, social, psychological, religious, and legal solutions often lag behind technology. First, new possibilities are created by technology, and then society has to develop ways to include, make sense of, and control the technology. Examples include a wide range of interventions, such as new reproductive techniques, services to impaired newborns, and life support for terminally ill people. According to Abramson and Black (1985), these three areas of medicine have altered traditional definitions of life, death, and the nature of personhood. Ironically, technological advances often increase the burden of the family caregiver. People who would have died before such developments occurred are sometimes living in very dependent states, and no matter how much professional and support assistance is brought into the home, families must bear the major part of the burden.

Brief interventions are consistent with the notions of the least invasive procedures first, informed patient consent (since treatment is collaborative), and respect for patient autonomy (Cooper 1995:28). Such interventions adhere to the principles of collaboration, competency, attending to client meaning systems, affirming individuality, and supporting problem-solving capacities and self-determination of clients. They begin with the problems that the clients define as important and empower the client to work toward solutions. These issues are elaborated in chapter 7.

Ethical Dilemmas. Today social workers face some of the most complex ethical dilemmas in the history of the profession (Manning 1997). For example, genetic research has improved ways of identifying people at risk for developing some diseases, but research lags in terms of prevention, coping with emotional ramifications, and treatment. Electronic databases allow the compilation of massive amounts of data and then raise concerns about privacy and consent. The current emphasis on cost savings and the constraints placed on professional helpers by funding sources (or by the organizations that employ them) also present ethical dilemmas.

Following are several disguised but real vignettes of ethical dilemmas. Included with each dilemma is the approximate year it occurred. Dates are given to demonstrate that some dilemmas remain perplexing, giving the social worker an opportunity to artfully address issues on many levels with clients. Other dilemmas are created as a result of technological advances. For example, in some situations, technological interventions have allowed people to live in circumstances that leave them highly dependent on the care of others.

Like those found in the *Hastings Center Report,* the vignettes presented here are meant to evoke discussion. They are difficult cases about which reasonable professionals can and do disagree. The goal is to reflect, understand one's reasoning, and try to resolve issues in client-supportive ways (Levine 1989:xiii). One such study from the *Hastings Center Report* concerns a 74-year-old skilled nursing facility resident who has Alzheimer's disease and who no longer recognizes his family or the staff ("Retiring the Pacemaker" 1997). His family and physician are clear that he would not wish to be medically supported in his current condition; however, no advance directive was signed. The family wishes to turn off his pacemaker, but his cardiologist refuses to discuss the option: "Is an implanted pacemaker a medical treatment that, once begun, can be withdrawn?" (Spike 1997).

1942. Social worker Harriette Grant has gone to Europe to work in a field hospital established to support men in combat. Her role is not clearly defined; she is helping any way she can. One day, Jim Wrightson, a young private who, after stepping on a mine, has had to have both hands amputated, asks Ms. Grant to write a letter to his girlfriend. She sits beside him and he dictates: "Dear Sue, I just wanted you to know that everything is fine here. I am getting plenty of rest and plenty to eat, and the medics expect me to make a full recovery."

Question for the social worker: It is the soldier's right to dictate the contents of the letter. Should the social worker raise issues for him? For example, should she ask, "Won't Sue wonder why you have not written this letter yourself?" Or perhaps it is reasonable that the social worker empower the soldier by following his direction and doing what he asks as supportively as possible.

1968. Ralph Haines, age 43, a Caucasian male, married with two children, employed as a city bus driver, in whom paranoid schizophrenia has been diagnosed, is about to be discharged after a three-month hospitalization in an acute psychiatric unit of a city hospital that is run as a therapeutic community. Mr. Haines was brought to the hospital from his workplace after he had spent several hours driving his bus along a route that he had created himself that morning. After several irate passengers whom he had let off the bus at stops of his own choosing had reported him to his employer, he was stopped en route and accompanied to the emergency room by his supervisor. At first, Mr. Haines deteriorated dramatically, but by the end of his hospital stay, on high levels of psychotropic medication, after daily group therapy and weekly sessions with his wife, he was adequately medicated, calm, and very quiet. Although he continued to hallucinate, he could relate on a superficial level quite normally. In this community, it is customary that, during a discharged patient's final group therapy session, each person who is present on the unit at the time (i.e., all staff and patients) provide whatever advice they can and wish the person well. Several staff members voiced their doubts about whether Mr. Haines should return to his job as a bus driver. However, the psychiatrist, who was also the unit director, assured the group that there was no reason why Mr. Haines could not continue to be a bus driver. He thought it would be detrimental for Mr. Haines to leave feeling that the group would not trust him to drive a bus.

Question for the social worker: What should the social worker do in this situation? Should the social worker advise Mr. Haines to discuss his condition with his union representative or his supervisor?

1984. Anna Scarpetta, a frail-looking 92-year-old widow, had multiple hospitalizations over a one-year period for a series of falls likely related to transient ischemic attacks. In each instance she rejected the social worker's offers of referral for home health care, meals-on-wheels, or elderly day care/senior services. Mrs. Scarpetta lived in a tidy, small two-story row house in a tight-knit neighborhood with a strong Italian identity. She and several other widows in the neighborhood watched out for one another. Although she had been unable to have children of her own, Mrs. Scarpetta was close to her niece, Karen Carfagno, who had grown up in the neighborhood and now lived within a half-hour drive.

Upon Mrs. Scarpetta's current three-day hospitalization for a fall that resulted in a concussion and severe bruising, Ms. Carfagno became insistent that the physician should "put her in a home where she will be safe." Dr. Franco Abruzzi, an older paternalistic physician who lived and practiced in Mrs. Scarpetta's neighborhood, agreed with Ms. Carfagno that this was the best plan. He asked the social worker to arrange nursing home placement. The social worker, who knew Mrs. Scarpetta well, met with her, found her to be well oriented and "sharp as a tack." Mrs. Scarpetta was adamant about returning to her home, despite the objections of her niece and Dr. Abruzzi.

Question for the social worker: Should the social worker follow Mrs. Scarpetta's wishes despite the risks or follow Dr. Abruzzi's orders?

CONCLUSION

Ethical and legal dimensions are major components of social work practice in health and mental health care. They determine the parameters of the work in relation to what social workers do, with whom they work, and the conditions in which they work. To function as advocates, social workers must behave with the highest ethical standards. In addition, they are compelled to understand deeply the laws and legal issues that can affect entitlement or restriction of the individuals and populations with whom they work. Lawyers working for social service organizations, professional and self-help advocacy groups, and Web sites for advocacy groups are excellent resources for information pertaining to laws and their administration.

The Place of the Social Worker in Health and Mental Health Systems

T his chapter provides social workers in health and mental health care with a range of concepts and tools, including graphic representations, that will help them to understand the systems in which they work. Such understanding helps social workers to gain leverage, to enhance what power they have in organizations, and to work more efficaciously. As social workers' power in organizations increases, their perceptions of service effectiveness also tend to increase (Guterman and Bargal 1996). More than anywhere else in this work, the concepts and tools are drawn from the business management literature, because scholars in that area make most explicit the relationships—or "fit"—between organizations, missions, goals and objectives, tools, and tasks. They are clear that "the tools are not to work harder, but to work smarter" (Drucker 1990). As is true for all social work, the effective use of the concepts and tools presented in this chapter depends on social workers' relationship abilities (Levinson 1992).

This chapter highlights the importance of an ecological perspective. Social workers begin with the goals of clients/consumers, populations, and/or communities and then stand back far enough to know how broadly the context has to be defined to most efficaciously help people reach their goals. Using the metaphor of a camera, social workers are asked to zoom out to see as broadly as possible, then to zoom in to the capture the essential dimensions of context. Thus this chapter also emphasizes understanding that informs action, understanding that helps the social worker to intervene with or on behalf of clients. In relation to organizations and systems, this means that social workers must increase access, freedom, and authority and know how to leverage their actions for maximum effect. Regardless of social workers' practice level or orientation, it is critical that they understand that, while some problems can be resolved at an individual or family level, others will require intervention on a broader scale, including the need to effect changes in organizations and communities (Netting, Kettner, and McMurtry 1998).

Much of this work involves visualization, viewing context broadly, and expanding the places where social workers and clients can be and the ways they can move in those contexts. It is the perspective of a social ecologist, a participant observer of the human habitat in social, economic, and cultural terms (Drucker 1959). This perspective also allows social workers in health and mental health care to step out, redraw, and regroup so that they can step in again refreshed, more willing to listen, and motivated again to work toward client goals. Perspectives are viewed as subjective frames because, like lenses, they bring some aspects of culture into focus while blurring others (Martin 1992). Boundary spanning is the key.

This approach to practice requires an ecological perspective on the part of mature, smart, disciplined, well-educated social workers who are able to understand very complex social, biological, psychological, economic, and legal systems. The approach supports not only the needs of clients but the continued viability of the social work profession in a range of health settings. Social workers with this kind of vision appear to be faring well in the current era. To help their clients as much as they can, they are willing to (1) redefine their jobs, (2) become more knowledgeable about new dimensions of the work, (3) learn new skills and adapt old skills to new situations, and (4) become expert about specific populations. They are adapting to the changing and fast-paced environment (Heifetz and Laurie 1997). So this chapter asserts that to practice effectively, social workers require autonomy, adaptability, an expanded playing field, and—most of all— a much broader, multidimensional, truly ecological perspective.

SYSTEMS

A system is "a regularly interacting or interdependent group of items [or parts] forming [a complex or] unified whole" (*Merriam-Webster's Collegiate Dictionary* 1993:1197; *Random House Dictionary* 1973:1444). One form a system may take is that of a group of body organs that perform one or more vital functions, such as the digestive system or the nervous system.

Or a system may be a group of devices or artificial objects or an organization forming a network, especially for distributing something or serving a common purpose, such as a telephone system, a heating system, a highway system, or a data processing system. A system may also be the structure or organization of business or politics or of society in general, or a form of social, economic, or political organization or practice, such as the communist system or the capitalist system. Or a system may be any formulated, regular, or special plan or method of procedure, such as a system for measuring or marking. All these examples suggest sets of relationships and arrangements of parts as well as different kinds of order. In the same way, concepts or means that are described as systematic suggest coherence, method, thoroughness, regularity, and/or classification. Thus systems have to do with pattern, relationship, coordination, predictability, and order. Altogether, a system is something that is brought together from many parts to form an organized whole. "Increasingly, understanding organizational context means knowledge about multiple, complex systems involving varied funding streams, auspices, professional and nonprofessional providers, and public, not-for-profit and for-profit agencies with varying degrees of authority" (Kerson 1997:24). To survive in today's climate requires constant attention to funding, costs, and efficiency in the delivery of services.

Increasingly, for reasons having to do with solvency and survival, health-related organizations are joining together to form systems of care with the dominant partners and deepest pockets, traditionally university hospitals and medical schools—or, lately, big business.

> Systems organization is an extension of the team design principle. But instead of individuals comprising a team, the systems organization builds the team out of a wide variety of different organizations. They may be government agencies and any number of private businesses, large and small; universities and individual researchers; organizations that are part of the central control organization charged with the task and directly controlled by it; others who may be wholly or partly owned by it but run autonomously; and yet others which stand only in a contractual relationship to the parent organization and are in no way controlled by it or even controllable. . . . The "model" which first made the systems structure visible as a principle of organization design was the National Aeronautics and Space Administration (NASA) in its organization of the U.S. Space Program in the 1960's. But while the large systems structure emerged as a design principle in a huge governmental program, it actually was first developed as a structure for businesses, and major future application is probably in business. (Drucker 1974:593)

In many ways, this book (in specific) and an ecological perspective (in general) are applications of "systems theory" to social work practice in health and mental health care. "The connection and influences among various systems are central to the ecological paradigm" (Greene and Watkins 1998:15). Many using an ecological perspective look to Bronfenbrenner's (1979, 1989) conceptualization of the ecological environment as a series of nested structures. Bronfenbrenner describes four concentric circles surrounding the developing individual. Closest to the individual is the *microsystem* (small-scale systems that involve face-to-face relationships). *Mesosystems* refer to linkages between two or more systems. *Exosystems* are linkages between systems in which an individual may not be involved, and *macrosystems* are the overarching social, legal, political, economic, and value patterns of a given culture. Of course, none of these levels is discrete. Given this perspective, the reader will find that chapter 3 of this book focuses on exosystems and macrosystems, and chapter 5 focuses on microsystems. This chapter focuses on mesosystems, linkages between two or more systems.

The following case example, involving a child with complex needs who lives in a rural Alaskan community, highlights the importance of context and perspective and also demonstrates the various systems within which the social worker had to advocate for the child.

Amy Rose was an administrative care coordinator and early interventionist in an early intervention program in rural Alaska. Mandated through the Individuals with Disabilities Education Act, the program serves developmentally delayed, disabled, and at-risk children from birth to 3 years old and their families. The Individuals with Disabilities Education Act (IDEA) of 1986 views the parent as the child's first teacher. However, a conundrum resulting from an increased demand for services in the face of drastic budget cuts in managed care organizations has caused the program to contract for therapy services at an hourly rate with part-time therapists, and this arrangement has negatively affected the quality of parent education.

Early intervention models typically include a care coordinator whose professional training varies from program to program. The care coordinator arranges for each referred child to receive a general developmental assessment as well as a more detailed assessment based on concerns identified by the parents or others. Referrers to early intervention programs include a range of professionals. In the rural settings, a village health aid or physician assistant typically refers a child for an assessment, which includes tests for vision and hearing development. If speech and language development are a concern, a speech therapist is included in the process, and if movement or motor skills are involved, a physical or occupational therapist is involved. Developmental assessment targets speech/language development, small and language muscle skills, social and emotional development, and adaptive or self-help skills. A written report describes findings and recommends specific services. In the state of Alaska, to receive priority services under federal funding, a child must demonstrate a 50 percent delay in one or more areas of development. State funding is used to provide services to children who have a lesser delay or who are at risk of a developmental delay (such as those exposed in utero to alcohol or other substances).

Federal law requires that an individual family service plan be developed for each child receiving ongoing services. Home-based services may include but are not limited to parent education; family counseling; educational programming; speech, occupational, and physical therapy; language stimulation; and motor encouragement. Providing these services is challenging in rural Alaska. Each community has a health care clinic, and many communities are inaccessible by road. This hub community, with a population of forty-five hundred, and its fifteen surrounding Native Alaskan communities, with populations of two hundred to five hundred people, are accessible only via small aircraft.

Generally school districts and social service agencies are grantees, because the major service components of IDEA are directed toward education and social services. For example, other early intervention programs with which Ms. Rose has worked were coordinated through community-based organizations providing social services to people of all ages with developmental disabilities. In this community, the regional health care corporation is the grantee. In some ways, such as having direct access to health care providers, being a part of a health care corporation is helpful to the program. However, early intervention is not a priority in the medical model, and working with a preventive proactive service in a system that is reactive and crisis-oriented is challenging. This is particularly true for a rural facility with limited capacity whose task it is to stabilize patients and transfer them to a larger community hospital for surgical procedures. Managers and directors in this setting did not understand early intervention, and services with that goal in mind were never considered important.

The early intervention program's staff consisted of Ms. Rose and a special educator. Since few professionals in Alaska want part-time employment, the state early intervention division developed a traveling team of therapists to support rural communities. Several times a year therapists from the various disciplines travel with the care coordinator to the surrounding villages. Once a year in each locale they set up a developmental screening clinic to identify children in need of services. Emily Qimmikpiauraq Beaver brought her 3½-year-old son, Joseph Iviayiq Beaver, to one such screening at a village clinic located on a sand-spit (a small, inaccessible point of land projecting into a body of water) in northern Alaska with a population of five hundred. Mrs.

Beaver described Joseph's and her own frustration with her inability to understand what he was saying. Communication worsened when Joseph's 5-year-old brother, who had been interpreting for him, began attending kindergarten. In his frustration, Joseph was having escalating temper tantrums, and Mrs. Beaver was increasingly concerned. When Ms. Rose assessed Joseph, she found a playful, curious child who enjoyed interacting but whose speech was almost incomprehensible. She suggested that during her next trip to the village she have the itinerant speech therapist assess Joseph's speech and language development. This was an unusual situation in that the early intervention program technically provides services to children only until their third birthday. Joseph was over 3 years old, and yet Ms. Rose was aware that the speech therapist for the school district, who was technically responsible for assessing children over the age of 3, was on medical leave and had been for quite some time. Ms. Rose was not sure how long it would be before anyone would actually be available to assess Joseph's speech and language development. With his mother's permission, Ms. Rose decided to allow Joseph to proceed through the early intervention program. At the same time, Ms. Rose made a referral to the school district and arranged an educational planning meeting to be held during the visit with the speech therapist.

When she examined his mouth, the speech therapist noted that Joseph had two uvulas instead of the typical single one. She told Ms. Rose that this can indicate submucous cleft palate, a medical condition in which speech is affected because the hard palate on the roof of the mouth does not develop, although the skin grows over it, making it less obvious than the more common cleft lip and palate. Because the hard palate is not developed, it is difficult to make sounds that require pressure from the tongue on the roof of the mouth (McKusick 1999). While this is a genetic condition that cannot be cured, treatment to address symptoms can include surgery, speech therapy, physiotherapy, occupational therapy, and remedial assistance at school (Marchett 1999). One surgical procedure, called pharyngeal flap surgery, when combined with speech therapy, helps children normalize their speech (Aergamaso 1999). This anomaly was previously documented in Joseph's medical records by a health aide, but no connection had been made between it and Joseph's difficulties with speech and language. It is important to note that Native Alaskan culture tends to be less verbal than Western culture, and it is not unusual for an older sibling to interpret for a younger child or for family members to worry little about a child's not talking very much.

The speech therapist recommended that professionals develop an educational plan and request a medical assessment. The educational plan was developed with the preschool for which he was eligible through IDEA. The speech therapist's suggestions included teaching some basic sign language to assist Joseph and his family in communicating immediately, as well as recommendations for stimulating the use of his mouth to make sounds. Because they would not be returning to provide services to Joseph, Ms. Rose and her colleague shared as much information with the preschool teacher as possible. In addition, the speech therapist agreed to mail information to the teacher.

The speech therapist made it clear that to determine whether this child did indeed have submucous cleft palate, a medical diagnosis would be necessary. "Velo-cardio-facial syndrome is the most common syndrome associated with a cleft palate without a cleft lip, although a cleft lip may also occur" (Marchette 1999:1). To receive the medical examination, the child would have to be flown to the hub community where medical specialists usually travel every couple of months. Ms. Rose worked with Mrs. Beaver to arrange an appointment during the next visit by the otolaryngologist. In addition, arrangements needed to be made for air travel to and from the village. Joseph was eligible for state Medical Assistance, and in Alaska travel to and from medical appointments is considered a medical expense, as is lodging if the appointment requires an individual to spend the night. For children, the state program also covers the cost of airfare for an adult to escort the child to the appointment. For Mrs. Beaver and Joseph to receive this aid, a physician's referral was required. To obtain a referral, Ms. Rose worked with a family practitioner through the hospital. She described the situation to him, and as he is a strong supporter of Early Intervention Services, he was willing to make the referral without having examined the child. The otolaryngologist did diagnose a submucous cleft palate but offered no suggestions for improving the child's ability to communicate.

Ms. Rose was convinced that medical options were available for Joseph, and she encouraged Mrs. Beaver to seek another opinion, although she knew doing so would be difficult because she would have to travel to Anchorage at her own expense. Because Joseph was not eligible for Early Intervention Services, the last contact Ms. Rose had with this family was to accompany them to the medical appointment. Figure 4.1 shows Joseph's ecomap before the visit to the otolaryngologist, and figure 4.2 shows it after the medical examination.

While doing this work, Ms. Rose became acutely aware of the difficulties presented by being proactive in a reactive environment. She believes these difficulties are universal, and yet they seemed magnified while she worked in rural Alaska. Shades of difference have to be understood.

Demographic differences [do not] exhaust the variations among subgroups of the poor. Although attitudinal differences are more difficult to define and identify, a wide diversity of world-views exists even within demographically homogenous populations. Thus, some poor are more alienated than others, some more upwardly aspiring, and some angrier. Where they fall on these dimensions has a bearing on how they will

FIGURE 4.1. Initial ecomap for Joseph Beaver.

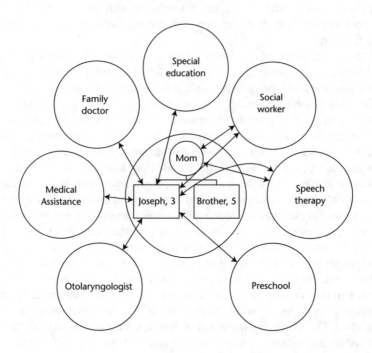

FIGURE 4.2. Ecomap for Joseph Beaver after consultation with the otolaryngologist.

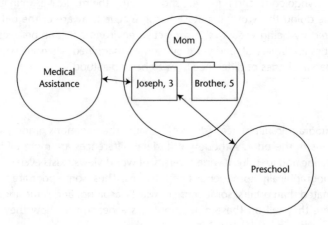

respond to particular efforts to involve them in organizing projects. (Brager, Specht, and Torcayner 1987:60)

Systems as Continua of Care and as Multihealth Businesses

In the contemporary parlance of health care delivery, the word *systems* refers to two separate entities. One use refers to systems that reach across the continuum of care and are made up of what used to be smaller units or organizations. Examples include large health systems whose flagships are a medical school and a university hospital and include community hospitals, health centers, home health and hospice services, and, sometimes, physician practices. The second entity referred to as a system is the multihealth organization:

A multihealth corporation is a health care organization that transcends the boundaries of the traditional hospital. Its organization is characterized by both horizontal and vertical integration. Horizontal integration refers to the combining of similar organizations, in this case hospitals, into a larger unit with the primary objective of enhancing market power. . . . Vertical integration describes the acquisition of other business entities that have an influence on the organization's flow of goods, services, or products or, stated in systems terms, on its input-output exchange. (Kaluzny and Hernandez 1988)

So multihealth organizations may resemble the systems developed around a continuum of care, or they may be business conglomerates that contract to provide health care of a certain type to large populations through a capitation system. One example of a multihealth corporation is a company that contracts with a state to provide mental health services under carve-out arrangements to Medicaid populations.

To be effective advocates and practitioners on every level of service, social workers in health and mental health care must be able to understand systems and organizations. As always in this ecological perspective, the assumption is that structure follows strategy, that these complex multihealth systems have been developed to accomplish the work in more efficacious ways. And as always, the focus is ultimately on tasks, on social workers' understanding organizations and systems in ways that will best help clients achieve their objectives. Social workers may find that relatively minor changes in their work or in organizational structures could significantly improve the work of their unit, organization, or system (Drucker 1974:46). The material presented in this chapter is meant to foster that kind of thinking.

To maximize their ability to help clients reach their goals, social workers must understand (1) the relationships within systems and communities; (2) their own position within systems and communities (that is, the authority afforded them and the latitude allowed them); and (3) the fit between their work, the mission of the system in which they work, and the needs and wishes of the community (Flynn 1992; Goffee and Jones 1996; Kettner, Maroney, and Martin 1999). Ultimately, good understanding, sufficient authority, and a fine fit allow social workers to maximize their work with clients and leverage that work to its fullest potential. To work in this way requires a wide lens, organizational savvy, effective tools and techniques, and superb relationship skills. The material is salient to all social workers, from those responsible for caseloads or small programs to those administering large programs and complex systems. All social workers are managing at least their own work as case managers, clinical social workers, generalists, or program or project managers. This information helps social workers to manage cases, projects, and programs and to address community and organizational problems. Knowledge of systems and organizations enhances social workers' power and helps them advocate more effectively for their clients, consumers, programs, and communities as well as for themselves. "Power is the ability to take one's place in whatever discourse is essential to action and the right to have one's part matter" (Heilbrun 1988:18). "Rather than power being associated with position, and therefore a position's occupant, new approaches to management locate control in the work process itself" (Weinberg 1996:202).

One's *place*, in this sense, means relative position in a series, position in a social scale, position in a sequence, position at the end of a competition, or a proper or designated niche. Social workers have to understand the position they must maintain in their organizations in order to have sufficient authority to advocate for and otherwise best help clients. While one dimension of *place* is geographical location, in the largest sense it includes the multiple arenas within which social workers function. Even in its most concrete interpretation, the place being described is probably not an office with one or two clients. Social workers have to be able to expand the boundaries of place to think in terms of all the systems with which their clients interact. They have to garner the knowledge and authority to move freely enough to accomplish the work. Organizational understanding allows social workers to assess more accurately how to influence group behavior and culture to help clients reach their goals.

Expert knowledge of organizations, networks, and systems allows social workers to maneuver through those systems and manipulate them in ways that enhance their abilities to help their clients. The verbs used here are meant to empower. To *maneuver* means to perform a movement in military or naval tactics in order to secure an advantage, to make a series of changes in direction or position for a specific purpose, or to use stratagems. The word *manipulate* comes from the French word *manipuler,* meaning to handle an apparatus in chemistry. Its common English definition is to manage skillfully.

The New Organization and the Need for Management

Citing revolutionary changes in ways of doing business over the last century, Peter Drucker (1959, 1998), the father of management theory, writes about the new organization with new capacities to organize highly skilled and knowledgeable people for voluntary, joint performance through the exercise of responsible judgment. Examples of such changes include the development of international banking; the Marshall Plan; the invention, refinement, and dissemination of computer technology; and the Internet. Not only did the rise of the new organization create new social realities, new definitions of leadership, new issues about power, and new problems of how to integrate professional specialists and managers into the organization, it also created the demand for the new discipline of management.

Applicability of Management Theory to Social Work

Management theory supports and enhances this ecological perspective for social work practice in health and mental health. Like social work, management is an integrating discipline that draws its expertise from many sources. The sources for management theory include engineering, psychology, sales, accounting, labor relations, and the military (Beatty 1998). Like the outcome measures being demanded of today's social workers in health and mental health care, management requires an operational mission that can be converted to clear, concrete, measurable objectives by which to establish, organize, and measure the work. Nothing is more salient to social work practice today than Drucker's long-incorporated concept of management by objectives, which speaks directly to outcome measures.

Objectives are set by determining what should be measured in each area and what the yardstick should be. Clear objectives enable one to (1) organize and explain the work in a small number of general statements; (2) test these statements through experience; (3) predict behavior; (4) evaluate the soundness of decisions when they are still being made; and (5) enable the practitioner to analyze the experience and, as a result, improve performance (Drucker 1954:65). Objectives should be derived from the goals and mission of the whole enterprise.

Basically, managing by objectives means that everyone (from individual clients and their relatives, to communities to line social workers, to social work supervisors to social work administrators) who is involved in any dimension of the work is managing that part of the work. Management by objectives also changes the conception of the job of the social work manager from supervising line social workers to cooperating with line workers to determine objective measures and goals, leaving them to achieve those objectives as they can. In this way, attention is placed on tasks and goals rather than on the worker. The work, and not the worker, is the object of supervision. The social work practitioner is the means for accomplishing the work, the conduit, the catalyst, not the end. Thus the supervision dimensions of management are related to the determination of objectives, goals, and measures of the social worker's productivity, including effectiveness. In the same way, social workers do not manage clients/consumers, programs, or communities, but rather their task is to inspire and their goal is to make productive the specific strengths and knowledge of each individual involved in the work (Drucker 1999:22).

Management by objectives was originally framed by Drucker as "management by objectives and self-control," with self-control being critical to the concept. Agreed-upon objectives are achieved through self-control. Self-control is a very important part of this concept. A great advantage of management by objectives is the possibility for people to control their own performance (Drucker 1954:130). Measurements need not be rigidly quantitative, but they have to be rational, simple, and clear. Information is freely shared because it is used for self-control, not for control from above. Similarly, social workers help clients and communities establish objectives and reach them through self-control. The principle of management by objectives is first and foremost about responsibility. Social workers must know and understand the ultimate goals, what is expected of them and why, and what they will be measured against and how. Self-control means stronger motivation, higher performance goals, and broader vision (Drucker 1974). Thus all who are involved in the work must be able to explicate objectives and ultimate goals, what is expected of them, and what criteria will be used for performance evaluation. Again, emphasis is on control of the work and individuals' control of their own work. One major difference between the two disciplines is business's comfort and social work's discomfort with the concept of control. This approach is not talking about the control of clients. Rather it underscores the importance of controlling the process in order to help the client maximally. The stance is highly compatible with the ethics and values of the social work profession.

This rich interpretation of management by objectives and self-control fits perfectly with the ecological reinterpretation of social work practice that is espoused in this book. One dimension of the fit has to do with the uses of control and self-control. Another relates to the emphasis on bringing together practice, policy, and action within a total scheme.

"'Practice theory'—what Loeb [1960] called a 'professional science'—leans heavily on both knowledge and philosophy, but it cannot end there. For a theory of practice is a theory of action, and action is not deducible from either knowledge or intention working alone. If we knew everything there is to know, we would still have to decide what to do; and if our purposes were impeccable, the action based on them would still not be self-evident. Each of these areas influence and limit each other in every specific situation; given the appropriate evidence, and given a set of valued outcomes, the principles of action provide the implementing force. Throughout any practice theory we might build, every step must show how we bring together science, policy, and action within a total scheme" (Schwartz 1994:333).

The following practice example illustrates one patient's relationships to the mental health system in the United States in January 2000.

In January 2000, the U.S. Secretary of Health and Human Services, Donna Shalala, sent a letter to the nation's governors regarding the strides that were made in enabling individuals with disabilities to receive necessary services in their communities rather than in institutions. The letter reminds the governors of the recent Supreme Court decision in *Olmstead* v. *L. C.* (1999), which affirms the beliefs that no person should have to live in a nursing home or other institution if he or she can live in his or her own community and that unnecessary institutionalization of individuals with disabilities is discrimination under the Americans with Disabilities Act (ADA) of 1990. The court's decision says that a state may be able to meet its obligation under the ADA by providing comprehensive, effectively working plans ensuring that individuals with disabilities receive services in the most integrated setting appropriate to their needs. The letter reminds the states that they must provide effective, fiscally responsible policies designed to increase access to community-based services.

The Olmstead case was brought by two women in Georgia whose disabilities include mental illness and mental retardation and whose treatment professionals thought they could live in a community setting. Their lawyers argued that their continued institutionalization was a violation of their right under the ADA to live "in the most integrated setting appropriate to the needs of qualified individuals with disabilities" (28 CFR 35.130[d]). Under the court's decision, states must provide community-based services when treatment professionals determine that such placement is appropriate, when the patients do not oppose the treatment, and when the placement can be reasonably accommodated. The court cautioned, however, that nothing in the ADA condones termination of institutional settings for people unable to handle or benefit from community settings (Westmoreland and Perez 2000). Following is the story of an individual who may not be able to live outside the state hospital.

Donna Hauck, age 50, has an extensive history of inpatient hospitalization for the treatment of severe mental illness. Schizoaffective disorder (bipolar type) and personality disorder (not otherwise specified) have been diagnosed. Short and overweight, with long brown hair, she attempts to present herself as dignified but actually appears as an older woman trying to look less worn by life by using too much make-up and a youthful hairdo. Figure 4.3 is a lifeline for Donna Hauck showing the pattern of her illness over time.

Ms. Hauck regularly cycles in and out of the state mental hospital. She does not believe that medication is responsible for her dramatic improvement. Each time she is discharged, she initially attends a partial hospitalization program and takes her medication as prescribed. However, as life stresses mount, Ms. Hauck gradually stops all treatment because she believes that the medication is causing her depression and her inability to think clearly and concentrate. As she further decompensates, she becomes delusional and agitated. Eventually her bizarre and threatening behaviors bring her to the county mental health court, resulting in commitment to the community psychiatric hospital.

Ms. Hauck's latest admission was precipitated by an event in which she started a fire. The fire department was called, and the accompanying police took her to the community hospital, where she was committed for treatment of her psychosis. Ms. Hauck's Medical Assistance HMO will cover a maximum hospitalization of sixty days, but stabilization usually takes about ninety days, with additional time needed for discharge planning. Eventually the staff from the County Office of Mental Health utilized one of their apportioned beds at the state hospital for further stabilization and discharge planning. Over the years, Ms. Hauck's need for hospitalization and the length of her hospital stays

FIGURE 4.3. Lifeline for Donna Hauck.

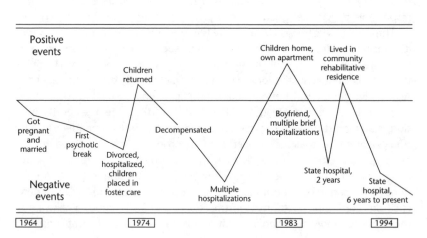

have increased. Her last hospitalization is one of eight state hospital admissions.

The state Office of Mental Health and Substance Abuse Services establishes requirements for admission to a state hospital, with regulations that follow the directives of the state Department of Public Welfare, which receives funding from the state and federal government and must satisfy the regulations of the federal Department of Health and Human Services. The impact of the law on treatment and service options can be seen in the current effects of the Americans with Disabilities Act on discharge initiatives. Also, the Supreme Court's decision in the Olmstead case reinforces the need for community placement for those who do not require inpatient care and has intensified the expansion of community-based services.

Patients who meet the criteria for an involuntary commitment are admitted to the state hospital. The Mental Health Review Officer who hears the case determines whether the petitioner presents enough valid evidence of a person being a danger either to himself or to others. In addition, the state hospital is not available for acute care; therefore all patients must have received treatment at a community hospital prior to admission. The state hospital administration then facilitates admissions from the individual community hospitals.

Every patient in the state hospital is assigned a treatment team that is composed of a psychiatrist, a social worker, and a nurse. The social worker's tasks include providing an accurate psychosocial assessment, participating in therapeutic interventions, maintaining communication with family members and significant others, and collaborating with the patient and community providers to formulate and implement an appropriate discharge plan.

Social worker Sophia Regal finds that working with Ms. Hauck can be both pleasant and very frustrating. Ms. Hauck is superficially cooperative, never disagreeing with what is being suggested; however, whether or not she will follow through with developed plans always remains a question. Also, she has an ability to find the silver lining in any situation but uses massive denial in her judgments. She is very forgiving of any wrongs that may have been done to her, a quality that consistently places her at risk for future abusive relationships. Impaired judgment and minimal insight significantly affect her problem-solving and decision-making capabilities. For example, she sincerely wants to live life fully and is quite willing to try new possibilities; however, her denial of her illness severely affects her ability to accept necessary medication and therapy. Because she has had long periods of moderate stabilization in the past with a minimal amount of medication, she cannot accept that at present her illness requires different medications to achieve the same quality of thinking. The social work value of self-determination is tested when Ms. Regal considers the need to protect this vulnerable woman. Advocating on her behalf requires a delicate balance between practice wisdom and knowledge of client's rights.

Each time Ms. Hauck's condition stabilizes, the treatment team recommends initiation of discharge planning. For her, stabilization requires a daily combination of Seroquel (600 mg) for disordered thinking, Paxil (40 mg) for depression, Topamax (400 mg) for mood stabilization, and Buspar (60 mg) for anxiety. On this medication she is fully alert, able to function during the day in the community, and able to sleep peacefully at night. Without depression, delusions, or mood fluctuations, she can relate to others quite effectively and can meet her needs with minimal assistance.

Ms. Hauck's family has cared for her for most of her life; however, with advancing age, they are no longer willing to provide her with a residence. She is eager to be discharged and has engaged a patient advocate to pressure the hospital for immediate release back to the community. She was able to contact the patient advocate by calling a toll-free number, and she requested that the advocate attend her treatment team meeting.

With Ms. Hauck's permission, Ms. Regal begins to formulate a plan that will accommodate her needs for housing, financial benefits, and aftercare. The County Office of Mental Health is notified of the plan to discharge Ms. Hauck, with an accounting of her resources. Applications are initiated for placement in a county residential facility with intensive case management services provided by the County Case Management Office. State hospitalization automatically establishes eligibility for these scarce and high-cost services, which are funded by the patient's county of residence. Financial benefits can be obtained through the Social Security Office, with eligibility established prior to discharge, or through the Department of Public Assistance on the day of discharge. Medical insurance and prescription coverage are also obtained through these offices. Once these services and benefits are in place, a firm discharge date is set, and aftercare plans can be established through the county mental health clinic.

Because Ms. Hauck has a long history of stopping her treatment and medications after discharge, the state hospital petitions the Mental Health Court for an outpatient commitment to the partial hospitalization program she will attend after discharge. This commitment can be converted back to an inpatient commitment if Ms. Hauck misses scheduled treatment appointments or begins to decompensate regardless of the treatment, thus avoiding serious decompensation before intensive treatment in a hospital setting can begin again. For Ms. Hauck, decompensation begins with difficulty sleeping, agitation subsequent to auditory hallucinations, and argumentative behavior. At this point, placing her back on her medication can fairly easily stabilize her. If treatment does not occur at this point, she will become increasingly delusional, agitated, and, eventually, assaultive. Contact with the police will then precipitate hospitalization. The likelihood of criminal charges increases, and Ms. Hauck will require a longer period of time for stabilization to occur.

While Ms. Hauck is in the community, the county mental health system will provide housing, usually in the form of a community rehabilitative residence or supported living arrangement. Intensive case management services, also provided by the county, will help Ms. Hauck access needed services and solve whatever problems she faces. Although in this case Ms. Hauck is quite capable of budgeting her own money, individuals who are not financially aware can receive money management services through Lifetime Support, a nonprofit organization that serves this population. Psychiatrists, therapists, and milieu settings, such as Freya House, which offers socialization and job opportunities, will provide treatment. Income is provided through agencies outside the mental health system, but the process of obtaining those benefits can be too daunting for those with mental illness; therefore, successfully securing these benefits is part of the discharge process.

Ms. Hauck's ecomap indicates how her life changes when the symptoms of her mental illness influence her life (figure 4.4).

Ms. Hauck's prognosis is guarded at best. Her history includes repeated noncompliance with her medication regimen and outpatient therapy. If coerced into continuing treatment, she will relocate and disappear from the mental health system. She will not resurface until she has totally decompensated and her psychotic behaviors bring her into contact with the police again. Her only hope for long-term stabilization is for her to accept the need for medication. One of the most frequent deterrents to medication compliance in women is weight gain, but the newer medications are showing promise in reducing this side effect.

Ms. Regal's job is to balance Ms. Hauck's needs and the community's needs within the financially constrained system of service delivery. Ms. Hauck has a right and a desire to live in the community. She has one personal financial resource, Social Security Disability Benefits. All other needs must be met by publicly funded programs. Ms. Regal's ability to engage Ms. Hauck in the planning process and her knowledge of the available programs and how to access them are critical for implementing a discharge plan that will give Ms. Hauck the best chance to remain stabilized in the community.

UNDERSTANDING THE PLACE OF THE ORGANIZATION WITHIN THE COMMUNITY

The term *community* can be defined in several ways that are useful for social workers in health and mental health systems. A community can be any size social group whose members live in a specific locality, share government, and have a common cultural and historical heritage. Thus a town or a college can be a community, as can a social group sharing character-

FIGURE 4.4. Ecomap for Donna Hauck.

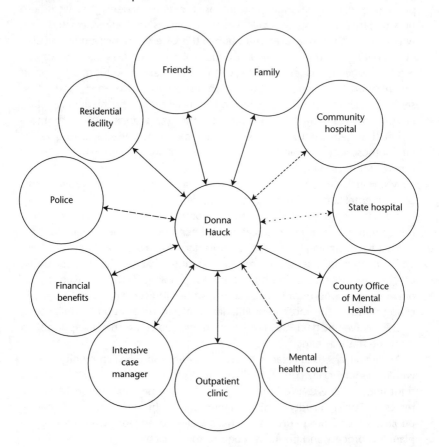

istics or interests and perceived or perceiving itself as distinct in some respect from the larger society. In that way, a community can be an order of nuns who live in many different countries but whose purpose, style of living, and differences from the societies in which they live make them a community. Also, many people who are deaf describe themselves as part of the deaf community, which has no geographic boundaries but is composed of people who have a profound common characteristic and see themselves as distinct from the larger society. Ideally,

> a community is a group of people who are socially interdependent, who participate together in discussion and decision making, and who shape certain practices that both define the community and are

nurtured by it. Such a community is not quickly formed. It almost always has a history and is a community of memory, defined in part by its past and its memory of the past. Communities continually evolve in relation to roles, economic structures, power holders and funding sources. Organizations must be responsive to their communities in the same ways that they are responsive to other external forces. (McMurtry, Kettner, and Netting 1992)

Since social workers in health and mental health care have to understand context and move between levels of practice, knowledge of communities is essential for every kind of practice.

Many social workers are ignorant of what occurs outside their offices and work inwardly rather than outwardly. They need more outside information to be effective (Drucker 1998). Social workers have worked in communities since Mary Richmond described the use of personal and community resources in improving the lives of families and promoted measures to deal with community needs outside the scope of her agency, either through legislation or the establishment of new agencies and services (Pumphrey 1986). Thus if all interactions occur within an office, social workers must still know the communities in which their clients live or through which they define themselves in order to understand the constraints on and possibilities for clients.

The following case example describes a reproductive health center that has too few clients in spite of a clear need for its services in the surrounding community.

Social worker Rosa Bonilla was hired by Women Living Well, a well-staffed reproductive health center that had too few clients. Most of the surrounding community were Spanish-speaking individuals who preferred a distant health center where several staff members spoke Spanish. By talking to many neighborhood residents, as well as a few shopkeepers, Mrs. Bonilla learned that although Women Living Well charged on a sliding scale and was more convenient, regardless of age or marital status, all the women in the neighborhood felt unwelcome there. When Mrs. Bonilla brought this information to their attention, staff members worried that increasing the neighborhood clientele would discourage their traditional middle-class clients from continuing to seek services there. With clinic support and staff involvement, Mrs. Bonilla held meetings with community representatives and some long-time clinic clients.

Suggestions that arose from those meetings about structure and outreach services allowed the clinic to expand its client base to serve its immediate community while continuing to serve its traditional population. Some of those suggestions were easy to institute. For example, signs and notices were posted in Spanish as well as in English, the entrance and waiting room were given a more welcoming appearance, and small articles were placed in community newspapers describing how Women Living Well welcomes all women who have similar reproductive health needs and share the mission and values of Women Living Well.

A foundation grant has allowed the health center to offer two special courses on how women can live well and take good care of themselves. One is offered in English, with beginning conversational Spanish mixed into the learning. The other is offered in Spanish, with an emphasis on how the women can communicate their needs effectively to professionals whose first language is English. Each course is held twice a week for twelve weeks, on a weekday evening and on Saturday morning, and each session lasts forty-five minutes. Between the two classes is a time for conversation and refreshment that draws participants from both courses. All staff members must participate in one of the two courses, and the time is considered part of their workday. Finally, Women Living Well has the staff member who checks clients out of the clinic ask for feedback about how they were treated and how satisfied they are. She logs these responses so that the director can review them weekly. In six months, staff members plan to do a simple in-house client satisfaction study to be sure they are drawing from a larger client base and are responding to the needs of all their clients.

Netting et al. (1998) provide a framework for understanding communities through which target populations are defined, community characteristics are determined, differences are recognized, and structures are identified. The target population is composed of people who need and who may benefit from assistance. Community characteristics include geographical boundaries (which may include physical or social barriers), units of health and human service programs, and service accessibility. The cultural values, traditions, and beliefs that are present in the community encompass all divergent views and value conflicts, including those of each racial, ethnic, gender, age, and class group. Struggling with value conflicts helps social workers know how much the community is committed to addressing the needs of the target population. This framework is described more fully in chapter 6.

Power and Participation

Social workers in health and mental health care have to understand the distribution, working, and machinations of power and participation in communities. To identify structure, the distribution of power, provision and allocation of resources, and patterns of service distribution that affect communities, social workers need to recognize locations of power. Also, they need to identify the primary sources of funding for health and human services, strong leaders within the health and human services community that serve the target population, and community power structure influences. To determine resource availability, social workers have to identify existing agencies and groups providing service, major funding sources, and needed and available nonmonetary resources. In addition, they have to understand organizational domain, what the organization does and who it serves, and the means by which the organization establishes its role within its environment.

In many ways, an organization's survival is a function of its ability to learn and adapt to changing environmental contingencies. The degree of an organization's dependence on some element of its environment is related to its need for the resources that that element can provide and inversely related to the ability of other elements to provide the same resource. Organizations that are perceived as threatening to an existing organizational configuration will evoke defensive reactions by established local organizations. In addition, an organization's survival is related to the formal agreements it has with other organizations that make up its task environment.

ORGANIZATIONS

To organize is to form into a whole consisting of interdependent or co-ordinated parts especially for harmonious or unified action (*Random House Dictionary* 1973:1014). An organization can be defined as a body of persons brought together to accomplish some end or work, or the personnel or apparatus of an agency, business, or institution. Most organizations are highly bureaucratized. Bureaucracy both persists and expands because this highly rational approach to structuring complex systems leads to greater efficiency and predictability (Etzioni 1964). Decoding organizational culture—that is, understanding the roles, norms, informal power structure, rituals, unwritten rules, and group dynamics that are operating in a setting—must be done by any participant in any situation (Scott 1989). Size, hierarchy, rules and expectations regarding behavior of social workers and clients or customers (role structure), division of labor, degree of bureaucratization, degree of centralization of control, and ethics and values shape the organization and create parameters for work.

An organization is an administrative or functional structure, or a body of persons organized to do some work. "It has become clear that organization is not an absolute. It is a tool for making people productive in working together. As such, a given organization structure fits certain tasks in certain conditions and at certain times" (Drucker 1999:11). For this chapter, organizations are the smaller units formed into a whole in order to act in unified ways. Examples include the hospitals, home care agencies, outreach services, community health efforts, and residences for specific populations that often make up systems of health and mental health care.

Organizations and Culture

Organizations can be viewed as elements of culture, while they also impose a culture on all their participants (Bielefeld and Corbin 1996). "Organizations socialize their members into the norms of the organizational subculture and thus into defining reality in the light of the overt and manifest functions of the organization" (Scott 1989:45). To understand the culture of an organization, one looks for metapatterns, the recurring tacit patterns of relationship that can be seen in intraorganizational behavior and culture. According to Ingersoll and Adams (1992:40), metapatterns from the cultures in which organizations that employ social workers are located include the following beliefs:

1. Eventually all work processes can and should be rationalized and are thus completely controllable.
2. The means for attaining organizational objectives deserve maximum attention, with the result that the objectives quickly become subordinated to those means even to the extent that the objectives become lost or forgotten.
3. Efficiency and predictability are more important than any other considerations.

To understand the culture of an organization, one must consider four levels of analysis: (1) the culture-at-large, that is, the social, political, and economic context within which all organizations are nested (and of which all organizations are elements); (2) the informal and formal structures; (3) interpersonal and group relations; and (4) the individual organization members' thoughts, feelings, and behavior. Within work organizations, metapatterns may be constructive, benign, or dysfunctional. They also have a contagious quality; they can spread by creating the conditions for their own contagion. Metapatterns, then, become part of organizational identity.

The following example shows the importance of understanding the community in which a homeless shelter is located.

Social worker Douglas Jackson was hired to help the residents of a homeless shelter. Several frustrating months later, he was told that the shelter was created because some homeless people had taken up residence in front of the courthouse, and powerful people who frequented the courthouse did not like seeing them. Because the purpose of the shelter was to keep the residents off the street rather than to help them live in the community, Mr. Jackson was stymied. Until he understood the real mission of the shelter, he could not advocate effectively or empower the residents. Mr. Jackson worked on multiple practice levels, asking questions, gathering information, narrowing the focus, learning about locations of power and the values of interested parties, and mobilizing resources. In those ways he gradually enriched his program and helped some but not all his "residents" to move from the shelter to other living arrangements.

Social work has understood the importance of organizations and the relationships of social workers and clients to organizations for a long time. For example, Jessie Taft (1937:18) wrote that "the worker's responsibility is mediated by the agency and what it can and cannot do." Also in 1937, medical social worker Dorothea Gilbert argued that social workers in hospitals were being ineffective with patients because they were so caught in conflicting responsibilities to the administration, the patient, and others. Social workers were put on the defensive and made to feel they had to justify themselves:

> Medical social work, always zealous in adjusting to the hospital, has necessarily changed as medicine has shifted its focus. In the early years, medicine had been largely preoccupied in the study of diseased parts. . . . With the resultant unprecedented growth of information about the physical manifestations of disease, emphasis both in teaching and in practice was placed more upon diagnosis than on the treatment of the sick person. . . . Developments in industrial medicine, psychiatry, endocrinology, and physiology . . . have focused more and more on what the social worker might have to say of the patient in his social setting. (Gilbert 1937:132)

Ultimately Gilbert was concerned about the social worker's greater affiliation with the physician and the hospital than with the patient. The medical social worker accepted the assessment of the physician and the needs for treatment as defined by the physicians and the institution, rather than working from the views of the patient who was working with her voluntarily. She thought rather that the social worker's role was called into being when the patient had to make a decision about accepting or rejecting the service or recommendations of the hospital or physician. Many of those issues remain today. It has recently been argued that "hospital social workers may be advocates for their patients, but they are also the handmaidens of physicians and frontline risk managers for hospitals . . . [and that] managing the dissonance between personhood and casehood on behalf of professionals and the hospital . . . is the central task of hospital social work" (Heimer and Stevens 1997:133, 135). These issues are also relevant to contemporary concerns about managed care and the ways those who pay for the services are orchestrating and constraining the work (Birenbaum 1997; Corcoran and Vandiver 1996; Sunley 1997). To be an effective social worker in health and mental health requires that one understand organizations and both intra- and interorganizational relationships. Neither advocacy nor case management in any form can be mastered without such understanding (Austin and McClelland 1996; Ballew and Mink 1996; Ezell 1994).

Most social work practice continues to be agency-based, that is, under the auspices of a particular organization, institution, or system. Social workers are representatives of their organizations, helping clients, consumers, and communities to reach their goals through enacting whatever dimensions of the agency mission apply to the social workers' particular work assignments. "The use of agency function and function in professional role gives focus, content, and direction to social work processes, assures accountability to society and to the agency, and provides the partialization, the concreteness, the 'difference,' the 'given' which further productive engagement" (Smalley 1970:106). Thus agency mission and purpose determines the content and focus of intervention. While the particularities of relationship reside between social workers and those they work with, social work roles reside with the organization. In this way, social workers always have backup; that is, the support and status of the organization are behind them. The laws that inform the organization, the administrative and supervisory hierarchy, the legal and community mandates, and the powers of the board of directors and the other professionals in the organization all lend authority to and support the social worker (Compton and Galaway 1998; Hammer and Kerson 1997; Kutchins 1991; Litzelfelner and Petr 1997). When social workers leave organizations, their clients/consumers/communities know that other social workers will replace them. Those social work roles and functions will be carried by others in the organization.

In the following example, a direct practitioner develops a solution to an organization problem.

Social worker Christina Hayes works at Children's Well-Being (CWB), an extended care facility for infants and children with problems such as failure to thrive and uncontrolled asthma. The facility is part of a large health system ranging from primary to tertiary care for children and adults. Most of the children are insured through Medicaid or State Children's Health Insurance

Program (Balanced Budget Act of 1997, Title XXI). The CWB mission is to "normalize" and stabilize the functioning of its patients so that they can live with their families and be as mainstreamed as their development allows. The children can live in the facility for as long as one year.

Nurses, therapists, and social workers working closely with parents complain regularly that they give parents the careful, clear instructions they need to care for their children, but many of the parents do not listen and jeopardize their children's precarious health. In fact, many of the children are brought to the emergency room when they are home on weekend or holiday passes and are rehospitalized or make many emergency room visits after they have been discharged from the program. This angers the staff because they know that, despite their best efforts, the parents have wrecked the children's care.

Before she became a social worker, Ms. Hayes worked as a teacher of persons with a range of developmental disabilities. Soon after she began to work at CWB, Ms. Hayes noted that several of the parents appeared to be learning disabled. Ms. Hayes, the nurses, and therapists reviewed the discharge list for the previous six months, and Ms. Hayes pulled all the records of the children who had gotten into medical difficulty when outside the facility. Information from records indicated that the majority of these children's parents did not learn to care correctly for their children, although they had indicated to the staff that they understood what they were being told but could not follow the written instructions. Ms. Hayes took this information to the head of CWB, who charged her with developing a program to address this need. At present, Ms. Hayes is instituting a social educational plan that will identify which parents are developmentally disabled and will teach them different ways to manage their children's illness. The objective is to demonstrate that applying the techniques used to teach those with learning disabilities to this special population of parents will reduce the number of visits children make to the emergency room and hospitalization rates. It may also be possible to compare time periods to demonstrate in monetary terms how much money the state is saving by paying for fewer emergency room visits and hospital days.

Ms. Hayes used her knowledge of certain illnesses and learning disabilities, her interdisciplinary team, her unit and its relationship to the larger health system, and the state's concerns about financial outlay to help her organization and its patient's families reach their goals. This example is a demonstration that a direct practice social worker can understand the system in which she works, her place in the system, and the fit between the mission of her organization and her work and can gain sufficient authority to improve services to individual clients (Applebaum and Austin 1990; Lewis, Lewis, Packard and Souflee 2001).

Organizational Mission

An organization's mission is its definition of purpose or reason for being. A shared mission is integral to the success of an organization (Peters and Waterman 1982). According to Drucker (1974), an organization's mission or purpose is an attempt to satisfy a need in the marketplace. The organization is defined by the desire or need that the consumer satisfies when obtaining a product or a service. Organizational mandates set out the requirements of organizations according to their charters or articles of incorporation or, when they are public organizations, as codified in ordinances and laws. The organizational mission is derived from these mandates. The mission statement of an organization

> establishes broad and relatively permanent parameters within which goals are developed and specific programs designed. A mission statement includes, at minimum, a target population and a statement of the agency's vision for what ideally might be achieved in collaboration between the agency and the target population. Mission statements are intended to be visionary and should be reevaluated when societal conditions are altered and when the problems that the agency was established to resolve are no longer present. (Kettner, Moroney, and Martin 1999)

A comprehensive mission statement should provide a basis for making decisions that should contribute to improved performance (Pearce and David 1987). Such a statement should include several basic elements: (1) the historical significance of the agency, (2) its distinct competencies (what the organization is uniquely equipped to do because of its location, personnel, resources, or historical position), (3) the needs it meets for specific patient/client groups or populations to be served, and (4) the environment that shapes its opportunities and threats (Williamson, Stevens, Loudon, and Migliore 1997). Examples of the latter are laws, insurance policies, and fears related to specific diseases or drug abuse. Also included should be (1) the principal products or services provided, (2) geographic domain, if relevant, (3) the organization's particular religious, ethical, or social philosophy, (4) the organization's self-image, and (5) the organization's desired public image, if different from its self-image (Duncan, Ginter, and Kreidel 1994). Duncan et al. (1994:22–23) cite the following examples of self-image (South Carolina) and desired public image (Connecticut). The mission of the South Carolina Department of Health and Environmental Control is to protect the public's health and environment. As the principal advisor to the state on public health, the department has the responsibility and authority to prevent, abate, and control pollution and health problems. The mission of the Connecticut Department of Health Services is to become the best state health department in the nation.

At times, organizations also devise vision statements, forward-looking aspects of purpose that identify broad long-term goals that the organization hopes to achieve that link its mission with its objectives. Vision is another concept that is "vital to an organization because it provides the energy and focus for learning. While adaptive learning is possible without vision, generative learning occurs only when people are striving to accomplish something that matters deeply to them" (Senge 1990:206). "A well-conceived vision consists of two major components: core ideology and envisioned future" (Collins and Porras 1996:66). Core ideology defines the enduring character of an organization and is made up of two distinct parts: core values (a system of guiding principles and tenets) and core purpose (the organization's most fundamental reason for being). Envisioned future also consists of two parts: what Collins and Porras call a ten- to thirty-year audacious goal plus vivid descriptions of what it will be like to achieve the goal. They say that they have found in their research that visionary organizations

often use bold missions—or what they prefer to call BHAGs (pronounced BEE-hags and shorthand for Big, Hairy, Audacious Goals)—as a powerful way to stimulate progress. . . . A BHAG engages people—it reaches out and grabs them. It is tangible, energizing, highly focused. People get it right away; it takes little or no explanation. A BHAG is a clearly articulated goal. Core purpose can never be completed, whereas the BHAG is reachable in 10 to 30 years. Think of the core purpose as the star on the horizon to be chased forever, the BHAG is the mountain to be climbed. (Collins and Porras 1996:73–74)

In comparing mission, vision, and objectives, mission statements are the longest-term and the least measurable. Vision statements rarely include numbers but are more specific than mission statements. Objectives are the shortest-term and the most measurable (Williamson et al. 1997). One strategic tip is to reevaluate the agency mission and goals regularly (Menefee 1997).

Following is an effective mission statement for a small social work program within a large health care system.

As part of the Star Healthcare Network, the STRIDE (Students Taking Responsibility in Drug Education) program is committed to providing high-quality prevention education services to children and youth in the city area. In partnership with the city school system, STRIDE educates students about the medical, social, and psychological consequences of substance abuse for the individual, family, and community. The basic goals of STRIDE are to increase students' awareness of the dangers of drug abuse and to decrease students' interest in trying substances. This unique school- and hospital-based education is provided through interactive presentations, discussions, and role-playing activities led by volunteers from the school system, hospital, and community.

The STRIDE program is committed to improving the quality of life for students and their families and recognizes the importance of collaborating with other community-based prevention programs in order to provide a comprehensive approach to the reduction of substance abuse, violence, and injury in the city. The STRIDE curriculum contains aspects of other educational programs, such as violence prevention, the promotion of healthy lifestyle choices, injury and illness and prevention, leadership training, self-esteem enhancement, and the provision of alternative activities for children and youth.

It is STRIDE's belief that it is important for children to be educated and encouraged in creative, cooperative ways by people from diverse backgrounds and professions. The STRIDE program offers persons who share this vision the opportunity to volunteer in each aspect of program service delivery and recognizes that the energy and enthusiasm of its dedicated volunteer base is its greatest strength.

The following example involves a home care and hospice organization that has been integrated into a large health care system.

The three organizational charts shown in figure 4.5 illustrate the evolution of the home care organization that has employed social worker Fay Sunshine from 1980 until the present. Each decade has brought greater complexity to the organization and has affected Ms. Sunshine's place and voice in the organization.

Management Styles in Multihealth Organizations

Successful social workers in health and mental health distinguish the bases of power, are sensitive to the sources of power, and are careful to keep their actions consistent with others' expectations (Kotter 1979). Social workers in hospitals and other health organizations have little formal power, are often seen as ancillary, and have to understand and use power that stems from sources outside the usual authority structure of their in-

FIGURE 4.5. Charting the evolution of a home care organization.

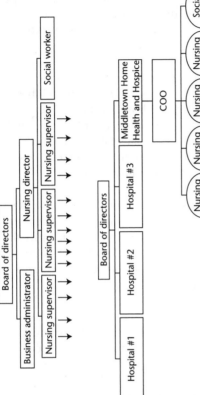
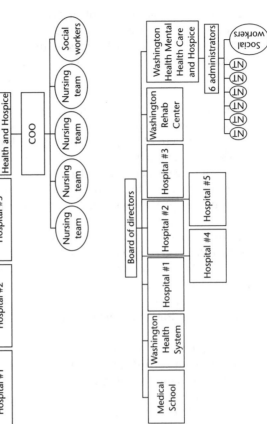

Organizational plan of Best Visiting Nurses when social worker Fay Sunshine began her employment there in 1980.

Organizational plan of Middletown Hospital System in 1990, when Best Visiting Nurses was bought and became Middletown Home Care and Hospice. Social worker Fay Sunshine continues her work in home care. Each of the organizations has separate social work units.

Organizational plan of Washington Health System in 2000, after it bought Middletown Hospital System, two other hospitals, and a rehab center. Social worker Fay Sunshine continues her work in home care. Each organization has separate social work units.

stitutions. Potential sources of such power are (1) having control over a critical resource that is necessary to organizational functioning, (2) possession of special skill or knowledge that the organization requires, and (3) charismatic power to influence other people to emulate one's behavior (Kenney 1990:27).

> Domains in which the social work director should be able to claim expert power for staff include, but are not limited to, the abilities to shorten length of stay, to ensure the psychosocial appropriateness of discharge, to provide medical crisis counseling, to link persons with appropriate financial and social services, to facilitate multidisciplinary decision making, to enhance physician-patient communication, and to increase patient compliance with medical treatment.

Three management styles are of particular value to social workers in multihealth systems: (1) multiple-option, (2) network, and (3) political. In regard to the multiple-option style, social workers have to identify themselves with the larger mission of social work in health care rather than with a particular kind of institution, such as a coronary care unit, a hospital, or a visiting nurses organization.

> [They] need to promote and integrate the value of social work's contribution at each stage and phase of the healthfulness continuum. An understanding, integration, and communication of preventive, primary, acute, post-acute, rehabilitative, and long-term care, is essential in solidifying the role of social work within a multisystem structure. . . . The notion of a coordinated continuum of care is not new to social workers but, until the emergence of horizontally and vertically integrated health care systems, few have had the opportunity and challenge of conceptualizing their practice and assuming program planning responsibilities in this multiple option context. (Kenney 1990:26)

The network style of management is characterized by open communication (laterally and diagonally), informality, cross-discipline structures, egalitarianism, and bottom-up decision making. These service organizations depend on (1) an educated and specialized workforce, (2) rapid information transfer, (3) high technology, (4) independent professional judgment, and (5) complex tasks requiring coordination across disciplines (Shortell and Kaluzny 1988). Here information is the critical issue.

The political style of management refers to the expertise and skill necessary to operate within the political realms of multihealth systems. Political management is defined as "the effective use of authority and power resources to achieve organizational and societal goals" (Kenney 1990:27). To succeed, the social worker must construct four interrelated systems: (1) a system that allows one to collect information in formats that support decision-making and performance evaluation, (2) productivity in the form of input and output measures (Who is doing what, to whom, and how much does it cost?), (3) quality assurance, especially in the forms of the appropriateness of social work plans and the achievement of outcomes, and (4) budgeting, which requires knowing how much a program or service will cost for a specified period of time (Kenney 1990). Social work within a multihealth system requires both subtle and substantive changes (Kenney 1990). Primary responsibilities still exist, but the emphasis on specific functions, the unit of attention, and the approach to implementation require shifts for social work practitioners in every level of service. Social workers have to balance sometimes conflicting corporate (if the organization is part of a large business), institutional, and professional identities (Kenney 1990).

Many management process models resemble social work practice and administration models (Argyris 1990a; Kotter 1996; Lewis et al. 1991; Patti 1985). Because they are process models, they must necessarily deal with issues of development, of becoming (Bailey and Grochau 1993). Also, management theory and social work practice share a common goal: enabling the unit of attention to reach maximal functioning. The goal of maximal functioning holds for the client, the program, the organization, the relationships between systems, and the profession itself. What Drucker (1994) refers to as "the theory of the business" is an overarching theme. Every organization, says Drucker, has a theory of itself, a clear theory that informs actions and decisions. For the theory to be most effective, it has to be clear, consistent, and focused. As realities change, the theory of the business must change along with them. The four specifications for a valid theory of the business are as follows:

1. The assumptions about environment, mission, and core competencies must fit reality.
2. The assumptions in all three areas have to fit one another.
3. The theory of the business must be known and understood throughout the organization.
4. The theory of the business has to be tested constantly.

Learning Organizations

To continue to be effective, organizations have to learn. To learn, an organization must have the capacity to study and interpret information in order to improve its ability to evaluate and make decisions (Hasenfeld and Patti 1992). Thus "a learning organization is an organization skilled at creating, acquiring, and transferring knowledge, and modifying its behavior to reflect new knowledge and insights. . . . Without accompanying changes in the way that work gets done, only the potential for improvement exists" (Garvin 1993). "Organizations are products of how their members think and interact" (Senge, Roberts, Ross, Smith, and Kleiner 1994:48). Thus, in a learning organization, people expand their capacity to create the results they truly desire, new thinking patterns are nurtured, collective aspiration is freed, and people learn how to learn together (Senge 1990:4). The following steps will build a learning organization:

1. Foster an environment that is conducive to learning.
2. Open up boundaries and stimulate the exchange of ideas.
3. Find effective forums for the exchange of ideas. (Garvin 1993)

Every organizational participant can foster learning organizations through an individual commitment to learning.

An empowering learning organization supports personal mastery, mental models, shared vision, team building, and systems thinking. Organizing information consists of three steps: (1) *enactment,* during which the organization takes in and acts on information; (2) *selection,* during which staff ascribes meaning to the information and applies it to the work; and (3) *retention,* during which organizations store meanings and actions that become routines for the organization. In any organization, problem identification is related to the organization's practices, as well as to the norms with which it evaluates actions. New information should challenge present practices and norms; it should help the organization examine its decision making and routines, rethink its norms, unlearn routines that are dysfunctional, and thus promote the organization's growth. This process of organizing information leads to work routines and service delivery processes that are known and understood by all who work in the organization, and thus it helps define the organization's culture and the way it functions (Cherin and Meezan 1998).

A constrained action repertoire adds to the stability of an organization but can discourage innovation and change. This kind of restraint leads to single-loop learning, defensive learning, or antilearning that prevents growth and change. A more positive model is double-loop learning, which produces a change in people's assumptions and theories about cause-and-effect relationships. In double-loop learning, organizations learn how to learn (Argyris and Schon 1978). Individuals are challenged to transform their current beliefs and actions into new ones that are more productive for the organization (Argyris 1991).

In a case study of the relationships and communications among members of the southeastern Network of Youth and Family Services, Kurtz found that four organizational characteristics were especially important: partnership, agreed-upon vision and mission, state-of-the-art knowledge and practice, and member effort (Kurtz 1998). Kurtz (1998:57) defined a network as an organizational interconnectedness for associating with others who hold similar interests, in order to develop and access ideas, information, support, and other resources that enable network members to improve what they are doing (such as provide a better service) or achieve a goal (such as the protection of abused children). All the participants pointed to the personal yet professional relationships they had with their colleagues in terms of problem solving, information sharing, interpersonal support, and a feeling of safety. There were continuous opportunities for member-member linkages and a horizontal leadership structure. Both vision and mission were mutually articulated. All the members thought that the organization was the knowledge and practice center for the area, and members related the success of the organization to their own involvement in and efforts for the organization. Members thought that the network affected professional and agency development, client involvement, and social change. In regard to social change, members said that the network had enabled them to become more involved and competent in advocating on state and national levels and also empowered the clients to advocate for themselves in the community. Thus they contribute to the overarching goal of social justice.

Host Settings

Host settings are organizations whose mission and decision making are defined and dominated by professions other than social work (Dane and Simon 1991). Partly because of this "resident guest" status, social workers are frequently called on to explain their roles and functions and to prove their worth and their relevance to the mission, purpose, and overall welfare of the organization. The collaborative process is a regular dimension of social work in such settings. Its effectiveness depends on particular knowledge, skills, and attitudes in working with others to meet clients' needs and to complete tasks (Dane and Simon 1991:212). Sometimes discrepancies exist between social work goals, mission, and values and those of the organization. An extreme example of this kind of discrepancy was relayed by a social worker who was responsible for deciding which prisoners could be admitted to the drug and alcohol treatment unit of a women's prison. Many of the other prison employees, especially the guards, thought that every woman who wanted to be admitted was lying about her addiction just to get away from the main prison population. The guards heckled the prisoners and the social worker and often told the social worker they were too busy to bring the prisoners for evaluation or brought them and, ten minutes later, reported that they had to be returned to the cells immediately.

Jansson and Simmons (1986) list five strategies that enhance credibility for social workers in host settings:

1. Articulate and publicize the relevance of the social work enterprise to the mission of the organization.
2. Be clear about social workers' usefulness in managing clients and consumers who are unclear about the appropriate use of services, treatment, and insurance.
3. Articulate social workers' ability to manage customer satisfaction, an important factor in regard to funding and public relations.
4. Network with coworkers and colleagues who are not social workers; never isolate social work from other service areas. For example, a social worker who was dismayed that her colleagues did not understand what she did organized a series of "Lunch and Learn" meetings hosted by the social work staff that allowed them to highlight their contributions to the organization's mission.
5. Build up the image of social work within the organization, because pressure often arises for social workers to demonstrate their worth.

In addition to these credibility-enhancing strategies, the social worker in a host setting must be seen to be useful. Jansson and Simmons (1986) describe capacity-building strategies that enable social workers to be administratively connected to the organization beyond the provision of direct services. Thus social workers must understand how the whole system operates and how they fit into it. These guidelines are true for any organization in which one might work, whether it is a social agency, a health care provider, or a business. Three key aspects a social worker must understand about the organization are (1) organization design and how it relates to organizational integrity as opposed to individual personalities, (2) the roles of people (that is, professional integrity), and (3) tasks and job satisfaction.

Shapiro (1992) outlines some approaches to cross-functional coordination that may prevent or alleviate some difficulties. Position definition and specialization of roles can help clarity but hurt integration. Also, one can create a closer informal social system and culture by having people with different roles and functions work proximally. "No single aspect or approach to inter-functional coordination is as important as the total system" (Shapiro 1992:367). The organization management must constantly provide the focus, rewards, and systems that inculcate interfunctional coordination to encourage team building, teamwork, and collaboration.

The following example describes the work of two social work consultants working over a seven-year period with a large organ procurement

FIGURE 4.6. Project timeline for the Looking Forward program.

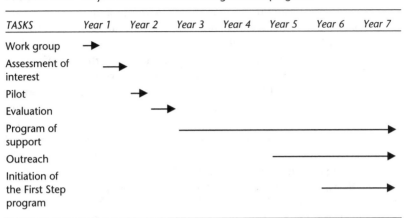

TASKS	Year 1	Year 2	Year 3	Year 4	Year 5	Year 6	Year 7
Work group	→						
Assessment of interest	→						
Pilot		→					
Evaluation			→				
Program of support				————————————————→			
Outreach						————————→	
Initiation of the First Step program						————————→	

organization (OPO). These social workers have specialized knowledge in organ and tissue donation and transplantation, as well as expertise in loss and grief issues and established professional credibility through personal and professional experience. The OPO pays the consultants, whose services are free to donor families. A project timeline, shown in figure 4.6, illustrates the breadth and length of the programming in which the social work consultants were involved.

Organ Procurement Organization (OPO) wanted to help family members and friends who had donated organs and tissues of loved ones who had died suddenly to deal with the deaths they had experienced. They asked the social workers to establish a program of support that would enable family members to develop the insight and means necessary to resume personal and professional lives as positively as possible. The program has three objectives: (1) to answer the questions families might still have about organ donation; (2) to help participants deal with the grieving that follows the sudden death of a loved one; and (3) to obtain feedback from donor families on how the OPO can better serve them. The social work consultants and several interested OPO staff members formed a work group to develop an appropriate supportive care program. To assess interest in bereavement services, a letter was sent to a thousand families who had donated organs of a loved one during the previous five years. The response was overwhelmingly positive.

Six months later, a pilot program was offered in four different parts of the geographic area served by the agency. The program consisted of four two-hour workshop sessions combining education and support. Each session provided information on different aspects of the grief process, a forum for answering questions related to organ donation, and a supportive environment for donor families to share experiences. A questionnaire completed by one hundred participants measured the effectiveness of the pilot program and assessed future needs. The results of the evaluation and the verbal feedback from participants confirmed that the program had met its objectives and needed to be expanded. Initiated the next year, the comprehensive support program called Looking Forward provided some services to families of donors and others to health care professionals. Services to families or donors include open and closed face-to-face support groups, telephone support groups, individual and family counseling, one-to-one peer counseling by trained donor family members, single-session seminars dealing with special topics (such as coping with holidays), and distribution of a brochure describing counseling services that accompanies the initial donor family letter.

The next year, an outreach program was initiated in which bereavement counselors routinely contacted all new donor families by telephone one month after the donation and kept contact for at least one year. Counselors offer support, discuss concerns, explain available services, make referrals, and facilitate written communication between recipients and donor families. Clinical issues for the donor families include the potential for complicated grief owing to the nature of sudden and often traumatic or violent death through suicide, accident, or murder; the possibility of complicated grief, such as the inability to acknowledge the reality of death; the belief that a part of the loved one is still alive in someone else (for example, one woman wanted to hug the recipient of her son's heart, hoping to feel her son's heartbeat); the possibility of finding comfort in the knowledge that something good has come out of a terrible tragedy, that the loved one has given a new chance of life to another human being; and the therapeutic effect of anonymous correspondence with organ recipients (Silverman and Worden 1992; Weisman and Worden 1976–1977).

Pleased with this collaborative relationship, OPO staff next asked the social work consultants to help educate and support medical personnel in hospitals and transplant centers. There are three components to the services to health care professionals: (1) the First Step, (2) debriefing sessions, and (3) individual consultation. The First Step is a program designed to help emergency room and trauma center staff familiarize themselves with organ/tissue donation and common grief reactions of individuals faced with a sudden death of a loved one. Debriefing sessions and individual consultations are provided to any hospital unit or personnel after deaths that have strongly affected staff members. Clinical issues for staff include the impact on personal life of transplant coordinators who have to face death on an almost daily basis and the impact of recurrent intense family grief, especially in long, complicated situations when the coordinator already suffers from sleep deprivation or is identifying with the family's situation.

Several professional issues arise when social workers assume this kind of role. First there is the question of whether to continue as independent consultants rather than becoming staff social workers, which would give less financial security but would provide the freedom to voice opinions that may conflict with administration and would enhance the ability to advocate for clients. To act effectively as consultants to this large, complex organization, the social workers had to understand the hierarchy and patterns of responsibility and authority, recognize individuals seeking similar goals, avoid turf conflicts, respect boundaries, build trust with staff, and gain the director's respect and trust.

Another set of issues that arises in this kind of setting has to do with timing. The implementation of the program took much longer than the social workers or the program director originally anticipated, especially when several departments collaborated on the project and the people involved had to accept new ideas.

Ethical, value, and legal issues that arise in such settings include confidentiality; anonymity; paternalism; self-determination; informed consent for clients and professionals; and legal protection of the OPO, transplant centers, and transplant surgeons. The Uniform Anatomical Gift Act of 1987 states that organ or tissue donation is an anonymous gift (National Conference of Commissioners on Uniform State Laws 1999). The OPO protects all parties' identity but sends donor families a letter with some information about the recipient of their donation including gender, approximate age, occupation, and marital status. Families value this information and often request updates on the status of recipients, which are provided indefinitely. Families also value correspondence with recipients, which has greatly increased since the inception of the Looking Forward program. The OPO is now encouraging transplant centers to ask recipients to write and thank their donor families. On the other side of the equation, however, transplant centers, surgeons, and center directors have traditionally believed that it is in the best interest of their patients, the organ recipients, not to receive any information about their donor. These beliefs clearly create a conflict.

Important questions remain: Is it beneficial for organ recipients and donor families to meet? Who decides who can meet and who cannot? What criteria are used for assessing individual situations? What if a recipient discovers the identity of his donor or has concerns about the donor's past lifestyle and believes his new organ might be affected by that lifestyle? Do recipients have the right to have some basic information about the donor before transplantation? With increased communication between the two sides and with the press often revealing the identity of one or both parties, more recipients and donor families are asking to meet. The OPO has begun to organize dialogues among professionals, patients, and donor families to explore ways to establish communication that will ensure that all parties' needs and rights are respected and met in a professional and responsible manner. Similar issues are discussed at the national level by the National Council of Donor Families.

When the OPO was first set up, its mission was to focus on the needs of potential recipients, to recover organs from donors who had suffered a sudden death, and to allocate these organs to recipients in an equitable fashion. It was generally believed that donor families were in too much pain to be interested in information about the recipients, that their privacy needed to be respected, and that they should not be contacted. Furthermore, the OPO did not perceive its mission to include services to donor families. However, as these families began to call transplant coordinators more frequently, express their grief, and ask for support, the OPO staff recognized that help was needed from professionals trained in grief counseling.

Counseling bereaved families is often an intense experience that affects professionals in a deep way and requires specialized training. To expect transplant coordinators to feel responsible for supporting past donor families on an ongoing basis while also approaching new families for donation would be unreasonable and unrealistic. During the pilot program it became evident that it was essential to separate the role of transplant coordinator from that of the after-care provider. Had this concept been presented some years earlier by an outsider, there would have been resistance. Now director and staff were ready to accept the consultants as valuable colleagues; they acknowledged that transplant coordinators could better accomplish their mission knowing that there was a mechanism for providing support to the families from whom they had obtained the gift.

A support program creates additional costs and great benefits for the OPO. Potentially explosive situations with families who might be unhappy with the organ donation experience can be diffused. Families for whom an empathetic listener provides an opportunity to vent frustration and resolve some ambivalence will present a more positive image of organ donation to individuals who come in contact with them. Most families of donors find solace in knowing that through organ donation some good has come out of their tragedy. Many become enthusiastic volunteers for the program. They lend an effective voice in reaching out to the medical community and public audiences on behalf of organ and tissue donation, and they find their involvement with the OPO to be therapeutic.

In the course of the past seven years, as the Looking Forward program has developed far beyond what was originally anticipated, many concerns and issues have arisen, some expected and others unanticipated (for instance, increased communication between recipients and donor families and requests for meetings between them). For the social work consultants, it has been a rewarding challenge to collaborate with an agency that trusts their clinical judgment and allows them the autonomy to implement new services for a population that had previously been neglected. It is also rewarding to see the OPO become ready to confront difficult questions and issues and examine its own mission. As a result, two sentences have been added to the OPO's mission statement concerning needs of donor families: "Work in partnership with the region's hospitals and health care professionals to ensure that the family of each potential donor is offered the option of donation in a sensitive and caring manner," and "Serve as a community resource by providing support for families of donors as well as transplant recipients and their families." By providing a professionally run support program for donor families, the Organ Procurement Organization has expanded and is now fully completing its mission. It continues to recognize its primary responsibility ("to improve the quality of life of patients awaiting transplantation by maximizing the availability of donor organs and tissues"), but it also acknowledges a moral responsibility to families who have made this gift of life at a most difficult time. It makes a commitment to assist them on the road to recovery, to bring closure around a tragic death and their generous act of donation.

These two social workers used the concepts of matrix management as they consolidated their positions in the OPO. In matrix management, each service line is drafted and articulated with the level of clarity that makes objectives meaningful and understandable and adds to a continuity of purpose and a consistency of application across areas. So the challenge is to build a matrix in the minds of all the professionals in the enterprise. This allows individuals to make the judgments and negotiate the trade-offs that drive the organization toward shared strategic objectives. It is more of a mind-set than a structure. The main components of matrix management are building an organization, building a shared vision, developing human resources, co-opting management efforts, and creating the matrix in the minds of all participants (Bartlett and Ghoshal 1992). The OPO example demonstrates that effective resource management involves the integration of individual thinking and activities with the broad organizational agenda.

Shared Populations and Social Work Linkages

Many advocacy and resource tasks involve social workers from one organization contacting social workers from other organizations. The relationships that first come to mind are between social workers in pediatric medical services and those in child welfare, or between social workers in hospitals and in home health agencies or nursing homes, or between case management services for those with mental illness and departments of social services. Generally, because these organizations tend to operate with fewer financial and other resources than are needed to do the work effectively, poor relations develop between them. Ideally, when interorganizational relationships involve populations of clients/consumers rather than highly individualized situations, the organizational leadership in all the involved organizations should rationalize the relationships.

One method used to address linkages for individual clients/consumers is the case conference (Indyk, Belville, Lachapelle, Gordon, and Dewart 1993), which is sometimes effective for the coordination of service. At least, it offers those who are trying to help a complicated client to relate more positively and personally to each other. At worst, such conferences inform little action because no one who is involved has any real authority over any services but his or her own. One example of excellent social service cooperation, Greater Access to Programs and Services, was established by nine agencies in a particular county who receive funding from a large foundation in order to serve the elderly with the goal of improving intrasystem referral to ease access to services for the elderly. Agencies included are a county mental health/mental retardation office, two visiting nurses associations, the county association for the blind, a senior volunteer organization, the local health system (which is part of a university health system) and several special services for the elderly. The Child and Adolescent Service System Program (CASSP) is a federal attempt at a solution to the problem of integrating services for children (Meyers 1993). In 1982, a national study found that two-thirds of all children with severe emotional disturbances were not receiving appropriate services and that there was little coordination between services. In response to that study, in 1984, Congress approved funding for CASSP, a partnership between the public (tax-funded) agencies that serve children that could include five different agencies: mental health/mental retardation; children and youth; drug and alcohol; juvenile probation and parole; and the school districts (Frankel, Harmon, and Kerson 1997; Karp 1996; Werrbach 1996).

Many differences, including divergent funding streams, levels and kinds of resources, and legal mandates, pull against such rationalization of relationship. Instead, social workers in health and mental health care resort to developing individual relationships with their counterparts in the other organizations on which their client/consumer populations depend for service. In hospitals, "social work case managers have traditionally shined in developing informal relationships with other agencies and programs in the community" (Netting, Williams, Jones-McClintic, and Warrick 1990:19). Such relationships are usually individual-to-individual rather than program-to-program or organization-to-organization. One social worker who works in discharge planning knows which kinds of clients appeal to which social workers in other facilities, and, using good marketing techniques, she matches client personality and behavior with the kinds of personalities and behaviors with which specific social workers in other organizations are most comfortable.

MAPPING DEVICES DRAWN FROM THE BUSINESS LITERATURE

Two business tools, the balanced scorecard and the organigraph, can help social work practitioners understand their place in the organization and leverage that place for maximum benefit to their clients. Both help social workers in health and mental health to span traditional boundaries.

The Balanced Scorecard

Although it was developed specifically for business, the balanced scorecard has broad applications for social work. I have modified the concepts and language somewhat for social work while remaining true to the balanced scorecard's original purpose.

The balanced scorecard helps individuals and organizations formulate strategies, because a disciplined measurement framework enforced by the Balanced Scorecard stimulates discussion about the specific meaning and implementation of the strategy (Kaplan and Norton 1996a, 1996b). Here strategy is defined as choosing the market and consumer base that the unit, program, agency, or institution intends to serve; identifying the critical internal organizational processes at which the unit, program, agency, or institution must excel to deliver the value propositions to consumers in targeted markets; and selecting the individual and organizational capabilities that are required for reaching the objectives of the consumer and the organization. Some of these objectives are financial (Kaplan and Norton 1996b:78). The Balanced Scorecard is meant to be top-down and to allow for long-term as well as short-term planning and evaluation. Nevertheless, it is useful on any level because it addresses fit, control of one's own work, finding ways to measure work other than money, as well as ways of enhancing work by being organized for systematic, continuing performance (Drucker 1998:174).

The balanced scorecard is used to measure long-term as well as short-term efforts and effects. While it measures in several ways, it is meant to be a total management system. The Balanced Scorecard was intended to be instituted by the chief executive officer of an organization, who then sends it down through the ranks to the line workers. However, the balanced scorecard is a useful tool for social workers on any level because all social workers must at least manage their own work and must understand how their work fits with their program or unit, the organization, and the system. Using the balanced scorecard also gives direct practice social workers data to help them advocate with managers for clients and programs.

Kaplan and Norton (1996a, 1996b) point out that the process of strategic learning starts with the clarification of a shared vision that the entire organization wants to achieve. The use of measurement as a language helps translate complex and frequently nebulous concepts into a more precise form that can gain consensus throughout the organization. Use of the balanced scorecard includes not only financial measures and targets but progress in achieving long-term strategic objectives. To track what an organization will need for future growth, performance is viewed from four perspectives: (1) financial, (2) consumer and payer, (3) internal processes, and (4) learning and growth. If one is managing a caseload, a program, or an organization, the scorecard card can attest to performance.

Performance is expressed through four processes: (1) translating the vision (that is, literally translating the vision of the organization into action at the local level through statements that are objective and measurable); (2) communicating and linking (that is, ensuring that long-term strategy is understood on all levels of the organization and that departmental and individual objectives are linked to it); (3) planning (that is, linking financial and other plans to use the scorecard to allocate resources and set priorities); (4) feedback and learning (that is, watching short-term results from all four perspectives and evaluating strategy while looking at present performance). The integrated perspectives provide a balanced picture of current operating performance and drive future performance (Kaplan and Norton 1996a). I would argue, however, that if one could get the attention of the highest level of management in the organization and be given sufficient authority, the scorecard could be adopted from any level as long as it spread to all other levels. This is true because ultimately the use of the scorecard allows for the discovery of insights that create value for the organization (Campbell and Alexander 1997).

For each perspective (financial, consumer/payer, internal practices, and learning and growth), one develops a chart. Within each chart, one answers a question by providing information about objectives, measures, targets, and initiatives. In regard to the financial perspective, the question is, To succeed, how should we appear to our shareholders? (Kaplan and Norton 1996a:9). Social work organizations might substitute, To succeed, how should we appear to our financial stakeholders? In regard to the consumer/payer perspective, the question is, To achieve our vision, how should we appear to our consumers and payers/customers? (Kaplan and Norton 1996a:8). Again, this question must be slightly altered for social work to define who we mean by the group that business refers to as its customers. Social work's customers are several kinds of stakeholders, including clients, family members, insurance companies, state legislatures, boards of directors, and any other groups that might have some authority over payment sources of service utilization. This perspective and its related question seem quite simple, even when one extends the concept to several kinds of stakeholders. Actually, the consumer/payer perspective is the most powerful connection to the world outside the organization. It is the dimension that relates most closely to the ecological perspective, to thinking about demands on the system, the values of those who will use and pay for the system, as well as the values of those who could be customers but who have chosen not to be. According to Drucker, consumer/payer values are the foundation for management policy, and noncustomers are as important as customers in relation to the future of an organization (Drucker 1998). Social workers must understand which groups are not using their services and why, just as we must understand to whom we are providing services. To think about this issue in still another way, Drucker (1998:174) points to marketing:

> The term was coined 50 years ago to emphasize that the purpose and results of a business lie entirely outside of itself. Marketing teaches that organized efforts are needed to bring an understanding of the outside, of society, economy and customer to the inside of the organization and make it the foundation for strategy and policy. . . . Yet marketing has rarely performed that grand task. Instead it has become a tool to support selling. It does not start out with "who is the customer," but "what do we want to sell?" and is aimed at getting people to buy the things you want to make. That's getting things backwards.

Once financial and consumer/payer objectives are established, an organization identifies the objectives and measures for its internal processes. Here the question is, At what processes must we excel in order to satisfy stakeholders? The final linkage to learning and growth objectives reveals the rationale for significant investments in teaching new skills to employees, in information technology and systems, and in enhanced organizational procedures. The investment in people, procedures, and systems produces innovation and improvement for internal processes, for consumers, and, eventually, for all shareholders (Kaplan and Norton 1996a:12). For learning and growth, the question is, To achieve our vision, how will we sustain our ability to change and improve? (Kaplan and Norton 1996a:8).

The measures should be developed from a program's strategy and should include outcome measures and performance drivers that communicate whether strategies are successfully implemented and how those outcomes will be achieved. While outcomes can be seen as lagging indicators, performance drivers can be seen as leading indicators of the program's strategy. "A good balanced scorecard should have an appropriate mix of outcomes (lagging indicators) and performance drivers (leading indicators) that have been customized to the [program's] strategy" (Kaplan and Norton 1996b:150).

The Personal Scorecard

One part of the balanced scorecard, the personal scorecard, is a tool to help individuals set goals for themselves that are consistent with the organization's goals. This is a starting point that all social work practitioners can understand and use.

Decisions affecting the entire [organization] and its capacity to perform are made at all levels of the organization, even fairly low ones. Risk-taking decisions—what to do and what not to do; what to continue to work on and what to abandon, what products, markets, or technologies to ignore—are in the reality of today's [organizational] enterprise (especially the large one) made every day by a host of people of subordinate rank, very often by people without traditional managerial title or position, e.g., research scientists, design engineers, product planners and tax accountants. (Drucker 1974:76)

"It is at the supervision subsystem level that the policies formulated at the planning stage are actually implemented. It is at this level that program goals and objectives are carried out in direct and tangible ways" (Lewis et al. 1991:279).

The personal scorecard dismantles the balanced scorecard for the employees. Personal performance measures are directed toward the three levels of information on the card: corporate, unit, and team/individual. The point is to identify for the individual worker the few items that have the biggest impact on achievement of productivity (Davis 1996). I see this as useful for social work practitioners even if their organization has not adopted the balanced scorecard. It can easily be used by an individual or a program or project leader who is clear about the mission (through the mission statement) and objectives of the organization. The measures provide guidance on where frontline employees should focus their efforts to influence the overall scorecard.

On this level, social workers articulate their objectives in ways that are consistent with unit and corporate objectives, pick initiatives they would take to achieve objectives, and define up to five performance measures for objectives and set a target for each measure.

Guidelines for the development of an employee scorecard are as follows.

1. The scorecard should be integrated with line, program, group, and organizational measures to keep the whole organization focused on the same set of objectives.
2. Line employees should be involved in the development of the measures; this allows wider ownership of and greater commitment to the measures.

3. In a unionized organization, the union should help develop the measurement system to be assured that the system will give the employees more control over their jobs.
4. Measures must be timely; that is, employees need immediate feedback so they can solve problems quickly.
5. The measures that are chosen should focus on the most critical aspects of performance, the ones that have the greatest impact on targeted performance goals.
6. New measures should be prioritized and balanced with other scorecard measures.
7. Measures should be made accessible to everyone in different departments and levels. If computer access is common, the information should be made available on-line. (Davis 1996)

For Feedback and Learning. Kaplan and Norton argue that use of the balanced scorecard allows for double-loop learning, that is, learning that produces change in people's assumptions and theories about cause-and-effect relationships (Argyris 1990b, 1991). The balanced scorecard describes the vision of the future for the entire organization, creates shared understanding, focuses on change efforts, and permits organizational learning. It makes cause-and-effect hypotheses among objectives and measures explicit so organizations can test strategies in real time and adapt as they learn. The balanced scorecard can ensure that this kind of learning will take place, because company vision is articulated in operational terms linking individual efforts to business unit objectives. Feedback is built in and elements can be modified, and the scorecard facilitates the kind of review that is essential to strategic learning. The balanced scorecard is for strategy implementation, not formation.

For Leadership and Vision. In this context, the leader does not have to be the boss. Having leadership qualities as a member of a team or as a case manager means creating and sustaining a vision. Leaders can be developed who can create and communicate vision and strategies, just as managers can be developed who can plan, budget, organize, staff, control, and solve problems (Kotter 1996). This is especially helpful when social workers have a particular mission related to a specific client group. They can see this material as providing the strategies that will make their vision possible. They bring the vision and may need help in sharpening their communication skills to be able to convey the vision and the strategies to accomplish it to colleagues in social work and in other professions. "Vision plays a key role in producing useful change by helping to direct, align, and inspire actions on the part of large numbers of people. Without an appropriate vision, a transformation effort can easily dissolve into a list of confusing, incompatible, and time-consuming projects that go in the wrong direction or nowhere at all" (Kotter 1996:7).

An eight-stage change process framework shapes the work: (1) establishing a sense of urgency, (2) creating the guiding coalition, (3) developing a vision and strategy, (4) communicating the change vision, (5) empowering broad-based action, (6) generating short-term wins, (7) consolidating gains and producing more change, and (8) anchoring new approaches in the culture (Kotter 1996). The steps must be taken sequentially, each step must be completed, and the action must build and develop in order to help maintain momentum. A good short-term win has to have these three characteristics: it must be visible, unambiguous, and clearly related to the change effort.

Thinking in this way helps social workers develop new strategies for reaching client goals. Leaders and those with a vision have to be resilient and capable of improvisation, wisdom, respectful interaction, and communication (Weick 1996). Improvisation means bringing to the surface, testing, and restructuring one's intuitive understanding of phenomenon on the spot, when action can still make a difference. Wisdom means a willingness to keep learning, to raise questions, and to be ignorant so that one can continue to learn.

> Respectful interactions have three imperatives: respect the reports of others and be willing to base beliefs and actions on them (trust); report so that others may use your observations in coming to valid beliefs (honesty); and respect your own perceptions and beliefs and integrate them with reports of others without depreciating them or yourself (self-respect). (Weick 1996:148)

The following example describes a program developed to meet a new need in the surrounding community. Other examples of uses for the balanced scorecard can be found in chapters 7 and 9.

A New Life provides transitional housing for people who are discharged from state hospitals and are not yet ready to live independently. Over the last year, staff members have noted that patients are more ill and have less ability to gain the skills needed for independent living. These are patients who lived in the state hospitals long after the mandate that everyone was entitled to live in the least restrictive environment. Thus they were clients about whose vulnerability staff continued to be concerned. A new program called Safely Home was developed congruent with the clients' legal right to the least restrictive environment. The overall goals of the program are to help the client find a home and live in that home in ways that meet the clients' expressive needs for stability, continuity, a positive identity, individuality, and a sense of ownership. Since the staff had a great deal of experience with transitional housing, their task was to develop the new housing arrangement with the same goals of protection and support in the least restrictive environment. They knew that many dimensions of the program were to be the same. For example, the housing had to be located within close walking distance to good mental health day programs, good counseling and medication services, grocery stores, and public transportation. They also knew that several service dimensions had to be different. For example, they calculated that the residents, who would live three or four to a house, had to be taught the following: (1) to get out of bed, wash, dress, prepare a simple breakfast, and make sure that the others were up and about also; (2) to walk to the day program at 9:00 A.M.; to come home from the day program at 4:00 P.M.; (3) with supervision, to prepare dinner, clean up, and return to transitional housing for the evening program; (4) to return home, prepare for bed, and go to bed. These daily tasks became the general client objectives by which the staff would be able to measure the success of the program.

This program was developed to respond to a very clear and urgent client need, but it served as well to help the parent organization of A New Life be a forerunner in providing this new kind of service. This not-for-profit organization runs programs in several states. As it replicates Safely Home in this and other states, it will enhance the standing and competitive advantage of the parent organization over other organizations that also manage services for this population. As state funding is always competitive, the new program will help its parent organization compete for funding in each state in which it operates.

Kaplan and Norton (1996a) argue that increased competition everywhere makes the need to integrate objectives and strategies across levels and functions more critical than ever. This is true for social work in health care as well. Again, the emphasis is on developing operational measures, on translating vision into action. These are measures that define a strategy designed for competitive excellence, rather than the traditional diagnostic measures that monitor whether a business is in control and can signal the occurrence of unusual events that require immediate attention. Kaplan and Norton and others who have used their system argue that it is often difficult to interpret objectives, strategies, and measures of performance throughout all levels of an organization. What transpires is that the workers believe that the top level is clear only about financial objectives, while the line workers must worry about production volume, quality, and service objectives. Often it is not clear how production, service, and quality translate into financial objectives, and it is the lack of clarity that is so frustrating and alienating to the front line.

Davis (1996) discusses General Electric's use of the balanced scorecard for its lighting group. As is true for many dimensions of today's working environment and certainly for many varieties of social work, having a team structure is critical in the development of a balanced scorecard. In the same way, team building and generic group skills are critical for social workers to help clients and to effect organizational goals. In Davis's example, group leaders provide protection, permission, and potency, guiding interaction; consolidating diverse elements; synthesizing communication, themes, and concerns; and summarizing, partializing, reframing, supporting, and confronting—the very same skills required for any kind of group work (Reid 1991).

The lighting group was organized on the lines of a functional product team matrix, with product line teams overlaid on traditional functional departments. This cross-functional structure was integrated at every level. Objectives that were articulated were critical and achievable. Manufacturing was assigned three dimensions: speed, quality, and cost. Speed refers to how fast the customer is served and also includes the inventory levels required to serve the customer satisfactorily. General Electric measured this through the percentage of on-time deliveries. Quality meant customer satisfaction with products and service that exceeded all competitor satisfaction levels. Cost referred to trimming expenditures on all facets of manufacturing. Marketing, engineering, and research and development were to address vitality, the innovation measure that was related to the introduction of new products. It is not difficult to apply most of these concepts to service provision in health and mental health care, as well as to achieving long-term organizational objectives.

The Highly Personal Scorecard

I would introduce one more level to the notion of the balanced scorecard—the highly personal scorecard. Since social workers are taught to be self-conscious and self-aware, and since so much of the work depends on relationship skills, one more level can be added to the balanced scorecard that can further enhance the work. The highly personal balanced score card reflects measures for the four perspectives that individual social workers have developed themselves (or with a supervisor or a colleague), which the social workers use to guide and measure their own work. Some of these measures may be based in work habits, group dynamics, personality traits, the social worker's meaning map (Ingersoll and Adams 1992), or the development of a new or evolving approach to the most personal and relationship-oriented dimensions of the work.

For example, one social worker working under great pressure as the discharge planner on three medical floors in an acute care hospital resolved to reduce the number of times she lost her temper to once a month for six months, once every other month for the next sixth months, and once a year after that. Another social worker working as an intensive case manager found that allowing herself to be intimidated by people who controlled access to resources that her clients needed was interfering with her ability to obtain resources for her clients. She even found that she avoided calling certain organizations because she found the employees to be bullying and humiliating to her and her clients. For her very personal scorecard she insisted to herself that she would begin by listing the resources that were most needed by her clients. She created the standard of beginning each day with the most intimidating call, and within a month she had solved the problem for herself. The last example involves a social worker whose organization used e-mail for all administrative communication. Because she was overwhelmed by the amount of work she had to accomplish and because she was sure she could not master the use of e-mail, she found excuses to avoid even turning on her computer. As a consequence, she often felt more overwhelmed because she was not getting information she needed as quickly as it was available. She made managing e-mail the issue for her highly personal scorecard and determined that she would come in each morning and turn on her computer before she took off her coat. Before she did anything else, she would check and answer her e-mail. And, of course, the improvement of scores such as these can enhance the work of the organization.

Table 4.1 is an example of a personal scorecard created by a social worker in an organization that provides services to those with a range of serious mental illnesses. Other examples of personal scorecards can be found in chapters 7 and 9.

The Personal Compact Between Workers and Employers

I would argue that in fact the success of the balanced scorecard depends of the employees' view of the organization. Just as other people do, social workers resist change. Their ability to grow with the organization depends very much on the personal compact that social workers and other employees have with their organizations (Strebel 1996). This compact is made up of the reciprocal obligations and mutual commitments that define the relationship between employee and employer. Three dimensions shared by all organizations are the formal, the psychological, and the social. Formal dimensions include documents such as contracts and job descriptions. The psychological underpinnings address the implicit relationships and involve feelings like trust and dependence.

Employees determine their commitment to the organization along the psychological dimension of their personal compact by asking:

TABLE 4.1. The Personal Scorecard: Progress for People

Organizational Objectives
1. Maximize individual responsibility and commitment by responding to people's basic goodness. Employees are trusted to believe in their potential to take on more difficult tasks.
2. View all human beings as having equal value and thus provide a milieu of trust, respect, dignity, and empowerment for clients and employees.
3. Support ideas and programs that are caring, innovative, effective, and efficient.

Organization Targets	*Scoreboard Measures*
Management—Administrative	
1. Provide centralized management services to all program units. (Organization maintains overall programmatic and financial responsibility.) 2. Day-to-day program operations are otherwise responsible for themselves.	Provide ongoing quality assurance, legal and technical assistance, personnel services, and overall management supervision, consultation, and peer review to all program units. Individual programs maintain operational guidelines for their unit staffs.
Management—Fiscal	
1. Centralized financial management.	Quarterly review and annual audit by independent accounting firm. Match program/client needs with available resources; develop and adhere to all program budgets.
Organizational	
1. Offer diversified programming for people with developmental disabilities, emotional difficulties, and physical handicaps.	Respond to 20 percent of program change/initiatives.
2. Continue to support and grow the Social Entrepreneur Support Program.	Hold two weekly brainstorming meetings. Support two new social service programs through this program. Maintain 50 percent of them for five years.

Unit Targets	*Team/Individual Initiatives*
A New Life Program	*Support Services for Mental Health Clients*
1. Meet changing needs of mental health population through flexible programs.	Assess community needs through six methods. Engage 100 percent clients in peer support activities.
2. Maintain clients in the community who are assessed as at-risk.	Minimum weekly contact with each client and biannual case conferences. Provide an individualized treatment plan for each client. Include all support services in each client plan.
3. Increase number of clients served.	Engage in four outreach efforts each month. Create promotional brochure.

How hard will I really have to work? And what recognition, financial reward, or other personal satisfaction will I get for my efforts? Are the rewards worth it? Individuals formulate responses to these questions in large part by evaluating their relationship with their boss. (Strebel 1996:88)

In the social dimension, employees gauge an organization's culture. The questions they answer are, Are my values similar to those of others in the organization? and What are the real rules that determine who gets what in this company?

Alignment between an organization's statements and behavior is the key to creating a context that evokes employee commitment along the social dimension. "It is often the dimension of a personal compact that is undermined most in a change initiative when conflicts arise and communication breaks down" (Strebel 1996:88). Compacts can be revised by drawing attention to the need for change and establishing the context for revision, initiating a process in which employees are able to revise and buy into new compact terms, and locking in commitments with new formal and informal rules. Again, the key is clarity of concept and clarity of direct communication.

The Organigraph

The organigraph, developed by Mintzberg and Van der Heyden (1999) to depict the workings of organizations, is so useful to the approach to practice espoused throughout this book that it is explained twice—once here and again in chapter 7.

While traditional organizational charts seem to indicate that all units are independent boxes that are connected through chains of authority, the organigraph looks at how people and processes converge and where ideas flow (figure 4.7). It maintains the conventional components of organizational charts: sets of people and machines and chains of command. And it adds two components: hubs and webs. In the hub, the process of managing brings together and coordinates the work of people who are intrinsically empowered. In the web, work is fluid and the facilitation of collaboration energizes the whole network. Social workers' ability to have adequate influence in their workplace and to be able to advocate for clients/consumers depends on their participation in hubs and webs.

Unlike ecomaps, genograms, or organizational charts, organigraphs often look very different from each other. Using the building materials of sets, chains, hubs, and webs, they assume the overall shape that presents the clearest portrait of an organization or system. Figure 4.8 shows an example that is explained more fully in chapter 7. Because the hub, the

FIGURE 4.7. Elements of organigraphs.

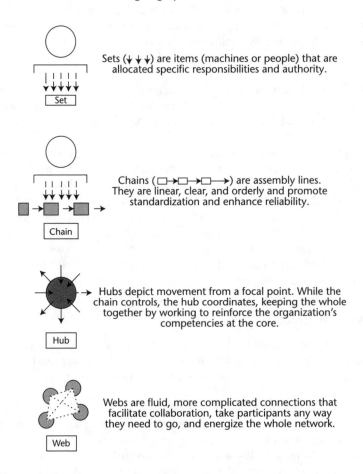

Sets (↓ ↓ ↓) are items (machines or people) that are allocated specific responsibilities and authority.

Chains (□→□→□→) are assembly lines. They are linear, clear, and orderly and promote standardization and enhance reliability.

Hubs depict movement from a focal point. While the chain controls, the hub coordinates, keeping the whole together by working to reinforce the organization's competencies at the core.

Webs are fluid, more complicated connections that facilitate collaboration, take participants any way they need to go, and energize the whole network.

Department of Case Management, is the center of the organigraph, the graphic closely resembles an ecomap.

An organigraph of a state hospital in which social worker Sophia Regal is responsible for planning safe discharge for patients who have serious and persistent mental illness is shown in figure 4.9. The web is represented by thick dashed lines, and the hub is represented by a circle. This organigraph takes into account a much broader context than the one in figure 4.8. For example, it includes the moral obligation of the mental health system, the societal stigma, legal entitlements, and financial constraints as parts of the ecosystem

FIGURE 4.8. Organigraph for the Department of Case Management at Fine Community Hospital.

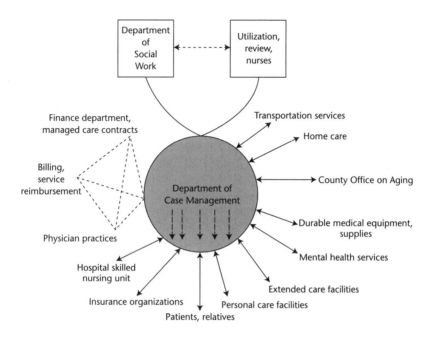

that must be taken into account to understand the organization and its responses to client/consumers. It demonstrates the relationships of Congress and the State Legislature to the laws and administrative bodies that affect the state hospital and its patients, as well as the relationships of the mental health court system, community hospital, advocates, and family members to the institution. The hub, the unit within the state hospital, is surrounded by a seemingly impenetrable thick line, and few relationship arrowheads point outward. Finally, the fluid web that facilitates communication includes the patient, social worker, treatment team, the County Office of Mental Health, and those who manage financial benefits.

CONCLUSION

The systemic and organizational information presented in this chapter is critical for social workers in health and mental health care to be able to practice effectively within very large and complex systems of care. The

FIGURE 4.9. Organigraph for a state hospital.

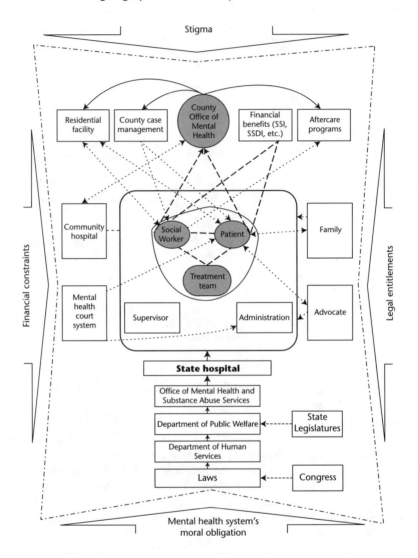

material is used to demonstrate the importance of maintaining the kinds of positions in systems and organizations that will yield sufficient authority for social workers to act as advocates, catalysts, and expeditors for their clients, consumers, programs, and communities. Systems and organizations are defined and placed within the notion of community. The new organization and the need for management concepts are reviewed. Organizational mission and styles are explored, and particular attention is paid to learning organizations, host settings, and interorganizational work. Finally, two new mapping devices are introduced, both of which are drawn from the business literature. Both devices, the balanced scorecard and the organigraph, help social workers in health and mental health care to locate themselves in the system and to leverage their positions in ways that can best expedite client, consumer, program, and community objectives. This combination of knowledge, skills, and mapping devices will support necessary boundary-spanning activities.

The Power of the Relationship Between the Social Worker and the Client System

With Judith L. M. McCoyd

A relationship is a connection, association, or involvement. For human beings, meaning is constituted through relationships, and the development of relationships through time is the basis of human activity from consciousness to culture. Relationships can create energy and support far beyond the sum of their parts: "Relationship is a human being's feeling or sense of emotional bonding with another" (Perlman 1979:23). It occurs between people when one is emotionally moved and the others experience a similar feeling, or when people feel, and their feelings are recognized, received, and felt *with* by others (Perlman 1979). This feeling of being recognized and "felt with" is one definition of empathy, a crucial element in the social work relationship. When most useful, helping relationships create a place of psychological safety that allows people to feel sufficiently secure to risk new thinking, learning, and experiences (Edmondson 1999). Good and bad, relationships have great binding power.

One of the hallmarks of professional social workers is the ability to use relationship to help clients, consumers, and communities reach their goals (Simon 1960). The objective of every social work relationship is to be able to engage, establish trust, and, through self-understanding and the understanding of others create a safe place where thoughts, feelings, and actions can be explored and positive learning can occur. The emphasis on the process of helping, using the art and nuance of the relationship itself to further the work of the client, is a central tenet of social work practice in health and mental health care. In every problem area or client system, the relationship between social workers and those needing help is paramount in the work. To attend to the helping process means dynamic involvement in the immediate interaction between social worker and client.

Thus relationship is one means through which social workers can leverage their efforts with clients, programs, and communities in ways that enhance the work. The most valued relationship, and the one that has been most studied and described, is the one between the individual social worker and the client (an individual, couple, family, or small group). However, social workers' abilities to relate to consumers, projects, programs, task groups, communities, and organizations are equally important to helping clients reach their goals. Relationship skills are critical to all dimensions of social work practice, from relationships with clients to defining, designing, planning, and maintaining programs and organizations. For example, through the development of individual relationships and through understanding client goals, social workers are able to establish the need for specific projects to reach the goals of groups of clients. If those projects work well for clients and organizations, social workers can use these project results to promote these programs in organizations and systems. Social workers can then establish stable, future-oriented programs that meet client needs while honoring organizational demands and constraints. Relationships, therefore, are another means of spanning boundaries.

Relationships evolve. Over time all relationships, helping and otherwise, change in meaning, need, intensity, purpose, satisfaction, and fulfillment. It is particularly important to understand the ways that relationships between social workers and clients change over time, as social workers respond to current client, program, or community needs. At times, social workers intervene actively to help clients to attain goals. At other times, social workers purposely assume a reflective stance in order to support their clients' own development of strategies and, at the same time, their clients' self-confidence. This chapter describes the varied and subtle dimensions of social work relationships and examines them in time from their beginnings to endings. All these dimensions of relationships—their importance, characteristics, functions, and changes over time—are examined so that social workers may consciously tailor relationships to the needs of clients and systems.

The following example demonstrates the importance of the relationship between individual clients and social workers, as well as the ability of a direct practitioner to affect organizational policy.

Eloise Braden, a new obstetrics social worker, stared out the window as Tina Meadows, her 15-year-old client, tearfully handed her baby to the foster care worker. She reflected on how far the young woman had come since she had first met her in the emergency room four days earlier. At that time, Tina was a frightened, uncooperative teenager in labor who refused to reveal her name. She had told no one of her pregnancy. Small and fair-skinned, Tina had been able to hide the pregnancy beneath the baggy shirts that were in fashion at the time. The emergency room staff had asked Ms. Braden to get Tina to cooperate and tell them whom they should notify.

Ms. Braden remembered the initial worry she felt about being able to accomplish these goals. Entering the room where nurses and physicians were yelling orders at the terrified young woman, Ms. Braden calmly approached, looking directly into her eyes, and said, "How about I keep you company through this?" During the next contraction, she held Tina's hand and quietly repeated the nurse's directions on how to breathe through the contraction. Between contractions, still holding Tina's hand, she asked if there was anyone that Tina wanted her to call. When the answer was negative, but Tina had begun to respond, Ms. Braden knew that the beginning of a relationship had been established. Because Ms. Braden had not pushed for an answer, Tina had begun to trust her. She gave her first name, and over the next hour of labor, explained her fears that her parents would find out about this pregnancy and be angry. Ms. Braden gently helped Tina to consider that they were likely to find out anyway.

After long discussion, Tina told Ms. Braden how to contact her parents and allowed Ms. Braden to call them. Ms. Braden met with Tina's mother when she arrived and was able to convey Tina's fears of nonacceptance and urge understanding. Tina's mother was upset and shocked but wanted to help her child. She was with Tina as she delivered the baby and was able to provide support. By the next day, Ms. Braden was acting as a resource to Tina and her mother as they explored options for keeping the baby or considering foster care or adoption. Alone with Tina, and treating her with support and respect, Ms. Braden helped Tina clarify her life goals to consider how the baby would fit with those goals. She also provided information about common emotional reactions to placement of babies, because Tina was seriously considering this option.

Concurrently, Ms. Braden was exploring hospital policy about working with potential adoptions, particularly the discharge policy. She was dismayed to find that the hospital discharge policy required that the baby be discharged to the biological mother and that any "handing over" of the baby be done off hospital grounds. The day before discharge, Ms. Braden met with the hospital attorney to discuss the rationale for this policy and to explore the possibility of changing the policy or making an exception. The attorney was adamant that this was the only way it could occur, despite Ms. Braden's provision of sample discharge procedures from other hospitals that allowed discharge to the foster care worker or other person designated by the biological mother. As change was unlikely to occur in the brief time frame available before discharge, Ms. Braden met to prepare Tina for the discharge.

Tina expressed a sense of "having grown up so much in the last couple of days" and was grateful for Ms. Braden's support during labor and mediation with her parents. After being apprised of all the types of foster care and adoption available in the area, Tina had been helped to make arrangements with a foster care agency of her choosing and had competently made the final arrangements independently. She asked Ms. Braden to be present when the foster care agency's social worker visited prior to discharge to sign papers, and Ms. Braden not only stayed with her but helped her to understand her rights.

Ms. Braden turned from the window to see her supervisor/director watching her. "Now what?" her supervisor asked.

"Now I gather other hospitals' policies and legal cases so that no one else ever has to do it this way unless she wants to!" Ms. Braden replied vehemently.

Ms. Braden met several times with the hospital attorney, Jonathan Berkowitz. While Berkowitz continued to support hospital policy, Ms. Braden continued to provide written sample policies from respected area hospitals, while also consciously working to develop a relationship with the attorney. Ms. Braden had to carefully develop a stance through which she could educate him without implying that he was not aware of the basic information. Berkowitz was under the impression that birth mothers would "intuitively recognize their baby" (even if they hadn't seen the baby since birth) and felt this protected the hospital from "turning the baby over to the wrong person." As he came to trust Ms. Braden's experience and the information she provided, he became willing to accept changes she suggested and to take them to the board with his support. Ms. Braden provided disguised case material for the board to "put a human face" on why the policy would both assist the birth mother and protect the hospital. The ability to demonstrate the benefits to both the client and the organization was critical to the board's eventual acceptance of the new policy. The new policy remains in effect, despite hospital mergers and managed care.

Tina checked in with Ms. Braden several times over the next few weeks and was sure she had made a good decision, despite the pain it involved. She received counseling for birth mothers from the foster care agency, and she visited Ms. Braden whenever she came in for gynecological appointments. She was happy to hear about the policy change and also exclaimed to Ms. Braden, "I could never have gotten through it without you." Ms. Braden was glad to have been able to make a difference for Tina through their work together and for her client population (women placing babies soon after birth) through the work of changing the hospital's discharge policy. Both of these dimensions of Ms. Braden's work, helping Tina to make decisions for herself and her baby and effecting changes in hospital policy regarding discharge of babies to biological mothers off the hospital grounds, depended absolutely on Ms. Braden's expert relationship skills.

COMMUNICATION

One salient dimension of relationship is communication, a process by which information is exchanged through a common system of symbols, signs, and behavior. It is also a technique for expressing ideas effectively. Thus communication is at the heart of the relationships between social workers and all those to whom they relate on behalf of helping clients or communities reach their goals. The use of words, tone, body, time, and affect carries messages to clients/systems about the workers' regard for them as evidenced in acceptance, respect, empathy, and genuineness. Social workers must be aware of how they use both verbal and nonverbal communication and why. This can be as simple as using a calm, quiet manner in a chaotic emergency room or carrying oneself with poise and determination when addressing a board of directors about a policy change. It involves choice of language and tone that are appropriate to the needs of the client. Social workers must be skilled at adapting communication to fit the client and the situation.

Communication is the dynamic aspect of interconnection, a structural system of significant symbols from all the sensory-based modalities that permit ordered human interaction (Birdwhistell 1970:95). Essentially, communication is "a complex and sustaining system through which various members of the society interrelate with more or less efficiency and facility" (Birdwhistell 1970:12). Communication, then, is that system through which human beings establish a predictable continuity (Birdwhistell 1970:14). As a form of communication, the social work relationship can be understood as a matrix that "elicits, permits, or prevents certain kinds of symbolic acts which we are better able to understand if we know the structural pressures imposed by the system" (Birdwhistell 1970:95). The social work relationship, therefore, is a system of shared meaning that exists within other systems that constrain it and shape its possibilities.

Communication can be defined as an interactive "process that gives, receives, and checks out meaning" (Compton and Galaway 1998:198). Key processes of communication are encoding, the process of putting a message to be sent into symbol form in preparation of transmission; transmitting, the process of sending an encoded message; receiving, the process of interpreting the message received; and noise, extraneous influences that distort messages going from the sender to the receiver (Compton and Galaway 1998). These steps are crucial in thinking about social workers' interactions. For many reasons, the potential for misunderstanding in health and mental health care is great. Disparities in language, symbol definition, labels, culture, and projection, among others, can cause communication to deteriorate unless they are considered and addressed directly. Consulting with the others in the relationship and asking for and providing feedback are important remedies for problems that are created by such interference. Interviewing techniques provide the tools for social workers to address these issues.

Effective mutual communication is the best tool for establishing important, positive connections with clients. According to Rogers and Roethlisberger (1991:108), the major obstacle to communication is people's tendency, from their own point of view, to evaluate and approve or not approve of the statements of others.

> When we think about the many barriers to personal communication, particularly those due to differences in background experience and motivation, it seems extraordinary that any two people can ever understand each other. The potential for problems seems especially heightened in the context of an [authority]–subordinate [or case manager–client] relationship. How is communication possible when people do not see and assume the same things or share the same values?

Nonjudgmental, reflective communication is often called "active listening." Active listening means attending perfectly and totally to the client. It involves reflecting back and summarizing what one understands the client to be saying until one is sure that the understanding is congruent with what the client is trying to communicate. This process allows the client to be heard and understood with acceptance and respect. It is important to listen nonjudgmentally while clients and consumers describe and explain concerns and pertinent history that they wish social workers to understand. Listening actively before evaluating becomes a gift that social workers can give clients and communities in critical contexts that are too often inattentive.

THE HELPING RELATIONSHIP

The ability to understand and use the power of relationship to assist clients is a key to effective social work. This has been a part of social work practice since the early days of the profession. As Jessie Taft (1937:3) said, "There is one area and only one, in which outer and inner, worker and client, agency and social need can come together effectively, only one area that offers social workers the possibility of development into a profession and that is the area of the helping process itself." Undergirding the helping process, the relationship between client system and social worker enables clients to feel sufficiently secure to risk new learning and new experiences. Regardless of the level of practice, collaboration creates the greatest opportunities for goal attainment. Whether clients are voluntary or involuntary, whether the focus is on a community or policy, or whether the relationship at hand is with colleagues on an interdisciplinary or multidisciplinary team, the nature and quality of the relationship has tremendous influence on the success of treatment/intervention.

Relationship is the essential base from which social workers and client systems work. It is the task of the relationship to be a conduit for change, a means of helping the client system reach desired goals. "A person has to be helped to understand and, further, to want what he needs, to move in his feeling/thought/action from one attitude or perspective to another" (Perlman 1979:51). The tasks of the relationship also include caring for clients, providing them with hope, and offering them a vision of something better.

LENDING A VISION

No matter what level of intervention the social worker is considering, a major part of the helping relationship involves the idea of "lending a vision" (Gitterman and Shulman 1994; Schwartz and Zalba 1971). Lending a vision is similar to the process of setting goals, but it also entails the quality of hopefulness and a belief that change is possible. Often clients and client systems identify problems in ways that indicate that they see no way out; they have a sense that nothing will improve. Other clients may arrive with the unrealistic hope that presenting themselves to the social worker will miraculously make everything better. In either case, it is not the role of social workers either to create dreams or to take them away. However, it is the social worker's responsibility to set realistic expectations with clients for work that can be accomplished. In creating realistic expectations with clients, the social worker lends a vision of what can be and helps the client system to envision more satisfying, manageable circumstances. In their book on group work, Schwartz and Zalba (1971:16) identify five major tasks the worker must address:

(a) finding, through negotiation, the common ground between the requirements of the group members and those of the systems they need to negotiate; (b) detecting and challenging the obstacles to work as these obstacles arise; (c) contributing ideas, facts, and values from [social workers'] own perspectives when they think that such data may be useful to the members in dealing with the problems under consideration; (d) lending their own vision and projecting their own feelings about the struggles in which they are engaged; and (e) defining the requirements and limits of the situation in which the client-worker system is set.

These ideas are timeless. The concept of lending a vision and helping clients to find their way toward this vision, to avoid or manage the obstacles in their path, is critical to assisting clients in accomplishing their goals.

In effectively functioning groups, the members take on this role of offering a vision as well, as illustrated by the following case example.

Nancy Hobbs, a 28-year-old Caucasian mother of a 3-year-old son, was employed as a nurse in a nursing home. During her first visit to the domestic violence support group run by the hospital's domestic violence medical advocate, Nancy told the group that she had been with her husband for eleven years. They had been separated for four months following the most recent incidence of physical abuse. During this incident, the neighbors called the police, and Nancy had filed criminal charges and had obtained a PFA ("protection from abuse" restraining order) to keep her husband away.

Nancy stated that the physical abuse had started during her pregnancy and that, although it was intermittent, it had escalated since then, occurring every few months. Her husband possessed several guns and had threatened her with them in the past. Nancy informed the group that she was staying away from her husband, except to arrange for visitation for their son. However, she told the group that she loved her husband, they were soul mates, and she knew he would change. She hoped to resume their relationship shortly and was reluctant to follow through with the criminal charges. Nancy confessed to the group that she believed she was equally responsible for the violence because she would sometimes fight back.

The other members of the group had all been separated from their abusers for more than six months. When one group participant asked Nancy how her life had been different during the four months of separation, Nancy stated that she had changed. She was not constantly worried about everything she said or did, no longer felt she was walking on eggshells, and had more energy for her child. Several women in the group talked about promises of change made by their abusers. They discussed what it was like to be free from constant fear. One woman had almost been killed by her abuser after meeting with him to discuss reconciliation. All the women agreed that it was difficult to stop loving their abusers. One woman who was actively struggling with the decision to return told Nancy that sometimes you had to let your head rule your heart.

By the end of the session, Nancy was less sure about reconciling and was clear about putting a safety plan into effect upon learning that a woman was most at risk for severe physical harm after she had left an abusive relationship. She made a commitment to return to group the next week. Thus the group served to lend a vision of the danger Nancy was in currently and also provided a vision of a life free of constant fear and self-monitoring.

Part of this work is helping people to develop their creative capacities. Fritz (1989) finds that most people believe they are not able to fulfill their desires. Indeed, he finds that many are told that they cannot have, or do, certain things that might allow them to realize their desires. Social workers can help to mitigate these beliefs by lending a hopeful, realistic vision and helping clients grow and unfold within the context of the helping relationship. Some of the qualities that are necessary for supporting such growth are warmth, acceptance, empathy, caring, concern, and genuineness.

ESSENTIAL SOCIAL WORK VALUES EXPRESSED THROUGH RELATIONSHIP

While mastering the skills needed for effective social work practice, one repeatedly encounters the importance of respect and empathy, the person-in-environment perspective, self-determination, cultural competence, and confidentiality. This message appears often because these values are at the core of social work. They relate to every level of social work practice in every setting. They are embedded within the NASW *Code of Ethics*. They reflect a basic part of Western ideology. Further, they allow the relationship between social workers and clients to be leveraged in ways that promote maximum growth.

Respect and Empathy

In social work, of the several values espoused regardless of the nature of the relationship to ensue, the first two are respect and empathy. They are part of the practice admonition to "begin where the client is." The critical feature of this kind of beginning involves eliciting clients' views of why they are engaging a social worker's assistance. Whether or not clients work with social workers voluntarily, social workers must begin with the clients' definitions of their difficulties. "To a great extent, the way the problem is defined determines the changes that will be sought through [the social worker's] relationship with the client, as well as the means for accomplishing them" (Fine and Glasser 1996:81). When discussing the nature and use of a contract between social workers and clients, social workers' understanding of clients' definitions of their difficulties is a key element in a successful working alliance. In addition to accepting the problem as defined by the clients and understanding the rationale behind it, social workers need to begin the treatment/intervention process wherever the clients are in thought, value, ability, and desire. Social workers must respect the positions of the people involved and know that people must work at their own level and speed. Respect is displayed in social workers' willingness to engage clients in relationships that are supportive, helpful, and in tune with clients' worldview, while never demeaning or denigrating the clients or their concerns. This means not only aligning the relationship with clients' goals but also designing the work plan from the perspective of clients' reality.

The quality of respect is closely tied to the second value: empathy.

> Derived from the Greek word *empatheia,* empathy may be described as a process of joining in the feelings of another, of feeling how and what another person experiences. Empathy is a process of *feeling with* another person. It is an understanding and appreciation of the thoughts, feelings, experiences, and circumstances of another human being. It is not an expression of *feeling for* or *feeling toward,* as in pity or romantic love. Rather, it is a conscious and intentional joining with others in their subjective experience. (Cournoyer 1996:6–7)

Empathy requires that social workers make every attempt to understand their clients' world. This involves truly listening to their story, their interpretation of their problems/issues, and their attempts at solutions. Like respect, empathy requires that any goal setting and intervention occur within the context of the client's worldview. This leads to the next social work value, the importance of seeing the client holistically.

Person-in-Environment

A third key value of social work is to view the client holistically, not to minimize any aspect of the client's world space. When considering clients and communities, social workers must understand people within their environments. One approach that has been developed to facilitate this view is called person-in-environment, or PIE. Using the PIE approach, social workers consider the internal, interrelational, and environmental forces that shape individuals. Clients and communities bring with them a myriad of connections, thoughts, beliefs, experiences, values, and possibilities. In viewing the client system from the PIE perspective, social workers diligently gather the data of clients' realities and then use those data to help them form a meaningful relationship and intervention plan. The approach requires that the client system be understood within the context of the environment and society.

This interpretation of social work practice encompasses work at every level. Environmental change through the promotion of social justice or the empowerment of oppressed groups or communities is within the social worker's purview when the PIE approach is adopted. Using the PIE perspective, altering organizational structure, community, policy, or societal norms become potential goals. The individual and family do not carry all the responsibility for accommodation to their environment.

Self-Determination

A fourth and paramount social work value is self-determination. Social workers recognize that their clients are the ones to determine what and how they will change or risk growth. Self-determination enables clients to make their own choices and decisions. Social workers promote this value through recognition of and respect for individuals' dignity, autonomy, uniqueness, and worth. The corresponding duty of the social worker is to respect that right, to recognize the clients' need for it, and to stimulate and help cultivate potential for self-direction by helping clients to see and use available and appropriate personal and community resources (Biestek 1957). The responsibility of the social worker is to provide information, to help discover alternatives, and to help remove internal and environmental barriers. While the subject of giving advice will be addressed later in this chapter, it is important to note here that giving advice as to what clients must do violates the value of self-determination. When giving advice, social workers often fail to trust that clients can develop their own solutions when provided with the opportunity to explore options and barriers. Self-determination requires that social workers allow client systems to make their own choices after the social worker has assisted in consideration of alternatives, barriers, and client capacities. Noncompliance is a moot point within the context of self-determination. Social workers adhere to clients' rights to self-determination, working with client systems to examine all the options and their ramifications. At this point, barring legal intervention or presenting a significant danger to self or others, clients are free to make decisions as they see fit.

Still, there are limits to self-determination. Besides the limitations enforced by law and the curtailment of behavior that may present a danger to self or others, the desires of clients must be balanced against social workers' responsibilities to the community (Compton and Galaway 1998). Hancock (1997:194) also suggests that the function of the agency be included here. Thus the concept of self-determination is relative in a world where choices are circumscribed by structural limitations of resource availability and by what is considered to be responsible behavior within a given community. As early as 1965, Perlman (1965:410) said,

> I believe self-determination is nine tenths illusion, one tenth reality. . . . But I believe self-determination is one of the "good illusions" basic to human development and human dignity and human freedom. Therefore, I am committed to supporting and enhancing the illusion and also making the most, the very most, of the exercise of that one tenth of it that is real, present, and possible in our lives. . . . [Nevertheless], we are members of a society so socialized, rationalized, organized, bureaucratized, specialized, and mechanized that there is less and less room for individual freedoms and choices.

People's choices are constrained by racism, limited financial resources, difficulty in interpersonal relationships, suboptimal education, job opportunities, and many social norms. Even so, health and mental health are optimized when people feel they have choices in their lives. A major theme in social work is finding areas of choice, helping to strategize about removing barriers, and promoting the use of the one-tenth that is self-determination, whether that "self" is a person, family, program, organization, or community. This, of course, requires attention to ethical responsibilities and, particularly, to confidentiality.

Confidentiality

The word *confidentiality* implies privacy, secrecy, and restricted access. It suggests that relationships classified as confidential are marked by intimacy and the willingness to confide. The promise of confidentiality is one way relationships are established. In fact, like the other values that are dimensions of the social work relationship, the practice of confidentiality is much more relative, complex, and contextual than definitions of the word suggest.

Confidentiality requires the ability to keep client system information private and unconnected to any identifying information, but most social work settings do not allow for true confidentiality. Therefore, what becomes most important is that clients be given explicit information about the scope and limits of confidentiality from the beginning of the helping relationship (Winslade 1995). In 1978, Wilson raised the following important questions: What do social workers promise when they promise confidentiality? Do they promise that what clients tell them will be known to no one but themselves? If they do make such promises, they are acting unethically, because the promise is not true. What clients tell them will, perhaps, be known to anyone who manages records in the organization (including the billing and finance offices). In the same way, it may be known by insurers' representatives, a supervisor, state or federal representatives who monitor (through the examination of individual records) agency compliance, and other staff. All social workers can truthfully promise, within the parameters of their own control, is that what clients tell them will be used responsibly and will be protected from misuse (Wilson 1978). In this era of managed care and computerized and electronically transferred records, confidentiality is a growing concern.

The NASW *Code of Ethics* (1996: section 1.07, p. 10) describes social workers' roles in regard to confidentiality as follows:

> Social workers should protect the confidentiality of all information obtained in the course of professional service, except for compelling professional reasons. The general expectation that social workers will keep information confidential does not apply when disclosure is necessary to prevent serious, foreseeable, and imminent harm to a client or other identifiable person or when laws or regulations require disclosure without a client's consent. In all instances, . . . the least amount of confidential information necessary to achieve the desired purpose.

Several exceptions exist to the confidentiality of communication between clients and social workers. In the following instances confidentiality may be broken.

1. If there is suspicion of any neglect or abuse to a child or elder, it is mandatory that social workers report the suspicion to the local Department of Protective Services.
2. If clients threaten to hurt themselves or another, measures must be taken to hospitalize the clients for the safety of those who are in danger and to inform those persons of possible danger (Fine and Glasser 1996). Even this exception is subject to interpretation and ethical consideration. Some legal commentary implies that *Tarasoff* v. *Regents of the University of California* (1974), decided in the California Supreme Court, is not necessarily binding in other jurisdictions (Bowman and Mertz 1996). Further, the distinction between the original decision in the Tarasoff case of a duty to warn is contrasted with the later ruling of a reasonable care standard, again meaning that no easily defined positions are available in the case of a client who is threatening to harm someone (Givelber, Bowers, and Blitch, cited in Bowman and Mertz 1996). (See chapter 3 for a discussion of the Tarasoff case.)
3. If a case is discussed in supervision for the purpose of a referral, getting advice on behalf of the client, or improving the social

worker's professional practice, confidence is also breached (Fine and Glasser 1996).

4. A more current breach involves submitted information to traditional insurance companies and managed care companies for third-party payment. Issues of confidentiality in relation to managed care present great challenges for the profession and our constituencies (Rosenbaum, Serrano, Magar, and Stern 1997). In such instances, a social worker may ethically breach confidentiality if the worker informs the client about the circumstances of the breach. The optimum situation involves discussion with the client about the need to disclose information, after which the client signs a release allowing sharing of personal information.

Compton and Galaway (1998:163–64) take the position that confidentiality is essential in certain circumstances, but limiting in others. They caution against using confidentiality as (1) a justification not to act, (2) a justification for protecting people from taking responsibility for their own moral behavior, or (3) a justification for failure to assist clients in building support systems and mutual support groups. Confidentiality is a negotiated condition of service, a resource the social worker can offer. In addition to ethical dilemmas regarding the duty to warn, Compton and Galaway identify three negative consequences to confidentiality that parallel these cautions:

1. The concept of confidentiality may be used to deprive clients of developing responsibility for what they do and say.
2. Confidentiality may be used to reduce options if clients and social workers become a closed system without access to other providers of services and resources who would need accurate information in order to be of assistance. For example, strict adherence to confidentiality might lead a social worker working with a pregnant teen to unreflectively adopt the teen's desire for secrecy. In exploring the conditions of confidentiality with the teen, however, the worker may enable the teen to consider and manage the ramifications of her pregnancy within her social environment. Further, the teen may find that she has a much more supportive extended family network than she had anticipated. This may reveal additional support resources that were unexpected.
3. The concept of confidentiality may reinforce notions of individuality in ways that demean or negate cultural practices that value broad-based support among family and community. These challenges are particularly true in health care settings. Conditions of confidentiality should be explored with clients/consumers to make sure they are not losing useful social supports through their

desire to keep difficulties confidential. Of course, this is not intended to imply that a breach of confidentiality by the social worker is appropriate, only that conditions of confidentiality need to be explored with clients so that they can make informed choices.

New laws and precedents have led to the duty to warn (see the discussion in chapter 3 of the Tarasoff case, which held that therapists are responsible to warn those whom a client has revealed he or she intends to harm) and the duty to report (as mandated reporters, social workers must report concerns about child or elder abuse to the appropriate local authorities). These responsibilities have created breaches in confidentiality. Laws governing confidentiality are not absolute and vary from state to state, and social worker–client communications are not protected in most states.

To divulge information about clients to other professionals or organizations, social workers must have written permission from clients to release such information. The client must be told about what information is disclosed.

CULTURAL DIVERSITY AND CULTURAL COMPETENCE

Respect for difference and cultural sensitivity have long been core social work values that were honored and tended to as part of a commitment to the profession. Now, increased understanding of culture and the effects of its expression on health behavior coupled with the changes in sociodemographics that the United States is experiencing have made ongoing education about cultural diversity critical for effective practice. Within the next two decades, those with minority status will make up the majority of the U.S. population (U.S. Bureau of the Census 1990). Because this is a multicultural society, social workers work with diverse populations who require multicultural understanding and the ability to intervene in ways that take cultural difference into account.

To paraphrase E. B. Tylor's classic definition of culture, culture is that complex whole that includes knowledge, belief, art, morals, law, custom, and any other capabilities and habits acquired by people as members of society (quoted in Wallace 1985:2). Thus it is "the transgenerational learning of all those categories of behavior that contribute to human adaptation" (Wallace 1985:3). The term *culture* refers to a pattern of ideas, a cognitive system consisting of a relatively small set of abstract propositions, both descriptive and normative, about the nature of the human self and society and about how people should feel and behave. Thus, shared uniquely by the members of the community, culture forms a template for all behaviors (Wallace 1985:9). Culture, then, is a way of looking at and being in the world. Underlying beliefs and values regarding "the way the world is" and the way people relate to one another are inherent to culture. To work effectively, social workers must understand clients' unique cultural heritage, as well as their own. This means that social workers must strive to attain cultural competence.

In the following example, the social worker must take into account the client's culture and that of the client's husband in order to advocate effectively for her.

Social worker Jean Billingsley, a member of a dialysis and transplant team, was asked to talk to Carol Hussein right away because Carol had asked to be taken off of the list of those waiting for a transplant ("One Hundred Years" 1995). Carol had been a patient for three years. Figure 5.1 shows Carol's ecomap. She had had one failed kidney transplant, but the team was hopeful that a second transplant would be more successful. Jean and Carol knew each other very well and in fact had been on a first-name basis for a long time.

Jean found Carol wringing her hands and crying softly. When Jean asked what was wrong, Carol began to sob and recounted that she had been on dialysis for three years, that she was too tired to be interested in sex, and that she and Ahmed, her husband, knew that they needed some help in the house. Ahmed had suggested that he return to his native Pakistan and find someone who would live with them and help with the housework. He had brought back

FIGURE 5.1. Ecomap for Carol Hussein.

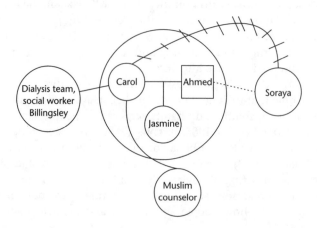

his young cousin, Soraya, who was not helping at all. Soraya was invading Carol's, Ahmed's, and their daughter Jasmine's privacy, and two weeks ago Soraya had announced triumphantly that she and Ahmed were married. Carol told Jean that for seventeen years she had tried to be a good Muslim wife and had made sure that Jasmine went to Muslim Saturday school. Jean said that she remembered when the team and family held their last planning meeting and Carol had told Ahmed that a second wife would not be acceptable. Again Carol cried, saying that she was so ashamed and could not tell anyone. She told Jean that when she had confronted Ahmed and Soraya, Ahmed had told her that she was English; she could cope. Soraya said that she had promised Ahmed that she would not tell anyone for two years, but she wondered aloud why should she have to wait. For the last two weeks Ahmed said over and over that he had made a terrible mistake, and their Muslim counselor told Carol that Ahmed should not have taken a second wife without her permission. Finally, Carol told Jean that she could not go through another transplant without support from Ahmed.

Jean very gently pointed out that Carol did have options and that she would like Carol to come talk to her a few times over the next few weeks to explore her options. She could, for example, leave Ahmed. Her benefits could support her and Jasmine. Carol responded that she wanted her husband back and that she wanted Soraya to be sent home. They discussed the constraints in Soraya's visa, and Carol said that she was afraid to call immigration because Ahmed would be terribly angry. Jean said very sweetly that she had met Ahmed, and she knew that they had had some rough times, but did Carol really think something awful would come of that? They agreed that before their next meeting Jean would call immigration to see if they could keep their sources confidential, and Carol would talk to Ahmed, who could decide to send Soraya back to Pakistan himself. Jean said that the sooner Carol's life got back on an even keel, the sooner she could think again about a transplant.

Carol and Jean met three more times to manage this crisis. Carol knew that the choices were hers and that Jean would support her in whatever she decided. Clearly, Carol and Jean had a well-established relationship that was built on social work values. They had some understanding of both cultures that are important to Carol and her husband, some understanding of immigration and immigration laws, and some understanding of renal disease and treatment (Bare 1997; Doolan 1997).

Cultural competence can be defined as possessing the information and relationship skills needed to understand, appreciate, and interact with persons from cultures other than one's own and using both knowledge and skills to further the work of clients and communities. Here the knowledge base includes the awareness of critical cultural values, beliefs, behaviors, and interactions that structure social and family life and affect social, psychological, and economic functioning. Cultural competence also requires self-awareness, acceptance of differences, knowledge of clients' cultures, and the ability to adapt helping skills to the cultural needs and capacities of clients and communities (Zayas 1997). Differences in sex, gender, race, culture, socioeconomic status, ethnicity, disability, and physical appearance can affect responses in clients and social workers (Woods and Hollis 2000). Social workers who are culturally competent can deliver professional services in a way that is congruent with behavior and expectations normative for a given community and that is adapted to suit the specific needs of individuals and families from that community (Green 1998). Social workers need to be aware of clients' and communities' origins, and the systems that accompany those origins, without assuming that all members of any given culture always think or act in the same ways. Attaining such cultural competence requires active and ongoing attention. Self-awareness ensures that social workers' understanding of clients is not distorted by unrecognized personal biases.

The cultivation of cultural competence is a discovery process that relies on an eclectic knowledge base drawn from several fields related to cross-cultural learning and communication, as well as traditional methods of social service education (Green 1998). Practicing in a culturally competent manner requires that social workers actively address and identify the personal meanings of racial and cultural differences in their work. Difference in another can be recognized and understood only when one is aware of one's own cultural norms, values, self-limitations, and capabilities. Difference is evident when it forces one to deviate from the familiar.

In many ways, all communication is cross-cultural (Compton and Galaway 1998). Even when the client system is from a culture perceived by the social worker as "the same," there will be differences that require that social workers begin by exploring the client's worldview.

James Green, a 67-year-old Caucasian Catholic retired builder, had had a very debilitating stroke. Mary Jackson, the social worker assigned to help him and his wife plan his discharge from the hospital, matched her clients in terms of age, ethnicity, religion, and social class. She assumed that the Greens had the same kind of marriage and relationship that she has with her husband and began to arrange for Mr. Green to return home on that basis. Fortunately, the Greens' daughter told Mrs. Jackson that her parents' relationship had involved years of adultery and abuse. While Mrs. Green did choose to have her husband return home, it was very important that Mrs. Jackson understand the critical issues involved in that choice, issues that her assumptions of similarity had hidden. Mrs. Jackson's assumption that she and Mrs. Green had the same kind of marital relationship could have interfered with her ability to help the Greens.

Culturally competent social workers are never condescending or patronizing. In fact, working from the premise that clients know a great deal about themselves and what is happening to them, culturally competent social workers become students of their clients. In the same way, they encourage clients to draw on the natural strengths inherent in their own traditions and communities, reducing (when possible) their dependence on services provided by outsiders or impersonal bureaucracies. They help clients make use of indigenous helping networks as well as mainstream social and health services.

Understanding individuals in their environment is integral to establishing a working alliance that has practical relevance to the client's life. Such understanding eases the stress of problem solving and communicating. This means sending clients clear signals of respect and positive regard as practiced in their culture, providing explanations for your questions, being familiar with available and relevant information about the clients' culture, and understanding how their relationship with you can be meaningful to them (Proctor and Davis 1994).

In attempts to be culturally competent, social workers often familiarize themselves with literature about the cultural practices of groups with whom they have a lot of contact. On the one hand, this research is valuable and provides needed background knowledge, but it also harbors a hazard. Knowledge of a client's culture can be used to enhance the relationship only when it is accurately applied. "When one ignores the heterogeneity of a population and offers prescriptions for social work practice predicated on a generic perspective, not only are specific subgroups neglected, but there is also a tendency to perpetuate stereotypes and racism" (Yellow Bird, Fong, Galindo, Nowicki, and Freeman 1996).

Additionally, culturally competent social workers consider the motivation for the contact. They explore the extent to which the interaction is voluntary. They understand the client's normative perception of the relationship. Clients may have had experiences that predispose them toward distrust of people like the social worker, whether owing to cultural differences or professional identity. To establish an effective helping relationship, one must understand the nature of these experiences and convey respect for cultural similarities and differences while continuing to have clients teach social workers about themselves. The answers to these questions help structure the relationship.

Cultural competence also applies to areas of spiritual culture. The Curriculum Policy Statement of the Council on Social Work Education now mandates practice content in religion and spirituality as well as the racial, ethnic, and socioeconomic cultural material that has been mandated since 1982 (Cascio 1998). Reluctance to explore these areas has been based on fears about dogmatic and rigid belief systems and concerns that religious beliefs could foster pathology as people "wait for God to intervene" (Joseph, cited in Cascio 1998:524). Spiritual beliefs, however, are integral to health beliefs and need to be approached in the same manner as other cultural beliefs. In developing an effective working relationship, exploring a client's spiritual beliefs while showing curiosity and respect for those beliefs allows the social worker to leverage the power of a client's spiritual beliefs in service to the client's goal accomplishment. "In these situations, one should deal with this difference like any other, by acknowledging the difference and taking a one-down position, and inviting the client to explain his/her beliefs to you. In no instance is it ever appropriate to impose one's spiritual values on a client" (Cascio 1998:525). With the client's permission, it is often appropriate to consult with the client's spiritual leader or representative.

Compton and Galaway (1998:65) consider the similarities of the Medicine Wheel of the Anishinabe to the ecological approach of social work. They note the wheel's origins in spiritual beliefs and ask whether social workers can apply some of its aspects to their practice. "Elders identify problems in terms of the spiritual relationship to the environment. Healing occurs primarily from the inside out (in the spiritual realm) and not from the outside in (in the environment). Can social workers, with their secular traditions, accommodate spiritual aspects within their practice?"

Although this example is applied to Native American communities, the message is clear. Without an awareness and willingness to learn about the spiritual beliefs of clients, we miss a powerful tool to enhance the healing power of the relationship. Particularly in health care settings where existential questions of "why me?" and "how can this happen to someone I care about?" occur, it is wise to incorporate spiritual support. When developing programs or working with communities, including religious and spiritual leaders not only provides needed information about cultural belief systems but often lends credibility to the program or organizational effort. In the same way that indigenous leaders are part of community organization efforts, members of the clergy and spiritual leaders have important roles as well.

RELATIONSHIPS AND PLACE

Just as clients' culture sets the tone for the beginning of the helping relationship, so too does the setting or place where the interaction occurs. Often, the first encounter is at a time of crisis for clients. Many of these first meetings occur in bureaucratic settings. Hospitals, mental health care centers, physician offices, skilled care facilities, and community health care centers are arranged to move people through their services, many times affording little privacy or space. Such settings make the establishment of an optimal helping relationship challenging. Finding ways to carve out a private, quiet, less pressured place for interaction will convey a level of respect for the client and allow the rapport building necessary to effective social work. "When no private area exists, social workers can create private space for themselves and their clients by using undivided attention, eye contact, voice quality, and body language" (Kerson 1997:29). While these settings are very familiar to those who work in them, they may feel quite foreign to others. Minimizing the strange and distancing aspects of a setting and "translating" its operations and norms allows clients and consumers to gain understanding and develop realistic expectations about the setting. Social workers have learned, for example, that when a child is to have surgery or experience some other frightening health intervention, it is important to arrange a preintervention visit to lessen the child's fears. Explanations about organizational protocols and attempts to have the setting accommodate to clients' needs fulfill the same function of familiarizing adult clients with an organizational setting.

Place takes on a different tenor when the social worker is in the community. There, social workers are in their clients' territory. Community-based social workers understand the nuances and benefits of community interaction. For direct practitioners in health and mental health, work in clients' homes has resumed a place it lost from the 1960s through the 1980s (Beder 1998). Entering the clients' private spaces, whether their homes or communities, requires extra attention to conveying acceptance of difference and awareness of clients' concerns that they or their possessions are being judged. Every home visit disrupts family routines to some extent (Beder 1998). Also, perceptions about the power of social workers who do home visits come into play. For example, many people harbor notions that child welfare social workers can remove their children if they wish to, and workers from the Department of Social Services can "cut off your check." These worries can combine with safety concerns on the parts of social workers to raise anxiety for all participants. Recognition of this anxiety along with a clear definition of the goals of the visit help to ease the interaction.

RELATIONSHIPS AND TIME

It is possible to establish an important relationship and to help a client in a single interaction. A social worker assigned to an emergency room in a busy, chaotic city hospital says she almost always sees clients only once. She has four goals for her interactions with each client:

1. No matter how much confusion there is around them, she listens carefully to each patient and family member to be absolutely clear about what they need from her.
2. She is absolutely honest about her ability and limitations to meet their needs.
3. She gives them a referral (in writing) to an agency, institution, or location within her own system where they are likely to get what they need.
4. She explains the role and availability of the social worker in the emergency room to assure them that she, or a colleague, is available to them at any time.

To accomplish these goals, the social worker must have excellent relationship skills. Even in this situation, she is aware of a time process in which she uses her skills to enhance the work of the client.

Time has many dimensions: the dimension of the individual contact; the dimension of the longevity of the contacts over time; and the dimension of beginnings, middles, and ends of the time used in each of the previous dimensions. It is important to be clear about expectations for time use at the beginning of every contact. Defining the number of contacts expected and the length of each contact allows for congruent expectations and provides mutual understandings about the nature of the relationship.

Today's relationships in social work practice in health and mental health tend to be of very short duration (as in brief solution focused psychotherapy or the emergency room setting described earlier). Or, they may be extended over a very long period (as in patients attending a clinic that focuses on a particular disease or set of symptoms over their lifetime, or a case management setting for those with serious mental illnesses or developmental disabilities). Likewise, a community-outreach social worker may work in the same organization with the same participants over several years (as in an AIDS outreach program). Or a community-outreach social worker may be assigned to an organization for a very brief period (as in a brief, intense community effort to immunize a population against a particular illness, or a research effort to collect data about a specific public health concern). In all cases, social workers must think through the effects of the use of time in a particular intervention so that use of time helps clients reach their goals. Because many client/community problems are ongoing and social workers may intervene on a short-term basis, social workers have to think of themselves and their client interactions as part of a continuum of care with which clients will be involved over the long term.

In the following example, a home care social worker has a brief meeting with a patient who will need care over the course of his lifetime.

James Naugle is a 46-year-old man with hemophilia and hepatitis C who, during hospitalization for a spiral fracture of his right leg, was told he was HIV-positive. Mr. Naugle lives with his 70-year-old mother, who had back surgery six weeks ago. His 50-year-old sister died of cancer six months ago. There is no other social support. Because Mr. Naugle was uncooperative in rehabilitation, he was discharged. On his first day home, he fell and realized that he could not manage without rehabilitation. Mr. Naugle wants to return to the rehabilitation center, but he will not be readmitted unless he agrees to be treated for HIV infection. Mr. Naugle, however, denies being HIV-positive. Since he has Medicare, the social worker, Sylvia Greenfield, can visit as necessary. On her first visit, Ms. Greenfield explored Mr. Naugle's understanding of his medical condition and received his permission to discuss his condition with his mother, with whom he has a strained relationship. They reviewed short- and long-term options. Some cognitive deficits affect Mr. Naugle's understanding of his condition and his relationship abilities. Figure 5.2 shows an ecomap for Mr. Naugle at the beginning of his visit with Mrs. Greenfield.

FIGURE 5.2. Initial ecomap for James Naugle.

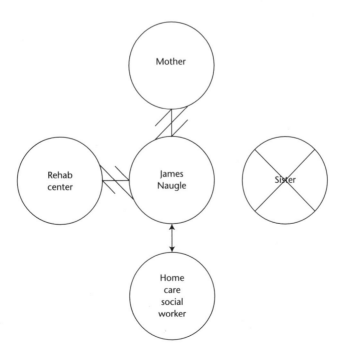

Ms. Greenfield's next visit found more tension and friction between Mr. Naugle and his mother. Ms. Greenfield allied herself with Mr. Naugle in order to help him think through his goals and how best to reach them. Building trust was Ms. Greenfield's major goal, and on each visit she found Mr. Naugle to be more receptive and trusting. During her fourth visit, Ms. Greenfield found Mr. Naugle willing to begin treatment in order to enter rehab, because he is convinced that this is his only route to being able function as well as he did before the fracture. Because Ms. Greenfield has advocated for Mr. Naugle with the rehabilitation unit, he will be readmitted. She has also notified the rehab unit that Mr. Naugle will accept HIV/AIDS education in order to more fully understand the importance of adhering to the treatment regimen. If the rehab unit cannot provide this kind of education, Ms. Greenfield has given them a contact at a local AIDS support organization who will visit and educate Mr. Naugle. Figure 5.3 shows Mr. Naugle's ecomap after his last meeting with Ms. Greenfield. Thus, in four visits in a very difficult situation, Ms. Greenfield successfully assessed the home situation, educated her client regarding his care

FIGURE 5.3. Ecomap for James Naugle after his last meeting with the home care social worker.

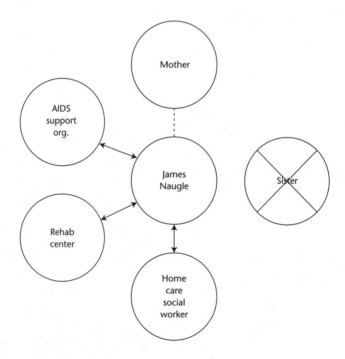

options, acted as an advocate and a liaison, and provided brief supportive therapy regarding the effects of illness and disability.

THE BEGINNING OF THE HELPING RELATIONSHIP

Every social work relationship consists of three phases: the beginning, the middle, and the ending. In this era of managed care, when many interactions may consist of one, two, or three meetings, social workers have to begin every relationship as effectively as possible, carry out all work that has to occur before the relationship ends, and then end in a way that supports client/community learning, summarizes the work that has occurred, and reminds those who have been helped that help will be available in the future and where they will be likely to find it. The nature of the relationship is to leverage all aspects to maximally promote client development and goal accomplishment. Within each stage, skills and characteristics of the social worker are used. Although not truly separable to stages, these skills and issues become more frequently utilized at various stages and are addressed under the appropriate time frame category. Nevertheless, many of the skills are interchangeable throughout the time frame.

The beginning of a helping relationship is a time of engagement and relationship building with clients, programs, and communities. It is usually the social worker's first opportunity to demonstrate social work's values to clients. First, trust is established and maintained. Until everyone involved is assured of the social worker's respect and trustworthiness, they may be reluctant to fully engage in the helping relationship. As social workers approach the first contact, it is important to consider what they know about the client and attempt to "put themselves in the clients' place."

When people feel that they have to seek help from others, they are frequently anxious and uncomfortable. To ask for help, they are admitting to themselves and others that they are unable to manage their own affairs. They are probably uncertain about revealing information to others. There is often a cultural component to their discomfort. In addition, they probably wonder whether they have sought help in the right place. They may be fearful that the people whom they are asking for help may not think well of them or that they may be asked to do something they do not wish to do. They may question the social worker's competency and honesty. "Experience has repeatedly shown that clients will be able to give more complete and less distorted information if initial tension is relieved and they feel safe enough to discuss their situations frankly" (Hollis and Woods 1981:110).

Beginnings mean that social workers need to remember how difficult it is to ask for help and watch for signs of clients' discomfort in this regard. Even when the client is a program or an organization approaching the social worker for consultation, fears about change may be operating and need to be anticipated. If asking for help is a problem, it should be addressed directly to minimize any barriers to proceeding with the work. This section on beginnings addresses the themes that resonate throughout the relationship and the importance of interviewing skills in enhancing client involvement in the work.

Recurrent Themes of the Relationship

Several themes and techniques that are established at this stage resonate throughout the relationship, including engagement, commitment, acceptance, empathic responsiveness, respect, mutuality, genuineness, self-awareness, and attention to issues of diversity. An ability to establish the helping relationship quickly and effectively is especially pertinent in the era of managed care because a decreasing amount of time is given to the relationship with an expectation of better outcomes. Conveying a sense of respect and mutuality allows the helping relationship to begin to develop. The following aspects of the helping relationship are critical to establishing and maintaining the relationship.

1. *Engagement.* In the early stages of a relationship, engagement—that is, the process of establishing a relationship between social worker and client—is a key task. Many refer to this process as building rapport. It is here that the social worker begins consciously and deliberately to develop the relationship. Social workers and clients need this kind of connection and trust in order to proceed with the work that the client hopes to accomplish. Working with people, no matter the systemic level of the goals, is a delicate art and skill. The first problem to be solved in any helping relationship is how to connect, how to become an ally of the person who wants or needs help (Perlman 1979:2). During this stage the social worker comes to know the client, the client's reality, and the client's goals for this professional contact. In individual contacts, the emotional bond between social worker and client is developed and sustained with the intention of supporting and enabling clients to work toward the achievement of their desired goals. "We want a compassionate connectedness along with the rent money, even if that relationship is limited to that one contact and that one need" (Perlman 1979:53).

2. *Commitment to the client system.* The social worker must be concerned for and committed to the client. This concern is expressed by protecting the client's privacy and ensuring that the client's needs are acknowledged.

3. *Acceptance.* Displaying positive regard for the client system in a manner that is free of judgment, with no assignment of blame, shows acceptance of the client and conveys respect for the worth of the individual, no matter what the client's current situation may be. Biestek (1957) defines acceptance as an action principle in which the social worker interacts with clients as they are, including their strengths and weaknesses, congenial and uncongenial qualities, their positive and negative feelings, constructive and destructive attitudes and behavior, while consistently honoring the clients' dignity and personal worth.

4. *Empathy.* When social workers experience and understand the reality of their clients' experiences and feelings, they exhibit empathy. This experience then guides social workers' intervention in using empathic responding. In this way, social workers can perceive sensitively and accurately clients' deepest feelings and communicate understanding of these feelings in language that reflects and matches clients' experience at the moment. This suggests that social workers have the skill to accurately assess and verbalize a client's state. Is the client gloomy or anguished? Is the program that is being considered responsive or unlikely to meet the needs of many of its constituents? Accurate reflection of the feeling and meaning states of the client system is key to the social worker's understanding and client's sense of being understood.

5. *Respect.* Respect comes from the social worker's belief in the dignity and uniqueness of each client. The social worker must have a deep-rooted respect for all clients and believe in clients' ability to be self-determining.

> As a social worker, you are likely to work with many people who differ from you in numerous ways. You may find that you do not especially like some of the people you serve. Some will undoubtedly dislike you. Nonetheless, as a social worker, you should maintain respect for and caring acceptance of all the clients you serve. . . . This ability to respect clients neither because of nor in spite of their attributes, behaviors, or circumstances is an essential facilitative condition in social work practice. (Cournoyer 1996:7)

6. *Mutuality.* Mutuality, which focuses on equal participation and accountability for all parties, is emblematic of the social work relationship. The social work stance is one of partnership in working through problems and negotiating solutions. Even in situations of community work or policy consulting, social workers work toward mutually determined goals, rather than entering a situation as authorities who have come to prescribe solutions.

7. *Genuineness.* Social workers who relate to their clients honestly exhibit genuineness. Honesty is essential to building trust. One demon-

stration of genuineness can be self-disclosure, social workers disclosing information about themselves in order to further the work with clients. Such information refers to the past history or personal experiences of the social worker. To some degree, the use of self-disclosure depends on the social worker's theoretical orientation. Those who oppose the use of self-disclosure often feel that it is harmful to "the therapeutic frame" (or blank slate), whereas proponents of self-disclosure believe it projects nurturance and strengthens rapport, enhances client trust, and aids the client in developing a new perspective (Anderson and Mandell 1989). Self-disclosure and use of self require self-awareness to make verbal and nonverbal messages congruent. Such self-awareness means that social workers can control their negative and defensive responses so that they will not harm clients (Northen 1995). In this way, they admit mistakes, fulfill contracts, provide rather than withhold knowledge, and tell the truth. Social workers who consider sharing information about themselves with clients should first ask themselves if they are providing the information for the clients or for themselves. Those social workers with little experience should examine the use of self-disclosure with those who are more experienced.

8. *Self-awareness.* Without awareness of one's cultural background, belief systems, professional self-monitoring, and value system, social workers become reactive and potentially threatening to a positive helping relationship. Self-awareness requires that the social worker have a good working knowledge of his or her family-of-origin issues, prejudices, level of self-esteem and assertiveness, self-control, and (especially in health care settings) comfort level with illness and difference. This self-awareness is imperative if one is to utilize the relationship to provide client feedback. Woods and Hollis (2000:241) recommend personal therapy as a way of promoting self-awareness. They caution that social workers who have an urge to rescue their clients, identify too closely with pain, or have an irrational fear of anger are likely to create dynamics that interfere with the therapeutic relationship.

Self-awareness also involves attention to issues of diversity. As discussed earlier, both social workers and clients come to the first interaction with cultural premises that define their worldview, including what they believe about the other person's cultural heritage. It is critical that social workers understand their own cultural heritage and its impact on the way they approach relationships. The ability to express openness to the cultures of others can come only from an awareness of the effects of one's own culture on one's relationship abilities. The characteristics and themes of the effective working relationship interplay to build trust and encourage client participation in the therapeutic process.

Interviewing Skills

The purpose of an interview is to collect data or information related to helping clients/consumers reach their goals. Ideally, interviewing takes the form of a conversation and incorporates the value base and recurrent themes described earlier. The skills involved in interviewing include attending, reflecting (feeling and meaning), paraphrasing, summarizing, confronting, questioning, and using silence. Social workers' use of these skills allows clients to be open and to share their concerns, the solutions they have attempted in the past, and the pertinent histories and goals for the work (Ivey 1994). Interviewing is purposeful and directed, limited and contextual, and involves specialized role relationships. The setting creates a context that defines the parameters of the interaction. The context defines the roles that participants play in the interaction. The interview defines the nature of the communication that has as its purpose creating a helping relationship with specified goals and responsibilities. Future communication is defined by those roles, goals, and responsibilities.

Client Involvement

Interviewing skills and communication techniques are likely to promote effective engagement of the client in the helping relationship. Raiff (1993:36) lists ten ways to encourage client involvement in a service or treatment plan:

1. Pay attention to the relationship and the process of relationship building. Pace the relationship; introduce the service plan only after there has been psychological engagement.
2. Involve the client from the beginning. Solicit the client's wishes; educate clients about their rights as consumers.
3. Pace the development of the service plan. Take the time to learn about client preferences and alter goals as gaps in needs and resources become apparent.
4. Plan in parts or partialize the work. Develop the plan in increments, using several sessions as needed. Do not overwhelm the client by promising too much or asking for too much change.
5. Emphasize client strengths rather than problems. Help clients to own the plan by emphasizing what clients can do, rather than what they are unable to accomplish.
6. The plan should reflect the person, be holistic and community-oriented not just focused on disability.
7. The plan must be individualized reflecting on what clients want to achieve and how those accomplishments fit with long-term goals.

8. The plan must be client-centered. Do not confuse agency-established criteria with what the client actually wants and needs.

9. Anticipate the possibility of failure. Do not give up if objectives are not met. Use failure as an opportunity to assess the objective as stated. Are the objectives realistic, valued and appropriate? What have you learned from the experience? Reinforce the client's ability to change and your willingness to help.

10. Remember: There is no such thing as one ideal treatment.

Contracts and Goals

A contract is the encoding of goals into a mutual plan of action to accomplish the goals. It is an agreement that clarifies the obligations and expectation of all participants. Thus the contract includes agreed-upon objectives, provides direction and continuity, allows all participants to monitor progress, and includes outcome measures through which all participants can evaluate the work. A contract also defines the means used to accomplish change. Therefore all elements in the contract should be mutually agreed on and should be a reflection of client self-determination. Expectations are clear about the timing and length of intervention. Such clarity involves reviewing agency regulations, client finances and other resources, external mandates (including the role of the court) for the involuntary client, and modes of intervention. Contract parameters are also established through the agency setting, the referrer, the funding source, program mandates, and so forth (e.g., the client must be "dry" for alcohol treatment). The multilevel impact of community, agency, and individual is felt strongly here. Often, these levels have their greatest effect when the client is involuntary or is considered noncompliant or resistant. Be wary of the latter two labels and sensitive to their origins. They are "red flags" indicating that the client and context (health care setting) are in conflict and that the social worker's mediation skills are needed.

The responsibilities of the client and therapist are discussed and clarified during this stage. This defines the framework and purpose of the relationship and makes both the client and the social worker accountable to the relationship. Appointment times are set and availability is conveyed. The contract also clarifies the boundaries (time, space, confidentiality) of the relationship, the expectations of each party, and the mutual goals of the relationship. In other words, it is the simple and clear map for the relationship. The contract can be formal or informal, written or verbal, and it should be regularly updated. In some ways the contract is reviewed, negotiated, and reformulated throughout the relationship. It is altered as the needs and capabilities of the client, program, or community are altered. In turn, the means of addressing the problems may change as well.

Often clients come with broad goals and need help to break down those goals into workable units. Goals like "I want to feel happy again" or "this program needs to function better" need to be broken down into tasks that can bring about the small changes that ultimately allow larger changes to occur. By splitting the broad goals into partial goals ("I will make one new friend"; "I will balance my budget"; "We will serve 10 percent more clients next year"; "We will have our clients provide written evaluations of our services"), goals become manageable.

This very difficult dimension of the work is called partialization. Many times clients can identify broad goals, but they have difficulty defining the small, more activity-based tasks whose accomplishment will allow them to proceed toward the overall goals. After social workers understand their clients' perceptions of their problems, they can begin to brainstorm with clients about ways to partialize goals. Partializing is a primary task in beginning the helping relationship. All work proceeds from there.

Sundel, Radin, and Churchill (quoted in Fine and Glasser 1996:88) provide guidelines for directing the course of action, prioritizing goals, and ordering priorities. The relationship's priorities, in order of importance, are as follows: (1) the clients' most pressing concern; (2) the behaviors that have the most negative consequences for clients, their significant others, or society (e.g., danger to self or others and child abuse); (3) the concern expressed by the referral source (e.g., involuntary drug-addicted clients who are sent for treatment by the courts and who may be participating as a way to avoid incarceration); (4) the behavior that can be handled most efficaciously, such as referrals for concrete help; and (5) the kind of behavior that has to be addressed before other needs can be managed (e.g., helping someone buy a uniform and shoes before she can obtain a position as a waitress, or helping a client learn to complete job applications before he can obtain employment).

Involuntary Clients

Many clients, whether individuals, programs, or community members, do not choose to participate in the services social workers provide. An example at one end of the voluntary–involuntary spectrum is the parent of a medically fragile child whom a Protective Services social worker had to remove from the home because the parent was unable to meet the child's needs. While the parent is required to work with the social worker, such work is rarely begun voluntarily. Reluctance may have many causes, from distrust of the system to avoidance of psychological issues. It also may be a way for people to exert some control in a situation that is out of control.

This is particularly true for clients within health care settings who may then be labeled as noncompliant. Often people do not wish to participate because they feel dissonance with the system the social worker represents. Many feel this because they are members of ethnic, racial, or gender minorities, or they are marginalized in other ways. "The circumstances of these persons' coming for service place unalterable limits on their right of self-determination" (Hancock 1997:212). Here, social workers find themselves between their clients' right to self-determination and legal and/or organizational mandates. Obligations to clients must be reconciled with legal and organizational requirements (Behroozi 1992).

If at all possible, the first goal is to help involuntary clients to participate more fully in the work. This can be accomplished by accepting their initial reluctance, avoiding premature confrontation, clarifying the social worker's dual role within the setting, and providing some sense of control and choice in selecting treatment goals and method (O'Hare 1996). Framing and then partializing goals can be a way to engage the client. In the Protective Services example, both the client and the social worker might be able to agree that the broad goal is "getting my child back." Agreement on the broad goal then allows partializing that goal, possibly as follows: (1) completing a parenting class, (2) learning infant CPR (cardiopulmonary resuscitation), (3) learning the prescribed care of my child, (4) making the home safe for my child, and (5) arranging for home nursing care. The most important factors in working with involuntary and nonadherent clients are being able to engage them in a helping relationship and locating areas of their lives in which they have some control.

Clients Who Find Compliance Difficult

In health and mental health care settings, it is common for medical professionals to consult social workers when patients are deemed noncompliant. Essentially, this means that clients are not adhering to the plan of treatment that the medical providers have determined is the best way to proceed. Many times, the noncompliance is indicative of the patient's attempts to gain control in a situation that feels out of control. At other times—for example, when teenagers with diabetes refuse to follow a restrictive program of diet, insulin, and exercise—it may also be a result of denial about the severity of illness. In either case, it is critical to establish a trusting relationship so that the social worker can assess the nature and etiology of the decision to pursue treatment in ways that differ from the expectations of medical providers. Sometimes, the difficulty is as straightforward as not having the financial resources to fill a prescription but being embarrassed to admit that to the physician. Providing information about available financial resources or linking the client with physician offices that can supply drug samples then becomes the key to solving the non-compliance issue. Other times, providing information about disease progression or discussing the client's fears of treatment can provide enough support to allow the client to decide to pursue treatment as prescribed. Or the client may provide a rationale for not adhering to treatment, in which case the social worker's role is to convey this rationale to the treatment team and to support the client's self-determination.

A word about language is in order here. Both *compliance* and *adherence* imply that the authority (usually the physician) has given an order and that it is the client/patient's duty to carry it out. This is in direct opposition to social work values of self-determination. Using O'Hare's (1996) guidelines for transforming involuntary clients into voluntary clients, social workers can join with clients and assess their understanding of the situation. When social workers are assured that clients are fully cognizant of the ramifications of not following medical orders, they have a duty to interpret the clients' position to the team and to educate the team about the role of self-determination. Building an alliance with clients is crucial to understanding their point of view, and any intervention designed to force adherence is antithetical to social work values. It should also be noted here that adherence or compliance tends to be judged in areas over which clients ultimately have control; therefore, it never works to try to force, scare, or bully them. This is as true for those who work with people with drug and alcohol problems or serious mental illness as it is for those who work with people with diabetes, hypertension, or AIDS. Ultimately it is up to the individual to decide whether to follow the regimen and to take the medication.

Giving Advice

Although it is important to provide information to those whom one is trying to help, it is generally not helpful to give advice. Providing solutions and dispensing advice may foster dependence and relegate clients to either passive cooperation or even passive resistance. Giving advice implies that workers believe that they fully understand the problem and are not stymied by it, as the client is. This sends the message that the workers are superior, a stance that is likely to inspire resistance as the client senses that he is not understood and is not given the opportunity to ventilate all the complexity of the problem and begin to find ego-syntonic solutions (solutions that fit the client's circumstances and worldview). Frequently social workers in health care settings have seen similar situations before and may feel they have the answer for the client or system with whom they are working. Often, a better technique, after full exploration of the client's view of the problem, is to share the information ("In the past I've worked with clients in similar situations and they tried X strategy"). This allows the client to consider that possibility, without prescription, and allows them to explain why that particular strategy might or might not work for them. This keeps communication open and further problem solving active.

Generally, giving clients advice about decisions or goals is risky. Giving advice about how clients can go about reaching goals is more appropriate, especially if it is unlikely that the client can think this through without help. Of course, the social worker should not refuse a request for advice in an abrupt or withholding way. When it is given, advice should be limited and should be provided in a tentative manner ("One possibility you might want to try is X") to minimize authority issues and subsequent resistance. What is given, then, is more a suggestion than advice.

THE MIDDLE OF THE HELPING RELATIONSHIP

While a beginning is a time of engagement and relationship building, a middle is a time of activity and use of the helping relationship to further the work. The contract is implemented, and all participants are working to fulfill goals. This stage of the relationship is focused on sustainment and intervention. In the middle of the helping relationship the work may be viewed as a form of gift exchange in which the social worker brings to bear a whole host of intervention skills. At this point in the relationship, a number of issues may arise for the social worker, such as transference and countertransference, resistance, partnership, self-care, and burnout.

The Client Relationship as a Form of Gift Exchange

According to Taft (1937:1), "The taking and giving of help are seen as two opposite but complementary currents in a single complex process on which social work must base whatever it hopes to achieve in the way of effective understanding of the client and conscious control over its own procedures." It may be helpful to explore the relationship as a form of gift exchange, not only because it involves a giver and a taker, but also because the concept of gift exchange demands that one explore the notion of reciprocity in such relationships (Kerson 1978b). To take without being able to reciprocate suggests that the relationship is not among equals. "It is far more difficult to take help than to offer it since, in taking it, the person acknowledges that he must, in so far as he accepts aid, be dependent upon and subject to the will of another" (Gilbert 1937:127). In the same way, the concept of gift exchange demands that one think through the sense of obligation one takes on when one receives and cannot or is not allowed to reciprocate. These are idealized concepts, but applying them to examples of the helping process adds a new depth of understanding. Thinking about gift exchange in real terms means that one must address the issues related to gifts and gift giving in one's family of origin as well as in one's present living situation. In the same way, it means that one must be willing to explore with clients what gift giving and gift exchange mean to them.

"'Tis better to give than to receive," and 'tis *easier* to give than to receive. In our society, self-reliance is a sign of strength. No one likes to ask for anything. It is easier to ask an organization for help than to ask an individual. Ironically, social workers generally like to be relied on, like people to ask them for help, and feel great when they can help others. Here we are, wanting to be in the powerful position of making a difference in people's lives, while at the same time we realize how awful it makes most people feel to have to receive help with life's tasks. People often feel even worse to have to ask for help with things that they think they should be able to do themselves. They feel they should be able to take care of themselves and those who depend on them. Acknowledging the difficulty of asking for help and truly listening to the struggle clients have in asking is a gift one can extend. Seldom in North American culture do people take the time to truly listen and attempt to understand another's experience. This is the gift social workers offer. Seldom are people expected to share their innermost thoughts and fears and make themselves vulnerable in another's presence. This is the gift that clients offer. Recognition of this two-way gift exchange goes far in promoting a partnership in the helping relationship. "The professional's task is to clarify the problems and the options, but the client's task is to choose" (Meyer 1993:46). Just as people may elect to refuse a gift that makes them uncomfortable, clients must determine whether the gift is one they can accept.

Issues Related to Receiving Gifts

In an editorial in *Health and Social Work,* Judith Ross (1992), then editor of the journal, wrote about social workers who had received gifts from representatives of nursing homes and companies supplying durable medical equipment and home infusion therapy. She raised questions related to the possible conflict of interest in accepting such gifts. "Is there a difference between accepting gifts for ourselves and accepting gifts for our patients? Is there a difference between gifts given to individual social workers and gifts given to a group? Does sponsorship of educational meetings or clinical programs come with no strings attached?" These are important questions to be addressed by social workers who are in a range of positions in many kinds of health care systems. In addition to being in positions to receive gifts, it seems that more and more social workers are in the position to give gifts because they are working for private companies wishing to solicit business from social work departments. Thus Ross (1992:165) gives the profession food for thought: "Social workers' relationships with patients . . . are based on trust. In accepting gifts, even small gifts, we may be violating that trust, adding to the costs of goods and services and ultimately violating an important social work ethic—that we must hold our client's interest above our own."

In some situations it is wrong for social workers to receive gifts. Whenever the courts are involved, receiving gifts raises issues about influence and confuses relationships. Many agencies and organizations have policies against accepting gifts. Certainly, the effects and meaning of gifts change the dynamic of relationships and must be explored. Part of this work requires that social workers think about the meaning of gifts in their families and cultures. This is another arena in which cultural competence is critical. For example, social worker Ellie Fisk works in a geriatric case management program whose purpose is to maintain people at home and avoid nursing home placement. She has several elderly Italian immigrants in her caseload. She visits all her clients once a month unless there is a crisis. Her agency's policy is that social workers should take nothing, including food, from their clients. But Ms. Fisk learned early on that if she did not accept a cup of tea or coffee and something sweet to eat, her clients were so insistent and insulted that her refusal was actually interfering with the relationship. This example is provided not because Ms. Fisk's solution was right or wrong but because in many situations social workers have to think through the meaning of their actions, understand the possible effects of those actions on their relationships, and make good professional judgments. Because the meaning of the giving and receiving of gifts is so deeply embedded in family life and culture, it is an activity in which social workers should have heightened awareness of transference/countertransference responses.

Intervention Skills

Tools used during the middle stage of the client relationship are clarification, confrontation, interpretation, reframing, attention to process and content, provision of information, and suggestion. Used to clarify the client's interpretation of the problem, clarification bridges the beginning and middle phases of the work. Clarification continues to be used as a tool to focus goals and choose and monitor appropriate interventions. It encompasses skills such as paraphrasing, summarizing, reflecting feeling and meaning, and empathizing. Each of these skills is used to assure clients that the social worker adequately understands their concerns and takes that understanding to greater levels of insight and action.

In the therapeutic sense, use of the word *confrontation* is somewhat different from its usual use. In this context, confrontation means reflecting back to clients some part of their behavior, thoughts, or feelings that may be maintaining or contributing to their problems. Social workers use confrontation to help clients become aware of issues or events that are interfering with their progress toward attaining their goals, as well as to enhance clients' motivation to work toward change. Essentially confrontation is used to challenge incongruities between clients' communications and behaviors, not to confront clients as people. This kind of challenge may take the form of contrasting clients' stated goals with their behavior. For example, a client may say she wants to lose weight in order to help control her diabetes, but she continues to eat all her meals at fast-food restaurants. The social worker might ask her to think about how her meals are helping her reach her goals. Community members may complain that there are too many auto accidents on their streets, but they may remain passive, waiting for the staff at the community center to deal with the Department of Transportation and the local news outlets for them. Again, the social worker might ask community members how their behavior is helping them reach their goal. This frames the confrontation as a question to which clients can respond. During this kind of discussion, other barriers to goal accomplishment may be identified.

Interpretation is another skill used frequently during the middle phase of work. It is a skill to use sparingly, since, like giving advice, it may evoke a sense of hierarchy and resistance. It is used to help clients see how their thoughts, behaviors, and actions are influenced by their current condition. Each of the sets of behaviors described in the discussion of confrontation could be used in interpretation as well, if the social workers, clients, and community members knew each other very well. However, these interpretations are best offered tentatively, with opportunities for the client to disagree with the interpretation.

Reframing, a similar skill, allows social workers to reflect back messages, but in a new perspective, often transforming a negative to a positive. This involves a subtle level of interpretation that then allows the client system to view the situation from a new perspective. For instance, in working with a person who arrives saying, "I'm here, but I'm a mess," a social worker might reframe the situation as follows: "You are in the middle of chemotherapy and still working—it is quite impressive that you are able to make the commitment to continuing our work together."

Sharing information is a crucial task during the middle phase of a client relationship. Clients need information about the setting and its functions and roles, especially regarding organizational policies and how the setting relates to larger systems and to other organizations and resources. This level of information supports all types of consumers in making the decisions that are best for them.

Finally, in keeping with the previous discussion about giving advice, social workers can use the technique of suggestion once helping relationships have been established and social workers are certain of understanding the client's concerns. Only then should one make a suggestion, thoughtfully offered to assist clients in their work. The example given earlier in this chapter of Carol Hussein, who was waiting for a renal transplant, includes several illustrations of suggestions. The social worker suggested that the client could leave her husband or could involve herself in the cousin's immigration issues.

Relationships in a Managed Care Environment

In this world of managed care and case management, with many social workers working under extraordinary time pressure, unless they are engaged specifically in the process of psychotherapy, it is easy to lose the focus on the relationship between social worker and client. Yet it is important for all social workers to cultivate the skills that foster effective relationships and to use those skills to help clients reach their goals. One way to enrich these dimensions of the work is through attendance at workshops given regularly on varied kinds of psychotherapy. This exposure enables social workers to apply what is applicable to their own clients and settings. This is not meant to demean or denigrate any of these psychodynamic approaches, which take years of training to understand and use to their fullest potential. Rather, it suggests that every approach to psychotherapy contains dimensions and elements that can enhance social workers' abilities to relate to clients. Learning and maintaining the skills of focusing on the relationship allow the worker to comment on the client's behavior in relationships. This then provides feedback for clients about how they are perceived and allows them to consider making changes, if any are indicated.

A Typology of Social Work Interventions

Over a social work lifetime and through later collaboration with her former student Mary Woods, Florence Hollis devised a typology that classifies the communication between social workers and clients or collaterals (Woods and Hollis 2000:121–27). This typology allows social workers to consider various aspects of the helping relationship and to classify those areas that have been used, as well as to open new areas for consideration.

The typology is divided into two broad categories: client–worker communications and person-in-situation, or environmental, interventions. There are six intervention methods within the client–worker communications category:

1. *Sustainment.* Communications designed to convey interest, understanding, confidence, and reassurance constitute the bulk of sustainment. Frequently, these are nonverbal cues, such as attentive posture, minimal prompts (repeating a word the client has used in

a questioning manner), nods, and smiles. Sparingly used supportive statements such as "You seem to be coping well with an enormous amount of pressure" or "It is to be expected that this would be difficult to deal with" reflect a level of understanding of the client's situation and sustain the communication.

2. *Direct influence.* This communication type is really a continuum of interventions that range from tentative suggestion through directive advice giving. As discussed earlier, giving direct advice is seldom appropriate to the social work relationship. Even so, suggestions such as "I wonder whether it might make sense to consider X strategy for handling this problem" or "Have you thought about trying to do X in that situation?" fall within the range of customary social work interventions in health care settings.

3. *Exploration, description, and ventilation.* These communications are designed to promote client disclosures through questions and other techniques. Although using minimal prompts and nodding are also involved in sustainment, the goal differs when they are used in this context. The exploration of clients' problems, motivations, and strengths, their descriptions of interactions and situations, and their opportunity to allow open expression of emotions are all goals of this type of intervention.

4. *Person–situation reflection.* Reflection of client communications is often a main goal of intervention. Woods and Hollis (2000) divide the types of reflection into six further categories: reflections of others (clients' own health or other aspects of the exterior world); client behavior (including its effects on others or on self); the nature of clients' behavior, thoughts, and feelings; the causes and provocations of behavior; self-image, values, and principles from an evaluative stance; and feelings about the social worker or the client–worker relationship.

5. *Pattern–dynamic reflection.* Communication for the purpose of reflecting back general patterns in the clients' behavior and the motivations behind the behavior are given a separate category. Much interpretive and analytic work is done with this type of communication.

6. *Developmental reflection.* Like pattern–dynamic reflection, this type of communication identifies patterns in client motivation and behavior; however, the focus is on historical developmental patterns. Framing reflections in terms of prior client development is a hallmark of this type of interaction.

There are three types of interventions within the person-in-situation, or environmental, category of interventions:

1. *Types of communication.* The first four types of communication are also used with collateral contacts (with the client's permission) as one works to help relatives, medical care providers, and others in the client's network to assist the client in reaching goals.
2. *Types of roles.* Roles such as provider of resources, locator of resources, interpreter of client to milieu, mediator between client and milieu, and aggressive intervenor between client and milieu (advocate) are all of use in environmental interventions.
3. *Types of resources.* Resources are also categorized as to the type of resource the social worker is providing, as well as to whom the social worker may refer the client, including resources such as the social worker's agency/setting, an organization in which the social worker is not employed, independent social work practitioners, and other collateral individuals (including those with instrumental, expressive, or professional relationships with the client).

Transference and Countertransference

Self-awareness, addressed in the earlier discussion of beginnings, is an important aspect of all work with clients. When the relationship is psychotherapeutic in nature, much attention is paid to understanding transference and countertransference, since they are considered integral to the work. However, transference and countertransference are important dimensions in every aspect of social work practice in health and mental health care. The intense relationships developed when people are in crisis frequently provoke the same transference reactions that are the core of the work in psychodynamic counseling. Interpreting these reactions for other health care providers may become necessary if clients' transference reactions to care providers become barriers to effective communication. It is important to note that all health care providers, too, can experience transference/countertransference reactions, which is why self-awareness is a key to providing effective social work service.

Psychoanalytic theory explains that people may displace feelings or attitudes that they experienced earlier toward a member of their family or other very significant person in their lives (Northen 1995:130). "Transference is the process in which the patient transfers to the analyst experiences from early relationships. As the transference evolves, the analyst learns of the past through the present and, by working through these transferences, enables the patient to approach new relationships without the 'baggage' from early ones" (Alpert 1990:159). Clients can interpret the current relationship between client and social worker in the same way, expecting the social worker to respond or act as these earlier figures did. Transference may be displayed through anger owing to the social worker's position of authority that can trigger past experiences with parents or bosses. The client may then express the hostility toward the social worker. Clients can also want to "be the only one," becoming jealous or intolerant of the social worker's other relationships. Clients can develop strong positive feelings for the worker, expressing these feelings as desires to have the social worker to themselves. They may have difficulty in sharing the social worker, feel strong overidentification, or experience prolonged dependency (Northen 1995:131). Unrealistic feelings toward the social worker are often titled "transference reactions," or "unconscious and inappropriate repetition of reactions and feelings from the past in a present situation" (Northen 1995:131). These feelings can be a good learning tool. It is important to address and process them as they occur. This is how the relationship itself can be used to promote growth. It is the work of the practitioner to bring the client into a participatory relationship based in present reality for optimum functioning.

Countertransference occurs when the social worker transfers feelings and reactions from an earlier relationship onto a client (Northen 1995). It involves emotional reactions, attitudes, values, and beliefs that the helper may have toward a client (Imhof, cited in Northen 1995:135). These responses can be harmful because of their influence on practice. They must be recognized and controlled to assure effectiveness in the helping relationship. "Unacknowledged and unmanaged countertransference can be countertherapeutic and may mirror oppressive sociocultural values" (Cantor 1990:14). Ruderman (1986) studied the countertransference themes of women therapists working with women. Most striking was the profound resonance, stretching far beyond empathy, that the therapists experienced, especially in relation to the issues of midlife (menopause and perimenopause in particular). Self-awareness and adequate clinical supervision help the social worker avoid negative countertransference reactions.

Working effectively in the helping professions requires "use of self," the particular way social workers combine knowledge and self-understanding. The social worker becomes the instrument of assistance, and the instrument is kept in tune via self-awareness and good supervision. Becoming professional helpers demands that social workers frequently reassess themselves as thinking, feeling, and acting persons in relationship to others (Hancock 1997).

It is important to realize that social workers also bring their own experiences, values, thoughts, beliefs, and desires to helping relationships. In attending to relationships, social workers must be aware of the clients, but also aware of themselves and their experiences in the relationships. This is a continuous process. Social workers must examine their own lives, including the sources of their preferences, values, thoughts, and actions. Being aware of oneself enables one to actively use self in relationship, prevents social workers from imposing themselves onto the clients, adds to cultural competence, promotes connectedness, and establishes healthy boundaries. Reid (1991) insightfully warns social workers to beware of narcissistic snares to "heal all, know all and love all."

The following case example provides a way of considering how the need for self-awareness becomes heightened as the work progresses into its middle phase. Issues of transference and countertransference arise, even though this is not a psychotherapeutic setting.

Danny Bennett, age 14, an African American residing in a suburban county, was referred to the public child welfare agency by his physician and the hospital social worker for "medical foster care." Danny's doctors had diagnosed acute lymphoblastic leukemia eleven months earlier. His father was found to be a suitable bone marrow donor, and a transplant operation was scheduled to occur in several weeks. Though the bone marrow had only five of the eight matching characteristics required, the risk was found to be justified, as without the operation Danny had a life expectancy of only four months. Danny's treating physician was most concerned by what she perceived as a lack of compliance with medical treatment by Danny's caretakers, including a pattern of missed appointments and medication errors.

Danny was in the midst of a chemotherapy protocol requiring a complex routine of carefully scheduled medication and appointments for spinal taps, tests, intravenous medication, and transfusions in preparation for the transplant operation. Any deviation from the prescribed course placed Danny at risk of relapse and/or toxicity. If Danny's operation was successful, he would be hospitalized for at least six weeks and would then require careful follow-up care at home. There were concerns that Danny's family might not be able to meet his needs. Eleanor Silverton, a Protective Services social worker employed by the County Department of Child Welfare, was assigned to assess the family situation and the adequacy of Danny's care. Ms. Silverton found that Danny, a seventh-grader, resided with his 30-year-old brother, Daryl Bennett; Mr. Bennett's significant other, Julie Matthews; and their two daughters, Talia, age 6, and Nakia, age 2. The family lived in a two-bedroom apartment in a racially integrated working-class neighborhood. Mr. Bennett, a high school graduate, worked for the post office; Ms. Matthews was a licensed practical nurse in a private doctor's office. Figure 5.4 shows Danny's genogram.

Danny's mother had died from a brain tumor when he was almost 2 years old. Daryl Bennett was then almost 17 and his sister, Ruth, was 15. Their maternal grandmother, who had serious cardiac problems, cared for Danny, with much assistance from Daryl Bennett, until her death, when Danny was 9 years old. Mr. Bennett then assumed custody of Danny, with his sister as an active participant in Danny's care. Danny had only sporadic contact with his

FIGURE 5.4. Genogram for Danny Bennett.

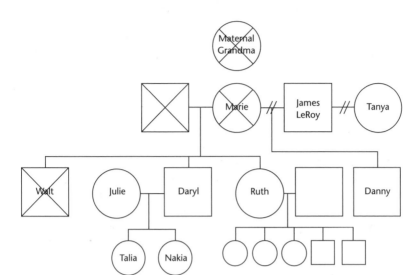

father, James LeRoy, who lived in a nearby city, but Mr. LeRoy did insure Danny through his employer-provided health insurance. Mr. LeRoy cooperated with testing to determine his suitability as a bone marrow donor; he agreed to be a donor but stated he could not assist Danny any further. Mr. LeRoy's ex-wife, however, continued to help with Danny's many medical appointments and had demonstrated her commitment to his care.

The assigned social worker met with much resistance from all family members, including Danny. Strictly observed family privacy rules made assessment difficult. The family distrusted the medical and social service systems that were trying to help Danny. Daryl Bennett missed appointments with the child welfare agency, school, and hospital personnel, often sending another family member in his place. Rather than perceiving the social and medical service systems as helpful, the family saw them as adding pressure to a difficult situation and as derisive of their capabilities and autonomy. Ruth Bennett and Julie Matthews spoke about their lack of satisfaction with Danny's medical treatment and wanted to have Danny seen at another facility. Health professionals described the family as "flippant" in their interactions. Mr. Bennett declined to answer questions about family income and social history. Danny's father, James LeRoy, was particularly secretive; he refused to give hospital personnel his telephone number and asked to be contacted only through his ex-wife. The agency social worker had not been able to meet with him.

Mr. Bennett and other family members denied all the concerns expressed by the professionals regarding confusion about Danny's medical treatment. While the hospital reported that Danny had taken the wrong dose of one medication, had taken the wrong medication on occasion, and had taken medication for an incorrect duration, Mr. Bennett insisted that either he or Ms. Matthews put out Danny's medication and that it was up to Danny to take it. Mr. Bennett reported that only once was a prescription not filled in a timely manner, and that was because the prescription was in his car, which had been impounded. Mr. Bennett acknowledged the difficulty in getting Danny to all his scheduled clinic appointments, citing demanding work schedules and the hour's drive to the hospital. He insisted, however, that appointments were kept.

It was clear that Danny required much more structured supervision of his medical care than the family could provide or deemed it necessary to provide. The expectation that Danny himself be responsible for taking his medication had resulted in potentially serious medication errors. Multiple caretakers bringing him to clinic appointments caused a lack of continuity in medication instructions and a failure to communicate problems at home. These concerns were clearly conveyed to Mr. Bennett by the agency social worker with the message that, if solutions could not be found, foster care would be considered. Mr. Bennett reluctantly agreed to Family Preservation services with the stated objective that a single family caretaker would assume complete responsibility for keeping clinic appointments and monitoring Danny's medication. Felicia Carter, the Family Preservation worker, assisted with transportation and coordination of appointments. The family did not fully cooperate with these services and missed appointments with Ms. Carter; however, Danny did keep his medical appointments.

Danny's loyalty to his family was clear from the outset. He spoke very positively about all family members, with the exception of his father, from whom he felt distant. Danny appeared defensive at the suggestion that he might need closer supervision of his medical treatment. He volunteered that he would refuse all medications if he were removed from his home.

Ms. Carter identified important strengths in this family, including family pride and great support for one another. Ironically, this pride and cohesion presented as barriers to the acceptance of help. The home was clean, nicely decorated, and well maintained. The family had high standards for education and parenting, and positive discipline was used. Danny was well liked by classmates and did very well in school, and the children were courteous and well behaved. There was a long stable employment history and a strong work ethic.

It was now two weeks before the scheduled surgery. Danny had to complete complicated tasks in those crucial days, including collecting all voided urine, taking medications, and keeping appointments. Ms. Carter had been working with the family for about five weeks and had serious doubts about their ability to accomplish all that was necessary. She talked about how differently her parents would have responded to such a situation and wanted to place the boy in foster care to ensure that he would be properly prepared for the operation.

Danny had experienced many losses in his young life, including the deaths of his mother, grandmother, and, most recently, his oldest brother in a drive-by shooting. He continued to experience the loss of his father, and he was now forced to rely on that father in a life-threatening situation. During the period before his transplant, Danny also faced the loss of his health and freedom. He appeared ambivalent about his father, the bone marrow transplant procedure, and his father's role in it. Much of the time, he was quiet and seemed depressed. His attachment to family members was evident, and probably echoing what he heard from other family members, he was most animated when protesting any action that he felt would undermine the integrity of his family. Perhaps this expression of protest toward several systems carrying great authority was the only way this family could manage in this very difficult period. Moreover, many of these prior losses entailed contact with "authorities," who may not always have been respectful and careful with the connections in the family. Transference could have the effect that any authority would be perceived as an additional threat to the family's integrity.

Felicia Carter, a 26-year-old Caucasian social worker married to an African American man, was helped by her supervisor to identify strong countertransference issues in working with these clients. She was very identified with Danny, talking about him (without referring to him by name, of course) to her own family, worrying about him in the evenings and on weekends. She found herself telling her supervisor and coworkers that this family did not do things as her parents would have and certainly did not act as her husband's family would have either. She felt that Mr. Bennett and Ms. Matthews should have been married years ago and that it was unfair to their children for them not to marry. After all, she would not bring children into this world without marrying. She found herself very angry with everybody in the family except Danny, especially with Mr. Bennett and Ms. Matthews, who were near to her in age. She was furious with James LeRoy, Danny's father, and could not conceive of the fact that he was absent with the exception of financial support and now his willingness to donate bone marrow. When she mentioned Mr. LeRoy, she would make a face and just shake her head. She could recognize cultural issues with this family that may have caused their suspicion of the systems involved, but even there, she thought they needed to get beyond their suspicions in order to help Danny. That they didn't made no sense to Ms. Carter.

Ms. Carter had several discussions with her supervisor about her responses to Danny's family. Although she was uncomfortable, she had to explore her own feelings about racial differences, what being married to someone of a different race meant to her, and especially her feelings about social class and economic status. Since Mr. Bennett and Ms. Matthews both had finished high school, and Ms. Matthews had been trained as a licensed practical nurse, Ms. Carter expected them to live according to the middle-class values with which she had been raised. She could accept that those clients whom she saw as very poor and uneducated would have other lifestyles, but she could not accept this from those she identified as members of her own class. Now that she was married to an African American, she could not alter her expectations based on race either. For Danny's sake and for Ms. Carter's ability as a social worker, it was urgent that she explore her countertransference responses. She did so in several intense meetings with her supervisor and learned to be less judgmental and more understanding of family dynamics.

Given Danny's history of losses, his attachment to his family, and their commitment to him, Ms. Carter and her supervisor did not believe his removal from the home should be considered, without a hazardous medical situation that would outweigh the social and psychological stress such an action would cause. Indeed, they thought that Danny's removal would aggravate his physical condition. Given his precarious medical condition, even if the agency assumed custody, Danny still might not survive the operation and the agency could be placed in a difficult situation. While Ms. Carter would not have hesitated to remove Danny from his brother's home if that were the only way to ensure treatment, she was not convinced that this was the case. While reaching this conclusion, however, Ms. Carter had to reexamine her own feelings. Having considered all aspects of the case, Ms. Carter and her supervisor continued to provide intensive services to Danny, and Ms. Carter continued to monitor her own feelings and responses.

Resistance

The term *resistance* is used to describe the response of clients who seem to fall into passive inertia or who actually oppose forward movement during the active phase of the work. Especially within psychoanalytic theory, work with the resistance through use of the therapeutic relationship is viewed as the heart of the work. Schlossberg and Kagan (1988) theorize that working with resistance based on social workers' self-knowledge and openness to their own feelings can facilitate change in severely dysfunctional families. Use of the relationship involves reflection of the sense of resistance and exploration as to the nature of its etiology. In the case example of Danny Bennett, the resistance to helping personnel can be viewed as a symptom of previous negative relationships with such people. It becomes a signal that the social worker will want to explore the client's prior experiences so that current helpers can differentiate themselves from previous ones to the degree necessary.

It must be said, however, that invoking the idea of resistance should not be used to avoid assessing the adequacy of the social worker's technique and style. "Some counselors and therapists have developed individual styles of helping that require their clients to join them in their orientation to the world. Such individuals have found the 'one true and correct' formula for counseling and therapy; clients who have difficulty with that formula are often termed 'resistant' and 'not ready for treatment'" (Ivey 1994:348). In this light, resistance may be a healthy response as the client avoids being subsumed. The social worker should coordinate the involvement of all systems, perform outreach, maintain respect, validate the client's system, avoid power struggles, and maintain a presence while addressing painful dilemmas that may inspire resistance.

Clients as Partners

In all helping relationships, clients and their families should be treated as partners. Nowhere is this illustrated more powerfully than in the book *Partnerships at Work: Lessons Learned from Programs and Practices of Families, Professionals, and Communities* (Bishop, Taylor, and Arango 1997), which provides information on family and interprofessional collaborative partnerships formed to help when children have special health needs. Bishop et al. correctly argue that only when social workers include families as partners can they expect children and their families to procure the services and supports they need. To form such partnerships, professionals must respect the needs of each family member, work with the family as advocate and counselor to fill gaps in service and in education, link with social services and health care, and recognize and use family members' skills and strengths to assist in overcoming obstacles and reaching their own goals.

For example, one organization, Peanut Butter & Jelly (PB&J), is a culturally sensitive family center in New Mexico where social workers and others work with families who need help with children with medical problems, developmental disabilities, and mental illness. The organization grew out of two mental health counselors' concerns that while their clients' needs for medication and talk were being met, the children were getting very little stimulation and attention. Their employer could not or would not address these needs; so the counselors began the work of PB&J as a volunteer effort. They now help one thousand families a day. Among PB&J's programs is a therapeutic preschool that works with parents and children together to strengthen parent-child communication and bonding, child development, parenting education, medical services, and support groups.

PB&J also offers a home-based services program that provides intensive services such as parenting training and infant development services for high-risk families who have had difficult relationships with agencies. Another program provides intensive parenting and independent living skills training for developmentally disabled adults and their children. One dimension of this program is a twelve-unit apartment complex in which parents and children can live in a supportive situation. The commitment PB&J made to children and families was the foundation of all their programs. They planned services with children and families around their self-identified needs and learned to work with each family's unique definition (Bishop et al. 1997:51–53). Another project educates parents about their rights under the Individuals with Disabilities Education Act.

Each of these programs illustrates movement from micro work with individual clients and families to programmatic levels of work. The social workers recognized client needs, generalized their findings to a population, and implemented programs to meet that population's needs. This involves work within the health care system and within community and governmental systems as social workers worked to assure funding for new programs. This is social work at its best, responding on all levels of work. Such work can be completed only in partnership with clients. Social workers' most important sources of authority are clients who reach an agreement with social workers to work jointly in defining problems and moving toward mutually agreed-upon objectives. Social workers are most likely to secure authority from clients if they focus on clients' goals (Compton and Galaway 1998).

Self-Care

An area that is often neglected is self-care for the social worker. Corey and Corey (1993:8, 62, cited in Hancock 1997:92–93) point out that social workers' own needs can work for or against being helpful to clients. Among such needs they list social workers' needs for control and power; to be nurturing; to change others in the direction of our own values; to feel adequate (particularly when it becomes overly important that the client confirm our competence); and to be respected and appreciated. Meeting these needs contributes to self-care. Alternatively, social workers must avoid the save-the-world syndrome or the cure-the-client quest. These pitfalls only serve burnout and disillusion and present unattainable goals. It is important for social workers to replenish their creativity and promote inner strength. Making time to cultivate significant relationships, engage in hobbies and social activities, contemplate during regular periods of solitude, and care for one's health (by regularly eating well, sleeping, and exercising) all go a long way toward effective self-care. Just as adult airplane passengers are told to secure their oxygen masks before assisting their children, social workers must ensure that *their* oxygen (self-care) is securely in place before attempting to assist others.

Poor self-care results in distraction from the helping relationship and may cause caregivers to distance themselves from people's pain by trying to act like an expert. Poor self-care also leads to burnout. Social workers who are burned out become unable to engage in the working relationship.

Burnout

Teachers of social work practice courses talk regularly to students about caring for themselves, having diversions from their very intense work, developing outside interests, taking the vacations they are entitled to, and leaving work at a reasonable time of day. Students are told that the goal is not just for them to graduate but to continue to be social workers for ten, twenty, thirty, or forty more years. There has been a great deal of discussion about burnout in the literature of the helping professions and business (Levinson 1996). Signs of burnout are (1) chronic fatigue; (2) anger at those making demands; (3) self-criticism for putting up with the demands; (4) cynicism, negativity, and irritability; (5) a sense of being besieged; and (6) hair-trigger display of emotions.

The same issues are true for those in supervisory positions who manage the work of others. Those who are in the helping position should say to themselves and to those whom they are helping, "At no time while I am helping you with this or any other problem will your problem become my problem. The instant your problem becomes mine, you will no longer have a problem. I cannot help a person who hasn't got a problem" (Oncken and Wass 1992:54). Assuring self-care and maintaining appropriate boundaries are the best ways to prevent burnout. The best cure for burnout is prevention.

It is critical that those in charge in an organization acknowledge that the work is psychologically and emotionally difficult and that they recognize that workers are vulnerable to burnout. Observing how long people are in certain kinds of positions and rotating them periodically into situations in which they can replenish themselves is a good management strategy. It is important to avoid always looking to the same people to rescue every difficult situation. Those in supervisory or management positions might monitor the length of workers' days, have work groups in which groups of workers move in and out of the most difficult assignments, and make sure that people have individuals and groups with whom to ventilate. The environment can be made conducive to self-care by giving plenty of space for recognition and for BLT (bright lights and trumpets) for those who are making a fine contribution to the work. Opportunities for physical exercise and expression are also beneficial. Supervisors and "managers should provide avenues through which people can express not only their anger but also their disappointment, helplessness, hopelessness, defeat, and depression. . . . When people in defeat deny their angry feelings, that denial of underlying, seething anger contributes to the sense of burnout" (Levinson 1996:160).

Some of these outlets can be provided only by the organization, but many are responses and protections social workers can develop for themselves. It is important to be watchful for signs of burnout in oneself and one's colleagues. Developing emotional, social, and physical outlets outside work and developing peer relationships within work settings provide the worker with needed support. Gomez and Michaelis (1995) note several correlates with burnout among human service providers. They have found that burnout is common in the human services because of conflicts between the expectations and ideals of people entering the field and the realities of the work. Social workers may anticipate fulfilling, helping interactions that are gratefully recognized by the client. In reality, they may be forced into brief encounters with clients who are resentful or who view them as one more cog in the bureaucracy wheel. In any case, the disjuncture between expectations and reality may give rise to burnout. Gomez and Michaelis also found that workers who had higher amounts of paperwork duties were more likely to experience feelings of burnout. Again, workers and social work administrators can use this information to modify responsibilities to minimize correlates of burnout.

ENDINGS IN HELPING RELATIONSHIPS

Endings are built into the beginnings of the social work relationship. The contract is critical because it sets the parameters for the relationship. From the start, the end of the relationship is foreseen as the time when the goals of the contract have been accomplished. The goal of this stage is to enable clients, programs, and communities to maintain the changes and sustain the growth they desire.

Termination

Termination is the professional, thoughtful, and masterful way social workers end their relationships with their clients. Termination in social work practice in health and mental health care begins with engagement. The reasons for termination include completion of goals, death, change in life circumstance for client or social worker, and, unfortunately, mandates by insurers or the cost of service, which may have become prohibitive. As part of self-awareness, social workers must know, understand, and be able to manage their personal styles of ending. For example, one social worker who had worked for more than twenty years in several health settings explained to her colleagues that she never had difficulty with endings. She just said she was leaving and left. A colleague's comments about her style made her think about how, as the child of an army officer, she had moved often with no good-byes and very few ties to former friends and acquaintances. She had become numb to the process and insensitive to the needs of her clients, who not only had different upbringings but had to add the loss of their social worker to the other losses they were experiencing.

It is important for all social workers to understand their personal styles of ending, including whether they prefer to leave first or be left. Social workers should think about times when they have ended relationships in ways that were avoidant, distraught, or matter of fact. They should reflect on whether abrupt endings have been part of their history. It is very important that social workers think about whether they have been unable to end relationships when it was necessary for them to do so. Often, there have been losses in social workers' lives that make separations or endings charged or very difficult. Awareness of these factors is imperative if social workers are to be able to effect healthy and productive terminations with clients. The termination phase of the helping relationship can affect the gains a client makes in treatment, how long these gains last, and the client's future growth (Fortune 1995; Woods and Hollis 2000).

The reasons for ending service can be varied. Common termination situations include the end of a planned, time-limited contract; mutual agreement that service is no longer desirable; unplanned changes in the service relationship (the client's schedule changes, the worker leaves the agency, the client or worker moves to another area, agency policies about length of service change, new limits are imposed by insurance companies, etc.); client's transfer to another social worker; or the client drops out (a unilateral ending) (Fortune 1995:2398). Ideally, service ends when a client and worker agree that it is no longer needed because agreed-upon objectives have been met.

Goals of the Ending Phase

The processes and tasks of termination are built into the helping relationship at its inception. These interventions are designed to help the client assess progress and the treatment process, generalize gains to other settings and situations, develop skills and strategies to maintain gains, assist in the transition to no service or to another service, and deal with the emotional reactions to ending.

Effective termination requires a great deal of attention and energy. It may be a highly productive period during which many objectives are achieved. "During the termination phase, clients typically evaluate their progress and their attainment of goals, summarize their work in treatment and evaluate the treatment process itself" (Fortune 1995:2399). Social workers also use termination to evaluate their own work. They ask themselves questions such as Have the objectives been achieved and the goals reached? Are clients able to maintain themselves within their environments? Are there areas that may require further work in the future, and have I assisted the client in identifying these areas? What are the financial constraints that still apply? Did excessive caseload contribute to a lack of success on any level? What have I learned about the most effective way to intervene with similar clients? Can clients or communities recognize the signs or issues that should cause them to seek help again? Will they know how to seek help when they need it? Ideally, questions about goal attainment, potential future work, and assessment of the effectiveness of the work are discussed with the client.

Preparation for a future without the social worker's presence is not necessary for all helping relationships, although relationships that have been long-term or intense benefit from this kind of essential groundwork. Critical factors in the reaction to termination are the reasons for termination, the amount of time spent in preparation for termination, the duration of treatment, and the client's previous losses (Fortune 1995:2399–2400). Activities during this preparation time may include homework assignments with longer periods of time elapsing between meetings, networking with others who will provide support once the helping relationship is over, and termination rituals that acknowledge the value each has had for the other (Fortune 1995:2401).

The following list constitutes a framework for considering goals of the ending phase of the relationship:

1. *Evaluate the client's readiness to end.* Whether the end date was specified from the beginning of the contract or goal accomplishment indicates the time has come to end the active work, client readiness to end must be assessed. Abrupt endings can negate much of the work that has been done. Woods and Hollis (2000:550) comment that "the range of responses is very broad and each client and family should be individualized. [Possible reactions include] euphoria, pride, gratitude for help given, shock, denial, anger, sadness, fear of aloneness, feelings of betrayal, disappointment, relief that a painful or inconvenient process is over, loving and/or hateful feelings toward the therapist." By eliciting the client's responses to ending, social workers lay the groundwork for solidifying the gains.

2. *Evaluate the work.* The process of evaluating the work is carried out by clients and social workers. Clients must be engaged in assessing the level of objective achievement. If they believe that objectives have been achieved, how do they account for the results? If they believe that objectives have not been achieved, how do they explain the lack of achievement?

Social workers want feedback about the most helpful and least helpful aspects of the work. This allows them to modify and develop practice interventions in relation to client feedback. This is true not only in work with individuals and families but also in work with programs and communities. The feedback allows the worker to adhere to the NASW *Code of*

Ethics regarding professional growth and also allows feedback about goals related to social justice.

3. *Reinforce strategies for maintaining goals.* A major task of ending is to preserve the gains made during the work. This involves ensuring that objectives were achieved and also requires strategizing about how to maintain accomplishments in the face of any challenges that can be foreseen. Particularly in this age of managed care and short-term interventions, it is imperative that social workers in health and mental health care prepare clients to maintain their progress even when the work is inactive. This may be done by reviewing the means through which objectives were accomplished, projecting what challenges might arise in the future, and considering what strategies might be used to manage those challenges.

4. *Assist in maintaining and preserving the new helping network.* Even if the work was very brief (a quick referral to a community resource), an important task of ending is to ensure that the new connections have been made and can be maintained. These connections can involve referrals one has made as well as informal friend and community networks that are in place to continue to provide support to the client after the social worker–client connection has ended. Ideally in helping relationships of a longer or more intense nature, the meetings between the social worker and client system can be gradually phased out, with longer time periods between each meeting. The purpose of these last meetings would be to support the transition and to assess the effectiveness of the new helping network.

5. *Say good-bye.* Clearly identifying an ending and acknowledging the meaning of the relationship is an important part of the end of the relationship. Although there is often an opening for future work, termination requires that the social worker be able to say good-bye and expect that the client system is ready to go on functioning well without ongoing use of the helping relationship. This, again, is a place where awareness of transference and countertransference responses to endings in the social worker's history is vital. This may be the first ending a client has experienced in which there is a planned movement toward ending without anger. This in itself can be healing.

Reactions to Ending and Termination

There are many reactions to termination. Clients may feel a sense of accomplishment and pride, and it is important for social workers to acknowledge the hard work their clients, programs, or communities have done. There may be a process of mourning the loss of an intense relationship involving feelings of denial, anger, loss, depression, and—finally—acceptance (Fortune 1995:2399).

Psychotherapists often refer to a phenomenon called "doorknob therapy." This comes at the end of a session when the client has a hand on the doorknob and is ready to leave but suddenly raises a complex issue. It is viewed as an attempt to stay in connection with the helping person. A similar dynamic may occur as the helping relationship draws to an end. The client system may seem to regress, losing gains accomplished earlier or identifying new and troubling issues. The work of termination requires careful preparation and reinforcement of gains. Social workers recognize the tendency toward "doorknob" regressions and do not overreact to them.

During this time, recognition of the value of the relationship is expressed and clients are assured of the social worker's positive regard. Review of what clients have learned reinforces progress. Discussing coping and mastery enforces these skills to maintain gains. Emphasizing problem-solving steps and skills that clients can use in the future brings about closure that is reaffirming and renewing for clients. Social workers do their best to ensure that supports are in place for clients and try to anticipate and strategize about future difficulties. They ease the transition by reducing dependence, reinforcing what clients do well, focusing attention on outside activities, and helping clients envision a future without the helper's presence.

Social workers' reactions to terminations are rarely discussed, but workers too experience a range of emotions when ending relationships with clients. Their own ending styles and reactions influence the process of termination. Social workers' feelings about clients and the work experience their usual manner of managing separations, and their current emotional and relational situations can all deeply influence the course of termination (Woods and Hollis 2000:544). Social workers' reactions, generally less intense than clients', are often related to pride in clients and the work they have accomplished and pride in themselves with regard to their skillful management of the work. Some ambivalence and sadness occurs for both clients and social workers at the end of a helping relationship. Unanticipated terminations are uncomfortable for social workers because they do not allow adequate closure for social workers or clients.

The conditions of the ending are also important. Review of the social worker's future availability can be reassuring as clients take their leave. When appropriate, return visits can be discussed. It is always important in these circumstances to assure the client that these possibilities are not raised in response to an inability to end the helping relationship. Also, the boundaries of the relationship, should future visits occur, should be clear. At no time should these arrangements be made to meet the worker's personal desire for ongoing contact at the expense of client growth and independence. When relationships are skillfully ended, both worker and client leave the helping relationship having benefited from the contact.

Endings can represent accomplishment, new beginnings, and independence for clients.

CONCLUSION

A relationship is a connection, association, or involvement. A helping relationship is one in which social workers assist clients to achieve their objectives. Such a relationship requires that social workers understand and manage many dimensions of the relationship, including the phases of work, the ways social workers carry themselves, and the unconscious forces (e.g., transference, countertransference, and resistance) that affect the work. Within the helping relationship, specific techniques are used and tasks are accomplished. When deeply understood and utilized properly, the helping relationship can assist social workers in leveraging the time and energy spent on work so that they have greater impact on clients' lives and goal accomplishment. The helping relationship is also the dimension of the work from which social workers derive the most pleasure and satisfaction.

The Nature and Tools of Assessment

This chapter explores the meaning of assessment, demonstrates the use of assessments in social work contexts, and discusses some specific tools for assessment that have been developed for social work and other helping professions. All practice concerns the gathering of information, making judgments and decisions, and then acting on those judgments. Assessment means making judgments about capacities, needs, and goals. Other words for this process are *evaluation, appraisal, examination, valuation,* and *judgment.* Although some use the term *evaluation* interchangeably with *assessment,* in this book, *assessment* will be used to refer to the collection of information and the judgments made prior to and concurrent with intervention. *Evaluation* will be used to denote retrospective consideration of information, judgments, and interventions.

Assessment is the basis for determining goals and objectives, developing contracts, and planning interventions. One could argue, in fact, that outcomes depend to a great extent on the social worker's ability to appraise the capacities of clients, programs, and communities and to match them with the most effective interventions. Assessment is also the process by which clients of all levels—that is, individuals, organizations, and communities—interact with social workers in order to decide whether their needs are being, or can be, met by social workers and their organizations

(Specht and Specht 1986). In some form, the process of assessment includes all parties.

Assessment is the process of defining a person, program, problem, family system, or community in ways that have the power to limit or further the client's access to goods and services of all kinds. The social worker gathers sufficient information about the background, resources, and characteristics of a client, program, organization, or community to understand the nature and scope of a problem and the capacities of the client or system in which difficulties are occurring to address the problem. This process occurs irrespective of one's level of practice or the nature of one's work.

Thus assessment is both a process and a product. The product, whether it is a diagnosis, a judgment, or a summarization, is often critical to the work that follows. Assessment is not only inextricably linked to the development of goals, objectives, and outcome measures, but is also often closely linked to funding. In turn, outcome measures relate closely to the evaluation of programs, projects, clients, and professional performance. Ultimately, the continued financial and social support of individual client systems and programs may depend on the ability of the social work profession to assess in terms that can be related to outcomes and then to report their work in terms of the defined outcome measures.

Assessment is a critical part of any social work intervention, be it community outreach, the development of a new program, or work with an individual or family. For example, certain kinds of assessments may follow individuals, institutions, and communities throughout their lives. An assessment of mental retardation, psychosis, personality disorder, or illness such as AIDS that is feared and misunderstood can limit possibilities for individuals far beyond what the actual symptoms of their conditions actually warrant. A judgment that the infrastructure of a neighborhood cannot support a community program can be equally devastating. The purpose of assessment is to have sufficient knowledge and judgment regarding a population to help people discover the best way to achieve their goals. Every assessment should be approached with a concern for social justice, respect for the client, and great delicacy. As a process, assessment must be sufficiently stable and consistent to inform action and to allow common understanding while remaining flexible enough to allow all participants to be responsive to new or newly understood information, change, and growth.

The assessment process is concerned with helping the social worker and client to think about and understand the meaning of events, circumstances, services, and relationships to individuals, families, groups, programs, and communities. This process takes time and requires the willingness to ponder, to step outside of one's own ways of making sense and into the thinking of others. Time and pondering are "two features that are hardly syntonic with the bureaucratic cast-iron mold of services in cost-cutting (at all costs) times" (Meyer 1993:x). Social workers are asked to determine whether there is a problem, need, or question to be answered. Generally, based on that determination, the social worker will plan some kind of action and then execute that action. Often, too, the parameters of the assessment will be determined not by the individual social workers but by the organization in which they work and the source of funding for the work. There is nothing internecine about this. It underscores the point that many dimensions of assessment are made outside the relationship between the social worker and the client or community. The funding source and organization act as a lens that limits what one looks for and what one sees. The social worker understands this, understands the limiting factors, and learns to see beyond and around the limits, keeping judgments reasonably focused in order to move forward into action.

Every assessment is bounded by problem definition. In the best of circumstances, the problem is defined by the client system. However, sometimes the definition comes from the state, the courts, funding sources, the nature of the agency or organization, or someone other than the client who is within the client's ecosystem (Gilgun 1994). Determining boundaries can be a complex task, requiring many kinds of knowledge, rigorous thinking, and informed judgment as to what should be considered part of the case. Once "inside" the circle of the case, there are yet more complex issues to air in the matter of assessment having to do with the reliability of judgments:

1. To what extent are the problem and situation being understood correctly?
2. Is it a unique phenomenon, or can it be generalized to other cases of its class?
3. If the case or situation is like other cases or situations, to what extent can social workers rely on existing systems of classification to shed light on the case? (Meyer 1993:26)

Reid (1989) notes another aspect of the assessment process. Though not directly linked to assessment of the client, program, or community, assessment also involves the selection of knowledge in empirical practice. That is, the social worker concurrently peruses the literature for methods of assessment and intervention that seem appropriate to the given circumstances. The social worker is expected to understand the products of social work and social science research in ways that allow the worker to choose appropriate strategies for assessment and intervention. The worker then "gives priority to products of research when these are available and applicable. . . . One intervention may have better scientific credentials than a second, but at the same time may have a poorer fit to a given case situation" (Reid 1989:169–70). This selection ultimately leads the social worker to the choice of intervention—a product of the social worker's assessment of the client, organization, or community's problem statement, the capacity for change, and the interventions available, especially those interventions that have been shown to be effective in research studies.

Since assessment is always related to the potential for some kind of action, the social worker must determine which dimensions of the client unit are amenable to change and which are not. Identification of the dimensions that are alterable then informs choices about possible interventions and allows the interventions to be tailored to the client's problem definition and ecosystem. "Some cases may be so straightforward that little assessment is required, but most cases that occupy contemporary clinical social workers involve complex, transactional phenomena" (Mattaini 1997:29). These complex phenomena require thorough assessment to guide intervention appropriately and efficiently. Assessment should include consideration of whether they lead to interventions that promote social justice or whether they contribute to client oppression.

THE HISTORY OF ASSESSMENT IN SOCIAL WORK PRACTICE IN HEALTH AND MENTAL HEALTH

To understand that assessment is a relative phenomenon and a social process, one must look briefly at the history of assessment in social work practice. This brief history demonstrates some ways that social workers have tried to absorb the complexity of problems in context, locate and understand the causes of the problems, and develop the tools that let them intervene effectively with and for clients. It is not meant to suggest that the earlier ways were foolish or unsophisticated or that today's theories and tools for assessment will be maintained over a long period. Rather, the history is another part of context that demonstrates that systems of assessment are cyclical and cumulative and will be replaced when better paradigms are found. Systems of assessment are products of their times and of available knowledge and expertise. Again, greater understanding of problems in context will yield more accurate assessments and thus more helpful interventions.

Over time, depending on the contemporary understanding of the causes of social ills, the social work profession has moved from placing responsibility for problems and their solutions in the hands of the community, the individual, the family, or society as a whole. As social workers' understanding of these problems shifts, the nature of assessment is altered as well. Also, since the profession continues to be made up of groups of individuals who work on very different levels of practice with different assumptions about problem responsibility and solution, disagreements about the nature of assessment continue no matter what the prevailing views of society are at the time. According to Meyer (1993:261), "In some ways, the history of assessment in social work practice has paralleled the history of social work itself, just as it has reflected social work's professional purposes, because what a profession chooses to focus on in assessment and what it recognizes as relevant and significant case data will ultimately define what it does." Meyer quotes Taft (1937:1), who wrote the following more than sixty years ago:

> There is a universal tendency in all human development to progress by extreme swings from object to subject, from the external, the physical and the social, to the internal, the psychological and the individualistic. . . . At one moment we place all truth in the outside world where we try to analyze the object as a separate entity; again we turn upon the self, the doer, and study him in all his subjectivity. Either concentration destroys or ignores the reality that lies only in the living relationship between the two.

Taft thought that practice had become confused by its inability to find its place between pure therapy and public relief. She reported that social workers in private agencies tended to identify themselves with therapists in a freedom to respond to individual need on an individual basis in contrast to public relief workers, who responded to categories of need with categorically rigid functions. The social workers in the field of public relief, on the other hand, were struggling with the dilemma of whether they should insist that relief was casework or whether they should repudiate their casework affiliation and perhaps put the relief function on a business basis (Taft 1937:13). These excessive swings from subject to object, from the psychological realm to public policy, continue to affect how social work understands problems and how it decides to intervene.

Social work's first specific term for assessment was *social diagnosis*. The term appears as the name of the first methods book in social work, because the author, Mary Richmond (1917), thought that the act of assessment defined the method. The diagnostic method consisted of gathering data about many dimensions of a person's life and then interpreting the data in order to begin to help the individual. Richmond (1917:357) defined social diagnosis as "the attempt to arrive at as exact a definition as possible of the social situation and personality of a human being in some social need—in relation to other human beings upon whom he in any way depends or who depend upon him, and in relation also to the social institutions of his community."

It is thought that Richmond choose the term social diagnosis for at least two reasons: First, she valued and understood the place of diagnosis in medicine and thought that social diagnosis would parallel medical diagnosis. Second, she was determined that social workers assess people as objectively as possible within their own social contexts. The term was meant to discourage the then friendly visitors' assessments of the needs or character of the individuals and families through the imposition of their own middle-class values and moral judgments. Richmond's approach to assessment was scientific and thoughtful. One of the problems with the schema, though, was that it required the accumulation of so many types of rich data that it impeded the social workers' abilities to act.

After World War I, social casework, and most particularly what was then called psychiatric social work, began to turn inward in terms of assessment and intervention. With the exception of community organization, relief work, and some forms of group work, direct social work practices appear to have put aside the dimensions of social context that Richmond thought were critical for understanding. Psychiatric social workers worked with shell-shocked veterans, and a great range of social workers began to embrace the theories and methods of Sigmund Freud. In the 1930s and 1940s, the diagnostic approach of social work almost abandoned social context for psychoanalytic theory. In the same era, during and after the Great Depression, when many more members of the middle class required assistance from the government and from social work, society viewed the responsibility for social problems and their solutions as societal rather than being located within the individual or family. Thus divisions increased between group work, relief work, and community organization on the one hand and family and individual work on the other. The kinds of family and individual work that are the focus of this book were then distinguished from other forms of social work and were referred to as medical and psychiatric social work.

Such divisions were partially addressed with the formation of the National Association of Social Workers in 1955. However, the divisions and divisiveness continue, in part, because of the range of problems that social work addresses, in part because of paradigms taught and modalities required for intervention, and in part because of differences in funding streams. The social legislation of the 1960s brought emphasis on social action, advocacy, and increased attention to community action. The turmoil of the 1970s had its own effect. The fact that the majority of psychotherapy in the country was delivered by social workers in the late 1980s and throughout the 1990s also affected the field and its processes of assessment.

Altogether, social work, even if limited to health and mental health care, is a diverse, responsive, poly-paradigmatic field that concerns itself with a wide range of problems and issues. Thus social work's approach to assessment is touched by its history, diversity, and issues. Whatever the context, the process of assessment is one of gathering sufficient information to make judgments that can inform action. Such information is a combination of what others have decided and what social workers gather in the form of reports, records, and test results from those within their own organization and referral sources, other service organizations who have had experience with the client, and the social workers' observations and direct discussion with clients, programs, or communities.

The following case example involves a frail older woman for whom the most positive solutions were found in a continuum of care through careful assessment. The social worker needed assessment skills on the direct practice, organizational, and community levels in order to help the client. In relation to direct practice, the woman's individual capacities and limitations and her social support network had to be assessed. Organizationally, four systems that provided services to the client required assessment. Finally, the social worker had to assess neighborhood and community resources in order to help maintain the client in the least restrictive and safest environment possible.

Minnie Oakman, a widowed 73-year-old African American woman, lives alone in her two-story row house. Both of her daughters live nearby (figure 6.1 shows Mrs. Oakman's initial ecomap). Once a month, Mrs. Oakman is admitted for an overnight hospitalization in the Clinical Research Center by her dermatologist for photophoresis treatment for her subcutaneous T-cell lymphoma. During one of these hospitalizations, social worker Susan Wright was consulted because Mrs. Oakman's daughters were increasingly concerned about her ability to care for herself. They thought that Mrs. Oakman was becoming forgetful and was not preparing meals or taking her medication as directed. Mrs. Oakman lives in an area of the city that is known to have heavy drug activity, and just before this admission there had been a shoot-out between police and drug dealers in the alley behind Mrs. Oakman's home. Although the Visiting Nurse Association was making home visits, the support they were able to give was limited, and visits were made only with an armed escort. Ms. Wright spoke to the visiting nurse, who shared the family's concerns. Mrs. Oakman's income (Social Security and a small pension totaling about $600 per month), and her Medicare were supplemented by Medicaid.

Mrs. Oakman was adamant about remaining in her own home, insisting that she was taking care of herself and that she did not need any additional help. The social worker advised the family that the City Corporation for Aging, through its waiver program, could spend up to 80 percent of the cost of nursing home care to provide home-based services to qualified older adults in

FIGURE 6.1. Initial ecomap for Minnie Oakman.

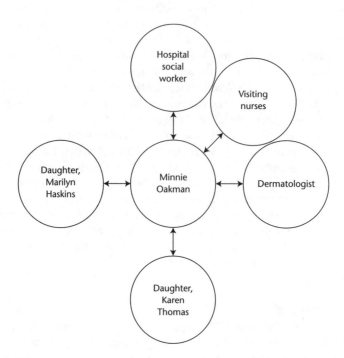

order to try to prevent nursing home placement. The family felt increasing support that might allow Mrs. Oakman to remain in her home was a good alternative. Ms. Wright made the referral to the City Corporation for Aging during Mrs. Oakman's overnight hospital stay, and there was no further involvement with Mrs. Oakman's daughters at that time.

One year later, when Mrs. Oakman was hospitalized for her routine photophoresis treatment, Ms. Wright was again consulted, as Mrs. Oakman's daughters wanted to obtain a power of attorney for Mrs. Oakman. An attorney had also suggested that they request a psychiatry consultation to assist them in their efforts to obtain legal guardianship. When Ms. Wright contacted Marilyn Haskins, one of Mrs. Oakman's daughters, she found that Mrs. Oakman had not allowed the assessment worker from the City Corporation on Aging to speak with her when she visited the home, and services had never been initiated. During this period and the ensuing eleven overnight hospitalizations, no one had contacted Ms. Wright. Now, Mrs. Oakman's daughters were convinced that Mrs. Oakman could no longer live at home. After reading Mrs. Oakman's chart, including the psychiatry consultation, it was clear that a simple power of attorney would not resolve the problem. The psychiatrist noted

Mrs. Oakman's diminished capacity, very poor short-term memory, and safety concerns should she return home alone (figure 6.2 shows Mrs. Oakman's eco-map at the time of this hospital stay).

The social worker consulted the hospital's risk management department, which stated that the patient could not be discharged until appropriate arrangements were made to ensure her safety. The family, physician, and other members of the treatment team were informed of this condition for discharge. The family was unable to make arrangements for the patient's supervision until nursing home placement could be obtained. Both daughters were single mothers who were the sole support of their family. Marilyn Haskins had recently returned to work after medical leave and had exhausted all her sick time and family-leave benefits. Karen Thomas, Mrs. Oakman's other daughter, had just been called back to work after a temporary layoff. Mrs. Oakman, who was

FIGURE 6.2.   Ecomap for Minnie Oakman one year later.

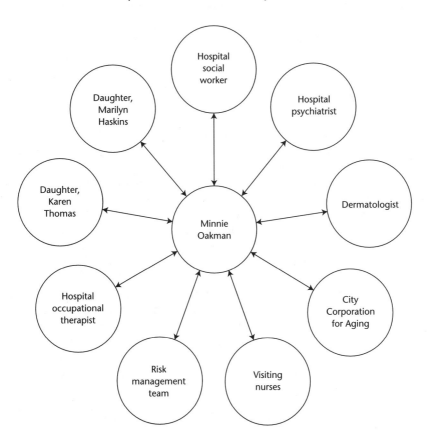

expecting to be discharged, also had to be made aware of the medical team's concerns. Although it is not equipped to deal with patients under these circumstances, the Clinical Research Center agreed to keep Mrs. Oakman there until her bed was needed. Staff members knew Mrs. Oakman well and were very supportive of her.

A nursing home grant application was begun immediately, and the family was advised to continue with guardianship proceedings. Throughout this process the family cooperated fully. An appointment was obtained quickly for the City Corporation for Aging assessment, and the family was asked to provide the necessary documentation for the application. During a visit to the patient's home, Ms. Haskins reported that there was evidence of both insect and rodent infestations, noting that rodents had obviously been chewing on food boxes. There were bags of garbage throughout the house, and a foul smell pervaded the home.

Both daughters were present for Ms. Wright's lengthy discussion with Mrs. Oakman. Throughout this process, Ms. Wright continued to explain to Mrs. Oakman that she had wonderful relationship abilities and that everyone liked her, but all the staff were concerned that she would not be safe at home because of her memory problems. Specific examples were given, such as leaving the stove on and forgetting to take medications. In fact, an occupational therapy evaluation had been obtained during which Mrs. Oakman did leave the stove on and never returned to it during the session, having completely forgotten about it.

During this time, the patient began to ask many questions about the nursing home. Her questions were answered by both the hospital social worker and the City Corporation for Aging social worker, who treated Mrs. Oakman with a great deal of respect. At the end of the interview the patient was amenable to going to a nursing home. The facilities coordinator made referrals to a number of facilities with conditional acceptances by several homes. The family was asked to visit the nursing homes in order to select one. Both daughters visited facilities over the weekend and selected one they both felt was appropriate for their mother. The nursing home was made aware of the family's preference for their facility, and they agreed to accept her with a letter of guarantee from the hospital, pending final approval of the nursing home grant. The family met with the admissions director and completed the necessary paperwork. By this time, Mrs. Oakman had been moved to a general medical floor. She had one-on-one supervision for safety, as she was in an open unit with access to the elevators. Transportation arrangements were made, and a copy of the chart was obtained to accompany the patient. The patient, family, and members of the treatment team were all advised of the pending transfer.

On the morning of the transfer, Mrs. Oakman's nurse told the social worker that the nursing home would not accept the patient. When their nursing staff called the hospital for report, they learned that the patient had one-on-one supervision, which they said their staff could not provide. The social worker contacted the admissions director who confirmed this. She next contacted the administrator of the nursing home and explained that although the patient required one-on-one supervision in the acute hospital setting, given her dementia and the safety issues this presented, she would not require this supervision in the nursing home setting. Obtaining a nursing report is usually part of the approval process for nursing home placement, and it was unclear why this information had not been made available to the facility. The nursing home is equipped with door alarms, and the patient is quite easily redirected. Also, unlike the hospital, the nursing home has recreational activities and a cozy lounge. Before the social worker could suggest that the administrator actually see the patient in the hospital, he volunteered to come to the hospital with both the admissions director and the director of nursing. The family was informed of this development. Upon visiting the patient in the hospital, the nursing home staff agreed that Mrs. Oakman was an appropriate candidate for placement in their facility. She would be transferred later that morning. The family was notified and said they would visit the patient the next evening after work. Figure 6.3 shows Mrs. Oakman's ecomap after she was transferred to the nursing home.

Several questions remain: First, is not part of assessment making decisions about who has the ability and the responsibility to intervene? Ms. Wright, from whose viewpoint this example is written, has no authority outside of the Clinical

FIGURE 6.3. Ecomap for Minnie Oakman after admittance to the nursing home.

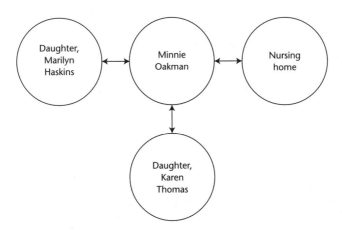

Research Unit. Some could argue that she dropped the ball by not following through and being sure that the City Corporation for Aging, Mrs. Oakman's daughters, and the Visiting Nurses Association were carrying out their responsibilities. However, her work is defined by her context, the Clinical Research Unit. One could also argue that in the twelve overnight hospitalizations between the first set of living plans arranged for Mrs. Oakman and the second, no one (not her daughters, the various agencies that did enter her home or did not, or the staff at the Clinical Research Unit) mentioned any change in status. One might presume that they were interested in assessing only her compliance, her affability, and her body's response to the photophoresis. Mrs. Oakman's self-determination was a very important part of Ms. Wright's assessment and her interventions. Until she was convinced that it was unsafe for Mrs. Oakman to return home under any circumstances, she supported Mrs. Oakman's wishes. When home became too dangerous for Mrs. Oakman, Ms. Wright used the same assessment skills to secure a safe place in a nursing home, about which Mrs. Oakman and her daughters were in agreement.

Mrs. Oakman's situation is an interesting example for several reasons. First, it is an example of the bread-and-butter work of today's social workers in hospital settings. Second, it establishes that assessment without networking and follow-up is almost irrelevant. Here, the first round of assessments were useful only in demonstrating the degree to which Mrs. Oakman's mental condition had deteriorated over another year. Third, it underscores the importance of assessing many dimensions in order to arrive at a rich understanding of a situation. Fourth, it affirms the importance of the social worker's understanding of psychological and social functioning, as well as her ability to make judgments about family, organizations, and systems interactions and relate to several organizations other than her own.

QUESTIONS TO BE ASKED IN ANY ASSESSMENT

To assess an individual, program, organization, or community, one must be able to answer the following questions:

1. Who and what make up the system you wish to assess?
2. What are the ecological boundaries that must be drawn to make sense of the situation?
3. What are the probable parameters based on access, proximity, entitlement, and need that help you draw ecological boundaries?
4. What range of services should be viewed as possible in this situa-

tion, especially in relation to the needs and capacities of the client system?

5. What are the client system's goals and objectives?
6. Are the goals and objectives realistic in the face of system strengths, capacities, and access?
7. Are objectives predrawn by organizations, legal mandates, or funding sources?
8. Which tools are available for assessment, and do those tools measure what the social worker has determined must be measured?
9. Is the biopsychosocial assessment sufficient to help the social worker and client system develop strategies to reach their goals?

One has to have a comprehensive understanding of the client's systems and needs before determining the extent to which dimensions of the systems have to be involved in the problem-solving process and before intervention. For example, a problem with a project might involve an entire program in order for the problem to be addressed. In the same way, an individual problem might have to involve family members, or a program's problem might well require the involvement of a larger unit in an organization. By the same token, an organizational problem may well be so interconnected with another institution that only through assessing the ability of both institutions to address the problem could it be possible to solve the problem.

The following case example involves an assessment that helped the relationship between two organizations who regularly had to work together to provide for the needs of deaf children.

Each time a student at the Roosevelt School for the Deaf needed assistance from the Department of Social Services (DSS), the principal and the school counselor had to argue with the social worker assigned to the case. Next, they would call the supervisor assigned to that social worker and ultimately call the administrator assigned to that division in order to arrange for the services to which the child was entitled. At the same time, the social workers at DSS thought that the school wanted exceptional treatment for their students, that most of the children were retarded, and that the families were demanding and manipulative. They did not see why deafness was such a big deal anyway. Victoria Hart, a social worker at the Department of Social Services, was deeply concerned about the problems the deaf children and their families experienced. First, she learned to sign so that she could communicate more clearly with the deaf children. However, she knew that if the issue were not addressed by both systems (DSS and the school), it would continue to be addressed on an individual basis and unsatisfactorily.

Ms. Hart asked herself the questions that have to be asked in any assessment. She knew that the system to be assessed included DSS, the school, and all the staff of both organizations who were involved in providing services to children who are deaf. Her goal was to increase each staff's understanding of the mission and needs of the other organization and the ways each organization could be most helpful to children who are deaf. She also knew that as a direct-service social worker, she needed the support of those in both organizations who had sufficient authority to make things happen.

Next, with the DSS supervisor and the school administrator in agreement, Ms. Hart organized a series of six brown-bag lunches over a six-month period for staff at DSS and the school. Each meeting had a specific topic and was led by one person from each organization, with Ms. Hart acting as facilitator. In those meetings, the staffs took turns teaching each other about the mission and structure of their organizations and what they needed from the other organization in order to be most helpful to their students/clients and their families. Representatives from the school educated the DSS social workers about deaf culture, and representatives from DSS met with all the school administrators and teachers to find ways they could meet the very real needs of the children and their families. Ms. Hart and a Roosevelt teacher made up a simple before-and-after test to evaluate the knowledge that staff gained from those meetings. Staff members felt that the tests were also useful for them to see what they were learning. All staff who had agreed to come attended at least three of the six meetings, and half attended all the meetings.

Those who attended the last meeting decided that in addition to educating everyone who was willing in both organizations, special liaisons were needed to become more expert and to work between the organizations. The liaison role was attached to specific roles in each organization (a supervisor at DSS and the guidance counselor at Roosevelt), so even if those people left their organizations, the liaison function would be the responsibility of the person who filled that position. The entitlements for children who are deaf would no longer have to be fought for one-by-one but would be protected through organizational intervention for this entire population. Thus, from a line position, Ms. Hart helped the staff from both organizations see the other organization as part of their constituents' system of care. By the last brown-bag session, the group was acting like a problem-solving team. Ms. Hart correctly assessed the problem as being about a population rather than about a series of individuals, and with very little authority, she helped both organizations provide better service to children who are deaf.

GENERALIZED APPROACHES TO ASSESSMENT

Of the many approaches to assessment in social work practice in health and mental health care, some are very general and others are highly specific. Many general approaches to assessment enable social workers to understand clients more broadly, on a deeper level and over time. This kind of vision of the client is also one of the hallmarks of social work. The profession sees clients not as the diabetic, or the day program of severely mentally ill, or the drunks' shelter, but as a person with diabetes, a group of people living with severe mental illness, or a place where those with problems resulting from substance abuse are sheltered. This holistic vision is always part of assessment.

In actuality, social workers are asked to help when existing solutions are not working—clients, programs, organizations, or communities are not working as they or others wish. Those who are individual clients are viewed as too dependent, too antisocial, or they are unable to carry out something that society expects. Most assessment tools function in the same way. Their purpose is to separate the "successful" from those who need help. In keeping with the values of the profession, social workers strive to balance the assessment tools required in their particular setting with the ability to see the strengths in the client system. In the same way, the social worker learns to assess strengths and weaknesses through gathering information about how the client unit has responded in the past and how the person or entity acted in adverse situations or perilous times.

Some assessment approaches are related to specific theories of social work practice. For example, the psychosocial approach stresses the relationship of the individual and the environment (Woods and Hollis 2000); the problem-solving approach assesses capacity for problem solution (Compton and Galaway 1998); the ego-oriented approach primarily assesses ego functioning (Goldstein 1995); and learning theory and the cognitive-behavioral approach assess the client's current behaviors (Gambrill 1999b; Rose 1981; Thyer and Hudson 1987). In such situations, it is also critical that social workers maintain the ability to assess in a general way the client system's ability to survive and prosper.

The Person-in-Environment Model

One current approach to generalized assessment is the person-in-environment (PIE) classification system that focuses on social functioning (Karls and Wandrei 1994a, 1994b). The system fits well with an ecological perspective and provides a useful structure for social work practice in diverse settings. Most social workers working in health and mental health settings must use more specialized assessment tools, but the important contribution of this and other similar approaches is the focus on social functioning. Most funding sources and organization missions relate social work practice to maximizing social functioning of clients and communities. This kind of assessment tool helps social workers to retain that focus. The PIE system also highlights the client system's strengths and coping abilities, locates the solutions to problems within the environment rather than focusing on the deficiencies of the individual, and does not require a particular intervention for a particular problem definition. PIE and its focus on social functioning helps to center and support the social worker.

The PIE schema allows the social worker to describe, classify, and code adults' problems in social functioning. Using the PIE system, the social worker describes the client in relation to four problem areas: social functioning, environmental factors, mental health, and physical health. Social functioning is described in relationship to specific roles and always includes the role with which the problem has been identified, the problems associated with the performance of those roles, severity and duration of the problems, and the client's ability to cope with the problems. Social roles used in the system relate to family, illness, other interpersonal roles, occupational roles, and roles found in special life situations—such as immigration, probation, or parole.

The final two areas for assessment within the PIE schema include gathering information about the client's health and mental health. With the client's permission, information gathering is carried out with all participants, including care providers. Assessment in all these areas (social functioning, environment, mental health, and physical health) helps social workers gather information systematically and provides a target for intervention.

The Strengths Model

A primary orientation for social work education is the strengths model, a very positive approach to social work practice that means seeing the strengths in the individual, in the organization, and in the neighborhood (Saleeby 1997). Strengths-based approaches are important in many health-related fields of practice, including mental health, solution-focused therapy, gerontology, substance abuse, health promotion, community and school work, and public social services. The strengths perspective lists a series of principles that guide practice:

1. Every individual, family, and community has strengths, assets, and resources.
2. While trauma, abuse, illness, and struggle are devastating, they are also opportunities for growth and sources of challenge and opportunity.
3. One cannot know the upper limits of an individual's capacity to grow and change.

4. Value individual, family, and community visions and hope.
5. Every environment is resourceful. (Saleeby 1999)

Elements of this approach include acknowledging pain, stimulating discourse, eliciting narratives of resilience and strength, and acting in context through education, action, advocacy and linkage, and normalizing and capitalizing on strengths. This is a disciplined approach that requires the social worker to think positively, carry hope and be highly resourceful.

The Biopsychosocial Model

The biopsychosocial model was developed in response to growing scientific understanding that biological/organic factors affect the functioning of individuals, their ecosystems, and their communities. In fact, the Council on Social Work Education deems biological understanding to be at least as important for social workers as social and psychological knowledge. Thus conditions as disparate as alcoholism, sickle-cell anemia, Alzheimer's disease, and schizophrenia are now thought to have biological bases. Programs and organizations develop in response to such biologically based entities or to biological symptoms. In some situations, as is the case of the deaf community, a culture develops around symptoms. This kind of culture is another way for a population to define itself and manage its presentation in relation to context. It also provides another definition of "health setting" for social workers.

To be maximally helpful in situations addressing specific illnesses, social workers must have a thorough understanding of the illness (Kerson and Kerson 1985). Understanding must include the natural history of the disease or diseases, their diagnosis, prognosis, extent, and limitations and the technologies used to treat them. Without such understanding, it is impossible to make judgments about people's capacities to carry out roles and tasks. For example, if a social worker were to assess the capacity of a mother with rheumatoid arthritis to care for her infant while the mother was in an acute stage of her disease and the social worker did not understand that many symptoms of the disease can be controlled through altered medication, the social worker might come to the conclusion that the mother could not physically fulfill her role. This could also well be true for a mother in a psychotic depression whose physical abilities to carry out the tasks of mothering might be intact but whose energy and relationship abilities might appear deficient. In both situations, the social worker must have an understanding of the natural history of the illness (what would be the probable course of the illness if the person were not treated), the intermittent nature of the course of the illnesses, and the probable effects of medical intervention.

One cannot assess someone's ability to parent, to work, or to live independently without understanding the impact of illness or disability on those life roles. Fine popular literature, dedicated disease-specific organizations (such as the American Cancer Society, Multiple Sclerosis Society, or Epilepsy Foundation of America), discussion with medical personnel, patient and family self-report, and carefully evaluated Internet sources all deepen understanding.

Assessment of Sexual Functioning

Social workers in health and mental health settings must attend to all the dimensions and ramifications of illness. In addition to the areas already mentioned, assessment of sexual functioning is also critical to a full bio-psychosocial assessment, not only for an ill person but for that person's partner as well. To provide a context for such understanding, social workers have to understand normal sexual development just as they understand other dimensions of development. Sexual functioning (the ability to perform) is different from sexual behavior (how one conducts oneself sexually), but both sexual functioning and sexual behavior have to be understood in relation to gender, sexual orientation, age, race, ethnicity, and social class (Burson 1998; Henry 1996; Icard, Schilling, and El-Bassel 1995; Lamanna 1999; Scheslinger 1996). This is also an area in which social workers have to understand their own functioning and attitudes. Many people may never have broached or discussed this intimate subject matter with anyone before, and the social worker's self-understanding is an important first step toward comfort with this level of intimacy (Rosen 1999). It is very important for social workers to understand the ways sexual functioning affects relationships, especially with sexual partners. Those who are affected most directly and their partners may interpret dysfunction as indifference or a lack of desire. Such pulling away can lead to disengagement when both partners may need the most intimacy and support.

Lister and Shore (1983) identify four spheres of sexual experience to be explored as part of assessment: (1) the biological and reproductive sphere, (2) gender identity and sex role behavior, (3) sexual activity, and (4) the influence of erotic and sensual stimuli. Nearly all people experiencing health crises find their sexual relationships affected at least minimally. When ill, few people retain their customary level of sexual desire or their sense of being desirable. These transient episodes often resolve quickly as health returns, but chronic conditions, long-term medication, and other ongoing symptoms and effects of illness continue to affect sexual performance and may negatively affect primary relationships as well as self-concept. Figure 6.4 is a visual assessment format that aids structured assessment and indicates areas of mutual influence (Gripton and Valentich 1983).

FIGURE 6.4. Sexual disability affects self, identity, and role (adapted from Gripton and Valentich 1983:56).

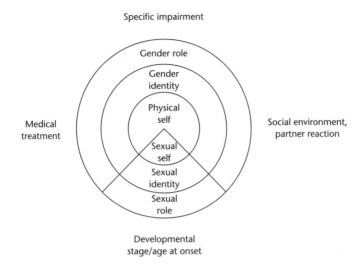

Specific impairment

Gender role

Gender identity

Physical self

Sexual self

Sexual identity

Sexual role

Medical treatment

Social environment, partner reaction

Developmental stage/age at onset

Social workers also have to understand how specific illnesses or conditions can affect sexual functioning at different points in the life span. For example, adolescents with developmental disabilities will have different concerns than will elderly people with varied physical or mental health problems (Schlesinger 1996; Zajicek-Farber 1998). Sexual functioning can be affected by an illness or condition, by the medical interventions (both surgical and pharmaceutical) used to treat the problem, and by psychosocial response to the illness or treatment (Kaplan 1995; Milstein and Slowinski 1999). Among the illnesses that can affect sexual functioning and sexual behavior are clinical depression, alcoholism, diabetes, and cancer (Spampneto and Wadsworth 1996). Diabetes tends to be associated with male impotence and/or difficulty maintaining an erection. There is some belief that maintenance of blood glucose levels may help mitigate this effect (Bechtel 1993). Medications, too, can decrease sexual desire or promote impotence. Many of the beta-blocker medications used for high blood pressure promote impotence. Many of the serotonin reuptake inhibitor–type antidepressants now available suppress sexual desire. One study of women who received chemotherapy for metastatic breast cancer reported that the majority were concerned that cancer would make them unattractive to their mates, were fearful of sex being painful, and had experienced decreased sexual desire since treatment (Makar et al. 1997). All these effects should be understood by social workers. Again, social workers working with specific populations, and those who wish to be population experts, must gather the knowledge required for in-depth understanding of effects on the sexual functioning of that particular population.

The most obvious populations for whom these issues arise are men and women experiencing surgery or other health procedures related to their reproductive tracts. Following hysterectomy and ovariectomy, women often experience a significant decrease in vaginal lubrication and elasticity, in addition to decreased sexual desire (Scialli 1999). Those experiencing hysterectomy may also find orgasm less intense owing to lack of uterine contractions as part of sexual response. Although gynecological surgeons now provide more information to women about these frequent side effects than they used to, being familiar and comfortable with discussing these effects and their impact on primary relationships is an important way social workers can assist women in their adjustment to surgery. In the past, many men who had surgery or radiation to treat prostate cancer lost sexual functioning permanently. New developments in nerve-sparing surgery as well as a range of medical devices have helped to address these devastating sexual problems (Meyer and Nash 1994; Walsh and Worthington 1995). Sensitive discussion of alternative methods of sexual expression opens the topic for discussion and allows the social worker to encourage open communication with the client's sexual partner and health care provider.

This approach suggests that social workers think about adverse effects on sexual performance, psychosexual development, gender identity, and social effects. Thinking positively, social workers should also discuss the areas of sexual functioning that clients continue to find satisfactory and rewarding, as well as those with adverse effects. One goal of this kind of assessment is to help the client understand whatever the physical limitations might be that are caused by an illness or a medical intervention, to explore and evaluate their continuing potential for sexual satisfaction, to mediate relationship difficulties stemming from sexual changes, and to minimize negative impact by supporting the client in his or her assertion of sexual expression (Gripton and Valentich 1983:62). This again underscores the importance of understanding the populations one works with and the customary medical treatments and their effects. Discussions with the medical providers about possible sexual side effects of common treatments are imperative.

In general, it is important for social workers to develop some ease in discussing sexual matters with colleagues and with clients. Becoming familiar with the range of normal sexual functioning, the natural history of sexual functioning for men and women, and the common sexual effects of health treatments on the populations with whom one works is vital.

Assessing these impacts, making appropriate interventions and referrals, and providing information is an important part of social workers' roles in health and mental health care. Social workers must assess the impact of this area of client functioning, use appropriate intervention and referral, and provide applicable information in conjunction with an ill client's health care providers.

SPECIALIZED APPROACHES TO ASSESSMENT

Assessments Specific to Particular Populations and Settings: The *Diagnostic and Statistical Manual of Mental Disorders*

Social workers who practice as parts of teams in highly differentiated services or who work in highly specialized systems are likely to use population- or setting-specific assessment tools. In many such situations, social workers may not make the official assessment but, to some degree, must work from it. For example, in psychiatric institutions, psychiatrists diagnose and then treatment is provided by a range by staff with varied or little professional education. In a geriatric setting, a physician must make the diagnosis of a specific level of dementia in order for people to receive certain services, but the services are provided by staff of varied backgrounds. Because social workers provide the majority of psychotherapy in the United States, and because it plays such an important role in the assessment of patients for all psychiatric and psychological services, social workers should have a deep understanding of the *Diagnostic and Statistical Manual of Mental Disorders* of the American Psychiatric Association (APA).

The fourth and most recent edition of the *Diagnostic and Statistical Manual of Mental Disorders* (DSM-IV) presents a classification system devised and published by the American Psychiatric Association (1994) that describes mental disorders and other conditions that may be a focus of clinical attention. The purpose of the manual is to help mental health practitioners make reliable diagnoses. This latest edition of the manual stresses two fundamental and overarching principles: parsimony and hierarchy. Parsimony suggests that clinicians seek the most economical, efficient, and elegant diagnosis that may account for all the available data. Hierarchy suggests that generally mental disorders exist on a hierarchy of syndromes that tend to decline in severity.

In some ways, DSM-IV has followed trends set out in the earlier versions of the manual, DSM-III (APA 1980) and DSM-IIIR (APA 1987). As did its predecessors, the fourth edition attempts to take an atheoretical approach to classification by describing the manifestations of mental disorders while rarely trying to account for the causes of disorders (Williams 1995). Also like its predecessors, the present edition includes a multiaxial system for evaluation (Williams, Goldman, Gruenberg, Mezzich, and Skodol 1990). This system allows for the evaluation of an individual's social, biological, and psychological functioning. It includes five axes, each of which addresses a different kind of information that is intended to help clinicians plan and predict the outcome of their interventions:

1. Axis I includes clinical disorders and other conditions that may be a focus of clinical attention.
2. Axis II includes personality disorders and mental retardation.
3. Axis III includes general medical conditions.
4. Axis IV includes psychosocial and environmental problems.
5. Axis V includes a rating scale that indicates a person's overall functioning. (APA 1994:25)

Axis IV in particular includes the kind of information that social work has always considered critical in assessment. The Global Assessment of Functioning Scale discussed later in this chapter is a rapid assessment tool that measures the information on this axis.

The authors of the fourth edition have continued the approach established in DSM-III of trying to make the manual useful for people in all cultures that exist in the United States, as well as cultures in other countries (Mezzich, Kleinman, Fabrega, and Parron 1996). Because evidence indicates that cultural factors influence a number of DSM-IV disorders, descriptions of culturally related features were added to descriptions of those disorders. Also, descriptions of "culture-bound syndromes," such as "possession," were added to some categories, and a glossary of culture-bound symptoms and an outline for cultural formulation were added to this edition.

In several ways, DSM-IV improves on earlier editions. One such advancement is the increasing reliability with which a diagnosis can be made by including specified criteria that allow clinicians to agree more easily about the presence or absence of a symptom or condition. For example, in describing the diagnostic criteria for a major depressive episode, DSM-IV states that five or more of the nine symptoms described must have been present for the same two-week period and must represent a change from earlier functioning. This allows for more objective judgment in the assessment process.

Another way DSM-IV represents a change and an update is in its inclusion of relational problems, that is, problems that do not reside in the individual but to which the individual is responding. Examples include parent-child, partner, or sibling relational problems, and relational problems related to a mental disorder or general medical condition. Even the language is meant to be more inclusive of varied practitioners. For example, it does not refer to the individuals who are to be evaluated as patients. The manual cautions that the arrival at a DSM-IV diagnosis is only the first step in a total evaluation that will culminate in the formulation of a plan of treatment.

Although it is widely acknowledged that each edition of DSM has been developed with a great deal of thought by highly educated and experienced psychiatrists, it continues to have many critics. Social workers are sometimes among the most vociferous critics (Kirk and Kutchins 1992; Kutchins and Kirk 1987, 1997). No matter what evidence its detractors present, no social worker can work in or with the mental health system without a deep understanding of the many uses and limitations of the current DSM. It remains the common parlance of mental health and is the basis for reimbursement for many if not most mental health services. Clinical social workers must understand and use the diagnostic criteria and multiaxial system of DSM-IV because the manual's language is the means through which mental health professionals communicate. Without this language, social workers would be isolated from other members of treatment teams and professionals in other organizations and systems (Williams 1995).

Because so many social workers work with the mental health system either as therapists or with clients in other sorts of social services who are receiving services from the mental health system, it is extremely important for social workers to have a reasonable understanding of psychiatric diagnosis. Now, with managed care companies controlling such a large percentage of mental health services and requiring a psychiatric or clinical diagnosis before allowing any treatment, the understanding of psychiatric diagnosis is even more important (Strom 1992). It is equally important to understand that diagnosis may have little relationship with prognosis. Depression or even schizophrenia may be diagnosed in a person who is able to maintain all important life roles, whereas someone else with the same condition may be unable to maintain any kind of work or family role.

Standardized Screening and Assessment Tools for Use with Individuals

The purpose of standardized screening and assessment tools is to predict the need for social work assessment and intervention. Several short-form assessment scales, called rapid-assessment instruments, were developed in the 1970s for use by practitioners in single-subject research designed to improve problem assessment and monitor progress (Hudson 1997; Levitt and Reid 1981). Over the years, social workers have debated the validity and utility of rapid-assessment instruments, but at present several of them are well accepted and commonly used, and many more multidimensional instruments are being developed and validated (Bloom, Fischer, and Orme 1994; Fischer and Corcoran 1994; Hudson and McMurtry 1997; Nurius and Hudson 1993b).

An assessment tool should help the social worker not only to judge but also to plan (Hudson 1997). The many standardized tools available for assessment have two purposes: First, they suggest that such assessments are generalizable and lead to a common understanding between professionals in unrelated fields. Second, they help professionals focus on a dimension that a particular funding source or organization deems important.

Use and interpretation of such tests require knowledge of validity and reliability as well as the ability to understand the results in relation to the culture and context of the client or client group. One helpful resource is the Walmyr Assessment Scales, a package of scales that measure self-esteem, peer relations, several dimensions of family relationships, anxiety and stress, depression, and several other items (Hudson 1992; Nurius and Hudson 1993b). Two other important sources are Miller's *Handbook of Research Design and Social Measurement* (1991) and Corcoran's *Measures for Clinical Practice*, volumes 1 and 2 (2000). Increasingly, such tools will be computerized. Parties will fill out the forms, the test will be instantly scored, and the results will be made instantly available to stakeholders such as social workers, funders, contracting organizations, referral sources, and the courts. The task of social workers and other helping professionals will be to interpret such test results as one part of an assessment. Otherwise, these quick, often unidimensional tests may serve only to pigeonhole, stereotype, or label those who have completed them. This, too, is about social justice and social workers' finding ways to protect and advocate for the most vulnerable populations.

Global Assessment of Functioning Scale

The Global Assessment of Functioning (GAF) Scale considers psychological, social, and occupational functioning on a hypothetical mental health–illness continuum. For example, someone who has superior functioning in a wide range of activities, whose life's problems never seem to get out of hand, who is sought by others because of his or her many positive qualities, and who has no symptoms would receive a score on the GAF of 91 to 100. Someone with moderate symptoms such as flat affect and circumstantial speech, occasional panic attacks, or moderate difficulty in social, occupational, or school functions, such as having no friends or experiencing frequent conflicts with coworkers would receive a score between 51 and 60. Someone whose behavior is considerably influenced by delusions or hallucinations or who has serious impairment in communication or judgment (such as being incoherent, acting grossly inappropriately, or having a suicidal preoccupation), or who is unable to function in almost all areas (staying in bed all day or having no job, home, or friends) would receive a score between 21 and 30 (APA 1994:32). This scale is used frequently by managed care companies and disability insurers to allow a standardized way of assessing client abilities and functioning and to evaluate progress.

The SF-36

The SF-36 (SF stands for social functioning) is a quality-of-life questionnaire constructed to survey health status (Ware and Sherbourne 1992). It measures the patient's social functioning as well as how health problems affect performance and relationships (Berkman et al. 1999). When its thirty-six questions are grouped, they make up eight scales: (1) limitations in physical activity because of health problems, (2) limitations in social activities as a result of physical/emotional problems, (3) limitations in usual role activities resulting from physical health problems, (4) bodily pain, (5) general mental health (ranging from well-being to psychological distress), (6) role activity limitation as a result of emotional problems, (7) vitality (ranging from energy to fatigue), and (8) general health perceptions. The measure takes no more than fifteen minutes to complete; it can be self-administered by anyone over 14 years old or may be administered in person or over the telephone. Scores are converted to a scale of 1 to 100, and higher scores indicate better functioning and well-being. The scale has been tested for validity and reliability (Stewart, Hays, and Ware 1988; Ware, Snow, Kosinski, and Gandek 1993). To the SF-36, Berkman and her group (1999) added twenty-one questions that were related to concerns of social workers in screening elderly patients in primary care. These questions relate to functional status as well as socioeconomic and environmental factors. Social work–specific screening factors include difficulties in (1) doing the laundry, (2) doing light housework, (3) following any dietary restrictions, (4) getting about in the home, (5) getting to appointments, (6) going shopping, (7) managing money/paying bills, (8) preparing food, (9) taking medications, and (10) using the telephone. Other factors include (1) alcohol/drug abuse, (2) appetite, (3) concentration, (4) dizziness, (5) falling, (6) hearing, (7) memory, (8) sex, (9) sleeping, (10) urinary incontinence, and (11) vision. While further study is necessary to demonstrate validity of the SF-36 as a standardized measure for the identification of elderly patients in primary care settings who need social work help, it is clear that this direction is an efficient and effective one for social work screening. It has been validated in the Medical Outcomes Study and the Health Insurance Experiment (Manning, Wells, Duan, Newhouse, and Ware 1986; Safran, Tarlov, and Rogers 1994). A short form of the Health Status Questionnaire called the SF-12 is also available (Kane and Kane 2000:221).

Activities of Daily Living

There are multiple forms of activities-of-daily-living (ADL) scales that assess patients' abilities to care for themselves on a daily basis. Measured activities include bathing, dressing, toileting, transfer/mobility, and feeding. Generally, these activities are graded on a three-point scale ranging from patients' requiring no assistance to some assistance to full assistance. The ADL scales are often used with elderly patients and those who are chronically ill in order to decide what care they need and at what intervals in order to maintain maximum independence (Bowling 2001). Kane and Kane (2000) describe reliability and validity results for several ADL scales and note that most include continence, though this is sometimes seen as a physiological issue, whereas the ability to toilet independently is an ADL issue. The Katz Index of Independence in Activities of Daily Living, the OARS Instrumental ADL, and Performance of Activities of Daily Living can all be found in Kane and Kane (2000), for use with populations who may be limited in their ability to complete ADLs independently.

The Beck Depression Inventory

The Beck Depression Inventory (BDI) is a specially designed self-rated scale that measures depression levels at the time an individual is taking the test but does not diagnose depression or verify its absence. For each of the twenty-one items in the test, four responses are possible. Attitudes and symptoms that are measured are sadness, pessimism/discouragement, sense of failure, dissatisfaction, guilt, expectation of punishment, self-dislike, self-accusation, suicidal ideation, crying, irritability, social withdrawal, indecisiveness, body-image distortion, work retardation, insomnia, fatigability, anorexia, weight loss, somatic preoccupation, and loss of libido. Responses to the questions on the BDI are assigned numerical values of 0 to 3, indicating the severity of the choice, and the total score allows social workers to measure the severity of patients' depression (Bowling 2001). This inventory is copyrighted and generally requires a fee to allow one to obtain the inventory and scoring interpretations.

Mental Status Exams

Of the multiple forms of mental status exams, four can be found in Kane and Kane (2000:76–83). They have the common goal of assessing the individual's awareness of their identity and context. The ten questions that follow make up the Short Portable Mental Status Questionnaire. This is part of the Duke University Multidimensional Functional Assessment, often referred to as OARS-SPMSQ.

1. What is the date today (month/date/year)?
2. What day of the week is it?
3. What is the name of this place?
4. What is your telephone number (or street address, if no phone)?
5. How old are you?
6. When were you born (day/month/year)?
7. Who is the current president of the United States?
8. Who was the president just before him?
9. What was your mother's birth name?
10. Subtract 3 from 20 and keep subtracting the whole way down.

The scoring is as follows: 0 to 2 errors, intact; 3 or 4 errors, mild intellectual impairment; 5 to 7 errors, moderate intellectual impairment; 8 to 10 errors, severe mental impairment. Add 1 to the number of errors if subject had only a grade school education. Subtract 1 from the number of errors if the subject had education beyond high school. Add 1 to the number of errors for blacks regardless of education criteria. One difficulty with the very widespread use of this test is that it may not be a valid predictor of functional difficulty in African American women who score below a certain level (Leveille et al. 1998). Although many may be uncomfortable with the differentiation of scoring based on racial identity, this practice began because it was part of the original rapid-assessment instrument and has been scaled using these scoring techniques.

The Interpersonal Support Evaluation List

The Interpersonal Support Evaluation List (ISEL) allows the person administering the test to assess the amount of social support available to the person completing the test. Four subscales allow assessment of availability of material aid, people to talk with, people to share activities with, and self-esteem. Items on the scale include statements such as "There is at least one person I know whose advice I really trust," and the respondent is to answer with "true" or "probably false." These types of social-support assessment instruments can be quite useful in health and mental health settings as the social worker begins to identify various levels and sections of the client's ecosystem for intervention.

GRAPHIC REPRESENTATIONS
FOR SOCIAL WORK IN HEALTH
AND MENTAL HEALTH CARE

Among the tools for assessment are graphic representations (see figures) or mapping devices that can also be used in determining strategies of intervention, in the work itself, and in evaluation. These mapping devices help social workers envision their work with greater breadth and over time. Many social workers in health and mental health now have new affiliations and organizational identities and are required to work in new ways with other disciplines and social workers in other systems. These mapping devices provide a useful shorthand for understanding and actually help social workers to see greater systemic opportunities for themselves and their clients.

Among the many mapping devices that are useful to social workers are ecomaps, culturagrams, genograms, linkage and network maps, neighborhood assessments, organizational charts, timelines, and strategic programming maps. These heuristic devices are taken from social work, organizational dynamics, business management, and strategic planning (Burkhart and Reuss 1993; McGoldrick and Gerson 1985; Meyer 1993; Mintzberg 1994; Mintzberg and Quinn 1991). Once taught, they are practical and easy to use; they are helpful throughout one's professional life and require only a pencil and a piece of paper. Each device, in its way, helps the social worker develop goals and objectives, make assessments, establish strategies of intervention, follow the course of his or her work as well as the work of others, and evaluate their work and the progress of clients and programs. These devices help the practitioner to (1) follow the social worker in the system, (2) follow the client through and across systems, (3) visualize the networks of services for client systems, (4) provide timelines with clear tasks and responsibilities, (5) engage in strategic programming, and (6) report succinctly to other organizations and other disciplines.

In his book *More Than a Thousand Words,* an excellent resource for a wide range of graphic visualizations, Mattaini (1993:3) reminds the reader that "throughout human history, people have used images for perceiving and communicating complex information holistically." Such is the purpose of all the attempts at succinct visualization that follow. Some are simply outlines that provide an overarching framework, guide thinking, and impede omission of critical categories of data. Others are complex visualizations filled with lines, shapes, and colors. All attempt to reflect the complexity of a case, piece of business, project, program, or organization; to incorporate time and movement; and to avoid a static and frozen quality. In this way, they evoke the multidimensional metaphor of film, of moving pictures with surround sound and rapidly changing images, rather than a photograph, a soundless picture frozen in time.

There are many devices for graphic visualization available to social workers. It is thought that intelligence and clarity in design reflect and enhance intelligence and clarity in thought (Tufte 1997). Their greatest problems are that they are unidimensional and static (Mattaini and Kirk 1991). They have been used by social workers in some form since the beginnings of the profession. An early example, created by Richmond (1901), is included in the preface. Each in its way allows social workers and those whom they are helping to condense a large amount of life information into an absorbable form. It is helpful to remember that these techniques are meant to increase understanding and promote action.

Timelines and Lifelines

Among the graphic visualizations useful to social workers are profiles, timelines, lifelines (table 6.1), life history grids (table 6.2), social support

TABLE 6.1. A Lifeline of Donna Hauck

Date	Events
1964	Got pregnant and married
1967	First psychotic break and hospitalization after birth of youngest child (intervening period stressful but manageable)
1974	Divorce, hospitalization, children placed in foster care
1975	Children returned home
1977	Decompensated because of stress and noncompliance with medication, substance abuse, hospitalization
1980	Multiple hospitalizations
1983	Beginning of good period, children home, own apartment, boyfriend, multiple brief hospitalizations
1990	State hospital
1992	State hospital
1992	State hospital
1992	Lived in community rehabilitative residence, left to live with a boyfriend
1994	State hospital
1995	State hospital
1997	State hospital
1998	State hospital
1999	State hospital

Note: Donna Hauck, who has a serious mental illness, is discussed in a practice example in chapter 4.

TABLE 6.2. Life History Chart for Bob Kelly

Age	Events
22	Obtained work in the state Department of Transportation Photo ID Center
21	Graduated from high school
17	In high school: sang in a quartet, lifted weights, and played wheelchair ball
16	Learned to use public transportation system for the disabled
14	Chose to use wheelchair for better mobility
5	Entered special education school where all therapies were available
4	Walked with a swing-through gait
3	Parents treated for alcoholism and reunited
	Braced so he could learn to walk
1	Parents began to drink heavily and separated
Birth	Registered with state mental health/mental retardation early intervention program
Birth	Born with myeolmeningocele

Note: Bob Kelly has been followed from birth to early adulthood in a spina bifida program (Schmid 1997).

mapping, and social network grids. Profiles simultaneously provide clinical ratings that allow clinicians to examine variables individually and collectively. Timelines, lifelines, and life history grids allow one to visualize significant events across time (Sheafor, Horejsi, and Horejsi 1991). Social support mapping allows the social worker to visualize and map a client's social support. Tangible, social, emotional, and advising support can be depicted through the use of different colored lines connecting with the client (Gaudin 1988). Social network grids use a grid to list the names of all the people who are significant in the client's life. The grid then lists the concrete, emotional, and informational support; how critical each is; the area of the client's life; and the direction, proximity, frequency, and duration of support (Tracy and Whittaker 1990). Lifelines can also be used to illustrate positive and negative events (Quam and Abramson 1991).

Ecomaps

Of all the visual tools used for assessment and strategizing in work with an individual or family client, the ecomap is the most useful because it allows the social worker and client to view almost all interactions with family members, institutions, and agencies, as well as showing the nature of those interactions on a single page. It was first devised by Hartman

(1978:370), who described it as "a simple paper and pencil simulation that has been developed as an assessment, planning, and interventive tool. It maps in a dynamic way the ecological system, the boundaries of which encompass the person or family in the life space."

Patterns and weight of the lines connecting items in the ecomap depict relationships between client systems and important individuals, agencies, and institutions. The use of light or heavy lines demonstrates the intensity of relationships. Circles with no lines attached demonstrate no relationship; arrows signal the direction of relationship; and continuous or broken lines show a smooth or stressed relationship. As the use of ecomaps has become more sophisticated, colors are used to define themes in the work, symbols show different environmental systems, and icons stand for individuals. What the ecomap is missing is a depiction of time, of the history of events, relationships between people, and the client and institutions. One way to address this problem is to develop a series of ecomaps over time that reflect changes in clients' lives. Thus the example of Minnie Oakman that was provided earlier in this chapter has three ecomaps: one that depicts her social network when she was first referred to the social worker, one when all services were put into place to support her home situation, and one that shows her supports as her mental state deteriorated and she moved to a nursing home.

Ecomaps can also portray motion, process, mechanism, and cause and effect. These aspects are especially helpful as ecomaps are used to portray multidimensional lives. Visually telling the story helps clarify relationships and points of difficulty. As with all tools, the participation of the client in the process of drawing and interpreting the ecomap enhances the map and furthers the work.

The following case example uses a genogram and two ecomaps to depict the relationships and interactions of a 15-year-old student who has tested positive for tuberculosis.

Ella Bogarden, age 15, moved from the West Indies to the United States three years ago with her father and six siblings (figure 6.5).Through routine testing at her school-based health program (SBHP), Ella tested positive for tuberculosis. When she did not return to the SBHP for her one-month follow-up visit, the nurse practitioner located her in school and found that she was not taking her medication, appeared to be depressed, and exhibited poor hygiene. The nurse referred her to Janet Edison, the health center social worker, who found her to be depressed and very isolated, with suicidal ideation. Ms. Edison arranged for Ella to have a psychiatric consultation at a teen crisis center. Ella's family was angry at her for discussing "family business" at school, and she withdrew from the SBHP staff. Ms. Edison and the nurse practitioner made a

FIGURE 6.5. Genogram for Ella Bogarden.

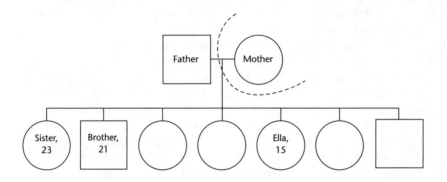

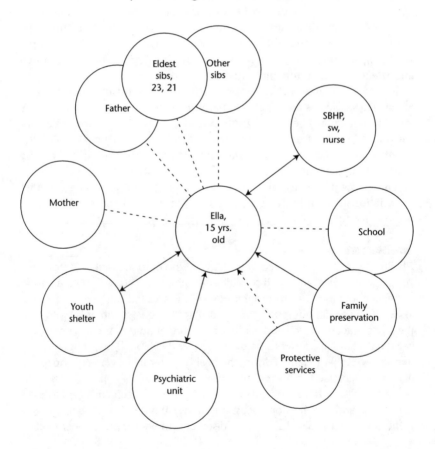

FIGURE 6.6. Ecomap for Ella Bogarden at outset of intervention.

home visit when Ella's mother came for a visit from the West Indies. After their visit, Ella was beaten severely by her older brother. At this point, many additional social supports were put into place for Ella, including a stay at a youth shelter, a psychiatric hospitalization, protective services, and intensive family preservation (figure 6.6).

When the family reached its goals, short-term family preservation terminated. Ella completed her course of preventive treatment for tuberculosis, is doing well in school, and although she is still having difficulty in developing friendships, she is receiving help from the social worker in that regard. She also has continued receiving Prozac from the teen crisis center and attends counseling sessions there. Ella's current ecomap is shown in figure 6.7.

FIGURE 6.7. Ecomap for Ella Bogarden after intervention.

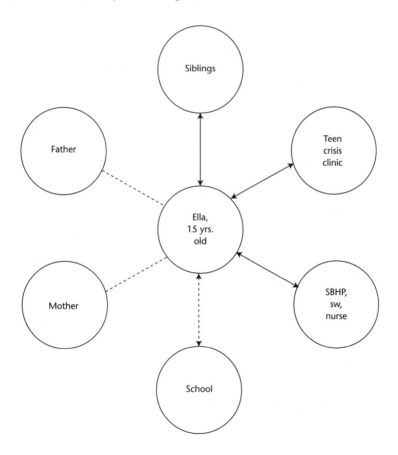

Genograms

Genograms are graphic representations of family relationships. According to McGoldrick and Gerson (1985:1), "A genogram is a format for drawing a family tree that records information about family members and their relationships over at least three generations. Genograms display family information in a way that provides a quick gestalt of complex family patterns and a rich source of hypotheses about how a clinical problem may be connected to the family context and the evaluation of both problem and context over time." Genograms are also useful in tracing patterns of illness or behavior within families.

By inserting brief descriptions beside each family member and using lines that indicate close ties, tension, or distant relationships, clients and social workers can begin to recognize patterns of repeated similarity in types of relationships, substance use, personality types, gender roles, and other patterns. This kind of visual exercise can help clients understand their behaviors and relationships within the context of their family history. So long as the key is clearly labeled and the legend explains the genogram, this tool can be used in any way the social worker deems effective. It is a powerful tool for helping individuals and families sort out responsibilities and determine what one can and cannot be responsible for.

The following two examples show genograms that depict important patterns of illness and relationship that proved to be key in the assessment of and intervention for the client.

Figure 6.8 shows a very simple genogram for Eliot Fox III, a 27-year-old, white, upper-middle-class, well-educated man who was referred to social worker George Jamison through his employee assistance program (EAP) because he was such a cutup that his supervisor was threatening to fire him. It was clear to Mr. Jamison that Eliot Fox was following the family pattern of depressive illness (Akiskal and Cassano 1997). Mr. Fox's consultation with a psychiatrist whose expertise was in the area of depressive illness resulted in a diagnosis of bipolar I disorder (APA 1994:696–97).

The EAP agreed to pay for six visits with the social worker, and during that time Mr. Jamison and Mr. Fox worked on many issues, including that of responsibility. Mr. Fox was not responsible for the depressive illness that was part of his family history, but he was responsible for taking care of himself. Mr. Jamison gave Mr. Fox a list of excellent reading material about bipolar disorder and recommended two different kinds of self-help support groups. For the rest of their time together, Mr. Jamison and Mr. Fox had two objectives: (1) they discussed and clarified the importance of staying on the medication that normalizes mood, moderating highs and lows, and (2) they reviewed and dis-

FIGURE 6.8. Genogram for Eliot Fox III.

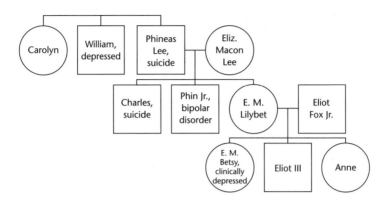

cussed ways to modify the behavior patterns that Mr. Fox had developed over the years to manage his anxiety and depression.

Figure 6.9 shows a genogram for Nan Ray, age 10, in whom acute lymphocytic leukemia has been diagnosed. The key indicates the meaning of each line, circle, and square. Most striking in this representation is the number of losses experienced by Sue, Nan's mother, and Sam, Nan's father. Sue's father has died, she is estranged from one sibling, and she has experienced the deaths of two children and divorce from her husband. Now she has a child with a terrifying illness. Sam's father has also died, and his 80-year-old mother is estranged from her two siblings. Thus regardless of the social worker's role with this child and her parents, she or he must be mindful of these deep cumulative losses.

The Culturagram

The culturagram is a quasi tool that has been developed to look at some of the dimensions of difference that social workers know to be important for understanding others (Asamoah 1996; Congress 1994). By 2015, more than half of the people in the United States will be from other than a West European background. Attempting to classify people through any single category, such as ethnicity or race, becomes more and more outdated. Such discrete categories are unusually rare in this country. For example, the

FIGURE 6.9. Genogram for Nan Ray.

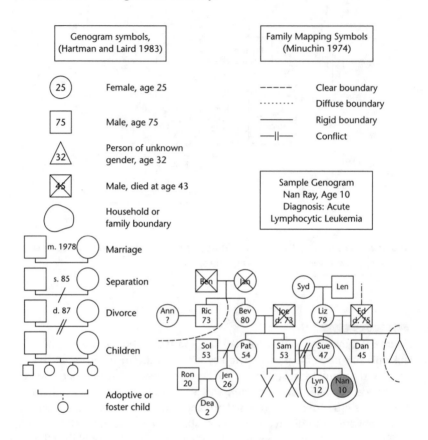

fastest growing racial category in the past two United States censuses was "other" (Spickard, Fong, and Ewalt 1996). Thus the construct of race itself is becoming increasingly fluid. Still, institutions in the United States, including schools, religious organizations, the courts, and facilities for the treatment of mental and physical illness, continue to act as if not only the great majority of those to whom they provide service but the providers themselves are white, middle class, and of Western European descent. Culturally diverse health beliefs such as spiritualism, herbal treatment, acupuncture, and vitamins are often devalued, although many of these alternative approaches are now being tested and some are routinely used in conjunction with traditional medical interventions. For example, it is common for surgeons to suggest that patients apply vitamin E cream to their skin to aid healing.

One way that culturally competent social workers can include assessment of cultural identity and context is by using a culturagram (figure 6.10). This vehicle is not as useful as the ecomap or the genogram, but it serves the purpose of calling attention to cultural difference.

The culturagram is based in an appreciation for cultural pluralism and the value in culturally diverse families pursuing their own styles, customs, values, and language and an appreciation of difference in the process of acculturation (Congress 1994).

Comprehensive and easy to use, the culturagram includes the following:

1. Reasons for immigration. Are there opportunities to return to the home country or is return prohibited?
2. Length of time in the community. Often, but not always, the longer a family has lived in the United States the more acculturated its members become.
3. Legal or undocumented status. Those who are in the United States illegally or without proper documents may worry that they will be deported. These people usually avoid interaction with authorities, including social services and medical assistance.
4. Age at time of immigration. Children acculturate more quickly than adults.
5. Language spoken at home and in the community. Often there is a source of conflict between children who speak English as well as

FIGURE 6.10. Elements of a culturagram.

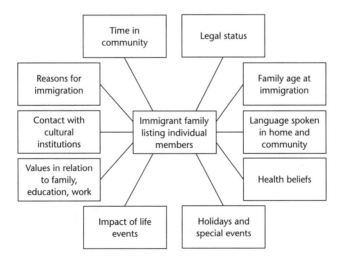

their native language and their parents who insist on speaking their native language at least at home.

6. Contact with cultural institutions. Remaining related to the cultural institutions of one's upbringing can offer positive support and can help maintain cultural identity.

7. Health beliefs. Many health and mental health problems are culturally bound, both in symptomatology and expectations about treatment.

8. Holidays and special events. Often even in the most acculturated families there is great value attached to certain life cycle events and rituals.

9. Impact of crisis events. Understanding the value of certain events and the subsequent impact on roles and family life is critical.

10. Values about family, education, and work. This area encompasses broad cultural beliefs and must be explored fully.

Ella Bogarden's family culturagram is shown in figure 6.11. Again, as with many other mapping devices, the culturagram provides a useful way to visualize important information about the subject's life. The elements in the culturagram are especially useful in working with those who have recently immigrated. However, the culturagram itself does not provide a focus for intervention or a way to prioritize, and it does not allow one to see change over time.

FIGURE 6.11. Culturagram for Ella Bogarden.

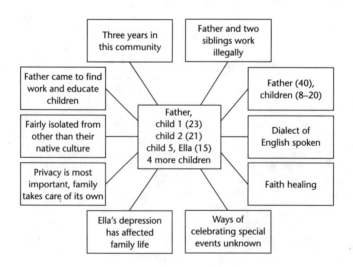

One of the dangers of focusing on blatant cultural differences is that more subtle cultural differences may be overlooked in those who appear to approach life and solve problems in the same ways as the professionals who are taking care of them. As Gary (1999:xi) suggests, "In its attempts to delineate the differences between ethnic groups, this approach to cultural diversity in the human services tends to deemphasize the diversity within ethnic groups and has the effect of promoting stereotypes." Sometimes, as in the following example, a dominant dimension in an individual's culture will bring her to conclusions that have to be understood as part of her "difference."

Felicity Gladstone, a white, upper-middle-class, middle-aged Presbyterian minister, noticed that she was having increasing difficulty swallowing. Her general practitioner referred her to an oncologist, who diagnosed esophageal cancer and referred her to a surgeon, who told her she needed an esophagectomy that should be done as soon as possible before the cancer spread beyond the esophagus. Over the years, spirituality had become increasingly important in Rev. Gladstone's life, and, in addition, many of her closest friends believed strongly in herbal and dietary cures and spurned traditional medicine.

When confronted with the problem of cancer of the esophagus, Rev. Gladstone decided to eschew surgery and opted instead for a wheat grass diet and guided imagery as her treatments of choice. She made an appointment with Linda Kaufman, a social worker who used guided imagery as part of her psychotherapy technique. Ironically, a friend of Ms. Kaufman's who was a physician had been cured of cancer of the esophagus through the surgery that had been recommended to Rev. Gladstone. Ms. Kaufman's friend had told her that this massive operation was the only cure for this kind of cancer, and if the cancer spread through the esophageal wall, it was deadly. Ms. Kaufman honored Rev. Gladstone's cultural differences and agreed to use guided imagery and other psychotherapy techniques to help her manage her illness and its treatment, but at the same time she urged Rev. Gladstone to go through with the surgery as soon as possible. Rev. Gladstone's then decided in favor of the surgery, which was successful, and she and Ms. Kaufman worked together through her recovery. For some, questions will remain about Ms. Kaufman's highly directive advice. Ms Kaufman thinks that she helped Rev. Gladstone save her life while honoring her cultural differences and coping strategies.

All the assessment tools that have been discussed thus far are seen traditionally as tools for what is commonly called direct practice, clinical social work, or even micropractice, but they have some utility for social workers on every practice level. Grouped in useful ways, they can help social workers in health and mental health to generalize from the individual to the population. In that way, they can help with program planning and organizational issues just as they can help with individual interventions.

These tools have great utility for every practice level. Likewise, tools that traditionally have been confined to indirect practice, program planning, or macropractice can be useful to those working in direct practice. In the following case example, the social worker used genograms and ecomaps to demonstrate patterns of abuse not only in families but in the suburban community being served by the hospital in which she worked.

Part of social worker Judith Ramsey's assignment in a suburban hospital was the emergency room. One of the situations in which she received referrals was in instances when women appeared to have suffered beatings. Generally, the women would not file charges against the men who had beaten them. Often, they would not give Ms. Ramsey the name of the perpetrator. Some of the women came to the emergency room more than once. If the beating resulted in a hospital admission, it was usually the woman's husband or significant other who took her home on discharge. When time allowed, Ms. Ramsey sat with the women and asked whether together they could create a genogram and an ecomap. If the woman was willing to complete the genogram, it was invariably filled with generations of some kind of abuse. Ecomaps showed increasing isolation and other problems on the part of the battered woman. Ms. Ramsey always referred these women for counseling, provided the phone number of a shelter, and gave them her card, but no one ever followed up.

Because this hospital is located in an affluent area, the administrators and chief physicians (almost all of whom are male) refused to believe that there was a problem of wife abuse in the area. Over a period of a few months, Ms. Ramsey and women who came to the emergency room because of severe beatings created eighteen genograms that depicted the abuse. All the names and other forms of identification on the genograms and ecomaps were disguised to protect all parties. If names had not been disguised, it is likely that, in this community hospital, employees would recognize the names of neighbors and colleagues on the graphic visualizations. Also, Ms. Ramsey realized that one of the emergency room nurses had made many of the referrals to her, and she thought about the fact that the chief of obstetrics and gynecology was concerned about battering.

Ms. Ramsey wanted the hospital to provide more help to this population. First, she wanted a social worker from the shelter to talk to all the emergency room staff about battered women, especially about how to recognize signs of battering and what the shelter and other similar services could offer battered women. Second, she wanted the hospital to allow trained volunteers, including some women who had been battered themselves, to come in to talk with a battered woman before she was discharged from the emergency room. She enlisted the interested nurse and physician, and together they convinced the chiefs of medicine and surgery and the chief executive of the hospital to allow the training, but not the volunteer effort. All three interested staff are sure that as the emergency room staff is sensitized to battering, the number of referrals that Ms. Ramsey receives will increase, allowing for data in the form of genograms and ecomaps that will convince the administrators that they have to find ways to better serve battered women.

Tools for Program, Organization, and Community Assessment

As is true in any kind of assessment, the purpose of assessing programs, organizations, and communities is to define need and capacity and then to devise interventions that match both. Programs nest inside organizations, and organizations are located in several ways within communities. Because the fit between programs and organizations as well as among programs, organizations, and communities is often crucial to the success of each, fit is an important concept for any discussion of assessment. The nature of program and organizational development is also circular. Thus an evaluation of one program or organization may provide the information needed to develop new programs, interventions, or even new organizations. Effective methods of assessment should yield not only clear directions for intervention but also the material (objective measures) needed to evaluate a program or intervention.

Program Assessment

Social programs are organized efforts designed to provide necessary services such as psychosocial intervention, education, medical treatment, job training, safe streets, welfare assistance, and recreation. According to Posavac and Carey (1996:2),

> [Program assessment] is a collection of methods, skills and sensitivities necessary to determine whether a human service is needed and likely to be used, whether the service is sufficiently intensive to meet the unmet needs identified, whether the service is offered as planned, and whether the service actually does help people in need at a reasonable cost without unacceptable side effects.

239

Seven areas ought to be considered in assessing the necessity for a program: (1) problem definition, (2) verification of existing services, (3) examination of results, (4) determination of which services or programs produce the best outcomes, (5) selection of programs that offer the most-needed services, (6) evaluation of program successes and failures, and (7) consideration of program side effects, if any.

During the problem-definition stage of program assessment, the task is to ensure that the program is being developed to meet unmet needs and that there is a fit between the way the problem is defined and the way the program will be developed. Another important element here is determining whether the necessary resources are available to meet the programmatic needs of the population toward whom the program is targeted. For instance, a program intended to reduce teen pregnancy by making sure that all participants were celibate and chaste. However, the teens came to the program eager to learn about and receive methods of contraception. Thus there was a poor fit between the program and the teens' needs. The resources the teens were looking for were not available.

A second area for assessment is verification of the services and programs that already exist. This is a two-step process in which information about similar existing programs is collected, and then each program is contacted to validate service delivery. There are many examples of programs that exist only on paper, but this step in the assessment process means that social workers must verify whether similar programs are active.

A third area for assessment is the examination of results. Once a program is implemented, data (results) should be monitored in an ongoing manner to ascertain whether program goals are being attained. Part of program development entails the identification of outcome goals. These goals then become the measure for assessment prior to interventions designed to modify the program. They also measure outcomes to ensure that the program is functioning adequately. There are several examples of this area and those that follow in chapters 7 and 8.

The fourth area of assessment is about determining which services and programs produce the most desirable outcomes. Comparison with similar programs or comparison of results over time can help the worker identify the strategies that promote the best results. Comparing results before and after the modification of a program can also provide information about what service provision is most effective. This assessment then guides intervention to modify the program in ways that promote the desired outcomes.

The fifth area for assessment is the selection of programs that offer the most-needed services. This means establishing priorities for which programs are most needed. This task requires that information be gathered about and from the community so that limited program resources can be targeted most effectively.

A sixth area of assessment involves ongoing monitoring of a program's successes and failures. This is done to maintain and improve the quality of the program. This task shows the ongoing circular nature of assessment-intervention/modification-evaluation-modification. There is a continuous goal of improving program effectiveness. This area of assessment is addressed more fully in chapter 9.

The final area for consideration in program assessment is that of determining whether the program has had any unplanned side effects. Just as clinical social work can incur side effects in the form of altered social relationships for the client, program participation may bring about unplanned side effects as well. These side effects must be assessed in order to minimize those that are negative and to modify the program to leverage any positive side effects. For example, program participation may bring about stigmatization of the clientele by the community, depending on the program. More attention to confidentiality/privacy boundaries, changing the visibility of the program, and universalizing the program are ways to diminish the negative unplanned effect of stigma. Also, good marketing of a program can attract new participants who may not benefit from present programming but for whom new programs could be developed. For example, a family agency developed a day service for those with Alzheimer's disease who live in the community. The early-morning staff noted that several family members chatted in the hall after dropping off their ill relatives. In response, the social worker developed an early-morning support group for relatives that meets once a week from 7:30 to 8:30 A.M. so that relatives can go from the group directly to their workplaces. The open and semistructured group sometimes has speakers but generally talks about the day-to-day difficulties of living with someone who has Alzheimer's disease. Partly as a result of the social worker's delightful sense of humor, the group even manages to share some good laughs about their loved ones and their lives.

Organizational Assessment and Mapping

The purpose of an organizational map is to provide social workers with critical information about the agency in which they work and the agency's relationships with other organizations. The map helps social workers to systematically gather information about the organization as well as its boundaries and context. Effective use of this tool leads to a basic understanding of the organization, while also clarifying some questions about which the social worker may need greater explication. One very helpful version of an organizational map is the organigraph, a description and examples of which can be found in chapters 4 and 7.

Figure 6.12 is an example of an organizational map demonstrating how a perinatal AIDS unit relates to other services within its health system, as well as to services outside its system on which its patients depend (Walther, Mason, and Preisinger 1997:83). For its particular patient group, the prenatal AIDS clinic is the hub for services needed to deliver a baby who is as healthy as possible. Thus the map shows the clinic's relationship to four other areas of the hospital that are critical to its patients: (1) the clinical trials group enrolls clinic patients in drug trials that may be helpful to pregnant women with AIDS and their babies; (2) the drug treatment program helps pregnant women manage addictions to drugs and alcohol; (3) the adult infectious disease clinic is the site for treatment of all infectious diseases, including AIDS; and (4) the pediatric HIV clinic cares for children born with HIV infections. Beyond the circle of hospital-based services, the map depicts community services that its patients use, such as day care services, disability payments, home care, legal services, drug-free programs, support groups, services to secure housing, and visiting nurse services. Thus this simple diagram shows the range of services available and their relationship to the hospital.

FIGURE 6.12. Organizational map of a community-based perinatal clinic.

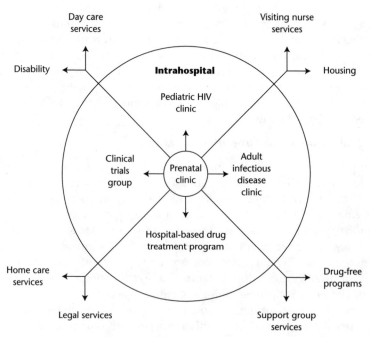

Hasenfeld (1982:235) says that human service organizations

> work directly with and on people whose attributes they attempt to shape. People are, in a sense, their "raw material" and human service organizations are mandated—and thus justify their existence—to protect and to promote the welfare of the people they serve. Therefore, they must conform to the implicit and explicit expectations of society that services are provided to their constituents in a way that also promotes the overall welfare of the public.

Social work practice is embedded in an organizational context, and most social work occurs within human service organizations. Brager and Holloway (1978:2) define human service organizations as "the vast array of formal organizations that have as their stated purpose enhancement of the social, emotional, physical, and/or intellectual well-being of some component of the population." The characteristics of the organization (mandate and domain, interorganizational relations, service technology, and structure of work) determine to a significant extent how social workers discharge their professional responsibilities. These characteristics structure and define the content of their relations and transactions with client systems. Thus organizational mandate and domain define the kinds of people and problems that social workers will meet and the kinds of clients with whom they will work; interorganizational relations affect the amount and kinds of resources to which social workers have access for their work; and available knowledge and technology defines the techniques and procedures available to social workers. Most important, to a great degree, the amount of professional discretion available to social workers is determined by the organizations in which they work (Hasenfeld 1992).

Organizational domain—what organizations do and whom they serve—is the means by which organizations establish their role within their environment. Recognition of the organization does not come easily or immediately, and generally a disparity exists between what an organization says are its boundaries (the claimed domain) and what these boundaries actually are (the de facto domain). Ultimately a mission that is shared and valued by the organization and the community is integral to the success of an organization. In any case, full assessment of the organizational structure allows social workers to intervene with organizations to enable them to meet their goals and the needs of the community.

Hasenfeld (1992:15–26) offers a system for mapping the critical elements of the agency; such mapping provides an initial understanding of the structure and operations of the agency. Although Hasenfeld calls this tool a map, it works more like a list, lacking the quality of visualization that is so helpful in some other tools. Even so, it provides elements that are necessary for understanding one's organization.

Hasenfeld (1992) begins his discussion by suggesting that social workers understand the agency and its interorganizational relationships. The organization's domain is the claim the organization stakes out for itself, the areas in which the organization will function, the range of problems it purports to address, services offered, the population eligible for services, the conditions that must be met for the population to receive services, and the population's qualifications. Organizational goals are the ends and outcomes the organization wants to achieve. Social workers must know and understand the mission statement and the agency's priorities, as well as the match of the program and agency objectives and the definition of problems or tasks that require a prompt solution.

The agency environment includes the composition and mobility of its population, its economic base, its tax policy and situation, and its relations with governmental, welfare, business, and industrial structures and housing and medical facilities. Hasenfeld stresses that social workers must understand their agency or institution's organizational set (its important and unimportant relationships with other organizations) as well as the groups and organizations with which it would like to develop a relationship and why it would like to do so. Hasenfeld notes that it is critical that an agency understand the problems it has encountered in developing linkages with other groups. Additionally, one must understand the nature of the communication between the agency and its organizational set, particularly the methods for receiving and processing information from the organizational set and the general environment, formal and informal channels of communication, the quality of information exchanged, and barriers to and gaps in communication.

Four propositions embody the dynamics of both resource dependency and domain setting:

1. An organization's survival is a function of its ability to learn and adapt to changing environmental contingencies.
2. The degree of an organization's dependence on some element of its task environment is directly related to the organization's need for resources that that element can provide and is inversely related to the ability of other elements to provide the same resource.
3. Organizations that are perceived as threatening to an existing organizational configuration will evoke defensive reactions by established local organizations.
4. The persistence (or survival) of an organization over time is directly related to the degree of formalization it attains in exchange agreements with other organizations constituting its task environment. (Wardell 1988:92–93)

Social workers should understand the planning, coordinating, and governing bodies that exist between the agency and its organizational set, the nature of representation to such bodies, resources, areas of conflict, power positions, and principal sources of legitimation. This kind of organizational knowledge is important whether one is working with individual clients, planning programs, analyzing policy, or doing community outreach.

Understanding market relationships is very important. All professionals working in or with health or mental health organizations must understand that their organizations are selling services and that to survive and prosper organizations must understand their markets. Organizations must know who uses their services and who might use their services but does not, a group that Drucker (1994) refers to as noncustomers. For example, a home care agency realized that its community did not understand that one could receive services at home without having been discharged from a hospital. Another agency that had always defined its mission as helping people with mental health problems realized that, if it redefined its mission slightly and found new ways of explaining its services, it could offer services to a range of people and their relatives who were trying to manage chronic conditions such as diabetes and stroke.

In the same way, it is important to understand complementary and competing services. Complementary services are those provided by external units that assist the agency in achieving its tasks with the clients, or that are given concomitantly with those of the agency, or that are given to clients upon referral by the agency. For each complementary service, social workers should understand the nature of the service provided, the kinds of clients being served, and the frequency with which these services are provided. Competing services also should be understood. Finally, social workers should understand regulatory groups such as the organizations, legislative or legal bodies, associations, and boards to which the social workers' organizations must be accountable and from which the organizations must receive formal and informal approval for domain and the legitimacy of activities (Hasenfeld 1992).

In terms of organizational analysis, Hasenfeld (1992) urges social workers to explore the formal and informal structures, technologies, and processes of their organizations. The kinds and uses of technology for measuring performance and control, its linkages to other components of the organization, and the methods for evaluating output are crucial. In this regard, Hudson (1997) believes that information-processing needs should be addressed from the level of the line worker up through the bureaucracy. In that way, computers will help practitioners with their work, and that work will produce the information the managers need to be accountable and to continue studying problems, interventions, and outcomes. Hudson (1997:74) suggests five steps:

1. Use psychometrically sound client self-report measurement tools.
2. Do not rely on practitioner-completed improvement rating scales.
3. Create social worker/client responsive computer systems.
4. Use computer measurement to practice, not only to evaluate.
5. Have evaluation of practice effectiveness be a background activity performed by the computer.

One way of measuring performance and control that is being used with increasing frequency is to look at the costs of a service per client or per program. Services and programs are assessed (prospectively) and evaluated (retrospectively) by cost. That is, payers want to pay providers the least amount of money possible in order to provide adequate services. At this point, while the social work literature contains very little information about social work's ability to cost its services, the issue is becoming more important to the profession and to social work's constituencies. Available literature, generally not comparative, demonstrates how to construct a budget but not how to cost out a service to a client, that is, to account for all the costs involved in provided services. For example, one study that examined mental health service utilization reported that the total expenditure per patient during the three-year period after discharge from a state mental hospital was $60,000, as opposed to $130,000 when patients remained institutionalized (Rothbard, Kuno, Schinnar, Hadley, and Turk 1999). Another study comparing costs of high-cost consumers of public mental health services with all such consumers reports that there is a need in the service system for using high-cost case management review techniques to control service utilization and lower costs for child and adolescent consumers of public mental health services (Schmidt-Posner and Jerrell 1998). Another study, which looked at consumers' willingness to pay for mental health services, learned that what consumers were willing to pay was too low to cover the cost of providing those services (Ogden and Ogden 1992). Another found that failure to detect and treat depression and anxiety disorders in older people may have major economic consequences (Livingston, Manela, and Katona 1996). It behooves social workers in health and mental health care to move in the direction of costing services. Although it is hard to account for level of complexity in working with different kinds of clients/patients/consumers, inadequate resources and services, insurance problems, and experience and skill levels of individual social workers, these difficulties are surmountable. Increasingly those who pay the bills will require that services be costed.

Also, it is important for social workers to understand decision-making processes, the roles and positions of key participants, the relative influence and power of each participant, the relationships formed (especially in terms of locations), bargaining and competition, the degree of participation of groups and clients, organizational constraints, methods developed to implement decisions, and the ways that decisions affect services. Control functions should be studied to understand the formal and informal processes for coordinating the work of staff members, departments, and clients. It is critical that social workers understand the management of conflict in terms of internal and external conflict, conflict resolution strategies and tactics, and functional and dysfunctional conflict. Communication must be understood in terms of systems for transmitting information within and outside the organization and ways information is evaluated. A good example here is that of social worker Judith Ramsey, who was introduced earlier in this chapter. Her awareness of power sources in the hospital (the chief of obstetrics and gynecology), her knowledge of outside resources (the women's shelter), and her knowledge of who makes decisions (the chief executive officer and the chiefs of medicine and surgery) supported her efforts to change organizational behavior.

Client profiles must be understood as well. If the clients are individuals or families, then age, sex, race, socioeconomic status, place of residence, and most frequent presenting problems should be understood. If the clients are organizations or associations, the social worker should understand the goals and functions of each; the services provided; the characteristics of constituent populations; and financial, personnel, and other resources. Social workers should also know the extent of the problem the agency addresses, the proportion carried by their agency, admission criteria, establishment of the criteria, the degree and kind of internal control, and the degree of client control by which types of clients. Procedures for initial client processing, the routes clients can take in an agency, the extent to which the agency depends on clients for financial support, agency freedom to accept or reject clients, and client representation in the agency should all be understood.

The position and image of the social work profession in relation to the client population and the organization should be assessed as well. Social workers must be able to assess the place of the profession within the organization that employs them as well as their individual relationship to the organization. Although this may sound frivolous when measured against the urgent needs and problems of client systems, it is ultimately very important in being able to act as an advocate for clients within a specific organization. The more respect and power the profession has within the organization, the more likely it is that the organization will respond to the ways the social worker assesses client needs and prescribes solutions.

An abbreviated framework for organizational assessment has been adapted from Hasenfeld (1992):

1. Identify the agency's task environment, assess its relationships with the community and its revenue sources, and identify its client population and referral sources
2. Analyze the organization by identifying corporate authority and mission and by understanding administration, management, and leadership style. Questions to be answered: (a) How are goals established? (b) What is the climate for supporting the achievement of goals? (d) Where are program-level decisions made? (e) How does information flow throughout the organization? (f) Who has involvement in providing feedback about performance?

An alternative approach to analysis is a systematic examination of a number of elements. Within each element, one assesses optimal levels of functioning. In that way, one understands the underlying cause as precisely as possible in the interest of solving long-term problems. The elements to be included are (1) organizational mission, (2) structure, including location, management, staffing, and workload of programs and services, (3) goals and objectives of the program's adequacy of funding, (4) personnel policies and practices, (5) management style, and (6) problem-solving and communication patterns (Hasenfeld 1992:257).

Assessing a Neighborhood

Understanding the neighborhood in which the agency or institution is located, as well as the one from which constituents or client groups are drawn, is critical for assessment regardless of the purpose of the social service organization. Asking the question Why do people live where they live? requires one to understand by exploring, describing, and defining the neighborhood. Thinking about the choice that clients or consumers have to leave the neighborhood if they wish, the degree of safety they perceive in the neighborhood, and whether the neighborhood meets the needs of its residents are other important questions. In the following case examples, understanding the fit between the neighborhood where an agency or institution is located and its clientele provides insights into clients' use of, and response to, services and even into clients' sense of self.

A geriatric case manager was assigned three Caucasian sisters whose ages ranged from 87 to 93. All widowed and without children nearby, they had lived together for many years. Each had different forms of chronic illness, and all three were quite frail, but they were cognitively unimpaired. The area where they had lived for so many years was now almost entirely populated by Latino/ Latina and Asian immigrants. They complained that they did not recognize the fruits and vegetables in the grocery store and that their old church no longer held services in English. Because they remained sprightly and adventurous for their ages, the geriatric case manager was able to help them become acclimated to the neighborhood. If they had been less able, they would have remained isolated and their fears would have increased.

A very old family agency with religious auspices has an AIDS/HIV counseling program. The agency has remained in the same neighborhood since its founding in the 1980s. During that time, the neighborhood has gone from wealthy to working poor, to almost abandoned, back to poor, and then it was gentrified to wealthy with a working-class periphery. Clients for this particular program travel from miles away and very different neighborhoods to receive services. One client told a social worker from the counseling program how the program's location affected him: "It is like a constant reminder of not only lost opportunities, but opportunities I never had." Another said, "I feel so bad when I leave the agency, just waiting for a taxi out front, and having people stare at me, I just do not feel like I belong." As a result, the agency is establishing a satellite office for the HIV/AIDS program in an affiliated church in a neighborhood near the homes of many of its clientele. It does not sacrifice its religious affiliation but brings its programming to a more comfortable place for its clients.

The second example involves multilevel work. Though the initial work is with individual clients, the social worker also assessed the neighborhood and organization. Further, the worker assessed the neighborhood to which the satellite was moved and worked to assist the agency in being responsive to its clientele. Knowledge of service availability and accessibility in particular neighborhoods can help the social worker decide when a client can be held accountable for not accomplishing tasks or projects. If the social worker knows that the client could not get to a specific service because of transportation difficulties or because the client worked during the hours the service was available, the social worker is less likely to define the client as unmotivated or uncaring. Also, if assessment is to be related to strategies of intervention, being familiar with neighborhoods can mean having a great deal of information about access, transportation, support services, and the like.

Neighborhood types can be understood in terms of social class, race, ethnicity, and patterns of identification with geographic boundaries and sociopsychological boundaries (Fellin 1995). Attention must be paid to the evidence of segregation, integration, and the changes in both over time. For example, many ethnic neighborhoods are seen by their residents as spatial as well as sociopsychological communities with strong familial and organizational ties. Sometimes, in racially or ethnically segregated neighborhoods, specialized institutions and services develop, and familial and organizational ties provide populations with essential social and cultural resources to cope with the problems of urban society. In some cities the segregated areas take on the characteristics of self-contained communities (Fellin 1995).

Warren and Warren (1977, 1984) have constructed a framework called "How to Diagnose a Neighborhood" in which they attempt to capture the distinctive helping networks in neighborhoods. Their purpose is to contribute a first step in planning outreach programs and organizing for citizen action. The result demonstrates how different populations solve problems. Thus those who plan services will be able to match the services with the unique culture, coping patterns and helping networks of a neighborhood.

Warren and Warren (1984:34) define a neighborhood as "an elementary-school district for several reasons, among which are that it is a compromise unit with an institutional focus, and that it provides a manageable area for observation within a limited time span." But they add that one must understand how residents define their neighborhood. It is probably true that people define their neighborhood in their own terms; that is, the elderly might not even mention the elementary school, church-going Catholics might define the neighborhood as the parish to which they belong, and those who live in rural areas might refer to the area served by their local post office as defining the neighborhood.

Warren and Warren's (1984) first advice regarding assessing a neighborhood is to get a feel for the location by looking around; use maps to outline neighborhoods; use the phone book to locate resources and informants; and use the library, local newspapers, and the chamber of commerce to identify and locate community organizations and contact people. The next step Warren and Warren suggest is to begin to tap into the neighborhood networks. Social workers should familiarize themselves with the area by driving and walking around to understand housing types and patterns and the level of activity in the neighborhood. Observation is to be combined with chatting with people who are outside. Warren and Warren's is a highly clinical approach, but their overall direction is very helpful for "getting a handle on" the neighborhood. The social worker should get a feel for the location, tap into the networks, and generally make use of what is there, taking note of houses for sale, the condition of the property, the availability and quality of stores, parks (Who frequents them? What facilities are available? What kinds of people are there, and how many?), the level of activity in the neighborhood, and people's reactions to each other and to the social worker. Also note the range of heterogeneity (Whom do you see? Whom don't you see?).

After social workers have completed observations and found people to talk to in the neighborhood, it is useful to compare notes with others who are in positions similar to one's own. Very often, people notice only what they have been taught to notice and ignore what they were taught not to see at their mother's knee. Children are taught to ignore dimensions of behavior their mothers view as impolite, dirty, or discourteous, and many times those dimensions are exactly the information social workers have to absorb. Even with a checklist, people rarely observe the same aspects of life. Comparing notes can only enhance one's observational powers.

Assessing a Community

"A community is a group of people who are socially interdependent, who participate together in discussion and decision making, and who shape certain practices that both define the community and are nurtured by it. Such a community is not quickly formed. It almost always has a history and so is a community of memory, defined in part by its past and its memory of its past" (Bellah et al. 1985:333). Community assessment is vital to social work practice on all levels of service. Work on the community level is often referred to as macro–social work or community organizing. It is generally done by invitation of the greater community, though this does not mean that all individuals and agencies within the community share the same goals. Especially if advocacy is involved, work with individuals, families, and programs also requires a deep understanding of communities. Part of the work of assessment is to determine what the community boundaries are, what its goals are, and who the "players" are. These players may be for or against the stated goals, but they must be incorporated into the work if the work toward the goals is to succeed.

Marti-Costa and Serrano-Garcia (1995) argue that any community needs assessment should be done only as a part of community development. Even when the assessment is a research effort, community residents should control interventions, and in that way researchers will be more responsive to their subjects. Thus their model of needs assessment has four phases:

1. Becoming familiar with the community involves a review of all written and statistical material regarding the community and several visits to

the community to gather the community's history, structures, and the processes by which one enters the community.

2. A core group is formed that is composed of both key community persons and intervenors. The creation of the core group has positive psychological and operative repercussions as this group directs and coordinates the needs assessment. The core group will have planning, coordination, and evaluation responsibilities throughout the process of intervention.

3. Task groups are formed that will engage in activities suggested by the needs assessment. Tasks will include the establishment of short- and long-term goals and the creation of an organizational structure. A general community meeting may be used for the purpose of forming the task groups, each of which will be related to needs assessment priorities. In addition, workshops and other social, cultural, educational, and recreational activities will be fostered that will have as their focus the development of skills to help community groups deal effectively with outside forces that rally against their efforts. These activities may focus on the development of leadership skills, skills needed to deal with service agencies, interpersonal communication skills, marketing skills, and organizational skills.

4. The fourth phase of community needs assessment is initiated after some short- and long-term goals have been met. This phase should involve the development of new goals to help bring together other community groups. Thus the phases begin again with more and larger groups that work in a circular fashion to enlarge the group and to broaden community development and support.

Netting, Kettner, and McMurtry (1998) provide another excellent framework for understanding problems and target populations as well as assessing community strengths and problems. Social workers become involved in macropractice through a specific problem, population, or arena. Each problem and population has specific related tasks. Guidelines for understanding a problem are composed of five tasks:

1. Problem identification involves devising a statement that identifies a target population, a geographical boundary, and the difficulty facing the population. For example, drug and alcohol problems have increased among the students at Lincoln High School to the point that truancy rates are up, students are afraid, and teachers say it is impossible to control student behavior in their classrooms.

2. Review the literature on the condition, problem, or opportunity. The challenge is to quickly develop expertise on the condition, problem, or opportunity. One must decide on the key literature and frameworks needed to understand the condition, problem, or opportunity.

3. Collect supporting data to describe the condition, problem, or opportunity, and to display the data in ways that will effectively and effi-

ciently make the case for change. "In collecting supporting data, the change agent should think in terms of the entire 'circle' of understanding, the community or organizational condition" (Netting et al. 1998:77). One needs information regarding local areas, but to bolster one's argument, it is also helpful to have information on the same conditions or problems at the county, state, or national levels.

4. The fourth task is to identify relevant historical incidents, such as when the problem was first recognized, the critical incidents that brought the problem to this point, and what was learned from earlier attempts to address the problem.

5. The fifth task is to identify barriers to problem resolution. After social workers understand the problem, the next step is to refine the problem statement, including speculating about the etiology of the problem. Understanding means gathering information about a narrowly focused problem within an allotted amount of time in order to make well-informed decisions.

The next problem is to understand the population, which involves reviewing the literature, including theoretical, ethnic, and gender perspectives. Another task is to explore past experiences with the target population and problem. This requires understanding this population's past experiences in dealing with the problem and the ways they perceive the current situation. Everyone involved in any change effort must understand the perspectives of everyone else who is involved and must want to reach a consensus.

Communities evolve constantly. Changes affect power distribution, economic structures, funding sources, and the roles that people play. Netting and colleagues (1998) provide the following example of developing a program for battered women of color.

Social worker Meg Browning was brought to the community to develop a program for battered women. The community had grown rapidly and was experiencing a higher incidence of domestic violence compared with other communities of similar size. Ms. Browning's first task was to encounter the community. She began by talking to police officers, social workers, medical personnel, and others with expertise in the area, and through them she located a few women who were willing to talk confidentially. Isolation was a big problem, but the community had many strengths. People were willing to acknowledge the problem and wanted to do something about it. The community sustained a rich mix of customs, traditions, and values. Several women's groups wanted to help, and a foundation was ready to fund a well-designed project.

Ms. Browning's next task was to begin to narrow the focus. While collecting data and defining boundaries, she noted that the problem of domestic abuse was presently addressed in several spots in the community. For example, three existing shelters for battered women served a segment of the community, and a counseling service was available, but only to people who could pay for it. The women who were not served were primarily Latina. Within the Latino/ Latina community, people sheltered each other, bearing a great financial burden. In her research of existing models of service provision, Ms. Browning found few models that focused on women of color. As a result, she began to speak to Latina women about how one could design a program that was sensitive and relevant, and in this way she encountered additional community strengths. Ms. Browning was able to identify a strong sense of community through informal associations. Also, two Latino/Latina churches had already selected domestic violence as their focus for the coming year and were willing to work with the social worker, and one of the churches already had a support group for women that had been in place for over a year.

Ms. Browning's next task was to mobilize the resources she had located. When she tried to find out who had the power in the local community, she had difficulty locating community leaders among people of color because they were not visible in the larger community. Her agency administrators and board were not sure they wanted to focus on Latinas, and the present shelters were not sure they wanted to call attention to the fact that they had not met the needs of people of color. The foundation wanted something innovative, with self-sufficiency promised in three years. Finally, the ongoing support group was concerned that they would lose their focus, closeness, and intimacy. Ms. Browning persevered and continued to collect information and ascertain feasibility. She also continued to include the perspectives of her battered women informants.

This continuing process illustrates the kind of circular process involved in all levels of planning, assessment, intervention, and evaluation. As information is collected, it allows the social worker to identify further areas, requiring collection of more information on which to base a sound and accurate assessment. Above all, this kind of social work activity requires vision, great determination, and an indefatigable willingness to advocate for clients against the odds.

WHEN CLIENT/COMMUNITY AND SOCIAL WORK ASSESSMENTS DO NOT MESH

Sometimes the clients' or communities' definition of the problem is not what social workers observe. At other times referrers define problems in ways that differ from the views of clients or communities. This issue should be raised with great care, because clients or communities ultimately should define the problems to be addressed. Sometimes a combination of distortions or defenses on clients' parts, which actually may work quite well for them in many areas of their lives, may interfere with their ability to address problems in effective ways. At other times, the problem may arise from a social worker's distortions or defenses. Again, an ecological perspective helps the social worker understand the bigger picture and thus add useful information in ways that help clients to redefine problems.

In the following example, the social worker provides support and education to help clients redefine their situation.

A social worker in a sickle-cell clinic heard several mothers saying that those of their children who had sickle-cell disease were their bad children. One woman even said that this was God's way of marking her bad child. The social worker began a psychoeducational support group for these women, educating them about the genetic determinants of the illness, the natural history of the disease, and its symptoms. She invited a physician and a nurse to two of these meetings and then had the women meet with her to process what they had heard. In six months' time, when on a routine visit to the clinic, the social worker asked the mothers to describe their children with sickle-cell disease. Not one used the adjective *bad,* and all described their children more positively.

In the same way, social workers who carry their own biases can easily misdefine a problem (Nurius and Hudson 1993b). Biases can be created not only by how individuals define problems but also by how organizations, funding sources, educators, and theories define them (Meyer 1993). There are several ways to work to avoid such biases. The first is to continually educate yourself about, and involve yourself with, the populations with whom you are working. For example, a practitioner working as an intensive case manager for the seriously and persistently chronically ill will find it helpful to know people with such diagnoses who are functioning quite well, as well as those who are having very difficult times. In addition, it is important to keep reading and to involve oneself in advocacy groups such as the National Alliance of the Mentally Ill, the American Cancer Society, and the Epilepsy Foundation of America to see multiple and rich dimensions of one's population.

Another way for social workers to avoid bias is to continually increase self-awareness by listening to their own responses and in particular for patterns of response that sound biased. Check out your perceptions with supervisors, peers, and other colleagues and with the clients and communities themselves. Also, when possible, as part of their assessment process, social workers should use preconstructed scales and other instruments of assessment to objectify their assessments (Hudson, Nurius, and Reisman 1988; Nurius and Hudson 1993a). Because the instruments are often biased themselves or are unidimensional, they are most effective when used with other forms of assessment (Mattaini and Kirk 1991).

CONCLUSION

Assessment is a complex, continual, and critical step for all levels of social work practice in health and mental health care. Assessment, as we can now see, is both product and process. The initial product is continually modified as new information emerges and as the social worker and the client system interact to work toward identified goals. Though frameworks of assessment differ in detail, all serve the purpose of clarifying the "who" of the client system, the "what" of problem definition, the "when" of historical material leading to identification of the problem, and the "where" or location of the problem. The assessment then begins to point the way toward the "how" of beginning intervention to mediate the problem.

In all cases, the result of the assessment process is some decision about action. It may be that the assessment indicates that no action is to be taken. Assessment must be closely related to the development of goals, objectives, and outcome measures. Throughout the process, the social worker is working as a catalyst, promoting as much information collection and organization as possible. Social workers advocate with the client system or community and others who are important to the work to provide accurate information aimed at eliciting goals and identifying the strengths the client system possesses to attain these goals. Social workers also assess any potential barriers to the accomplishment of objectives and work to minimize these barriers.

Time constraints are an increasing issue in assessment, especially in the managed care environment. With only 1 to 1½ hours (or sometimes as little as twenty minutes) to complete many pages of diagnostic material, some intake workers adopt a nontherapeutic approach to this task. In reality, clients and communities have to be understood from their own point of view. Sensitivity to apprehensions and perceptions must be considered by social workers through all their interactions with clients and communities. Simply discussing problems tells one very little about "how the client goes about the ordinary business of living" (Goldstein 1983:269), which is what the social worker actually needs to understand.

At all times, and at all levels of service, the worker is conscious of the structural, cultural, and interpersonal context of the client system. It is important to understand the cost of services to clients, whether individuals, programs, or communities. Cost and value are very much intermingled in our society; understanding cost provides more information and control to social workers and clients and may allow social workers to adopt or find new ways of offering services. Increasingly, and especially in relation to managed care, assessments and interventions must be understood in terms of cost and benefit, the cost of the solution, whether the payer will pay for the solution, and how much the payer will pay. As competition for the right to deliver services increases, the emphasis on outcomes, costs, and benefits will increase. Overall, "costs" means dollars spent, time spent, personnel required, emotional or physical costs to the client system, and costs to those who are involved in some other way. Today, again in the managed care environment, cost is measured as dollars spent over time. Little else seems to matter. Thus social workers must become savvy about the costs of their services and whether they can provide them in ways that measure outcomes and that are most efficacious. A full assessment allows identification of these costs in ways that allow the social worker and client to work together to minimize costs and maximize benefits.

The charge to assess multiple levels in an ecological manner around the client system may seem overwhelming. "Theoretically, there is no end to what a social worker might have to know in order to practice, given the bio-psycho-social focus of cases. Some relief of this burden to know everything has been provided through efforts to specialize, to sector out aspects of professional interests and activities" (Meyer 1993:15). Once one familiarizes oneself fully with the population with whom one works most closely, the multiple layers of assessment and multiple levels of intervention become more manageable.

Social Work Interventions: Planning, Contracting, Setting Goals, Developing Objectives, Strategizing, and Working in Teams

This chapter discusses the processes of planning, determining goals and objectives, strategizing, and contracting with stakeholders in general (i.e., everyone who has a stake in the work, including those paying for the services, providers of care, employers, and family members) and clients in particular. An ecological perspective is critical to all these interventions because it allows social workers and their organizations to understand and then respond to changing needs in their environment. Social workers have to be able to identify the driving forces that affect their organization (Christensen 1997). Because teamwork is essential to all these tasks, it is also covered in this chapter. Especially since interventions are systems-based and thought to be parts of clients' care over a continuum, every intervention must be thought of as one of many means of assistance perhaps over the lifetime of an individual, family, or community. Since social work often attends to problems that society cannot solve, social workers can even see themselves as parts of teams that may not ever meet face-to-face but that work for and with a client in different time periods. Focusing all these actions is the determination of objectives, measurable signs by which progress can be evaluated because "the work of the organization or the unit can only be enhanced by being organized for systematic, continuing performance" (Drucker 1998:174).

PLANNING

A plan is an intentional method of achieving an intended end, a detailed formulation of a program of action to devise or project the realistic achievement of specific results. Often a plan is a customary method of doing something that is created from a base of experience, a set of relevant data, or a review of the experience of others. While planning always implies mental formulation, it sometimes includes graphic representation as well (Christensen 1997; Kaplan and Norton 1996c). Thus a plan can be a plot, a formula, a system, a set of actions, a procedure, a design, or an arrangement. Planning involves the establishment of goals, policies, and procedures for a social or economic unit. To practice social work in health and mental health care at any level, social workers must plan their activity in relation to the goals that stakeholders have established.

Until it translates into work, the best plan is only an intention. A productive plan is one that is supported through the commitment of necessary resources, including the willingness of key people to attend to specific tasks. The test of a plan is whether management actually commits resources to action that will bring results in the future. A plan must mirror the realities of the organization's environment, and the resource allocation process must mirror the plan (Christensen 1997). Unless such commitment is made, there are promises and hopes, but there is no plan (Drucker 1974).

To plan is to have a method of formulating purposes and actions before acting. The word *plan* suggests thought and rationality. While planning occurs on many levels, this book focuses on two levels: the planning of programs and the planning of interventions to address particular situations. Although most social workers in health and mental health care are not directors or presidents of the agencies or organizations for which they work, they must understand how planning at the organizational level works. They must participate as fully as possible in order to gather the knowledge needed to best advocate for programs, for clients, and for their professional standing within their organizations. The latter is necessary because more recognition within an organization means that professionals will have more control over the conditions of their work and will be in better positions to help clients reach their goals. Program planning requires an understanding of the political and social environment, organizational and management concepts, and budgeting (Crow 1995). Effective planning requires an ecological perspective, fine relationship skills, an understanding of the effort necessary to carry out the plan (in terms of funds, time, and energy), and the ability to develop and write a comprehensive plan.

When discussing and writing about planning, it is common for professionals to use the word *strategic,* as in "strategic planning" and "strategic

FIGURE 7.1. The planning and control process.

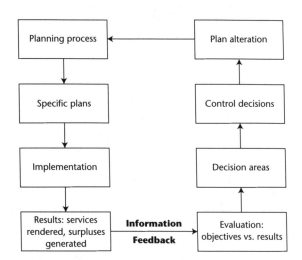

programming." The word *strategic* evokes a sense of urgency, shrewdness, and resourcefulness. In fact, it is more useful to separate thinking about planning and strategy. While planning is routine and built in to the regular calendar of an organization, strategy is a way to push the boundaries of the routine. Using a military analogy, one might plan the roles, training, and command of the armed forces, but once in battle, skirmishes would be strategic work. One could argue that thinking strategically had to be part of every planning process, and every strategy had to be executed planfully, that is, with great care and as rationally as possible. So, while I honor the language used by others who choose to describe their work as strategic planning, I think it is most useful to separate the concepts. I will continue to weave the word *strategic* into this discussion of planning, but I will also separate strategizing and planning.

Figure 7.1 is a map of a planning and control process that can be used to think about planning and control of the work. The steps and the order listed on this mapping device are necessary no matter what the plan is. Following these steps will provide participants with sufficient information and feedback to adjust the plan to match needs and resources.

The following practice example helps map out the process. It begins with a general planning process, moves to specific plans, then to plan implementation, and then to results. Information and feedback from the results allow evaluation. Areas of decision are derived from the evaluation, control decisions are implemented, and as a result the plan is altered so that the process can begin again. Such a process is built into the cycles of an organization. The larger process is predictable and is part of the life of the organization. Control of the work and the ability to alter the work based on results has to be built into the planning process.

Located in an ethnically diverse neighborhood of about thirty thousand residents where almost half the children live in poverty and there are high rates of drug abuse and crime, La Tienda de Ayuda para las Familias, a neighborhood drug crisis center, is in a storefront that had been the scene of confrontation between drug dealers and the police in which many were injured and a police officer was killed. La Tienda was conceived by the Institute, an organization that has developed innovative solutions to problems of crime and drug addiction for almost fifty years. Earlier, a study conducted by the Institute and others demonstrated that half of those on probation in their city who had enrolled in nonresidential treatment programs dropped out within thirty-seven days. The center's staff knows that the criminal justice systems' rewards and punishments are rarely enough to rehabilitate addicts. Because the Institute believes that family-oriented interventions can reduce drug-related domestic problems and improve users' chances for recovery, they focus on family and neighborhood and not the drug user. This focus distinguishes La Tienda from other programs (Zweben and Fleming 1999).

La Tienda's overarching goal is to fortify families' abilities to help their drug abusing relatives to address their problems while living at home ("Center for Families" 1996:2). La Tienda has three primary objectives: (1) to reduce intrafamilial harm caused by substance abuse, such as theft, domestic violence, and family breakup, (2) to improve the effectiveness of conventional outpatient drug treatment for addicts whose family members use the center, as measured by longer stays in treatment, reduced drug use and criminality, and fewer arrests and violations of criminal justice community supervision, and (3) to reduce the use of jail to punish relapse when a family member is willing and able to help the addict persevere in treatment.

Funding for the center is a collaborative effort that involves many kinds of stakeholders. The Institute, with funding from one local government agency and one federal agency, provides planning and management, and thirty businesses have contributed services and construction materials. At the Institute, ideas for research and programming come from staff experiences in institutions such as courts, schools, jails, and other city institutions. The Institute designs, operates, and evaluates demonstration programs with the goal of locating government programs and new nonprofit organizations that will continue the innovative work. La Tienda is funded as a five-year demonstration project for $900,000 per year. Research at the center is ongoing and supplies rapid feedback (see chapter 9), which allows staff members to alter services as they learn which are most valued. When operating fully, the center can manage 750 crisis intervention/walk-ins and family case management for 150 people annually.

The bilingual staff provides walk-in services, family case management and crisis intervention services to the neighborhood. Walk-in services are available to everyone in the community who may have a problem with a friend or relative. Services include providing facts about health and housing as well as sponsoring workshops and educational groups that provide information and encourage discussion among neighbors. Examples include sewing circles, yoga classes, and parenting groups. Crisis intervention services are structured so that staff members are available via a twenty-four-hour hotline when drug users are arrested, when they quit treatment or relapse, or when there are family, child custody, or housing problems.

Family case management services are meant to strengthen the ability of the family to support the addict during a period of treatment and criminal justice supervision. Families are provided with case management services under the following circumstances: (1) when there is positive family support toward the addict's recovery, (2) when the addict is a defendant, parolee, or probationer in the criminal justice system, and (3) when the family does not have the financial means to purchase these services. The center uses protocols developed by noted centers for family therapy and dispute resolution. Family case management services do not provide treatment or supervision to addicts, but they do refer for treatment and collaborate with probation and parole officers, programs that are alternatives to incarceration, health-related services, ambulatory care facilities, and grassroots health agencies.

Family problems the center grapples with are (1) disagreements among family members, (2) substance-abusing relatives refusing involvement with the center, (3) family members not wishing to be involved with an addict, (4) widespread family drug use, (5) the family's dependence on income generated from illegal sale of drugs, and (6) undiagnosed mental illness. Interagency problems include difficulty in maintaining positive relations with programs that have approaches to drug problems that differ from the center's approach, as well as difficulty in maintaining the center's voluntary alliance with families when courts or others want to require the services.

Evaluation of the center's work is related to its primary objectives (reduction of intrafamilial harm and jail time and improving conventional drug treatment). Each week the number of people walking in for the first time and those who either return to the center or follow up on referrals within one month are counted in separate categories with return or referral follow-up of at least 30 percent being the goals. Regarding family case management, the number of people who begin and remain engaged for at least three months are counted with a goal of 50 percent retention. Staff members also track the percentage of people receiving family case management services who notify the center within twenty-four hours of an addict's violation of probation or parole or rearrest, with the goal being 80 percent.

In addition to internally generated rapid feedback, research on the center will be conducted in two phases; (1) a form of process research focusing on the planning and implementation process, and (2) an impact evaluation that will study the program's effect on clients and community. Thus La Tienda's program is an example of an effective planning process that begins with clear needs that are seen in the community; it involves all stakeholders, is flexible and responsive, has clear objectives, has sufficient personnel and financial resources, includes built-in evaluation mechanisms, and considers both present and future needs.

Structuring a Planning Process

Planning is a process of developing and directing resources to meet specified needs. The process includes fact finding, problem definition, goal setting, implementation, feedback monitoring, and evaluation. It can be defined as a disciplined effort to produce basic decisions and actions that guide the definition (mission and purpose) of an organization and what it does. The planning process helps the organization in the following ways (Yankey 1995):

1. It provides a common purpose for future development.
2. It clarifies future direction.
3. It improves performance.
4. It develops expertise and teamwork.
5. It explicates procedures for making decisions and establishing priorities.
6. It develops ways for responding to community needs.
7. It enhances internal morale and commitment.
8. It raises funds.
9. It positions the organization in relation to its environment and its competition.
10. It educates stakeholders.

To structure a strategic planning process social workers must decide who should be involved, which kinds of background material participants need prior to beginning the process, who will lead the process, where responsibility lies, how results will be communicated, how frequently the process will be reviewed and by whom, and who is responsible for interacting with external groups in preparing the plan (Williamson, Stevens, Loudon, and Miglior 1997:32–36).

Henry Mintzberg (1994:210–14), a leading management thinker, says that strategic planning is invoked by managers to give themselves the "illusion of control." Mintzberg is highly critical of strategic planning because effective planning requires conditions of stability, controllability, and predictability (Mintzberg and Lampel 1999). Because planning must respond to and be built on what is in its headlights, he argues, it cannot respond to turbulence or tumult. If the plan is frozen in time, conditions had better be stable (Mintzberg and Quinn 1991). Because the annual strategic planning process in most organizations is barely altered over time, strategic planning often does not fit the context of the organization (Hamel 1998).

Mintzberg's contribution is to alter the strategic planning approach to keep the process timely and sensitive to its environment. In this way, the process is both routinized and responsive. He prefers the concept of strategic programming, moving the conventional model of strategic planning out of formulating and into implementing. Even strategic programming should not be viewed as the only planning method but should be used only when an organization requires the clear articulation of its strategy.

According to Mintzberg, strategic programming consists of a series of steps. First, codifying and calibrating the strategy means clarifying and expressing it in terms that are sufficiently clear to make it operational. In that way, the consequences can be worked out in detail, everything that can be is taken into account, and hurdles and inconsistencies are eliminated. In this approach the implicit is made explicit, and plans are refined to a few primary efforts or thrusts to which an organization can commit its resources and by which it can evaluate its performance. The process itself increases commitment and agreement. So the notion of contracting is built into the planning process.

Mintzberg also wisely suggests that work should be articulated by using familiar terms, images, and metaphors that people feel comfortable with and understand such as "social justice," "starting where the client is" and "empowering the consumer" rather than by imposing unfamiliar labels and language. The following techniques are used to create metaphors:

1. Listen for metaphors.
2. Whenever possible, use an individual's own metaphor.
3. Keep metaphors simple, and use as few words as possible.

If individuals seem unable to relate to a particular metaphor, do not insist on its use (Reid 1991). To illustrate one use of metaphor, Reid provides an unforgettable example drawn from a group in which a member described herself as a pinball bouncing off people and never developing real connections. The group used this metaphor to describe someone who could not develop or sustain relationships (Reid 1991). In the same way, the director of a large health care system's social work department says that the positive reframing metaphors from Ericksonian hypnosis (Matthews 1997–1998; Overholser 1994) help her to administer and supervise. For example, bridging is a favored device. When social workers complain to her about the nature or pace of the work, she helps them to build a bridge to the positive side of the situation, at which point they remember that the institution is financially secure and their positions are secure. She has used the word *bridging* so often that it has become a metaphor for recasting situations in more positive ways (Kopp 1995).

The second step in strategic programming is the elaboration of the strategy. Here, in action planning, consequences are broken down into a scheme that begins with substrategies, proceeds through various kinds of programs including sequencing and timing or scheduling, and results in specific action plans that state clearly what must be done to actualize the intended strategy. Thus each primary thrust is divided into steps and substeps that are assigned to individuals resulting in a timed sequence of actions. In the third step, the elaborated strategy is converted from action planning to performance control in terms of budgets and objectives. "Objectives are restated and budgets reworked, policies and standard operating procedures reconsidered, to take into account the consequences of the specific changes in action" (Mintzberg 1994:340).

The Organigraph

Mintzberg and Van der Heyden (1999:90) have devised a tool called the organigraph, which depicts how organizations really work (figure 7.2). They say, "the organizational chart treats everyone and everything as an independent box. And every one of those boxes is connected by a vertical chain—that is, a chain of authority." Instead, the organigraph focuses on how processes and people come together and where ideas have to flow. It does not eliminate little boxes from organizational charts, but it introduces new components. The two conventional components in the device are sets of items (machines or people) and chains (assembly lines). The newer components are hubs and webs. In the hub, managing occurs at the center, bringing together and coordinating the work of people who are intrinsically empowered. In the web, the work is fluid so that collaboration is facilitated and the whole network is energized.

In the following example, an organization called Support Services provides state-funded transitional housing for men discharged from the state hospital to learn life skills needed to live independently. The state refers men with lower functioning abilities who are not able to make the transition without assistance. Strategically, with the state's support, the organization

FIGURE 7.2. The four philosophies of managing depicted in organigraph.

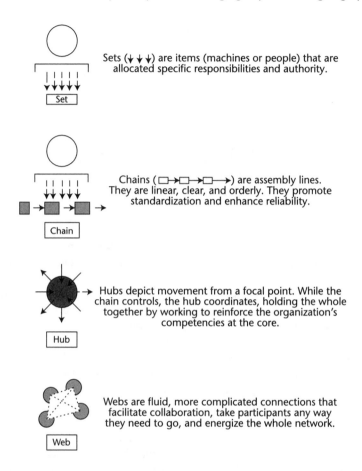

Sets (↓ ↓ ↓) are items (machines or people) that are allocated specific responsibilities and authority.

Chains (□→□→□→) are assembly lines. They are linear, clear, and orderly. They promote standardization and enhance reliability.

Hubs depict movement from a focal point. While the chain controls, the hub coordinates, holding the whole together by working to reinforce the organization's competencies at the core.

Webs are fluid, more complicated connections that facilitate collaboration, take participants any way they need to go, and energize the whole network.

has developed a new program, called Extended Supportive Housing, to meet the needs of the clients, the state, and the organization. Figure 7.3 shows the organigraph for the formation and support of the new facility.

Ralph Burns (42) and Gregory Kramer (45) were discharged from the state hospital five years ago and have been living at Transition House, a halfway house for people who are newly discharged from the state hospital. Before that, Mr. Burns had been hospitalized nearby for fifteen years with the diagnosis of schizophrenia (undifferentiated type). Mr. Kramer had been hospitalized in a distant state for 7½ years with the diagnosis of organic brain syn-

FIGURE 7.3. Organigraph for the formation and support of Elysium House.

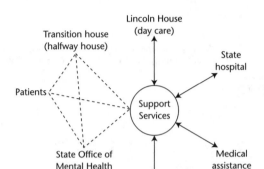

drome owing to acute alcoholism. On discharge, Mr. Kramer came to this program because his immediate family lived in the area. Transition House is funded by the state as a mechanism by which people with serious and persistent mental illnesses can make the transition from the hospital to independent living. The state had set a maximum length of stay at two years for each resident; however, each year when the state reevaluates Transition House, the house asks that an exception be made for Mr. Burns and Mr. Kramer because they are not yet ready to live independently. Because they have a very low income, Mr. Burns and Mr. Kramer would have to live in the most minimal boardinghouse in an unprotected environment.

Lately, the state has been referring men who are at much lower levels of functioning than those for whom the program was designed. The State Office of Mental Health has warned the program that Support Services will have to provide services for such people in greater numbers. The solution arrived at by Support Services staff is to create a new program called Extended Supportive Housing , located right around the corner from Transition House and a short walk from Lincoln House, where all the residents go for day care. This extended supportive housing, called Elysium House, is suitable for three residents, so Alva Jones will live there as well. Mr. Jones is compatible with Mr. Burns and Mr. Kramer in that he, too, is very passive and depressed, and he will not prey on the other residents.

In addition to the cost of renting the property, the primary cost of the program will be to staff the house for three hours every day in the late afternoon. A staff member will be with the men while they prepare and eat dinner, take their evening medication, and go to Transition House for the evening program. For five days a week, the residents will continue their day program at Lincoln House, a day center for the seriously mentally ill, and otherwise they will live independently. Thus Elysium House fits into the current continuum of care, gives the clients protection and increased independence, fills the needs of the state, and is much less costly than Transition House because of lower staffing needs. Support Services is the hub around which activities revolve. For Elysium House, the new program to begin and remain supported, a web has been created that will facilitate collaboration and energize the entire network.

Thus the planning concepts that have been discussed are easily applied to nonprofit human service organizations (Menefee 1997). For example, strategic management is the process of transforming goals into actions— an annual business plan that includes budgets, performance standards, and accountability criteria that generate outcome measures for agency and employee—with an emphasis on efficiency, effectiveness, and financial solvency (Menefee 1997:14). Two statements that undergird the concept of strategic administration parallel the person-in-environment model and the ecological perspective:

1. Managing the relationship between the agency and its environment is essential for survival and will mean the difference between agency growth, maintenance, or decline (Schmid 1992).
2. Administration is strategic when it concerns itself with the welfare of the organization vis-à-vis its environment (Hasenfeld 1992).

Strategic administration includes the following three dimensions: planning, management, and leadership. Planning involves assessing the agency environment, identifying and prioritizing fundamental policy issues, developing long-term goals to address them, and creating methods for achieving them. Management entails transforming strategic goals into action. The activities of management have to do with translating the organization's mission statement into the realities of service provision, collecting data that reflect stakeholders' concerns, and measuring performance of the staff and clients. Leadership, the third dimension of strategic administration, involves actively managing the external environment and delegating the management of daily operations to others in the organization (Schmid 1992). Thus effective executive directors must primarily be networkers and relationship builders in order to fashion and support relationships that effect policy and financial support for their organizations and clients. Social workers at every level have to understand these dimensions in order to best advocate for clients and leverage their work and their impact to the fullest possible extent.

Because so much social work involves interacting with representatives of other organizations and systems, all social workers must be relationship builders and networkers. In fact, if social workers note repeated similar problems with other systems or representatives of other organizations, they must exercise these leadership functions in the manner of a rapid feedback evaluation. In that way, direct practice social workers can alert those with greater authority in their organization that these problems can be solved only on the organizational level.

For example, a social worker assigned to the oncology service of a community hospital had great difficulty coordinating volunteers to help patients in whom breast cancer had recently been diagnosed because the representative of the local division of the American Cancer Society thought that the hospital volunteer service was in competition with the society. The social worker gathered information about all the patients who needed and wanted volunteer assistance and presented the information to the society representative while asking for her help. One result of the social worker's efforts was that the American Cancer Society began to work with oncology service staff and agreed to train and supervise volunteers who work with breast cancer patients. (See also the case example involving the Roosevelt School for the Deaf in chapter 6, pp. 211–12.)

Strategies for success can also be reviewed using the concepts of planning, management, and leadership. With regard to planning, agencies have to revisit their sources of revenue regularly. If agencies are dependent on one source for referral, they may find themselves in great difficulty if the source they depend on develops problems. For example, a social worker in a small home care agency reported that all her agency's cases came from one community hospital that had closed because of financial difficulties. Service diversification is one strategy to address this kind of problem. Many private, not-for-profit health and mental health organizations are totally dependent on Medical Assistance payments. Some states are so slow in making such payments that agencies are forced to borrow money to meet their expenses. In relation to management, agencies should run like businesses with an emphasis on efficiency, effectiveness, and financial solvency. In relation to leadership, organizations must act to preserve the legitimacy of the agency's services through marketing, fundraising, public relations, advocacy, networking, and politicking. Social workers should be part of all these tasks.

Phases of Work

In the approach taken here, it is necessary for the social worker to think about the phases, or stages, of work in two different ways. One is work in the largest sense, meaning what kinds of interventions a client, project, organization, or community might need over time. The second is what kinds of interventions the client, project, organization, or community might need from that social worker and those in his or her system and other systems. Both points of view are necessary to help optimally with a chronic problem. Also, now that most payers in health and mental health care are willing to pay only for brief, intermittent, and highly focused interventions, social workers need to think of clients receiving help in powerful bits over time rather than through one relationship lasting many months or even years.

Systematic Planned Practice

Planning systems have also been developed for social workers to use in planning direct practice. One such framework, called systematic planned practice, was developed by Rosen, Proctor, and others over several years (Proctor and Rosen 1983; Proctor, Rosen, and Livne 1985; Rosen 1993; Rosen, Proctor, and Staudt 1999; Zeira and Rosen 1999). In focusing on the primary decisions of the treatment process, this approach supports practitioners' making explicit practice decisions based on their best knowledge, values, and skills. Components of intervention planning (which Rosen refers to as treatment planning) are client problems, decisions on how to dispose of client problems, and outcomes. Outcomes are ultimate (goals of intervention have been reached), intermediate (the numbers of changes that have to occur in clients or their environments), unplanned, or sequencing (what smaller problems have to be solved on the way to reaching the clients' ultimate goals). Within intermediate outcomes are worker outcomes (such as achieving a clear diagnostic conception of the client's problems) and instrumental outcomes (pursued by the social worker to attain some other desired outcome). The framework is meant to be applicable to any level of practice. The mapping device that Rosen has developed is shown in figure 7.4.

Strategic Thinking

The following practice example describes the methods for strategic thinking used by Frank Leonardi, a social work consultant who was asked to help an AIDS service organization confront itself—that is, describe its current mission, functioning, and difficulties—in order to plan for a strong future. Leonardi used the techniques of brainstorming and creating driving-force maps described in Christensen (1997).

First brainstorming session. This is how staff members described AIDS Assault in their first brainstorming session with Mr. Leonardi: AIDS Assault is a 15-year-old AIDS service organization (ASO) that began its work with the dual objectives of raising community awareness of HIV/AIDS and disseminating information regarding protocols for the treatment of people with AIDS. Over time AIDS Assault has become a service organization that primarily provides case

FIGURE 7.4. Systematic planned practice (Rosen 1993:97).

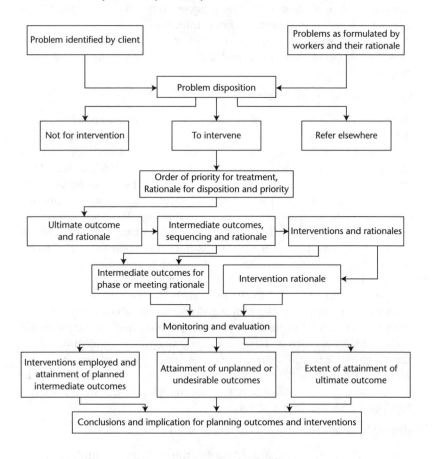

management; medical, hospice, nutrition, legal, bereavement, and loss and grief services; support groups; drug protocols access; and drug and alcohol rehabilitation for those who have AIDS and are acutely ill or dying. Figure 7.5 depicts AIDS Assault's first attempt to map a driving force.

In addition to AIDS Assault, six or seven other ASOs with similar missions serve the same metropolitan area. Of these, two see the African American community as their constituency, one sees the Latino community as its constituency, and one (which has traditionally been affiliated with middle- and upper-middle-class gay men) is now being compelled by its funding sources to reach out to a broader constituency. In addition, several hospitals and at least two religiously affiliated social service organizations provide similar ser-

FIGURE 7.5. AIDS Assault: First attempt to map a driving force.

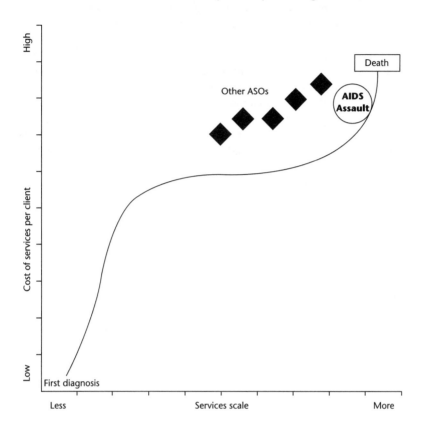

vices. At this time, the client base for AIDS Assault, and all its sister organizations, has changed to a poorer and less empowered socioeconomic population made up primarily of women, African Americans, and Latinos, of whom a significant percentage abuse drugs and/or alcohol. When the organization began, its client base was composed primarily of white, gay, middle-class men. At the same time, all the organizations are experiencing declines in funding from the government, private donors, and other sources. The decline in funding has increased competition among all the AIDS-related organizations.

Second brainstorming session. At the second brainstorming session, which was conducted to help the organization describe where it would like to go, AIDS Assault reviewed three arenas: economic situation, services provided, and competing service providers. With regard to funding sources, staff members decided that they could improve funding from the government, other private and public agencies (including local businesses and corporations), and private donors by creatively expanding services to adapt to the changing nature of the illness. Regarding services, they thought they should expand their offerings to include services for those living with AIDS as a chronic illness. This would include a back-to-work program for those with AIDS whose medical situation was stable and who were able and willing to go back to work. This service would use some of the research done in work/ rehabilitation with other populations with hidden disabilities (including mental disabilities). AIDS Assault would partner with a local organization that has received funding to conduct research in HIV/AIDS work-related issues. With regard to competition, the new back-to-work services would make AIDS Assault unique in the area. It would be the first to offer such services to its clientele and could be a model for other AIDS service organizations, both locally and nationally. Figures 7.6 and 7.7 depict AIDS Assault's second and third driving-force maps respectively.

FIGURE 7.6. AIDS Assault: Changing the map to reflect greater insight.

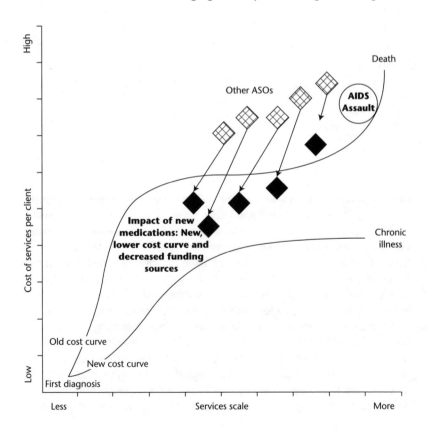

FIGURE 7.7. AIDS Assault: Final map of driving force.

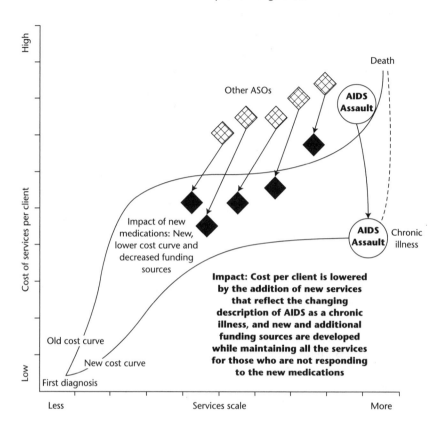

Coming up with a coordinated, detailed plan offering explicit guidance about an organization's activity to which everyone in the organization agrees is very difficult (Christensen 1997). Christensen describes three necessary stages: The first is the identification of the driving forces in an organization's environment through brainstorming in small teams and regrouping to begin to cluster ideas. The expression "driving forces" refers to the economic, demographic, technological, and competitive factors in the organization's environment that constitute threats or create opportunities. Part of this experience involves mapping the driving forces (figures 7.5, 7.6, and 7.7). The second stage, also begun in small groups, is the creation of a visual tool for discovering the root cause of a phenomenon affecting the organization. Teams draw maps for the driving forces that were summarized during brainstorming. At this point team members should search for the few factors that could bring about the hypothesized result and plot those factors on the axes of a matrix or diagram (Christiansen 1997). They should redraw and reuse the matrix until they are convinced that they understand (1) why the expected result will probably occur and (2) what would have to be changed to create a different outcome. After teams think that mapping is complete, they must pass the maps all around the organization for input and correction. This should be a several-week process. Next, a strategy should be formulated that addresses the driving forces. Again, there is a brainstorming session, then small teams should group the ideas pasted on each map into related clusters and draft a summary statement. Generally, ideas cluster around functional areas. Some teams may disagree about what to do. According to Christensen, disagreement is often a symptom of a poorly defined driving force. It is wise to stop arguing about what to do and instead ask whether there is a driving force that the team has not yet defined behind the problem.

Next a strategy matrix is developed to show how the organization might address each driving force by creating a prioritized list of driving forces at the top of each column, with the major functional groups in the organization listed at the left of each row (Christensen 1997:153). The strategy statements that were created to address each driving force can then be inserted into the appropriate cells of the matrix. Then at the right of each row, the strategy teams should summarize the functional strategy for each group in the organization. In the cells at the bottom of each column, they should summarize the strategy for addressing each driving force. Stage three incorporates the resources (including funding and personnel) that are necessary for strategy implementation. Resources must mirror the plan. Table 7.1 is an excerpt from AIDS Assault's Strategy Matrix.

The focus should be accordion-like, so that it can be altered as needed. The lens can be adjusted to include what is required to accomplish the work. A key factor is understanding the conditions in the environment and then altering strategic direction to fit changing needs in the environment (Christensen 1997). Thus management theory presents the best frame for looking at the client, the organization, systems, the social worker, and the work since the work of the functional school, with the exception of certain specific articles such as "The Triangle: The worker, the client, and the agency" (Lieberman 1982). Outcomes are critical and clear. Leadership is defined in ways that are useful to all social workers, and the essential place of teamwork is confirmed.

TABLE 7.1. An Excerpt from AIDS Assault's Strategy Matrix

	Driving Force 1: AIDS Assault's costs of services per client are high relative to other ASOs in the region. Only one other ASO has higher costs. Also, funding from traditional sources has decreased.	Driving Force 2: New developments in medical treatment that allow people to live longer with AIDS press ASOs to develop new services for their client base.	Driving Force 3: ASOs must maintain traditional services for individuals who do not respond to the new treatments or to whom the new treatments are not available for economic reasons.	
Work Groups	Strategy Statements in Response to Driving Force 1	Strategy Statements in Response to Driving Force 2	Strategy Statements in Response to Driving Force 3	Summary Statements of Each Function's Strategy
Development (Funding)	Locate new funding sources for the development of new services. Continue funding established services through traditional and newly identified sources.	Locate and submit proposals to government agencies that support back-to-work programs and services for those on HIV/AIDS-related disability who are capable of returning to or beginning work.	Develop joint proposals with regional ASOs for collaborative work that will lower the cost of service for each ASO by reducing overhead and pooling resources.	Develop sources of funding for the development of new services while maintaining established services.
Client Services	Explore means of lowering the cost of service per client while maintaining quality. Include the possibility of collaborating with other ASOs or agencies in the region to provide full service.	With full client participation, develop new services. Include outcome measures that demonstrate service effectiveness.	Provide outcome measures for established services to demonstrate effectiveness to funding sources. Improve client access to the new medical treatments.	Find ways to reduce cost of services per client. Develop new services while maintaining established ones. Evaluate the effectiveness of new and established services.
Administration	Find methods for lowering the cost of service per client, including creative partnerships with local ASOs and government agencies	Broaden the services that have been developed and implemented by Client Services.	Maintain established services while reviewing means for lowering costs (e.g., a collaborative ASO hospice would maintain an established service through pooled resources with lower overhead).	Direct and provide contacts to Development and Client Services to help secure new funding for new and established services. Include outcome measures of effectiveness in the effort.

CONTRACTING

Contracts are agreements that clarify relationships, making them more rational and predictable. Although contracting occurs on all levels of social work, it is discussed here as a part of an organizational planning process; that is, plans are drawn as part of the regular work of the organization or long-term program. Contracts are developed between the organization or program that did the planning and those with whom they need to clarify relationships. In direct social work practice, contracts are also drawn between social workers and clients that clarify the structure, content, and expectations of that relationship. Thus contracts are drawn as part of the individual planning process between social workers and individuals, families, or groups regarding the conditions, structure, goals, and objectives of the work that social workers and clients will address together. Therefore, all contracts are ways of arriving at an agreement, of making the expectations and actions of those on one side of a relationship clear and understandable to those on another side.

Social workers in health and mental health care work regularly with many kinds of implicit and explicit forms of contracts. For social workers to work effectively (even with an individual client with a highly specific concrete goal, such as obtaining a prosthesis, gaining access to a day program, or finding a bed for the night), they must understand the range of contracts that underpin, frame, allow, and protect the relationship and work of the social worker and client. Again, an ecological perspective allows the broadest understanding of the uses of contracting in health and mental health care.

Contracts exist on many levels: The system in which the social worker is employed must agree to follow the terms set out in all laws and policies that affect it. Every third-party payer contracts very specifically with each system regarding conditions and level of payment. Public authorities contract with private, not-for-profit programs to provide services or collaborate in a range of services (Libby 1997; Mulroy and Shay 1997). Patients sign contracts with hospitals and other health care systems. Social work departments contract with the organizations that employ them to settle the limits, conditions, and terms of their services. When social workers work in what have been referred to as "host organizations" (in which social work is not the primary mode of care), a kind of contract exists between representatives of the primary profession in that organization and social workers that lets each profession know what it may expect from the other (Dane and Simon 1991). Sometimes, as in court-ordered treatment for drug or alcohol abuse, there is a contract between the client and the court and its officers as representatives of the state, as well as a contract between the court and the organization that agrees to provide services to the client the court sends for treatment.

One recent concern is social workers' participation in provider networks that compete for the contracts with managed care organizations to deliver mental health services. Such relationships with managed care organizations are controversial in relation to definition, length, and depth of service (Gibelman and Whiting 1999; Hodgkin, Horgan, and Garnick 1997; Stroul, Pires, Armstrong, and Meyers 1998). In the full range of social work practice, from a federal or state advocacy effort to a community outreach service, from a hospital discharge plan to counseling regarding drug or alcohol abuse, a contract also always exists between the client and the sponsoring organization.

Finally, there is the contract, implicit or explicit, between the client and social worker in terms of what behavior each may expect from the other, the goals for their work together, and the means by which they intend to attain those goals (Neugeboren 1996). Contract is the keystone, cynosure, and linchpin of the social worker/client relationship, because mutually agreed-upon obligations and expectations contribute to the establishment of norms for the relationship, and transparency and trust in the relationship enhance the work (Goffman 1972; Kerson 1997). The effectiveness of written as opposed to verbal contracts between social workers and clients is a matter for debate. Effectiveness may depend on the specific kind of system, work, and clients. Some think that contracting within a relationship results in overarticulation, stultifies the development of a relationship, and interferes with transference and creativity. Certainly, a simple, written contract clarifies an agreement. It may be, too, that an official signing by all involved parties adds the kind of ceremony that demonstrates the importance of the terms to all parties.

Following is an example in which a halfway house for people with serious and persistent mental illness uses contracting to help its clients.

A halfway house for people with serious and persistent mental illness who have been discharged from a psychiatric hospital but are not yet ready to live independently requires that each new resident sign a contract. The document has some general house rules, such as one stating that no alcohol is allowed on the premises and another stating that each resident must be active in a work-related program, actively searching for paid work, or engaged in paid work. It also includes additional terms mutually agreed-upon by the new resident and the staff. These include therapeutic agreements such as a very quiet and shy resident agreeing to have verbal interactions with residents and staff on at least five occasions each day, and another resident, who was as garrulous as the first was quiet, agreeing to entertain himself by reading or listening to music by himself for a least one hour each day. The contract is signed in the living room of the house by the new resident and staff members. When residents are ready to live independently or when they are asked to leave because they have broken the terms of the contract, there is another public meeting in the living room to review the terms. Thus the contract plays an active role in residents' work throughout their stay in the halfway house (Donovan, Blanchard, and Kerson 1997:481–504).

> *The contract.* A new Hope House resident enters into an elaborate set of agreements. Hope House is probably the most demanding environment the resident could choose: more demanding than being in an institution or living alone. Every day, residents weigh the benefits versus the effort. No drugs, alcohol, violence, stealing, sexual relations, or suicide gestures are allowed at Hope House. Violation of any of these cardinal rules leads to immediate dismissal; a resident who has violated one of these rules is given one week's notice to leave. However, unless a contract specifically stipulates that a resident may not drink, individuals are free to drink outside the house, as long as the drinking is not disruptive to the house and does not interfere with the resident's progress.
>
> There is no curfew at Hope House. Residents can come and go anytime. Everyone has his own key to the front door. Residents are free to go away on weekends. They are, however, expected to be at Hope House during the week and are required to be at house meetings on Monday evenings and to be at dinner Monday through Thursday, unless excused. Everyone must cook for the house and clean up one night a week together with another resident. Everyone has one assigned house duty a week, for example, cleaning the second-floor bathroom. These duties are checked twice a week. Failure to complete a house duty results in being assigned extra duty the following week. Staff gives assistance as needed to help residents complete tasks.
>
> Each resident must maintain a day program that can include working, going to school or day treatment, doing volunteer work or sheltered work, or looking for work. In any case, residents are required to do something constructive during the day. We discourage people from using sickness as an excuse to stay home. If a resident's day program is looking for work, he is expected to make a minimum of two job contacts a day and to hand in a job contact sheet describing these activities at the end of the week. Residents are also expected to take their medication as prescribed. In certain instances staff may help residents with medication by using means such as reminders or pill cad-

dies. The ultimate goal is for residents to take their medication more reliably by themselves.

The first six weeks are a trial period. At the end of that time, the staff makes a decision regarding whether the person should be fully accepted into the program. If the person is found unready to meet the demands of the program, he is asked to move out. The contract between the resident and the agency is complex and remains very much a live issue during the course of his stay. All these policies are discussed at the time the individual comes for an initial tour, again at the interview, and again at the time of admission. New residents are given a handbook.

The agreement between the resident and the case workers is that they will meet regularly during the resident's stay to set goals, review progress, and deal with whatever personal matters are at issue. In addition, the social worker will direct the resident toward needed community resources and, if necessary, advocate for the client. Residents are told when they come in that anything they say will be shared freely with other Hope House staff. The staff teaches skills in areas needed for clients to become more independent. Skills to cope with recurrent symptoms are particularly important (Donovan et al. 1997:489–92).

SETTING GOALS

Goals and objectives are the solutions that social workers and clients work together to attain. They are realistic and achievable aims. In social work practice literature, goals are often referred to by various terms, such as outcomes or treatment objectives (Carlton 1984; Germain 1984; Hepworth and Larson 1986; Monkman 1991; Woods and Hollis 2000). Here, they are meant to be grand, overarching directions that are desired by clients. They may not be concrete and/or measurable, but some of their dimensions can be couched in measurable terms as objectives or outcomes. Ideally, goals are owned by the client, be it an individual, a family, an organization, or a community; it is the social worker's job to help the client articulate the goals and plan the interventions that will help clients reach those goals. Goals formulated by the social worker, family, organization or staff, court or legislation—anyone other than the client—are less likely to be attained (Woods and Hollis 2000).

Goals help structure the social worker–client relationship and the work itself. They provide purpose and direction. To be most effective, goals have to be important and of sufficient significance to motivate the client, but they should also not be written in stone. As needs and situations change, the social worker and client have to be sufficiently flexible to alter goals or even cancel goals that are not helping the work. The establishment of goals usually occurs after initial assessment and before the planning for and implementation of interventions (Rose 1995b). However, in this era of brief work, all these steps can occur during the initial meeting of the social worker and client. For example, a widowed, middle-aged white woman who lived alone and had begun to abuse alcohol since her husband's death five years before was referred to a social worker by an employee assistance program. In the first of three sessions, the social worker addressed confidentiality, treatment recommendations, and the system for reporting back to the employee assistance program. Concern about losing her job and being in a counseling situation helped the client progress in self-evaluation and exploration of her options for managing her drinking problem (Corwin and Read 1997).

Organizational Goals

In addition to having to understand and help realize client goals, social workers must be able to do the same for organizational goals, "units of information that are understood by organizational members to define preferred collective outcomes at a specific moment in time" (Maynard-Moody and McClintock 1987:126). Thus organizational goals clarify the collective purpose of the organization and, as a consequence, help individuals collaborate for action. A close examination of broad organizational goals often reveals them to be ideals that bring meaning to an organization. In the same way, a close look at the many goals in complex organizations highlights multiplicity, ambiguity, and conflict, but such complexity yields rich organizations that are able to respond to the changing needs of time and context (Amason 1996; Jehn 1997).

"Goals are statements of expected outcomes dealing with the problem that the program is attempting to prevent, eradicate, or ameliorate. Goals need not be measurable or achievable. They simply provide programmatic direction. . . . Goal statements are also political statements and are written in such a way that they tend to build consensus" (Kettner, Maroney, and Martin 1999:96). For example, in the personal scorecard in table 7.2 (for a full description of the balanced scorecard, see chapter 4), a goal of a chapter of the Multiple Sclerosis Society is to end the devastating effects of multiple sclerosis. This is not the way that the organization measures its performance or evaluates itself; rather it is a higher hope, a grander vision that acts as an overarching superordinate direction for the organization.

In the following practice example, a social worker uses the personal scorecard to strategize and leverage her position in the organization.

TABLE 7.2. Personal Scorecard for a Social Worker at a Chapter of the Multiple Sclerosis Society

Organizational Objectives
1. End the devastating effects of multiple sclerosis (MS) (mission statement).
2. Maximize quality of life for people with MS and their families.
3. Increase public awareness of MS.
4. Maximize financial support to MS cause.

Organization Targets	*Scorecard Measures*
Fund-raising	
1. Initiate more planned giving services, such as estate planning, wills, etc.	Create a planned giving marketing brochure. Market at 50 percent of chapter events.
2. Increase community campaigns: volunteer run/walks, dance-a-thons, craft shows, bingo, etc.	Two additional events per year.
3. Raise additional research dollars for national organization.	Give 5 percent more than the required 40 percent.
Public Relations	
1. Increase media coverage of all chapter activity.	Media coverage for 100 percent of fundraisers, 50 percent of services events, and special-interest stories.
Overall	
1. Increase volunteer-driven work efforts.	Write job description for newly appointed volunteer manager.
2. Increase chapter membership: MS clients, family members, friends, health care professionals, etc.	Create process for recording all chapter contacts. Improve management of data and increase membership by 10 percent.

Unit Targets	*Team/Individual Initiatives*
Services	
1. Reduce gaps in services.	Build relationship with employment consultant. Fill newly created advocacy position. Identify staff/volunteer to oversee updating of information and referral database.
2. Improve client/chapter network.	Achieve 75 percent prevalence rate in all counties. Track four clients/month as case management. Make monthly follow-up calls to 50 percent of newly registered chapter members.
3. Increase ongoing programming.	Pilot community-based wellness program in a nearby town.
4. Initiate project MS-Knowledge.	Provide orientation about MS and chapter services to all new nonservices staff. Market chapter brochures at a minimum of six professional community education programs.

Team/Individual Measures	*Targets*
1. Promote strong foundation of programs and services.	Increase current staff (one) and volunteers (three).
2. Community networking with clients and professionals.	Cosponsor two professional education programs. Pilot MS Community Wellness Club (ten members).
3. Work with consultants to reduce gaps in services.	Build relationships in work with employment, advocacy, etc. (three new collaborative relationships).

Sarah Wells had worked for a chapter of the Multiple Sclerosis Society for four years and had learned about the balanced scorecard in a continuing education course. She thought that using a balanced scorecard would be a nonthreatening way to encourage her organization to institute some performance measures. Here the balanced scorecard is not used from the top down as its originators meant it to be. Rather, Ms. Wells used it as a direct practitioner/ program planner to move this small organization to think in terms of performance. The scorecard incorporates planning, determination of goals and objectives, contracting, and strategizing. As much as possible, the scorecard has explicated terms that are measurable. In fact, Ms. Wells's use of the balanced scorecard is a kind of strategy. Most of the work is accomplished by a variety of interdisciplinary teams made up of professionals and volunteers who involve clients directly in most phases of the work.

The use of the scorecard was effective with the organization's personnel because it allowed them to relate the organization's mission and goals to the work of the individual employees in terms of measures and targets. Basically it was a way to understand relationships between mission and tasks, between individuals and the organization, and between present and future levels and kinds of work. Using precise numbers to set targets for work objectified the work in new, useful, and productive ways.

The personal trait that Sarah Wells thought most interfered with accomplishing her work was her consistent feeling that her colleagues did not think that what she did was very important to the organization. She decided that if she carried herself and did her work as if she and it were important to the organization she and her role would be viewed more positively. Therefore, Ms. Wells included this very personal goal as she introduced the balanced scorecard to her organization and as she worked for it to be adopted as a way of planning and providing feedback for the work.

Types of Goals

It is helpful to think about goals as they relate to service, treatment, and process (Rose 1995b). Among service goals are survival goals having to do with the future acquisition of resources necessary for survival, obtaining enough information to make informed decisions, and obtaining the concrete skills necessary for achieving survival goals. What Rose calls treatment goals are also called goals of direct practice, those goals that the social worker and client agree they will work toward together. In direct practice, goals are both general and situational; that is, they are meant to help clients learn what they need to manage in a specific situation and also learn to generalize from that situation to others like it. While treatment is usually a word associated with clinical work, the notion of generalizability is as important in community and program contexts as it is for individuals and families. For example, a child with epilepsy has to learn to manage his response to his classmates' reactions to his seizures, and it is hoped that he will generalize that experience to other situations in his life. But social workers have to work as societal advocates so that epilepsy is better understood by everyone and so that the popular media's negative, distorted, and antiquated depictions of those with seizure disorders will be addressed and corrected. Similarly, a community might organize to force traffic to slow down in areas where there are many accidents, and it is hoped that the community will generalize from that experience and use similar strategies to make more positive changes. Among treatment goals are the acquisition of coping skills, which enable clients to cope with stress-, anger-, and anxiety-inducing situations. Other treatment goals are the development of effective time management skills and problem-solving techniques. Finally, process goals are those necessary for the effective use of the social worker/client relationship, such as contracts clarifying the expectations that social workers and clients have of each other as well as the structure of such relationships.

Goal Formulation

To formulate goals one must work directly with the client to develop goals that are agreed upon and sufficiently explicit so that both social worker and client can monitor their work together. Length of time has to be a factor in such monitoring. If goals are long-term or involve a great deal of work and many personal and resource accommodations, it is helpful to break down the time frame into intervals at which client and social worker will review their progress. This is especially helpful when clients are managing chronic conditions or situations. Goals work best when they are cast positively instead of negatively. Subgoals can also be used when goals are very broad. For example, a neighborhood group that wants to improve community safety determines that first it will improve relations with the police department, then form a team to accompany children to and from school, and then work to secure better street lighting.

Goals may range from concrete and highly specific items, such as obtaining a place to live or a wheelchair, to intangibles, such as emotional states and feelings. It is easier to achieve success when the goal is to distribute information about hazardous waste or refer a teenager to a school-based health center. It is much harder to measure success when looking for behavioral change, such as having community members contact their legislators about the disposal of hazardous waste or evaluating teenagers' familial, school, and peer interactions as a result of the school-based health clinic referral (Kelley and Stokes 1984; Maher 1987). The first set of goals is highly concrete and measurable. The second can be objectified, that is, viewed in terms of behaviors that are measurable. However, the second set involves many more tangible and intangible variables that are much harder to measure. This issue will be discussed in greater depth in chapter 9.

Goals and Diagnoses

In individual or family work, it is critical for the social worker to explore the relationship between the diagnosis of the client and the establishment of goals (Kerson 1997). Diagnosis is often determined by a member of another profession, generally a physician. Diagnostic terms such as *epilepsy, schizophrenia,* or *AIDS* are labels that tell the practitioner very little about functional ability (see chapter 6). These tend to be the kinds of diagnoses that cause clients, family members, and helpers to limit goals and, too often, to limit hope. Thus, in terms of the establishment of goals, the social worker's approach is to be realistic but positive, grounded but hopeful. If social workers use diagnostic information to limit goals, to limit the use they believe a client can make of a professional relationship, or to triage clients into categories that receive no service, social workers are allowing diagnoses to restrict their work.

Goals and Missions

Goals are tied directly to the purpose or mission of the organization through whose auspices the work occurs. This is a very simple notion. One goes to a bakery for bread and a butcher shop for meat. If the client comes to a family therapy institute because a child is having problems, the institute and what it is established to provide will have the goal of reordering family interactions. If the child's problems occur in a school, it may be that counseling in a school-based center will focus on the child and not the family. This notion is especially obvious when a complaint is physical. If a patient has trouble walking and is referred to an orthopedic clinic, the clinic may address the physical problem but do little to investigate the individual's living and working environment. If goals often do not match mission or purpose, perhaps the purpose should be altered. In fact, understanding needs using an ecological perspective might lead social workers to see that the purpose or mission of an organization might have to be altered in order to meet the needs of its present clientele.

Goals and Outcome Measures

It is not accidental that *goals, outcomes,* and *objectives* have become almost interchangeable terms. The insinuation of outcome measures into goal setting has made it necessary for social workers to be more definite, categorical, and concrete in helping clients set goals. Expressions such as self-actualization or feeling better about oneself can be goals only in the most rarified of practice situations. Unless the client is a self-pay private psychotherapy patient, some third party wants progress reports in highly concrete terms related to material or behavioral results. The present emphasis on outcome measures and the increased demand of third-party payers that social workers justify their time and their expense by proving that their clients are reaching their goals means that goals will increasingly be concrete and/or measurable. To be measurable, goals must be objectifiable; that is, it must be possible to describe them in concrete terms. Being able to report progress in these terms supports the client, encourages the client to continue to work, and assures others such as third-party payers, the courts, and other authorities that progress is being made. This allows the professional relationship to continue to be supported. The use of outcome measures will allow social workers to prove their results and their economic value to their organizations and funding sources.

Many goals are related to helping clients live outside of institutional arrangements and live as independently as their capacities will allow. Placement can be foster care, a psychiatric facility, or a nursing home. Those goals, tightly related to outcome measures, are often false and short-sighted. After all, it is possible that parents and children may be better off with children in foster care or adoption, that some frail elderly persons must be in the protected environment of a nursing home, and that some people with serious mental illness whose symptoms are not responsive to medication or whose symptomatology does not allow them to comply with medical regimens may benefit from an institutionalized environment. According to Tracy (1995:978),

> One such issue is increasing dissatisfaction with the prevention of placement as the sole outcome measure. Although it has been argued that, strategically, placement is an important policy focus, there are significant practical and methodological problems in relying on placement prevention as an outcome measure. Placement is not an adequate measure of clinical status. Some placements are clearly necessary, but even when placement is prevented, it cannot be assumed that the child and the family are necessarily safer, happier, or functioning better.

Goals and Resources

Goals must also be related to the resources of the organization as well as to the level of resources available outside the organization. Cost-effectiveness will continue to be expected and must be demonstrated. "When principles of effectiveness-based program planning are used, program success can be measured and documented. All indications are that this type of documentation will be increasingly required for future funding" (Kettner et al. 1999:108–9). Thus service providers have to ask whether programs and services to clients are cost-effective and whether similar results could be achieved at lower cost. At the same time, it is critical that social workers think about finding ways to increase and redistribute resources for clients and programs. Not to do so is to limit the possibilities for clients in the same way that they can be limited when their capacity to change and grow is underestimated.

Although it is unusual for social workers in health and mental health care to control a "pot of money" to deliver services to a population of clients, this seems the smartest way to relate client/organization/funding source goals with best use of resources. This method is often used in business as well as in parts of medical care. For example, a state gave one social service agency $1.2 million to provide services to six hundred clients who are presently working part-time and whose goal it is to be financially self-sufficient. The agency has the discretion to use the money for whatever clients may need to further the work, such as helping with auto insurance or day care, in addition to providing a range of counseling and referral services.

Short- and Long-Term Goals

Increasingly, funding sources, policies, and organizations require that social workers work only with short-term goals. Some exceptions are services to people with chronic conditions such as spina bifida, cerebral palsy, Alzheimer's disease, severe learning disabilities, or serious and persistent mental illness. Even in such lifelong situations concerning illness or disability, the roles for social workers are often seen as providing short-term solutions in a chronic situation or crisis. Part of the solution to this problem is for clients and social workers to be aware of and discuss long-term needs and goals while working to address immediate goals. Thus, in the same way that social workers have to learn to think of themselves and their clientele as parts of very broad and deep systems of care, while attending to smaller segments and time periods they have to focus on long-term goals while attending to immediate needs and goals. Short-term or immediate goals and short time periods can be thought of as segments in clients' continuous care. It is as if the social worker takes a photograph and a movie, a close-up and a panoramic view all at the same time.

Goals and Ethical Constraints

Although goals are to be determined by clients, they must be within the ethical guidelines of the social work profession. A managed care company that imposes gag rules that prohibit staff from discussing treatment options the company does not wish to pay for would be an example of an organization in which a social worker could not work ethically. Union members whose goals were to physically intimidate nonmembers could have social workers work with them to no greater extent than a social worker could condone a man's beating his wife because she did not agree with him.

Possible Negative Repercussions of Goals

Sometimes, the planning process yields unanticipated consequences (Clapp 1995). One community-based approach facilitated neighborhood empowerment by allowing neighbors to guide each phase of problem solving. Here, coalition building and ongoing neighborhood activities were crucial. The designated neighborhood was a four-block area of an inner-city community. The organizing process was adapted from other organizing models (Bracht, Kingsbury, and Rissel 1990) and generic planning models (Lewis, Lewis, Packard, and Souflee 2001).

The organizers were asked by the Head Start staff at one target site to address the neighborhood drug problem. To assess the problem, the social workers collected existing data, held community meetings, and tracked social indicators. As related by Clapp (1995:53),

> The most striking indicator of neighborhood problems was visual. The first time the social workers visited the neighborhood, there were dozens of people in the street selling drugs. The organizers formed, implemented and evaluated their strategy and then identified several issues that would affect the neighborhood's ability to maintain the positive effects of intervention. There were issues related to membership, barriers to maintaining effort, evaluation issues and one major unintended consequence, that drug dealers moved just outside of the four-block area and set up shop in a contiguous neighborhood.

There are unplanned consequences of all work, some positive and some negative.

Goals Versus Objectives

Although the terms *goal* and *objective* are frequently used interchangeably, here they are distinctly different. Goals are overarching hoped-for outcomes that may or may not be measurable, whereas objectives are measurable incremental steps toward achieving the overall goal. The following is an example that demonstrates the relationship between goals and objectives: A social worker working with a client who was depressed and isolated helped the client develop the goal of leaving the house each day to do a specific positive activity that involved other people. The objectives were drawn into a contract that resembled a daily schedule and named a specific activity; so for one month, each Sunday the client would go to church, each Monday she would wash her clothes at the self-service laundry, each Tuesday and Thursday she would go the senior center for lunch. The hope of social worker and client was that meeting these measurable objectives would help the client to reach the goal of being less depressed and isolated.

DEVELOPING OBJECTIVES

Objectives call for quantifiable results, specific measurable outcomes of activities. Outcome objectives clarify the anticipated effects of interventions on the client, population, or organization. They focus on problem reduction or an improvement in life quality. Effective outcome objectives translate goals into specific and measurable terms. Thus interventions are designed to attain defined outcome measures. Patti (1985:84) states that "objectives are operationalized statements of program intent that express in specific, observable, preferably measurable terms those changes (outcomes) the program seeks to produce within some designated time period." Three criteria can be used to determine if, and how, the objectives can be met: measurability, manageability, and context.

For example, the goal of a federally funded, state-monitored Healthy Start Program is to build a supportive safety net for at-risk mothers and their infants in order to reduce infant mortality and morbidity rates. Objectives for the program include the following: (1) providing psychosocial assessment and enrolling 90 percent of the project's annually projected target, four hundred new clients, and (2) providing at least three community referrals to each assessed client.

To make objectives most useful and therefore most measurable in evaluation, it is helpful to have action plans accompany each objective (Patti 1985:85). For example, one objective of the program is to provide psychosocial drug education and information and referral to community resources for drug and alcohol treatment. An accompanying action plan could include

- Disseminating brochures outlining the effects on babies of their mothers' drinking alcohol or using drugs, and brochures with information about local substance abuse programs listing locations, telephone numbers, hours, and the kinds of services provided
- Including questions about, and discussion of, individual substance use each time the expectant mother comes for service and also at the time of delivery

- Asking local substance abuse treatment centers to suggest ways to market their services to Healthy Start clients

A problem with searching for measurable objectives is that, rather than measuring their results, people tend to measure their work volume (Kaplan and Norton 1996c). Thus report figures can appear better than the work might warrant: a five-minute visit may be counted as follow-up; handing someone a brochure may be counted as drug education. "To formulate objectives one has to be explicit about the results that are to be achieved (outcome objectives), the means by which the results will be achieved (process objectives) and the activities or tasks that are necessary to achieve them. A good objective is clear, specific, measurable, time-limited and realistic and represents a commitment" (Kettner et al. 1999:97). Effective objectives are similarly understood by everyone who shares in the work. They are measurable in some way. The measurement criteria are incorporated into the objectives, and the objectives must specify results, including changes in conditions and numbers. Outcomes, including subsets of activities, are clear about who has responsibility for the process. According to Kettner et al. (1999),

One way to ensure clarity (and later, measurability) is to develop objectives that have action dimensions. Examples of these would include statements that begin with verbs such as write, list, increase, reduce, terminate, or demonstrate. Examples that use vague and nonbehavioral (i.e., not observable) referents might include statements that begin with verbs such as understand, know, realize, feel, believe, or enable.

The following example lists the objectives devised for a client at Hope House.

A. Obtain employment.
   1. Make at least two job contacts every day.
   2. Register with two vocational development programs.
   3. Apply to the Office of Vocational Rehabilitation.
   4. Attend occupational meetings on Monday afternoons.
B. Maintain employment.
   1. Attend work regularly despite feelings of nervousness.
   2. Discuss work problems with Hope House staff.
C. Develop a support system.
   1. Continue to spend two hours every day in common areas of the house.

2. Make an effort to stay up until at least 8:00 P.M. four nights a week.
3. Do at least one recreational activity every week once you have income.
4. Work with the social worker on developing interests and hobbies.
D. Save money.
1. Develop a budget with the social worker once you have income.
2. Open a savings account and begin to save for an apartment by the second week of employment.
E. Watch for early symptoms of illness.
1. Discuss with staff any concerns in this area.
2. Develop two new ways to handle stress.

The elements of a situation or condition that the social worker is expected to change, as well as the time frame (in terms of months, days, and years), must be specified. The outcomes in terms of products, results, and milestones or benchmarks should be articulated. The criteria by which results will be documented, monitored, and measured must be clear. Additionally, the identity of those responsible for implementing and measuring achievement of the objective must be specified. Thus names and positions should be part of the documentation of task and outcome responsibilities.

A primary goal for people with disabilities is to remain in their own homes. Their families are often eager to continue to provide a home but may lack sufficient access to support services, such as day programs or respite care, to do so. The traditional way people are matched with services is that programs develop vacancies and then clients who are suitable for those openings are identified. The desire was to turn this process around: to identify an individual's needs, then to develop services to meet those needs. Thus it was thought that services would be individualized in ways that would maximize the chances for people with disabilities to stay at home. In the following practice example, people with disabilities are given enhanced opportunities to remain at home.

One state has developed a program called Family Driven Support Services (FDSS) in which family members of a person with a disability are required to identify what they would need to enhance that person's opportunities to remain in their family's home, as opposed to being admitted to an institution. Families begin by answering the question What will it take for your family member who has a disability to remain in your home?

During the assessment period, families are encouraged to think creatively about how best to answer this question. They often need support in learning how to identify their own needs, as for many years they have been presented with programs with a vacancy and asked whether they are interested in that service. The support service starts with the assessment and then looks for services based on the needs identified by the family.

Some of the services that have been purchased under FDSS for people with disabilities and their families include the following:

1. John's family obtained a new refrigerator so that medications could be stored safely. The family income was low. The refrigerator they had was old and unreliable, but they could not afford to replace it.

2. Ann's family obtained a stair glider that enabled Ann, who has a physical disability, to travel independently between the first and second floors of the house. Most houses in the area are row houses that have more than one floor. This equipment enabled the family to remain together without embarking on a search for single-floor housing, which would be hard to find in their community at any cost.

3. Antoinette's family purchased a membership for Antoinette and another family member in the local YWCA. This provided recreational and leisure opportunities for Antoinette in a setting that included people with disabilities as well as those without them. The family member provided the additional help that Antoinette needed to participate in the Y's programs, such as swimming and aerobic exercise.

4. Stephanie's family used FDSS to purchase school uniforms so she could attend a private school.

5. Jim took horseback riding lessons using FDSS funds. In addition to providing respite for the family, the activity enhanced Jim's self-esteem, and according to his family, led to more harmonious home relationships.

Each person with a disability whose family receives FDSS funds must live in the community. If individuals with disabilities are institutionalized, they are no longer eligible for FDSS. While it is not always possible to avoid institutionalization, many families are receiving needed supports under FDSS, and this allows family members with disabilities to remain in their family home for as long as possible. There is even a monetary benefit to people's continuing to live at home. Family Driven Support Services have also been demonstrated to be cost-effective, compared with the cost of institutionalization. The FDSS program serves as an excellent example of the relationship between goals and objectives, the importance of being able to measure objectives, and the success of programs that have been planned with sufficient resources, measurable outcomes, and goals that are the same as those of the client.

STRATEGIZING

Strategies are action-focused, careful plans, methods, or series of maneuvers for obtaining specific goals or results. They are a means for people not to work harder but to work smarter (Drucker 1990). It is helpful to remember that the word *strategy* has military roots, and in that context it refers to the work of a commander-in-chief, the art of projecting and directing the larger military movements and operations of a campaign. Both the concept of strategy and the content of this chapter are meant to empower the social worker. Strategizing, then, supports social workers in seeing the biggest picture, thinking positively, leveraging resources, and acting on the assumption that with great care, knowledge, and effort it is possible to obtain a myriad of goals and results. According to Hamel (1998:10),

> Like all forms of complexity, strategy is poised on the border between perfect order and total chaos, between absolute efficiency and blind experimentation, between autocracy and complete adhocracy. . . . Circumstance, cognition, data, and desire converge, and a strategy insight is born. The fact that strategy has a significant element of serendipity to it shouldn't cause us to despair. . . . The question is, how can we increase the odds that new wealth-creating strategies emerge? How can we make serendipity happen? How can we prompt emergence?

Social workers in health and mental health care are most exposed to concepts related to strategies when they are involved in strategic planning exercises. At this point, many have participated in a myriad of these exercises that seem unrelated to the realities of practice and are rarely implemented. The announcement of another planning session often sounds like a waste of time. Nevertheless, strategizing can be part of a planning process or separate from it. The overall point is to think and act strategically. It is this desire to have the element of critical thinking ever present everywhere that causes the word to be used as verb or an adverb in every title and topic description. Thus there are strategic plans, strategic innovations, strategic programs, as well as thinking strategically, planning strategically, and the like. But, in all cases, the word *strategic* implies that one should think critically, act smart, look carefully forward, be aware of friends and foes, be ready and know how to work systems.

In the following case example, strategies were devised to extend the preparation for adult life for individuals who are developmentally disabled.

The Individuals with Disabilities Education Act (IDEA) of 1986, amended from the Education for All Handicapped Act of 1975, mandates free, appropriate education for students with disabilities until they are 21 years old. This important legislation curtailed the discretion of school district personnel. Before IDEA, such personnel assessed students with disabilities on an individual basis and could refuse school admission even though a student met all requirements placed on students without disabilities, such as residency, age, and immunizations.

Even with the advent of IDEA, problems remain. Families and other advocates must learn the distinctions between school programs for students under 21 years of age and services for adults with disabilities. At age 21, the entitlement to education under IDEA ends, and families often have little information about future alternatives. This problem is confounded because, in order to maintain confidentiality, the school district refuses to release names of such students to the community agencies that can provide services once students turn 21.

While the school district is the primary access point for education for the student under age 21, families must deal with at least three agencies when they search for job-training and placement services for adults with disabilities. The base service unit or community mental health and mental retardation center controls services funded through the state mental retardation system. The Office of Vocational Rehabilitation provides funds for vocational evaluation, job training, and job coaching services, but a provider of job-training and placement services must be identified, as the rehabilitation office's role is limited to paying for the service. Numerous contacts must be made to meet the requirements of each of these three agencies.

A large city chapter of the Association for Retarded Citizens has assembled representatives from agencies involved in helping students to make the transition from the school system to community-based job-training and placement services. High-level officials from vocational rehabilitation, the school district, mental retardation services, and provider agencies, as well as family members and individuals with disabilities, are committed to this interagency problem-solving effort. The group meets quarterly.

Objectives from this group include

- Educating family members regarding whom to contact to make plans for after high school
- Educating school district personnel to begin the planning process early, while the students are still in school
- Problem solving among the agencies who will share records once the individual and family give consent
- Identifying physicians who are willing to do the required medical examinations
- Persuading all parties to work within in an identified time period in order to minimize the time gap between school district programs and job-training services

Susan and John Stout were desperate for services for their daughter, Melissa, who was turning 21. Because Susan and John work outside their home, and Melissa cannot be left alone, care and supervision as well as training opportunities were an issue for her. Because the Stouts knew that the entitlement for services would end when Melissa became 21 years old, they made contact with their base service unit when Melissa turned 20 years old. The groundwork laid by the interagency group smoothed the process for planning for Melissa's life after high school. The Office of Vocational Rehabilitation was contacted about Melissa during her final school year so that school district personnel could describe Melissa's needs and provide necessary records. The parents learned about the various providers of service and selected an agency with experience with people like Melissa. Melissa left high school in June, and in September she entered a job-training and placement program that is funded through the Office of Vocational Rehabilitation. The result of interagency collaboration was a fairly smooth transition for Melissa.

Strategizing and its related concepts can contribute to the social work enterprise. For example, it is useful to understand that the major concepts of strategic planning are similar to social workers' plans for work with clients: (1) determining the purpose of the work, (2) conducting an external/internal or ecological analysis, (3) setting objectives, (4) developing strategies, (5) operationalizing plans including individual objectives, strategy action plans, and performance appraisal and reward, and (6) determining how the work will be evaluated and monitored or controlled (Steiner, Gross, Ruffolo, and Murray 1994; Williamson et al. 1997). Strategy options are alternative courses of action that are evaluated before an organization makes a commitment to a specific course of action that is outlined in a strategic plan. Too often, because of a powerful belief system or particular themes in its history, an agency proceeds with a particular modality or style of relating to clients without reviewing options. This is as true for direct practice as it is for work at the program or organizational level.

Devising a good strategy requires an understanding of two fundamental points: the benefit of having a well-articulated, stable purpose, and the importance of discovering, understanding, documenting, and exploiting insights about how to increase value. If the strategies of agencies or institutions are evaluated in this way, one agency or organization can create more value than other organizations do (Campbell and Alexander 1997). If a social worker working with a client or program is being studied regarding strategy use, it is to make the work more efficacious. The process of developing a winning strategy is messy, experimental, and iterative, and it is driven from the bottom up. The fundamental building block of good strategy is insight into how to create more value than competitors can. "These insights normally focus on practical issues and point to new ways of doing things" (Campbell and Alexander 1997:46). Defining purpose, discovering insights, and combining the two into a strategy is difficult.

Often, organizations are more familiar with strategic planning than they are with the concept of strategic intent. According to Hamel and Prahalad (1989), planners ask themselves, "How will next year be different?" while those who work with strategic intent ask "What must we do differently?" Planning is about programming, a rote activity, but strategizing is a quest that is never rote (Hamel 1996). While programming often is developed or altered through planning processes, strategizing can more often lead to projects, more constrained in relation to time and resources, but perhaps with greater scope and vision because they are less bounded by the routinized constraints that are part of planning processes. Strategies can be more spontaneous, can align roles and tasks that are not usually seen together in an organization, and can be less hierarchical than planning activities might be.

Hamel and Prahalad (1989) explore two contrasting strategy models, one of which leads to an entire organization's learning to maximally leverage resources. The less successful model focuses on the problem of maintaining strategic fit between resources and opportunities so that those determining the strategy trim their ambitions and goals to match available resources. Traditional planning with its criteria for rewards, definition of the markets served by an organization, and acceptance of current practice all work together to tightly constrain the range of available means with innovation remaining an isolated activity. In this model, growth depends more on the inventive capacity of individuals and teams. The model focuses on the problem of leveraging resources, of finding ways to enhance available assets. The difference in emphasis affects how the organization fares over time when compared to others that are similar. If an organization leverages resources to reach seemingly unattainable goals and so must accelerate organizational learning, new rules can place the organization at an advantage. With strategic intent, the planning process typically acts as a feasibility sieve to appraise flexible means with improvisation to reach clear ends (Hamal and Prahalad 1989:66). Managers at all levels must participate in the broad direction implicit in their organization's strategic intent as well as understanding its implications for their own positions.

Hamel (1998) sees five preconditions for the emergence of strategy: (1) new voices (a highly participative, pluralistic process), (2) new conversations (dialogues that cross traditional boundaries), (3) new passions (i.e., giving everyone involved voice in the future of the organization because people do embrace change when they see a positive return), (4) new perspectives (i.e., new conceptual lenses that aid organizations' reconceiving themselves, their customers, their competitors, and therefore their opportunities), and (5) new experiments (i.e., small, risk-avoiding experiments that maximize an organization's rate of learning about which new strategies will work and which will not).

Following is a direct practice strategy that carried all of Hamel's necessary preconditions and transformed agency programming.

Reena Gupta, a new voice, was a foster care worker whose clients were in care because their biological parents' substance abuse or mental illnesses interfered with their ability to parent. The agency visits that she arranged for biological families were unsuccessful. Some parents did not show up, and parents who came interacted very little with their children. At first, Ms. Gupta, who had recently immigrated, thought that this was the way American parents interacted, but her colleagues told her otherwise (new perspectives and conversations). Determined to enhance the interaction in biological families, Ms. Gupta instituted a program in which she participated in each family session (new passions and experiments). For each session, she brought materials that were developmentally appropriate for each child and taught the families how to interact with the children using the materials. She found that the parents were more comfortable and more satisfied with the visits so that they came more frequently and participated more freely. Ms. Gupta's children also returned more quickly to their biological families than did the children assigned to other agency social workers. Since her objectives were measurable, and her means could be replicated by the other social workers, Ms. Gupta appealed to the supervisor of foster care to institute this structured and professionally run visiting program for all the agency's foster children. Within a year of the program's being instituted, the return rate to biological families improved for the entire agency. Thus this strategy, devised by one direct practice social worker who was new not only to the organization but to the country as well helped the agency reach its goals.

TEAMWORK

The conduit for everything that has been discussed in this chapter—planning, determining goals and objectives, contracting, and strategizing—is teamwork. In the narrowest definition, the team is the client unit and the social worker is the representative of the organization. The team could also be all the workers in an organization. To advocate for clients, to act as case managers, and to act in concert with those from other agencies and organizations, social workers have to participate in interorganizational teamwork. Teamwork includes face-to-face (or at least computer-to-computer) assemblages who, through relationships in reasonably small groups, act as teams to solve problems and create service structures (Compher 1987; Compton and Galaway 1998; Poulin, Walter, and Walker 1994; Saltz and Schaefer 1996). The ability to work with, for, and through groups is critical in every kind and level of social work in health and mental health care.

Teamwork is one version of the many varieties of group interaction that social workers in health and mental health care must master. Team learning is a collective activity in which relationships are more important than material objects, and discussion generates creative collective thinking (Kurtz 1998). While group work or group therapy may be understood as interventions with client groups, task groups and teamwork must be understood as vehicles for working with colleagues, members of other professions, and other kinds of collaborators.

Teamwork as Strategy

Teamwork is essential to almost every part of social work practice, but it is most important in developing and implementing strategies on the organizational and program level, as well as on the level of the individual client or consumer. In the 1980s there were quality circles, and now there are self-directed work teams (Denton 1999). "The discipline of team starts with 'dialogue,' the capacity of members of a team to suspend assumptions and enter into a genuine 'thinking together.' The Greek *dia-logos* meant a free-flowing of meaning though a group, allowing the group to discover insights not attainable individually" (Senge 1990:10). Organizational experts have long condoned the importance of teams that are charged with particular foci, given increased autonomy, and encouraged to work outside the box. High-quality decisions depend on "active cooperation of the team members. To effectively usher a decision through this complex web of operational details, team members must understand and commit to a decision" (Burgelman and Grove 1996).

In the following practice example, a team worked together to form a cancer support group developed by and for African American women.

The Women of Faith and Hope Group is a church-sponsored breast cancer support group in a black community. Its name signals to prospective participants that a very important coping resource among black women is their strong sense of religiousness and faith in God. Although there are many support groups for women with breast cancer in the larger community, very few women of color attend these groups.

The group was planned by an advisory board consisting of parishioners from Canaan Baptist Church and professional black women from the community, one of whom is a social worker with special expertise in breast cancer. Begun by an African American breast cancer survivor who is a member of the church where the group meets, the group is attended by women in greater numbers than are usually seen in such groups; twenty to thirty members attend each meeting. Its location in the black community and in a church adds credibility to the group. Discussion topics are culturally relevant, and speakers direct their presentations to the issues of black women. For example, church elders attending the group anointed with oil those women who requested this intervention, and when invited to address the group, a dietitian presented ways to prepare traditional African American delicacies using reduced-fat recipes. To honor black women's strong sense of family, husbands, partners, and children are invited to attend meetings, and meetings always include time for testimonies of God's intervention in one's healing process.

Building Teams

Before creating teams, organizations have to clarify the teams' purpose and direction, and they must be certain that the teams are necessary to the organization. This first step requires substantial study and planning (Dewar 1999). "A true self-directed team has to be able to change the order of the task, have some control over budget and the power to make decisions. To grow your own teams: have a plan and stick with it, make sure that team members are in frequent contact with each other, give teams a clearly defined target and a way to get there, measure performance and have as an ultimate goal the creation of self-directed work teams" (Denton 1999:53). A working coordinator and, if possible, a facilitator who is a process coach must be assigned. Issues regarding interdisciplinary teams in which one profession traditionally has more authority than others have to be resolved before the work begins (Griffiths 1997). Team members must have expertise related to the task or must be given additional training to make their full participation possible. A team that chooses problems within its own area of expertise has a much greater chance of success. Typical steps in the team work process are to identify several problems, select one problem, collect data, analyze that data, develop solutions, pick best solution(s), implement solutions(s), and follow up (Dewar 1999). Cooperative learning is key (Magney 1996).

In the following example, strategizing and teamwork are used in discharge planning.

In her study of discharge planning in one urban hospital, Clemens (1995) argues that there are several solutions to the problems created by shortened hospital stays: Discharge planning should be handled by one department staffed jointly by nurses and social workers. A team of social workers, nurses, and physicians could assess each patient, thereby removing structural barriers to information and permitting access by clients to their full range of options and also promoting greater collaboration between health care professionals and clients. The hospital should work to develop other means of prompt and safe discharge, such as a step-down unit. Such a unit would facilitate discharge of high-risk patients and alleviate concerns about legal liability. The Medicare extended-care benefit would pay for care in such a setting and provide the hospital with additional revenue (Clemens 1995).

Brief, intense discharge planning, one result of very short patient stays in acute settings, makes the contributions of social work even more critical for the creation of a safe, optimal plan for patients once they leave the acute care setting. The Department of Case Management (DCM) of Fine Community Hospital has proved to the hospital that it is critical for discharge planning and that it can save the hospital a great deal of money in the process. Directed by a social worker and made up of social workers and nurses, the DCM reaches its goals through work with patients, families, payers, the hospital finance department, community resources, ancillary services, and admitting physicians. A full description of this work can be found in Hammer and Kerson (1998). The DCM accomplished its goals by renaming the department from two consolidated departments of Social Work and Utilization Review, reviewing all tasks that made up the work of both departments, training most staff as generalists with specific expertise, developing a role with the finance department, and establishing measurable outcomes (Gibelman and Whiting 1999). The organigraph in figure 7.8 demonstrates the critical web of activity between the departments of finance, billing, and case management and the physician practices.

As part of this work, the DCM developed several resources, including bibliographic references for developing language for communicating with finance officers and managed care company representatives. A primary objective was to reduce the number of days for which managed care companies deny payment to the hospital. The DCM found that most unpaid days were due to delays in service, disparities in needs assessment between physicians and payers, and medical practice patterns. Members of the DCM became mediators advising the finance and billing departments and physician practices about levels of care, participating in contract negotiation, and monitoring development and implementation of critical pathways. One result of the DCM's work was that the number of acute days for which managed care companies denied payment to the hospital has been quartered (Hammer and Kerson 1998).

FIGURE 7.8. Department of Case Management at Fine Community Hospital.

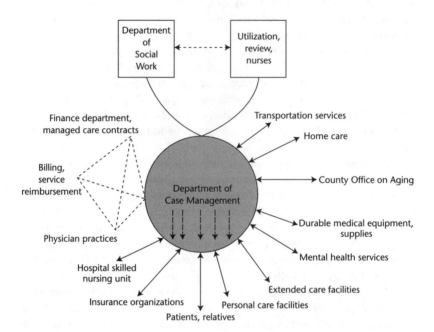

In the following practice example, the social worker does strategic intervention with a managed care organization on behalf of a client.

Marie Pugliese, 68 years old, was admitted to a community hospital with respiratory failure and subsequently became dependent on a ventilator. The prognosis was fair to good that she could be successfully weaned off the ventilator, and her discharge plan included transfer to a facility that (1) had a specialized ventilator unit where her physician practiced; (2) was within walking distance of her spouse, who did not drive; (3) was the hospital to which Mrs. Pugliese would return in an emergency, and (4) had a bed available within two days. The managed care organization (MCO) offered a facility that had a bed available the same day, was twenty miles away, required three different busses for what would be a two-hour trip to the facility, and had no staff physicians with whom Mrs. Pugliese's physician was familiar.

The MCO case manager did not see any problems with her discharge plan. The hospital was willing to accept a reduced rate of skilled payment ($210.00) versus an acute payment of $889.00 to keep the patient to await the bed at the desired facility. The social worker convinced the patient's physician to call the MCO's physician appeal hotline to argue that the patient should stay at the present hospital so that her care would be continuous and would meet her physical, medical, and psychosocial needs. Since a bed was available at another facility, the MCO determined that the patient no longer required an acute level of care. That meant that the hospital would not be paid any rate in an acute bed, even though the hospital agreed to accept a skilled care rate. Also, the hospital would be denied any payment if it chose to keep the patient for two days until the other facility was available. The family was kept closely informed of these discussions by the social worker and physician.

When family members asked if there was anything they could do, the social worker suggested contacting the MCO case manager, the medical director, and the patient's employer, who purchased the benefits from the MCO on behalf of the patient. Even though the family contacted all three and the employer contacted the MCO, the hospital was still denied payment. Still, the hospital made the administrative decision that the patient should remain until the bed was available at the ventilator facility. Subsequent negotiations between the MCO and the case management department resulted in an agreement with the MCO that the hospital would receive a grace day for discharge planning at a reduced rate to accommodate such instances.

CONCLUSION

This chapter has described many of the planning dimensions of social work practice, the planning process, determination of goals and objectives, contracting, and strategizing. Each of these dimensions is most likely to be successful through the use of teamwork, and each involves the clients or populations with whom social workers intervene. These aspects lay the groundwork for interventions. Thus planning, contracting, the determination of goals and objectives, and strategizing are all part of the work that helps people reach their goals.

Social Work Practice Interventions: Advocacy, Brief Work, Case Management, and Work with Groups

To intervene means to arbitrate, mediate, get involved, intrude, interfere, or come in or between so as to modify or hinder. It also means to enter or occur as an unnecessary condition or characteristic; to appear, come, or lie between two things or two periods of time; and to interfere, usually through force or threat of force. The meanings vary according to the degree to which the parties desire the presence of the person who is coming between, with "mediate" or "arbitrate" being the most positive and "interfere" the most negative. Although social workers view and wish others to view the work positively, social workers *do* use relationship and advocacy skills and knowledge to place themselves between clients/consumers/communities and the societal elements, populations, psychological dynamics, and people that have the potential to either hurt them or interfere with their access to the services they are entitled to. The most explicit and vivid examples are both historical and contemporary. In the early days of health-related social work, social workers toiled alongside the police to locate those with syphilis or tuberculosis and bring them to clinics for treatment. Now there are certainly times when social workers and the police work together in violent situations involving child, spouse, or elder abuse or persons with serious mental illness who cannot be brought safely to treatment facilities in any other way.

Viewed in this light, the overarching tools for social workers in health and mental health care are relationship and advocacy. Chapter 5 discussed in detail the power of the relationship between social workers and clients/consumers/communities. This chapter moves from the power of the relationship to focus on the four types of interventions that are most critical for social workers in health and mental health care: (1) advocacy, (2) brief solution-focused work, (3) case management, and (4) group work. The systems understanding and management techniques described in chapters 4 and 7 are also considered a part of social workers' technical repertoire. Each intervention can work like a bellows, expanding or contracting depending on the definition of the problem, the setting, and the capacity of the client system to benefit from the intervention.

Thus an intervention is an act of stepping in or intervening in any matter so as to affect its course or consequence. In contemporary social work practice in health and mental health care systems, interventions are rarely singular. Even if a social worker is involved in a simple interaction with an individual client, the social worker is part of a system of services or supports that may be called on in the future by the client or by another person in his or her network. Strategies will typically involve an amalgam of professional interventions, family and other social supports, and governmental, voluntary, self-help, relational, informational, or in-kind interventions. These may not occur at the same time, and may be carried out by more than one social worker, but the social worker is part of a large network of helpers moving in and out of work with the client system over time. In this chapter, particular attention is paid to the relationship between self-help and professional help, as well as to interdisciplinary teamwork.

Social work practice interventions include advocacy (with advocacy being seen as a strategy in its own right and as part of all other strategies), brief solution-focused work, case management, group work, and community organization. Group work is further broken down into self-help and professionally facilitated groups and is differentiated by whether the goal is insight- or task-oriented. Group strategies will also be discussed as tools for work with individuals, families, organizations, and communities and in relating to other social workers, to interdisciplinary teams, and even in to adversarial situations. Thus group techniques are used in management, problem solving, psychotherapy, resource development, and community work.

I understand psychotherapeutic theory and techniques to be useful in every kind of social work practice in health and mental health systems. However, to "apply wholesale the methods of any brand of psychotherapy, from psychoanalysis to behavioral modification, is to ignore the goals, the mission, the cause, and the objectives, the raison d'être of social welfare and casework" (Tolson 1988:14). Effective social work practice in brief work, case management, group work, or advocacy requires a deep psychological understanding of self, individuals, and groups and the relationship of each to context. Psychotherapeutic techniques are some of the tools that all social workers must possess.

It is important to remember that interventions should be closely tied to assessment, problem definition, resources, capacities, goals, and objectives. Contracts between various interested parties, especially between social workers and clients/consumers/communities, should explicate interventions. Interventions are the methods social workers use to address the problems they and their clients have defined. Interventions include tools, methods, and approaches from a panoply of disciplines including social work, psychology, and business. Method is "a systematic process of ordering one's activity in the performance of a function. Method is function in action" (Schwartz 1971:22). Similar skills are required for many methods. All require the understanding of others and the ability to relate. Often the language is different and the playing field is larger for work with organizations and communities than it is for work with individuals, families, and groups, but the relationship, negotiating, and advocacy skills are similar.

The overarching practice example for this chapter depicts the work of two social workers, one trained in clinical social work and one in program planning and advocacy. They are employed in two separate systems and approached the same problem area from their separate vantage points. Nevertheless, they both contributed to the life of a child, his family, and the state program that funded the services he needs to survive in his home.

Opportunities for Independence is a center for independent living that serves people with disabilities in a large city in the northeast corridor. The program it was advocating for in this example is Medical Access for Child Health. Approximately five weeks before the passage of the new state budget, the governor announced plans in which the budget of the State Health Department's Special Needs Division was cut from $16 million to $6 million. The Special Needs Division funded medical, social, and respite services for nine types of children's special health needs. Included were children who use ventilators, as well as those with other conditions such as cystic fibrosis, spina bifida, Cooley's anemia, and sickle-cell disease. The governor claimed that the cuts would not affect the program.

When Opportunities for Independence staff members attended Parents Day at the Caring for Ventilator-Assisted Children in Their Own Homes (CVACH) program, parents, who had already written to their legislators to oppose the cuts, asked for help in additional strategy development. Staff members from some of the affected programs met together but were prohibited from advocating for their programs. The parents wanted to increase their advocacy activity, but they needed guidance. Two Opportunities for Independence staff members, social worker Rebecca Gutman and education specialist Shelley Acevedo, worked with the parents to form a coalition, visit legislators' offices, hold a press conference at the seat of the state capital, and involve legislative staff from the children's hospitals. The Opportunities for Independence team helped the parents launch a parent coalition effort. Parents from the CVACH, spina bifida, and cystic fibrosis programs responded, and parent coordinators were chosen to promote family participation, legislative awareness, and media coverage. Parents wrote to their own legislators as well as to those in positions of power in the state house and senate. A former attorney general of the United States, who had helped form the CVACH program, wrote a letter opposing the cuts to each member of the legislature. Newspapers were contacted, and press in the two largest cities in the state responded. Affected parents and children attended a press conference at the state capitol that was covered by various media. In an emotional hour on the steps of the state capital, children who were able to participate told stories about their lives, and parents, many of whom held up enlarged pictures of their children with special health needs, described the critical nature of these programs. C-Span featured the press conference in its entirety, both live and again later the same day. The outcome was an amendment to the budget that restored most of the funding.

The CVACH program was again threatened when the health department decided to restructure it using a managed care model that provided funding only for a medical director and one social worker and cut most CVACH social services. The program launched a letter-writing campaign, and one hospital's government relations staff lobbied heavily. The budget was again amended to cover all CVACH services. From this second experience, it was clear to Gutman and Acevedo that Opportunities for Independence had to develop formal guidelines and procedures to help the concerned parties to respond to future financial cuts and similar issues. (This kind of organizational learning through the process of evaluation is discussed in chapters 4 and 9.) In consultation with all their colleagues at Opportunities for Independence, the social work/ education team created guidelines for a Medical Access for Child Health response that allowed them to be prepared to avert the next crisis and to think about extrapolating from those experiences to develop guidelines through which Opportunities for Independence would be able to respond on the national as well as state level.

Figure 8.1 is an organigraph drawn by the Opportunities for Independence team of social worker and education specialist. They envision the campaign to save the funding levels for the special needs division as an emergency sailing vessel with a hull, made up of the five programs and populations, that was deepened to include the government relations staff and finally was further strengthened by the press and other media. The sail, to be taken down when

FIGURE 8.1. Organigraph for Opportunities for Independence.

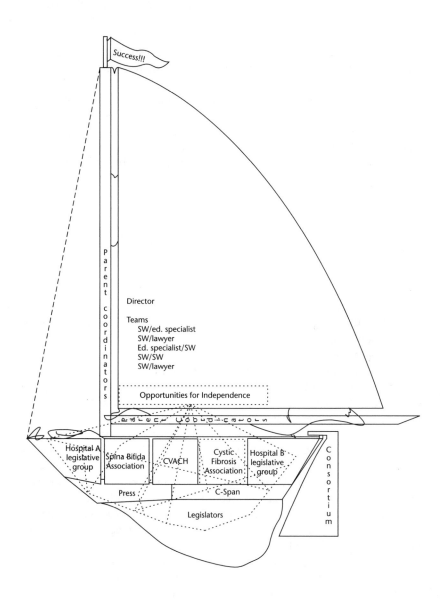

it is not needed for energy or direction is the Opportunities for Independence staff, including the team that worked directly for this effort and all the other administrators, lawyers, education specialists, and social workers who make up the organization. Finally, the mast is the parent coordinators, whose determination, ability to learn, desperation, and pride helped them pull the endeavor together. The web ties all the elements together with no hierarchy, infighting, or searching the limelight.

Thus Gutman and Acevedo used advocacy techniques and relationship skills to further the goals of their clients. In addition, they used teamwork, brief work techniques, management approaches, and group skills to mobilize the various constituencies to work toward their common goal. In this example, they interpreted intervention as mediation (between groups that were used to proceeding alone) as well as interference (their own organization and others chose to interfere with the funding levels that the state had decided were sufficient for a specific program).

Chris Scattergood is a social worker for the Caring for Ventilator-Assisted Children in Their Own Homes (CVACH) program located at a large hospital for children. In this case, Ms. Scattergood's role was to plan for the safe discharge of Matthew Grantham, a 6-year-old boy who was ventilator-dependent as the result of a severe traumatic injury resulting in a state of severe paralysis. He was quadriplegic with minimal movement of his upper extremities and had no spontaneous respiration at all. Ms. Scattergood was to help assess the possibility of a safe and effective reunification of Matthew with his biological mother. Mrs. Grantham possessed limited resources (minimal family support, low socioeconomic status, uncertain professional services capable of addressing care needs around the clock in the region) and had limited experience caring for her son's complex and sophisticated medical needs. Mrs. Grantham had been overwhelmed by Matthew's needs and had refused to try to care for him at home when he was released from acute care and rehabilitation. If Ms. Scattergood decided now that Mrs. Grantham could care for Matthew, her role was to facilitate Matthew's move home to his biological mother. Figure 8.2 is an ecomap for Matthew Grantham.

To assess the appropriateness of this or any other "discharge plan" or transition to home for a ventilator-dependent child is complex and incorporates the expertise and coordination of multiple professionals and organizational systems whose underlying purposes are sometimes in opposition. In this instance, a county division of Children and Youth Services (C&YS) was under significant pressure to move Matthew because the foster parents who had been responsible for him since his discharge from the rehabilitation hospital

FIGURE 8.2. Ecomap for Matthew Grantham.

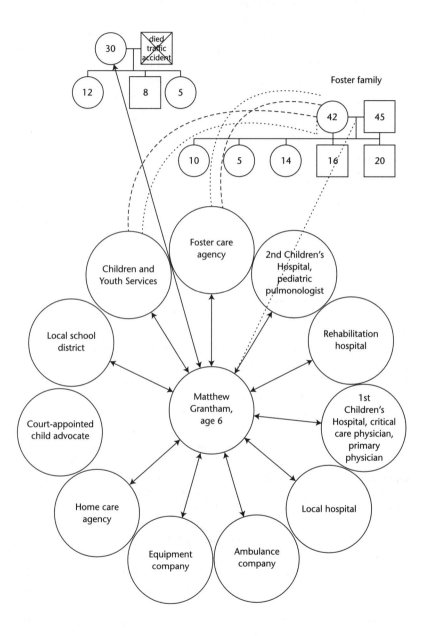

no longer felt they could fulfill his needs. As a result of poor communication between the foster care agency and C&YS, the C&YS social worker had to prepare for a new placement within three to four months, a short period of time for this type of placement.

After several conversations with the foster parents, the C&YS system, and the biological family, the nurse coordinator and Ms. Scattergood, provided information regarding (1) discharge and care guidelines for ventilator-dependent children as compiled by experts from two hospitals; (2) regional resources to provide home modifications and help evaluate the appropriateness of home care nursing and the durable medical equipment vendor providing technical and respiratory services to the family; and (3) potential foster care placements or care facilities established in the care and coordination of discharging a ventilator-dependent child to home, as well as other medical professionals most familiar with the individual characteristics of this child's care.

A key factor was facilitating communication between the ventilator specialist and the diagnostic pediatrician regarding the care plan that had been adopted during the medical crisis. Strategies listed in the order they occurred were (1) to interview the foster family, (2) to offer the assistance of Children and Youth Services, (3) to initiate contact with the biological parent, (4) to inform and confer with the specialty physician, (5) to investigate funding for skilled nursing, (6) to find a transitional facility placement, (7) to discuss transition to home with the nursing care agency, (8) to refer to contractors specializing in home modifications, (9) to serve as a liaison between the pulmonologist, diagnostic pediatrician, and C&YS social worker regarding final opinions on Matthew's initial transition from his foster care home to his biological home, and (10) to provide resource support and assistance during Matthew's final discharge from the transitional care facility following the training and preparation of his mother as well as his backup care provider.

This case presented multiple challenges for everyone involved. The role of the CVACH program is to provide support and technical expertise to families and other professionals serving the home care needs of ventilator-dependent children. In this instance, the Department of Children and Youth Services was legally responsible for this child's well-being, yet the department staff had a very limited perspective on the complexities of caring for a child on life support. Although she obviously cared deeply for her son, Mrs. Grantham had reservations about her ability to care for her son's needs over the long term. Assessing her commitment and the social support that was available to her were important first steps in trying to safeguard the interests of the patient.

A crisis erupted when plans to admit Matthew to a pediatric center fell through just days before the foster parents had adamantly stated that Matthew could no longer stay with them. Attempts were made to initiate another plan that would bring Matthew home for no longer than two weeks with twenty-four-hour coverage. Discharge recommendations for the ventilator-dependent population require thorough caregiver training and backup support. Neither of these elements could be guaranteed in Matthew's situation. Bringing together the medical team responsible for Matthew's care and the C&YS worker responsible for this placement, Chris Scattergood facilitated an alternative plan to admit Matthew to the local hospital for children. Initially, Matthew's physicians viewed this temporary solution as optimal, but plans moved forward to have Matthew live with his mother with around-the-clock care. Matthew's mother did avert one medical crisis during this stay using very basic skills that she had learned from the foster mother.

In Matthew Grantham's case, under financial pressure, two systems with different directives adopted a plan that could have resulted in tragedy. With training and a successful transition to home, Matthew is now happily reunited with his family with solid local professional supports in place. This situation required that the clinical social worker be skilled in advocacy, teamwork, and techniques related to short-term work, case management, and group interaction.

Both of these examples focused on one program, Caring for Ventilator-Assisted Children in Their Own Homes. In the first example, the goal was to save the funding for a broader program of which CVACH was an integral part. The goal of the second example was a safe and successful discharge to his own home for a 6-year-old ventilator-assisted boy. In both examples, there was an overarching need for advocacy. Both examples also used advocacy, teamwork, and relationship techniques, as well as techniques drawn from brief, solution-focused, and group work and a range of management techniques.

UNIT OF ATTENTION

It is traditional in social work to categorize interventions according to the size and kind of units with which social workers are working and the nature of the intervention. Thus for many years social workers were taught according to whether they intended to work with individuals, couples, families and/or small groups, communities, programs, or administrative units. These divisions are no longer viable. Many of the traditional categories have been dismantled, but a common strategy of advocacy permeates all approaches. Thus to devise interventions, social workers think in terms of what their clients need rather than what particular approach they have been taught. As advocates, social workers present and argue the client's cause when necessary in order to accomplish the objectives that have been agreed to by client and social worker (Compton and Galaway 1998).

Once again, funding and policy have great impact on the kinds of interventions social workers use. Often particular ways of working are defined in policy statements or required by funders; one example is the current use of brief treatment. Although social workers may be confined to particular strategies that are determined for them, it is critical that all social workers in health care understand the range of possible interventions so that they can direct their clients to other social workers or other organizations that may meet needs that are outside the purview of a particular social worker or organization. For example, a social worker in a mental health center heard from several of her clients that they were having difficulty convincing the management of their housing that there were revolting fumes in the halls. Although it was not part of the social worker's job to deal with the housing authority or to involve her individual clients with each other, she suggested that each client who complained be in touch with the local housing advocacy organization. She called the organization herself to let them know of the situation. In addition, she called the local hospital and asked that the pediatric clinic keep track of ill children from those apartments and alert the Department of Public Health and the housing advocacy organization. It was not necessary for the mental health center social worker to do the work in regard to the housing situation, but linking and advocating helped her to help and empower her clients.

ADVOCACY

Advocacy involves active support; it may imply speaking on behalf of a cause, but it is equally applicable to speaking on behalf of a client. Through advocacy, issues are raised on behalf of people who are affected by specific practices and policies. Mobilizing asks people to find their voices, to stand up for themselves, usually in response to an immediate situation (Kahn 1995). This includes case advocacy, in which a social worker helps a client, individual, family, or group meet a specific need. It also includes cause or class advocacy, in which similar unmet needs are grouped and organized into advocacy activity by a group of people within an agency, a section of an organization, or a combination of professionals and community people (Erickson, Moynihan, and Williams 1991). When social workers advocate for the population with whom they work, they are engaging in cause or class advocacy. In the first practice example presented in this chapter, parents were empowered to advocate for themselves in ways that allowed needed funding to continue—class advocacy. When the social worker made alternative discharge arrangements for Matthew, she was advocating for him—case advocacy. Advocacy involves efforts to empower others to advocate for themselves, as well as efforts of the social worker to advocate for clients.

Empowerment is often the first goal in working with clients/consumers/ communities. Social work's values of self-determination and social justice support empowerment. By helping people advocate for themselves, either alone or collectively, social workers teach skills that allow clients to manage their futures by applying these skills to new situations.

"Empowerment is defined as achieving reasonable control over one's destiny, learning to cope constructively with debilitating forces in society, and acquiring the competence to initiate change at the individual and systems level" (Pinderhughes 1995:136). Many disempowered people react to their lack of power by internalizing projections, identifying with the aggressor, becoming guarded (so that they are called paranoid) and/or oppositional (and thus viewed as stubborn and uncooperative). Social workers can assist clients to locate their sources of power, to find their voices, and to strategize about the most effective methods for advocating for themselves. This leads to gains in social justice growing from the efforts of the people most informed about the situations of oppression. Additionally, it promotes feelings of efficacy and inclusion when efforts are successful.

Social workers do not empower people. Empowerment is a reflexive activity, a process capable of being initiated and sustained only by the subject who seeks self-determination (Simon 1990). Empowerment can be facilitated only when the client/system/community is open and interested in developing these skills. Additionally, even when the goal is empowerment, there are times when social work advocacy on behalf of the client is also necessary and appropriate.

Advocacy requires commitment, determination, and even passion to pursue efforts on behalf of individuals or groups despite opposition (Sunley 1997). Often an adversarial stance is required (Ezell 1994). Even so, there are times when adversarial stances can be minimized by provision of information, gentle confrontation about the inconsistency of widely held values and current policy, or by co-opting opposition. Resnick and Patti (1980) provide multiple strategies for advocating from within organizations and agencies to make changes that promote responsiveness to clients and populations. When social workers are aware of social injustices, it is incumbent upon them to advocate for those who are being wronged and to help people advocate for themselves.

The managed care environment makes advocacy especially difficult, since so many managed care organizations are removed from service providers by geography and many layers of bureaucracy. This distance makes the contact and relationship required in advocacy more challenging. Additionally, social workers are often in the uncomfortable position of being compelled out of concerns for social justice to advocate for clients against their own employers' policies. Resnick and Patti's (1980:200–14) classic strategy for changing organizations from within involves three analytical tasks in preparation for promoting change: (1) determining the goal and identifying the desired change clearly; (2) assessing people and sections of the organization that are likely to be resistant to change and identifying probable reasons for that resistance; and (3) selecting strategies to minimize resistance and enlist those with power to support the change.

Regardless of the level of practice, advocacy is inherent to all social work. Case advocacy and the facilitation of empowerment are present in all direct practice. As social workers understand their population's worries, their own concern for social justice compels them to act as advocates. Thus advocacy, like relationship, is part of every social work intervention.

BRIEF SOLUTION-FOCUSED WORK

Brief solution-focused work uses a strengths perspective and "provides confirmation and coaching in the dynamic use of the self and in specific strategies for rapid assessment, promotion of patient ownership in outcomes, and finding a positive future focus" (Parker 1997). The goal of brief solution-focused work in health care is to increase positive patterns. What the client wants drives the work. It requires creativity and imagination and a sophisticated use of time, place, structure, and organization on the part of the social worker, especially in terms of the use of metaphor, and of positive recasting. It is important to note that social work has employed brief techniques since its beginnings. Examples include crisis intervention, in which an external event has been too great for an individual's capacities to cope and the social worker helps the client to regain her or his equilibrium (Parad and Parad 1990). This kind of approach is also more congruent with the help-seeking models of poor and working-class clients as well as those who represent many kinds of cultural diversity (Corwin and Read 1997; Wells 1994).

In the following practice example, a client combines professional therapy with self-help to achieve her goals.

Anne Brownstein is a 24-year-old single Jewish female who has been in recovery from an alcohol and drug addiction for the past four years. She presented to Jewish Family and Children's Service with severe depression and suicidal ideation after an argument with her current boyfriend and was assigned to social worker Dorie Josephson. In her initial interview Ms. Brownstein complained of severe mood swings and extreme anger at men. She reported that arguments with her boyfriend trigger rage that then shifts to thoughts of her wanting to hurt or kill herself. She reports a long history of troubled relationships with men that have triggered this reaction before.

Anne Brownstein grew up in a very troubled family. The youngest of three siblings, she was aware from a very early age that her father was unfaithful to her mother and that her mother harbored a murderous rage toward her father and often spoke to her daughter about it. Ms. Brownstein's behavior reflected the family's problems. She was arrested three times for underage drinking and once for shoplifting. She admits to a long history of shoplifting that persisted even after her recovery from drug abuse was well under way. While she has for the most part ceased this behavior, one shoplifting incident occurred shortly before she entered therapy. She sees this as one more example of addictive, compulsive behavior that she struggles to control.

Ms. Brownstein began daily drinking at 13 years of age, diet pills at 15, marijuana at 16, and episodic experimentation with acid at 19. She has not used any drugs or alcohol since getting sober with the help of Narcotics Anonymous four years ago. Ms. Brownstein identifies herself as a recovering alcoholic and drug abuser who is coming into treatment now because her addictive thinking and behavior (not drug use) have caused the problems she is now having.

Ms. Brownstein's situation illustrates two concerns this Jewish family service agency is facing today. One is the growing number of Jewish people who are addicted to alcohol and drugs, a presence the Jewish community has largely denied in the past and struggles now to find ways to address. This Jewish family service agency is one of the few local Jewish agencies that is confronting this problem, and it is encountering the obstacles that frequently arise when charting new territory. The second concern illustrated by this case is the lack of financial resources to provide long-term therapy for this type of client. Funding for such a client, who has a low-paying job and no benefits, used to come through subsidized sliding-scale fees that were low enough that the client could pay without payment becoming a burden. Clients whose diagnoses fell on the Axis II personality disorder scale, as Ms. Brownstein's does, were often long-term users of outpatient therapy. Today, with the shrinking of charitable funding and diminution of publicly funded insurance and limited managed care insurance payments, it is no longer possible to provide clients like Ms. Brownstein with the very low fees of the past. While sliding-scale fees still exist, they are usually too high for most clients to remain in long-term therapy. Therefore, the agency must find ways to meet those clients' immediate needs through short-term intervention.

One way to address this problem is to limit treatment goals and then combine brief therapy techniques with other kinds of resources. The current managed care model of brief treatment focused on symptom reduction can serve as a guideline for providing this service, whether the client has a managed care insurance plan or is paying for his or her own services, as Ms. Brownstein is. Various models of short-term work, such as solution-focused therapy, offer techniques that help the clinician develop and carry out an effective short-term treatment plan. What enables Ms. Josephson to deal with the long-term concerns of someone like Ms. Brownstein, who will obviously need support over a longer period of time than therapy can provide, is the inclusion of the twelve-step program as a means of providing long-term support at no significant cost to the client.

Ms. Brownstein is a good candidate for this treatment. She is already deeply connected to a twelve-step recovery program and is working with a sponsor to help with the maintenance of her sobriety and with support and feedback when other behaviors become obviously compulsive and counterproductive. Ms. Josephson is not concerned about relapse because she knows that Ms. Brownstein's mastery of the twelve-step program is deeply developed. Relapse is often a problem for women who have been emotionally or sexually abused. As Ms. Brownstein goes deeper into therapy, working with the twelve-step program and her sponsor, while not absolutely assuring continued sobriety, allows for more exploration of old, painful issues than would have been indicated had she not had a solid support program.

This intervention also has the advantage of discouraging the development of transference in the therapeutic relationship. Both the brevity of the treatment and the emphasis on Ms. Brownstein's own coping mechanisms and abilities helps minimize the transference, as does the decision not to explore her feelings about Ms. Josephson. Ms. Brownstein, having had previous experiences in therapy, brought up such feelings quite a bit initially, but Ms. Josephson's shifted the focus onto how Ms. Brownstein coped with feelings in her relationships with her sponsor and her boyfriend, the two areas of major concern to her. This helped her keep her focus on these concerns and rather than on the therapeutic relationship. Ms. Brownstein uses positive reframing frequently to enable Ms. Brownstein to appreciate the successes and improvements she is experiencing.

A major concern is the power of Ms. Brownstein's anger, combined with impulsive verbal outbursts followed by suicidal ideation stimulated by arguments with her boyfriend. From the second session, Ms. Brownstein has been encouraged to make a list of messages she can tell herself and actions she can take when unwanted impulses arise. She is to keep this list on her person at all times. The contents of this list have been developed in the therapeutic work to increase her understanding of herself, her actions, and her reactions.

Since Ms. Brownstein is bright and insightful and already has some understanding of some of her issues from her previous therapy, she has worked in this way quickly and effectively. Ms. Brownstein wrote on the card during her sessions, and Ms. Josephson made certain that the ideas, wording, and actions came strictly from Ms. Brownstein and not from the social worker. This intervention both minimizes the transference and increases Ms. Brownstein's sense of mastery and ability to tackle her own problems.

Ms. Brownstein has now decided to stop treatment because she wants to return to school and feels she cannot financially manage both school and therapy. This decision occurred after Ms. Josephson's vacation had interrupted treatment. At a different time and with different goals, Ms. Josephson might have interpreted this as Ms. Brownstein's anger and worked with the transference. However, in brief solution-focused treatment, it seemed in Ms. Brownstein's best interest to pursue school and terminate treatment.

Ms. Brownstein was treated in eight sessions over a three-month period. At termination, she was still active in Narcotics Anonymous and was working with her sponsor appropriately. She continued to use her card to understand and control her impulsive tendencies, and she reported that she felt she had a much better mastery over her anger and suicidal feelings than she had previously. If these issues, or others, arise at a future time, Ms. Brownstein knows she can come back into therapy. She also knows that she has the ability to use therapy and the other resources in her life in a productive way, and this knowledge in itself may be her greatest asset.

Rationale for Brief Solution-Focused Work

If, as is now expected, most future health and mental health services will be compensated by prospective reimbursement (capitated payment), then counseling and psychotherapy will be brief for most clients. "Under these circumstances it is easy to lose sight of the fact that there are nonfiscal reasons for the use of brief therapy" (Pekarik 1996:1), but "a growing recognition of the reciprocal influence of physical and psychological factors has underscored the importance of mental health services within an adequate health care package" (Wells 1994:4). Both of these trends have led to an emphasis on active, short-term approaches. Still, it is critical in using forms of brief work that social workers distinguish brief approaches to treatment from the policies that mandate their use. Although policies regarding the containment of costs have made brief work a prime approach, and many times, the only approach that insurers will cover, it is "a serious and purposeful therapeutic endeavor" (Wells 1994:19) that brings a demand for accountability by managed care companies and other service contractors.

To maintain the integrity of brief work, practitioners must move away from the dangers inherent in utilizing it simply as a response to the demands and mandates of payers and maintain therapeutic control by integrating it into the mainstream of therapeutic education and practice. "The more fully practitioners recognize the legitimacy as well as the utility of brief work, the more likely they are to retain control of its implementation" (Wells 1994:274). Planned short-term work has a long and respected tradition as a treatment strategy and philosophy that has been developed through understanding client preference, treatment outcome, and research on treatment attrition patterns. Many of the structured elements in brief work resemble those of the functional school that were explicated in the 1930s (Dore 1990; Robinson 1978). Reid and Shyne (1969) presented a carefully researched rationale for brief work in the 1960s. For example, Pekarik (1996:16) cites statistics from a 1981 study conducted by the National Institute of Mental Health showing that the median number of sessions attended by clients was about three and one-half; 63 percent of clients terminated before their fifth session, and 75 percent of clients terminated before the seventh session. There was no client (diagnostic or demographic) subgroup for which the majority of clients attend more than ten sessions; at most, 36 percent of clients continued for the ten visits that were prescribed. Single-session therapy information shows that 25 percent to 50 percent of clients use only one session of therapy (Wells 1994:259). Another study at a community mental health center showed that the dropout rate for time-limited work was half of that for open-ended work (Sledge, Moras, Hartley, and Levine 1990). Other studies comparing time-limited and long-term care have reported equivalent outcomes (Budman and Gurman 1988, 1996; Reid 1997; Smyrnios and Kirby 1993).

Brief work utilizes treatment strategies from almost all theoretical orientations; therefore social workers can add dimensions of brief work to their current ways of working (Pekarik 1996:9). For example, the psychodynamic and cognitive behavioral approaches are easily used in brief work. Following are some examples that Budman and Gurman (1988:69) provide on the adaptation of traditional techniques to a brief format for object relations, ego psychology, and cognitive theories. Object relations theory explains that relationship patterns and personality themes are constantly reinforced from infancy through adulthood. While these reenactments may occur quite unconsciously, it is often the discomfort or stress that clients experience as a result of these pervasive interpersonal environments that leads them to seek help. The impetus for treatment here offers a framework for looking at a present stressor and a focus on the here and now. Ego psychology explains that experiences over time lead people to develop rules of operation, or "maps." According to Budman and Gurman (1988:68),

Experiences and perceptions attached to them become automatized. Since the map is rarely in a person's conscious awareness, it is not scrutinized and updated with the passage of time. It is, instead, re-inforced by the outcomes of the person's selective behavior and per-ceptions. Symptoms are generally the result of the client's making the best choice among options determined unconsciously by those associations available in his or her map.

Cognitive theory assumes that faulty learning and patterns of thinking and behaving (conscious or unconscious) create a template for behavior. The potential for insight with this approach lends itself well to long-term treatment, but the intervention techniques are highly operationalized and therefore are easily adapted to a brief format.

These brief references to specific theories highlight the fact that whether clients present with past or current issues, identifying how patterns of interaction are developed and maintained is central to the helping process. "A general strategy in achieving focus is to look for the cognitive, behav-ioral, and affective coping patterns of clients. Insofar as they become overly rigid and unhelpful, these coping patterns may become potential treatment targets" (Cooper 1995:39). Budman and Gurman (1988, 1996) believe that loss, developmental dysynchrony, and interpersonal conflict are the most identified reasons clients seek treatment. Regardless of how a problem is stated or what theory informs the work, people seek help only for what they are prepared to face.

In the present environment, time is compressed for social workers in most health and mental health systems, including acute hospitalization, rehabilitation, home care, and many day programs. Despite the height-ened interest in efficiency, effectiveness remains critical, and effectiveness requires building relationships with clients/consumers/communities and their social supports in order to gain the trust that is necessary to achieve positive outcomes. Here, relationship building, like all the other elements in brief work, is heightened and intensified. With less time available, team-work and interorganizational relationships are even more critical. Neces-sary information must be gathered quickly and succinctly from other health care professionals, and face-to-face contact and other direct com-munication are increasingly rare. Instead, communication depends on various electronic devices such as voice mail, pagers, and e-mail. For some social workers, this fast pace heightens the excitement in the work and prevents boredom. Others disagree, expressing frustration with the work-load and the increase in paperwork, concern that they are moving too quickly to do their best work, sadness that they cannot establish the level of relationship with clients that brought them to the field and nourished them, and the feeling of never being caught up. Frustration also exists with the time consumed in locating attending physicians, community resources, and insurance reviewers (Farley 1994).

Many brief approaches work from the premise that the client is ready for change. People seek help when they are in great enough emotional pain (Budman and Gurman 1988). Knowing the impetus for seeking help and locating the momentum for change is central to this approach. Thus an early and excellent question to ask in brief work is, Why now?

The Elements of Brief Solution-Focused Work

Many elements that are common to brief work distinguish it from traditional psychotherapy approaches but are very familiar to much health-related practice, including discharge planning and public health outreach for those with communicable conditions. Among these common elements are a limited but flexible use of time, a clear, specific work focus, limited goals that are negotiated with the client/consumer/community, a focus on present stress, rapid assessment, a high level of social worker and client/consumer/community activity, and the eclectic use of combinations of strategies and techniques. The most central of these elements are rapid assessment and a specific work focus (Cooper 1995).

The process of clarifying and focusing begins with initial contact, whether it is a telephone call or a face-to-face meeting. A preliminary assessment is completed by the end of the first session, and already active intervention is taking place (Corwin and Read 1997). In a rapid assessment, the social worker gathers information on current and past functioning relevant to the client's current problems, uses that information to understand the client's problems, and identifies the focus and gathers enough information about it to formulate a treatment plan. Termination is introduced at the outset as well. The social worker says, "We have this many sessions," or "we have only this time together." In this way, and in others, the work is highly structured. The clear explication of structure presents an honest and open picture to the client/consumer/community. The social worker is "showing her hand," sharing information, sharing power.

In the following practice example brief work consisting of three sessions helps a client alter her drinking behavior.

Mrs. Spina, a widowed, white, middle-aged woman, was referred to an employee assistance program in a family service agency for help with alcohol abuse (Corwin and Read 1997). The agreed-upon goal was to alter Mrs. Spina's drinking behavior by having her regularly attend Alcoholics Anonymous meetings and meet with social worker Elizabeth Read, who uses behavioral management strategies to help clients change their addictive behavior.

Ms. Read helped her client identify the internal and external triggers warning that she was likely to begin to drink and then devise specific plans for how she would manage those situations. Ms. Read also helped Mrs. Spina restructure her day so that it was no longer completely focused on drinking, and Ms. Read provided behavioral strategies to manage cravings and stresses (Corwin and Read 1997:439).

A comparison of the brief work with Mrs. Spina and Anne Brownstein demonstrates the versatility of this approach. Both are white middle-class women who need help with substance abuse problems. Mrs. Spina, although isolated, has a substantial work history, the crisis of her husband's death, and a newly developed problem with alcohol. It may be that the three sessions with a clear psychoeducational approach may be sufficient to bring Mrs. Spina back to the level of functioning that preceded her problems with drinking. On the other hand, Ms. Brownstein's longer-term difficulties and reliance on alcohol and drugs from a much earlier age may indicate that she will need many additional interventions for longer periods for what may be considered a chronic concern.

In brief solution-focused work, each individual session can be considered as a whole in itself. While the emphasis on the first session sets the purpose, brief work can be described, in effect, as a series of first sessions (Cooper 1995:33). Looking at the work in that way raises three basic questions to be answered in each self-contained session:

1. How is the client/consumer stuck (what is maintaining the problem)?
2. What does the client/consumer need to get unstuck?
3. How can the social worker facilitate or provide what is needed to make a positive change?

Here, the social worker thinks in terms of what and how rather than why. Versions of this approach are both familiar and comfortable to many social workers who have diverse roles in health and mental health care settings. Those who work in acute care services, who are discharge planners, activists, case managers, managers of certain kinds of programs, and those who work as organizers think in these ways because this is what their work calls for. Even many social workers who work "long-term" with clients/consumers/communities have learned to develop short-term goals and contracts within long-term relationships. Such foci keep the work fresh and keep everyone working. Those who do psychotherapy are using these techniques as well. The techniques of brief solution-focused work are applicable to and can be incorporated into all types of social work practice in health and mental health care systems.

In this kind of work, patterns of the past are used only to help mobilize forces in the present, not to sort out the past (Parker 1997). Small groups (which could be work groups or families) are used for brainstorming. Every interaction is seen as an opportunity to learn, as part of the creation of a learning community. Social workers using brief solution-based therapy are very assertive, active, and focused and encourage their clients to be the same. The effectiveness of every intervention depends on the therapeutic relationship, and every intervention is used to focus on problem resolution. Clients are actively involved continuously throughout the process. A regular question from the social worker is, What do you think we need to do here? For example, a 75-year-old woman seems stuck on her abuse as a child, and she is looked to for her own solution when the social worker asks her what her advice would be to some young person who has recently dealt with abuse (Parker 1997). Occasionally, the social worker raises questions such as Are we working? or What are we working on? These questions help refocus the work when clients' dialogue becomes tangential to the identified goal (Schwartz 1962; Schwartz and Zalba 1971). Social workers are honest about wanting direction from clients/consumers/communities.

Metaphors and visualization exercises are often used to intensify and heighten the process and lend a sense of control to the client. Parker (1997) provides several superb examples in her videotape series on brief solution-focused work. For example, she suggests that social workers reframe situations to make clients the heroes of their own stories and lives. By identifying the clients' strengths, methods for coping in the past, and problem solutions they have used before, the social worker can frame possible solutions in the clients' own language and using the clients' own metaphor. The overarching hero metaphor works to help clients begin to frame themselves as heroes of their own stories and to understand the capacities they bring to the situation. Heroes, she says, have to leave home (comfort) and overcome fears to slay the dragon. Heroes often don't want to make the journey. On this trip, she asks, which tools will you take?

In working with a terminally ill and very depressed man who likes to fish, Parker (1997) says, "I'm casting, I'm casting, and I'm not getting a bite. Can you help me?" She provides another case example of a retired army colonel who was providing total care for his wife who was severely chronically ill and whose children were very worried about him. She took the story the colonel told about his ways of commanding and applied his approach that had worked so well in the past to the present time and his present problems. Metaphors she drew upon were marshaling forces, diagramming the battles, making decisions about who was to carry which roles, and loyalty, not just to wife but to self. In another example, visualization plays a powerful part in giving an ill woman some sense of control and power. This woman, who is aphasic and partially paralyzed as a result of a stroke, was an art teacher. The social worker drew out the "steps to home" on a computer. The picture (figure 8.3) shows the pathway from the hospital to the rehabilitation center to the client's home and simply and concretely displays the steps that will occur between this acute hospitalization and the return to home. Although they could not promise the patient that she would be home in two weeks, the social worker and the physician thought that she would be home in that time. Thus each block in the steps to home represents a day.

Even this simple computer-generated drawing would not have been the social worker's way of expressing time, progression, or goals, but she thought that visualization could be important to this art teacher. This, then, is an example of the social worker's effort to match her work to the client's needs and capacities. She caught the client's attention and, through this simple drawing, helped her think positively for herself and know that the professionals taking care of her saw home as their goal just as she did. The introduction of novelty is critical; that is, the social worker introduces to the client a novel way of thinking, feeling, or doing (Cooper 1995; Hoyt 1994). Novelty captures the client's attention while also providing a metaphor that allows broadened frames of reference. This may inspire new ideas about solutions to problems or coping mechanisms. It also may become a story-tool that the client may return to after the work is done.

An ever-present element in brief work is the use of homework, again another method that broadens the impact of the contact between the social worker and the client. One talks about the problem and solutions and then goes home to work on the problem and try out the solutions. Clients/consumers have to see how the homework relates to solving their problems or they will not be committed to doing it (Wells 1994). All assign-

FIGURE 8.3. Drawing made to assist client's visualization of the steps needed to get home.

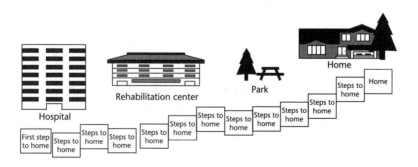

ments must make clients feel they are affecting their situation and must build confidence and hope as they are completed. Assignments keep clients focused on the goals they set and help them to work toward those goals between sessions. Most important, homework helps change "stuck" behavior by developing new skills.

The discussion of a limited number of sessions and the use of homework may work together as marketing for brief therapy. Providing a limited number of sessions offers hope that goals can be achieved in a defined time period and that one *can* feel better. This also serves to help social workers and clients/consumers to adhere to a clearly defined focus or objective (no one can do it all at one time). In turn, the clearly defined focus supports the assignment and follow-up of homework and tasks and averts shifts of focus and digression from goals and progress. This combination of finding new ways of thinking about old problems and rehearsing new behaviors through homework is often referred to as cognitive behavioral therapy. Cognitive behavioral therapy is a brief solution-focused modality that has shown great promise for effectiveness with many difficulties, including anxiety disorders, depression, and obsessive-compulsive disorder.

CASE MANAGEMENT

Because case management uses whatever modalities and vehicles the social worker can call on to meet the needs of the client, it both subsumes traditional social work practice methods and obviates social workers' defining themselves by a specific traditional method such as clinical social work, group work, or community organization. Case management appeals greatly to proponents of managed care and to managed care companies as well because its monitoring function appears to contain costs. Of course, by capping spending per program or per client, managed care can build cost containment into case management. Even if case management is not organized in this way, having one practitioner responsible for organizing and evaluating the care of a client would make it more likely that the individual would understand the cost of total service. In the same way, if a case manager is expected to function as a gatekeeper, allowing someone access to a service or denying access, the manager also can prevent unnecessary spending. As discussed in relation to advocacy, this dual role may cause ethical dilemmas when advocacy for the client and gatekeeping come into conflict, but this does not always have to be the case.

The appeal of case management is its fit with an ecological perspective, its emphases on relationship, interactions of multiple systems and helpers, and networking of all kinds of services. Social workers are case managers whose primary mission involves helping people link to the resources of their community. As is true for an ecological perspective, this linking function, especially linking with informal support systems, addresses the interdependent nature of individuals and communities. The focus is on the client's interaction with the network of services that are necessary to meet the goals of client and payer. To be an effective case manager means that the social worker must be a skilled clinician who can relate to the most difficult client groups and help such groups to progress.

Case management, which has been in existence in some form since social work began, is gaining in popularity. In its most highly bureaucratized and least effective form, it is simply paper shuffling and a way to hold organizations accountable for the money they are paid to manage a dependent population. At best, case management is a sensitive and skillful way to monitor the progress of a dependent population while providing fine relationship- and resource-building services. Following are five ways in which case management has developed recently: (1) increased use of case management teams, (2) interagency teamwork, (3) integration into the community, (4) greater use of informal helpers, and (5) firms that provide intensive services (Ballew and Mink 1996).

Teams work with a primary case manager to help clients/consumers and sometimes their families function within the community and prevent hospitalization or institutionalization. Examples are intensive case management of adults with serious mental illnesses, wrap-around services for children who are mentally ill, and services for the frail elderly. Interagency teamwork sometimes occurs when a funding source notes that the same client groups use the services of several agencies, and service may be improved and made more efficient through coordination of those agencies. For example, children who are developmentally disabled may require the services of the Department of Social Services, the mental health system, and the school system (Frankel, Harmon, and Kerson 1997; Karp 1996; Michelsen and Kerson 1997; Weiss and Kerson 1997). Coordination is thought to prevent redundancy, mixed messages, and confusion.

Most populations who are assigned to case managers fit two criteria: (1) they are dealing with several concurrent problems for which they need extensive help from several different kinds of helpers, and (2) they have special difficulty in using help effectively (Ballew and Mink 1996). Because the expertise of the many helpers is rarely discrete and also rarely encompasses a way to address every client problem, there are often authority issues and territorial disputes among the helpers.

Debate over the Role of the Manager

If case managers have sufficient authority, part of their role is to coordinate helpers and to mediate and resolve territorial disputes. For example, school personnel may be in conflict with home health care personnel and foster care workers about the responsibilities for care of a medically fragile child.

In the same way, personnel from various organizations, including the police, may not agree about the care needed for a seriously mentally ill individual who becomes violent when he stops taking the medication, which he is sure is the cause of his problem. The case manager helps to resolve these conflicts, ensures that everyone is clear about who is responsible for what care, makes certain that all the client's needs are being met by some entity.

Among many hotly debated issues in case management is the issue of whether the case manager works directly with clients or only coordinates the work of others. Many managed care organizations prefer that the case manager have minimal direct client contact, believing that such contact diminishes the case manager's ability to act as a gatekeeper. Others are concerned that direct client involvement leads the caseworker into the role of providing direct services instead of managing and coordinating others to provide those services. On the other hand, social workers frequently define their work through their relationship with the client, something that is difficult if not impossible to do without direct contact. Attempting to do this work without direct knowledge of and interaction with the client or consumer is not case management; it is paper shuffling. The task of the case manager is to work with clients to identify need, to identify and overcome barriers to using effective intervention, to help surmount the barriers, to find and build relationships with all possible helpers, and to coordinate services and relationships to those services until problems are resolved (Ballew and Mink 1996).

The Stages of Case Management

Most case management models include several stages encompassing assessment and planning, coordinating, facilitating, and monitoring services (Austin and McClelland 1996; Jackson 1995). Another model includes assessment, development of a plan, procurement of a service, monitoring and advocacy, tracking, and evaluation (Wolk, Sullivan, and Hartman 1994). None of these processes are linear; all require continuous reassessment and fluid movement among all the phases. The activity level remains high and intense for social workers (Werrbach 1996). Engagement continues throughout the relationship, and assessment, planning, and implementation are adjusted to changes in clients/consumers and the situation.

Following are descriptions of six phases of involvement in case management. They very much mirror the phases of other kinds of intervention; however, the role of the social worker and the need to balance capacities and responsibilities of others besides the individual social worker and the individual client/consumer make this category of intervention different.

1. *Engagement.* In the engagement phase, the case manager and client/consumer decide whether they can work together. If they decide to proceed, the social worker continues to build trust, clarify roles, and negotiate expectations.
2. *Assessment.* In the assessment phase, the case manager identifies strengths, determines the balance between needs and resources, and ascertains the barriers to using resources in connection with the clients/consumers, family members (if they are involved), other social supports, and service providers.
3. *Planning.* In the planning phase, together, the case manager, client/consumer, family members, other social supports, and service providers identify goals, specify appropriate goals for various people, and develop an action plan. If the plan is to succeed, all interested parties have to be involved.
4. *Accessing resources.* In the phase for locating resources and making sure that clients/consumer have access to those resources, goal accomplishment involves social workers' linking clients/consumers with resources, negotiating and advocating with those resources, helping clients/consumers develop internal resources, and assisting in overcoming barriers.
5. *Coordination.* In the coordination phase, case managers organize and coordinate the efforts of everyone involved, gain agreement to common goals, and monitor and support all helping efforts.
6. *Disengagement.* The disengagement phase concerns termination. During that time, case managers evaluate results, identify signs of disengagement, structure the disengagement, and help determine ongoing responsibility. (Ballew and Mink 1996)

Again, since case management is not and cannot be linear, these phases should be viewed as flexible, supporting work based on individual capacities and intermediate goals as well as on the needs and capacities of clients/consumers and their social supports over the longer term.

Frequent Locations for Case Management

Case management is frequently found in child welfare, probation services (particularly for youth), services for the frail elderly, services for those with serious mental illnesses, services for people who are developmentally disabled, services for medically fragile children, hospice services, services for those with AIDS, and services for those who are addicted to drugs and/or alcohol. Members of these populations are likely to have biological, psychological, and social problems for a long period, and they sometimes become the responsibility of the state. In some cases, technological advancement may eliminate certain populations from that list, as it has in the past. For example, in the years before effective preventive measures had been found for polio and syphilis, social workers worked as case managers for many with those illnesses. When a like cure or treatment is found for persons with AIDS, that population will not require case management services from social workers. However, since the numbers of frail elderly are likely to continue to grow as technological advancements allow society to treat people for many illnesses that used to result in death, case management services will probably increase for that population. Also, many people who require case management also have multiple long-term problems. For example, many people who are seriously mentally ill, many youth on probation and many of those receiving case management services because they have AIDS also have substance abuse problems, and most frail elderly have many other problems as well.

Kanter (1996) provided the following excellent example of case management through a managed care company for a man with both psychiatric and medical illness.

Paul had brittle diabetes and was not taking care of himself; his mother and father had died very recently. Paul's managed care company employed Joel Kanter to provide comprehensive case management involving psychological and environmental interventions. Joel realized that Paul could not use insight-oriented psychotherapy but that he still had to grieve his losses and begin to manage his diabetes. In addition to understanding the complex psychodynamic issues that prevented Paul from caring for himself, Joel also had to learn a lot about diabetes and the simple dietary strategies that Paul's psychological problems were preventing him from using. To aid Paul's grieving process, Joel and Paul made at least three visits to Paul's parents' gravesites. Additionally, Joel helped Paul develop more collaborative relationships with caregivers. Joel also says that he had to contain his "intense countertransference responses to Paul's guardedness, passive aggressiveness, and seemingly self-destructive neglect of his own health" (Kanter 1996:365).

It is interesting to note that an indemnity insurance program would never have funded this work with Paul. The managed care company agreed to this approach because Paul was a high-risk patient who had been a high utilizer of services. The insurer also had to be confident that Paul would remain with that managed care company for a long time. "In a competitive insurance climate where employers, employees and other insured persons often change insurers, there will be less financial incentive for insurers to 'invest' in their customers' health; keeping that in mind, policymakers should consider the value of supporting stable relationships between insurers and their customers" (Kanter 1996:366). The managed care company's representative working on Paul's case with Joel was a registered nurse. She commented that the company thought Paul was "at great risk for medical and psychiatric recidivism because of his clinical instability and the relationships between his psychiatric diagnoses, social situation, and medical history" (Kanter 1996:367). In the nurse's commentary, she mentions that as competition between insurance products intensified, case management programs started to focus on patients with the chronic illnesses that required expensive care. For these patients managers planned care that would be more cost-effective than care without such planning.

Kanter's account identifies four obstacles to planning for Paul's care: (1) finding a skilled nursing facility whose staff could manage diabetes, that was on the bus line, and that would take a psychiatric patient; (2) convincing the insurer to pay for services outside the benefits listed in the benefits contract; (3) educating Paul, his employer, Joel, and the multiple caregivers and providers on handling medical emergencies while teaching Paul to assume responsibility; and (4) managing the legal and financial requirements for guardianship, estate settlement, and group home placement.

Kanter's account lists the following costs of Paul's care (in 1996 dollars). For the year before case management, the cost was $53,000; the year case management began, the cost rose to $84,000; the next year, the cost was $39,000; and the next, the cost was $9,000. The cost was so high in the first year because of legal difficulties resulting from Paul's financial situation. In the second year, the costs were so high because Paul had a stroke, a not uncommon consequence of diabetes. Joel concludes that the costs were still warranted because Paul's medical and psychiatric improvement, independent functioning, and the cost reduction over time have justified the initial treatment plan. The key element in the success of the plan was the value base, skill level and perseverance of the case manager.

Following is another example of case management in a clinic for evaluation of children and adults with developmental disabilities. In this situation, the social worker could have confined her work to an initial client/ family assessment through a single home visit with a team member. Instead, the social worker assumed the role of case manager with the permission and participation of the client's grandmother and caretaker in order to support the grandmother, to locate services that were critical to the child's development, and to help the client and family gain access to the services.

The primary mission of the University Affiliated Program at Children's Hospital is to improve the health and welfare of children and families who are affected by disabling conditions, chronic illness, or other special health care needs. The program provides assessment and treatment services through specialty clinics. One of these clinics, the Core Clinic, serves as a model demonstration and training clinic for comprehensive interdisciplinary evaluation of children and adults with developmental concerns. Social work is one of thirteen disciplines represented in the Core Clinic, including audiology, dentistry, health administration, nursing, nutrition, occupational therapy, pediatrics, physical therapy, psychology, psychiatry, special education, and speech/language pathology.

For social workers, the interdisciplinary setting presents challenges in areas of role definition, activities and responsibilities, and assessment. A case management approach within an ecological perspective provides an excellent framework for social work practice. The social workers act as case managers when all families are interviewed in their homes in order to establish rapport and to begin to build relationships before the patient comes to the clinic for the first time. In this way, social workers also gather information, observe individual and family dynamics, and gather social and community information for the interdisciplinary team. To clarify roles and responsibilities in this complex process involving so many kinds of professionals, the social workers, patients, and family members draw ecomaps to be used by the entire team (figure 8.4). This shared process builds rapport and helps families and patients visualize their relationships with various organizations and supports. The ecomap is useful to the team throughout the evaluation process. This case example illustrates work with a family seen in the Core Clinic. The information, assessment, and recommendations were drawn from the home visit and ecomap evaluation, with additional information drawn from other discipline assessments.

Kia Morgan, a 9-year-old African American girl with cerebral palsy, mild mental retardation, and a communication disorder, was referred to the Core Clinic by her pediatrician. Kia's grandmother, Grace Morgan, who was also her legal guardian, had told the pediatrician that she was very worried about Kia. Her concerns about Kia's development were in three primary areas: peer relationships, school performance, and speech and language development. According to Mrs. Morgan, Kia could not read and often had difficulty with verbal communication. Kia had just begun attending a new school, and her grandmother had grave concerns about the appropriateness of the school placement. An individualized educational program (IEP) meeting was scheduled at her school, and Mrs. Morgan asked the social worker for assistance with the IEP, as well as with finding the optimal learning environment for Kia.

Kia lived with her maternal grandmother (Grace Morgan), her grandfather (Ben Morgan), and Alan, her 6-year-old brother. She had been removed from her mother, Charlene Morgan's care when she was 3 months old because of her mother's substance abuse problems. Her brother was removed later for

FIGURE 8.4. Ecomap for Kia Morgan.

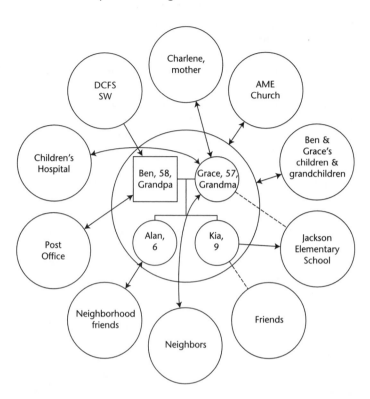

the same reason and placed with her grandmother as well. On removal, Kia had been placed in foster care. She had been in two foster homes, with the second very positive placement lasting five years. Two years before her referral to the Core Clinic, Kia's foster mother had died suddenly, causing Kia considerable stress and emotional disruption. Following their foster mother's death, Kia and her brother had been placed with their grandparents. According to Mrs. Morgan, when Kia and her brother first came to live with her and her husband, Kia cried often, especially at night, and appeared to be quite saddened by this loss. Over the last two years, however, Kia's emotional status had improved in the stable and caring environment provided by her grandparents.

Kia had poor relationships with peers at school and in her neighborhood, and she interacted only by fighting. Most of the time, she played with her 6-year-old brother, did her homework with her grandmother's help, played with her computer and electronic games, watched television, or listened to her radio. Kia would continue the same activity all day unless her grandmother encouraged her to do something else. Both Mrs. Morgan and her daughter, Charlene, believed that Kia would return to her mother someday, but the social worker thought that Charlene would not be able to take on the responsibilities of a child with multiple disabilities in the foreseeable future. Charlene lived nearby and visited her children approximately twice a month. She did not know the identity of Kia's father.

When social worker Vanitha Desai and the occupational therapist from her team visited the family, Kia greeted them outside her home where she was playing ball. She acknowledged the visitors but appeared to be shy around strangers. The neighborhood appeared to be relatively safe, with many children playing outside. Mrs. Morgan and Kia were present for the entire interview. The house was comfortable, clean, and well organized. Many family photos and religious materials were displayed throughout the room. The family's religious affiliation provided them tremendous support, and they were all involved in church activities. The many family photographs displayed indicated the importance of family.

Mr. Morgan was a long-time postal clerk, and Mrs. Morgan was a homemaker who had raised three children of her own. Married for thirty-five years, the Morgans had a stable, caring relationship. Mrs. Morgan spent most of her time taking care of the grandchildren and transporting Kia to her many medical appointments. Alan appeared to be a well-adjusted 6-year-old with no developmental concerns. Church and family connections contributed to the well-being of all the family members. Kia was the only family member with no peer relationships. Mrs. Morgan was a concerned caretaker. She had actively investigated numerous resources within her local community and was diligent about keeping the multiple appointments Kia required for her complex problems. Mrs. Morgan valued education and felt she set high but realistic and attainable goals. She thought that Kia had made tremendous progress in the last two years since living in her home; she had a longer attention span, took less medication, and performed simple tasks around the house such as taking phone messages. Although Mrs. Morgan mentioned that Kia had difficulty initiating activities, Kia did so twice during the home visit. During the interview, Kia sat next to her grandmother and continually tapped her foot. Generally quiet, she answered a few questions.

Mrs. Morgan reported that Kia's physical development was not delayed. She ambulated independently, rode a bike, and "did everything other kids do." However, Kia's speech and language development were a major concern to Mrs. Morgan. Kia was unable to read and had a "tiny voice" (spoke in baby talk). She reportedly had difficulty initiating activities and conversations and had trouble expressing herself. It took her a long time to search for words.

Recently, Kia had moved to a new school because her old school continued only through third grade. Mrs. Morgan reported that Kia did not adjust well to change, so this transition had been difficult for her. At the time of the home visit, Kia attended Jackson Elementary School and was in the fourth grade. Jackson was an integrated school with two options for children with special needs: SED for children with severe emotional disturbance and MSD for children with multiple severe disabilities. Some of the children who were in regular classes left the classroom for special assistance.

Kia was placed in the SED class with seven other students and three teachers and was mainstreamed for regular physical education and music. Although Mrs. Morgan had requested speech therapy in school, Kia was not yet receiving it; Ms. Desai helped her to obtain speech therapy. While Kia had received counseling at her previous school, she was no longer receiving this service at her current school.

The Morgans clearly had resources adequate to meet their physical needs, and their neighborhood was a safe and comfortable environment. The family drew strong support from their church, and Mrs. Morgan had a very close relationship with a neighbor who lent support on a daily basis. The ecomap indicated that intervention was needed in two areas. The various reports of the interdisciplinary team confirmed Mrs. Morgan's goals and the issues that were clarified in drawing the ecomap.

First, Kia's current school placement did not meet her educational needs and was not enhancing her potential for peer relationships. Given Kia's cognitive deficits, a special education class rather than one for children with severe emotional problems would be beneficial both for learning and for opportunities to socialize. The comprehensive assessment completed in the Core Clinic, with Ms. Desai serving as case manager, provided Mrs. Morgan with the ammunition to demand that all appropriate and needed services be given to Kia for the optimal educational experience, including the necessary speech and language services to address her substantial delays.

Second, Kia's lack of peer interaction was detrimental to her development. Given these concerns, it was imperative to assist the Morgans with alternative school placement and services, as well as to find an alternative source of peer contact that would improve Kia's quality of life. One important resource that Ms. Desai located for the Morgans was the King Center, an agency for those with developmental disabilities and their families. Ms. Desai's referral provided important resources that met the family's needs. This included respite care, which gave Mr. and Mrs. Morgan relief from the stresses of caring for Kia full-time. For peer socialization opportunities, Kia attended a camp for children with similar developmental concerns, and she joined one of the regional center's softball teams. In addition, the regional center gave the Morgans tickets to a variety of sporting events so that the family could spend more relaxed, enjoyable time together.

The Morgans welcomed new experiences and relationships. Mrs. Morgan demonstrated openness in her constant desire to get all the services Kia needs and to connect with health care providers and informal networks as well. Charlene, Kia's mother, has minimal contact with the family. She visits twice a month. She is currently free of drugs but feels unable to care for Kia at this time.

The social worker as case manager made a referral to the Division of Mental Health at Children's Hospital. This became another source of support for the Morgans. Kia has been in individual therapy for several months. She has become less shy and more talkative, and improvement in school has been reported. Ms. Desai also assisted Mrs. Morgan with school IEP meetings and exploration of school placement resources, and she facilitated use of regional center resources. The individual and family therapy has been important in bolstering the supportive nature of the family-environment system and addressing the multiple losses Kia has experienced throughout her life. Thus the Core Center social worker's acting as case manager helped to locate and access a number of critical services. She provided support and information to the already resourceful Mrs. Morgan and thus helped Mrs. Morgan to optimize Kia's care.

GROUP WORK

Group work can be an effective intervention that allows group members to solve problems that they have in common (often self-help or task groups) or to work on problems that members need to solve in their individual lives (often therapeutic, professionally led groups). Depending on social workers' beliefs about the purposes of group work, they may have very different strategies and goals for groups. Although it is often difficult to assemble groups in open and voluntary settings, there is no doubt that they are powerful tools for support and education, helping individuals to understand their presentation of self and effect on others, raising consciousness, and empowering people to act as change agents.

Whether groups are functioning as work units, therapy modalities, or social gatherings, socializing techniques are critical for understanding group dynamics. "In time, a group will turn into a social microcosm of the participant members . . . every person will begin being him/herself" (Yalom 1985:30). The ways that individuals experience groups mirror their interactions in other social situations. Likewise, "every group evolves a set of unwritten rules or norms" (Yalom 1985:118). Taking this factor into account clarifies why membership in some kinds of groups requires careful selection.

Likewise, it is vital that group leaders have the capacity to sculpt their roles to fit the needs of the group members. Leaders must be able to manage interactions to the degree that individuals feel safe to do the work of the group. In group therapy, for example, therapists must create an atmosphere of psychological safety in order to help participants explore negative personality issues, try on new behaviors, and experience new socialization outcomes. On many levels, every kind of group—from a task group to one formed expressly for psychotherapy—must create the conditions of psychological safety. Without a feeling a safely, no sense of trust can develop, and without trust people are unwilling to risk the exposure necessary for personal growth, problem solving, or organizational growth (Cohen 1999; Gummer and, McCallion 1995).

The more important a group's members and facilitators consider it to be, the more effective it may become. Believing in the importance and power of the group enhances its ability to help. Other factors that are important for the development of group cohesiveness are "the feeling of belonging" and universality. According to Yalom (1985:51), "The importance of belonging . . . can hardly be overestimated. There seems to be nothing of greater importance . . . and nothing more devastating than exclusion." Everyone has experienced the power of childhood peer groups and adolescent cliques and, at any age, being part of or left out of the social in-group. We rely on groups for approval, acceptance, and continual validation of ourselves and our value systems.

In the following case example, the social worker is the coordinator of a parenting program that is based in a community hospital. The primary mode of service delivery is group work.

Cynthia Rowlandson, a Caucasian 19-year-old woman, has a 13-month-old son, Andrew, who was placed in foster care shortly after birth. Ms. Rowlandson had been using drugs and alcohol before her pregnancy and claims to have been clean for the past two years. She has no experience in caring for children, and her ability to create a safe, healthy environment is very much in question. She lives with her own parents at present and wants to take care of her son. The court has told her to take parenting classes before it will consider placing her child with her. To assess this young mother, social worker Sharon Enderby used observations of Ms. Rowlandson's presentation of self; observations of Ms. Rowlandson's communication with her mother, her child, and Ms. Enderby; and informal conversation and self-report from Ms. Rowlandson and her parents when they attended several parenting groups. The groups are informal and supportive, and attendance is voluntary.

Sharon Enderby uses parenting discussion groups to teach and support healthy parenting practices. Among the groups she leads are an informal parent drop-in discussion group, a parents-of-infants discussion series, a workshop of summer safety and first aid, an infant/child cardiopulmonary resuscitation (CPR) group (in which there is training in basic CPR techniques and choking intervention), a parents-of-toddlers discussion series (in which topics emerge such as developmental norms, structuring a child's day, sleep, effective discipline, eating issues, toilet learning, and coping with anger), a parents-of-adolescents group, and a postpartum exercise program. Ms. Rowlandson has attended several sessions of the parents-of-toddlers discussion series, while her parents attended the one for parents of adolescents. The following overarching issues and concepts are addressed in each group:

1. *Normal child development.* The coordinator helps parents bring their expectations of their children in line with reality (many parents expect children to reason and behave like small adults).
2. *Healthy patterns and modes of communicating and relating.* Developing healthy patterns of communication improves not only adult/child relationships but adult/adult relationships as well. Helpful communication skills are active listening, using "I" statements, using communication to enhance self-esteem, giving choices, and promoting problem-solving techniques.
3. *Identification of the strengths one possesses that would support effective parenting.* Here the coordinator builds confidence and teaches group members about supporting themselves with resources and social supports.

Ms. Rowlandson's primary issues are deep misunderstandings about child development that lead her to expect behavior and control that are impossible for her child to meet; authority, jealousy, and control issues with regard to her relationship with both her mother and her son; a need for more education that will lead to a job with which she can support herself and her child; a range of work-related concerns; concerns about the very poor relationship she has with her child's father; and the need to learn more about appropriate male/female relationships. Ms. Enderby's interventions with Ms. Rowlandson include teaching her about child development, reframing her descriptions of her behavior in ways that support self-esteem, and modeling behavior in terms of how Ms. Enderby talks to Andrew. Ms. Enderby's interventions with Ms. Rowlandson's mother include helping her to understand the limits of her involvement and helping her to improve communications with her daughter through modeling active listening.

There are times when the parenting focus does not fit the needs of a group member. For example, a group for single parents discusses parenting issues in general as well as those unique to single parents. One new member who wanted to spend her time discussing the singles scene in the area was disappointed with the focus on parenting and chose not to return. However, the young women who make up Ms. Rowlandson's group not only learned a great deal but related very well. The last couple of meetings were so positive that the whole group adjourned to have lunch together in the hospital cafeteria.

In Ms. Enderby's considerable experience, parenting classes and workshops that are carried out well by knowledgeable professionals with fine group skills are highly effective. In addition, learning about healthy parenting can improve family relationships dramatically. Foster care agencies and hospitals can be effective partners in helping women learn about parenting, but funding such programs continues to be a problem because health insurance does not cover parenting classes. Ironically, the courts increasingly say that they will not consider returning a child in foster care to its parent or parents unless the they take parenting classes, but the child welfare system will not pay for parenting classes, and parents must pay out of pocket. While Sharon Enderby's program charges only five dollars a session, even that cost can be prohibitive. Therefore, she has to find outside funds to defray costs and sometimes has parents who are willing to pay more than the charge.

This program also functions as a marketing device for the community hospital in which it is located. The community is diverse; a mix of affluence, social class, education, and race is represented in the groups. The community hospital in which the parenting program is located draws from very mixed neighborhoods, and Ms. Enderby has been determined to have that mix reflected in the groups. This program has a small budget (about $40,000 a year) in a department whose director reports to the vice president for community development of the hospital. It is clear to the director that the hospital supports the program as a marketing device, and the coordinator is then responsible for marketing the program within the hospital, especially to local physicians and the community, with a broad mailing list and many community postings of programs.

Decisions That Structure a Group Experience

To form a social work group, social workers must decide on the purpose of the group, the characteristics of the members, activities to be performed, the degree to which the group will be the unit of attention (as opposed to each individual member being a unit of attention) (Schwartz 1971), the number of meetings the group will have, the length of each meeting, the place where the meetings will occur, and the role of the social worker. Traditionally, with the exceptions of self-help, support group, and community action efforts, it has been much easier to convince people in residential settings to take part in group work than it has been to motivate people to come to an organization specifically for group work. In residential situations, clients/consumers are often required to participate in groups. In nonresidential settings, it is very difficult to motivate busy clients with many other responsibilities to come for group interaction. They have to be helped to believe that such interaction will make a difference in their lives. Therefore, it is imperative that social workers believe strongly that group interaction will make an important difference before they can motivate people to be involved in a group (Thomas and Caplan 1999). It also is important to allow enough time for the group to form and for enough people to come regularly that they form a bond with each other and with the social worker. Once the core has been established, it is possible to keep the group going even if some members participate less regularly.

Among many dimensions, groups vary in their leadership, the task or tasks they are to accomplish, their time frames, and their size. Historically, social workers have adhered to one of three prevailing models of group work:

1. The social goals model focused on the social worker's role in enhancing individual growth and learning through the use of democratic participation in the pursuit of social action.
2. The reciprocal model focused on the social worker's role as a mediator who engages group members in reciprocal relationships and a system of mutual aid within the group in order to meet common goals.
3. The remedial model focused on the social worker's interventions with each individual in the group, the group itself, and other social systems in order to reach individual and social goals.

Very simply, the purpose of the social goals model is to move members to social action, the purpose of the reciprocal model is to build a mutual-aid group, and the purpose of the social goals model is to treat individual members. It remains useful to think about which of these models social workers have in mind as they begin to form groups. The structure, roles, and functions of groups following each of those models will vary as a result of the group's purpose.

The size of the group merits early consideration as well. For example, most psychotherapy groups benefit from a relatively small membership of five to eight individuals. Small groups are also seen as an excellent modality for empowering individuals. They can create "the perfect environment for raising consciousness, engaging in mutual aid, developing skills, and solving problems and [provide] an ideal way for clients to experience individual effectiveness in influencing others" (Gutierrez 1990:151). Alternately, many mutual self-help and psychoeducational groups are able to sustain much larger numbers. Groups can also be open-ended, with members coming in and out freely, or they may be closed, with a set group membership and often a limited number of scheduled sessions.

Types of Groups in Social Work Practice

Psychoeducational groups, psychotherapeutic groups, support groups (including both the professionally facilitated and the self-help varieties), and task groups commonly occur in social work practice in health and mental health care systems.

Psychoeducational Groups. Psychoeducational groups provide information and psychological support in a variety of formats. They commonly focus on an individual disease that patients and family members must understand in order to provide the best self-care and support. Health systems, hospitals, and outreach groups related to specific diseases will offer series related to the natural history of a disease (what happens to the individual if the disease is left untreated), possible forms of medical intervention, sources for durable medical equipment, and sources for social and psychological support. For example, a Parkinson's disease outreach network with a social worker as coordinator sponsors a monthly series of groups with guest speakers covering subjects of interest to those with the illness and their relatives; a psychoeducational group for those with diabetes focuses on self-care issues regarding diet, exercise, and insulin management, along with the psychological issues related to the disease; and a group for caregivers of those with Alzheimer's explores the alterations in the capacities of an individual who is moving through the stages of the disease and the psychological issues that those changes raise for both those with the illness and those who provide care.

Des Jarlais and Stepherson (1991) discuss three intensive prevention programs that demonstrate reductions in risk behaviors among homeless HIV-infected gay men and homeless youth. This is also an example of how group work can benefit broad groups of people, including those who are not directly involved in the group interaction. The interventions are based in social learning theory and involve the following: (1) a minimum of ten sessions, (2) assertiveness and coping skills training, (3) acquisition of knowledge and positive attitudes toward safe acts, (4) identification of individual personal risk behaviors, (5) structured and continuing support for behavior change, and (6) group meetings to develop and enhance open support and social norms for safe acts. Thus these types of groups can provide a mix of support and psychoeducation for participants while also providing a broader societal benefit.

In the following practice example, a psychoeducational group is held in an urban middle-school-based health clinic.

A small, privately owned and operated health clinic, housed in a middle school in a large city, serves students between the ages of 11 and 14 who are in grades six through eight. The clinic, now 6 years old, is sponsored by a privately owned African American health agency that is funded by public and private sources. The agency runs programs that include a health center in another neighborhood, a teen health program in a local high school, and other community health initiatives. The clinic is funded through a privately owned African American HMO. Both the HMO and the health agency are staffed by African Americans for African Americans.

The middle school is located in a primarily African American community. While the community's family income level ranges from very poor to middle class, almost all the student body is from very low income families, with a large segment coming from multiproblem families. To the east of the school is a high- and low-rise public housing project, and to the south is a small development of newer, well-kept privately owned homes. Older row houses are located to the west and north of the school. Among the institutions located within a five-block radius are a community mental health agency, a Catholic church with a grade school, a public grade school, a district health center, a church-run nursing home, a private psychiatric hospital, and an active YMCA. Several corner variety stores are in the neighborhood. It is a dangerous place to live. The community has a teen pregnancy rate of 10 percent of live births, an infant mortality rate in excess of twenty infant deaths per thousand live births, and very high rates of substance abuse, sexually transmitted diseases, and violence-related injuries, including homicide.

Staffed by a director who is a licensed social worker and two medical assistants, the clinic provides a full range of health services to registered students. A pediatrician provides medical coverage one morning a week, a nurse practitioner provides the medical coverage other mornings, and a clinical social worker provides mental health counseling and consultation one day per week. The mental health services include individual counseling of referred students, group counseling, and some parent and family counseling. Through this site students also have access to the larger community health service.

Groups have been established as a response to the great number of registered students who have experienced significant trauma. Examples of such trauma include the death of a significant loved one (usually a parent or caretaker), drug-addicted and/or incarcerated parents and family members, and a parent or significant family member with a chronic physical or mental illness. The director and the consultant have developed two groups: (1) the Grief and Loss group for students who have experienced the death of a loved one, and

(2) the RAP (Reaching Adolescent Potential) group for students who have a parent who is drug-addicted and/or incarcerated or who have experienced family problems with severe physical or mental illness.

Referrals come from clinic and school personnel, family members, and the students themselves. To determine whether a student is appropriate for the group, the clinic director first interviews him or her. Next, the consultant talks to the referred student about the group in an informal contracting process exploring the student's desires and the group's expectations. For balance, each group is made up of students with different styles of relating and levels of cognitive functioning.

The students in the Grief and Loss group have experienced the loss of one or more family members or caretakers. In one group of six, one student's mother, the only surviving parent, died the previous year. Another student was living with an aunt and grandmother because his mother died when he was about 10 years old and his father was incarcerated; then, his grandmother died while he was attending the group. Another young student was living with her adoptive father. Her adoptive mother died the previous year from cancer, and her biological mother died from AIDS when she was much younger. Several years earlier, she had witnessed the death of her younger sister, who had been born with AIDS. This student does not have the disease. One student's father and another student's mother had recently died of cancer.

Of the students in the RAP group, one, whose parents were divorced, lived with his father who was on dialysis. One student had just returned to live with her mother, who had completed a drug recovery program. One student's mother was released from prison during the school year. Her favorite uncle had died several years earlier, and another uncle was in prison on death row. Another student lived with a foster family; his mother was mentally ill, and his father, who lived in another state, had little contact with him.

The groups are time-limited, meeting once per week for forty minutes for ten-week cycles. Membership can change at the end of a cycle. A psychoeducational approach is used. To structure a predictable and safe environment, the groups follow a similar structure with different content. Group goals are (1) to help students realize they are not alone in their experiences and feelings, (2) to normalize and familiarize students with specific feelings and other pertinent information associated with specific trauma, (3) to help students put words to feelings, (4) to help students connect feelings to behavior, to help students talk out versus act out feelings, (5) to help students learn about themselves, (6) to provide students with information about stress, and (7) to help students learn to talk with one another without put-downs. The role of the facilitator is (1) to provide an emotionally and physically safe environment, (2) to plan group activity, (3) to facilitate group discussion, (4) to provide active direction when needed, (5) to model listening to one another, (6) to model ways to talk about self to others, (7) to monitor behavior and communication when necessary, and (8) to provide conflict resolution within group process when necessary.

Each session begins with hellos and a review of rules. Among the rules are the following: be respectful, no put-downs, speak one at a time, it's okay to pass, be positive, it's private and confidential, and stay focused. A feeling check-in follows in which each student is given a chance to say how he or she is feeling. The student usually begins with the sentence "I feel ___ because ____." At times there is brief discussion of what is happening with a student. Students can come up with their own feeling words or choose from the feeling chart in the room. Next, the facilitator introduces a stimulus activity, a brief written or verbal exercise or a video to focus the discussion on specific content. (Table 8.1 lists some of the stimulus activities these groups have used.) This allows for an informal discussion relating the stimulus activity to the students' own experiences with family, peers, and so on. In the wrap-up circle that concludes the session the students hold hands and briefly summarize the group focusing on supportive, positive comments about contributions and effort.

The amount of trauma in these students' lives is overwhelming. The incredible resourcefulness of the families and coping of these students is always evident. In planning the groups, it has been important to match the group with the developmental and cognitive level of the students, with particular understanding of the emotional impact of the types of trauma in the lives of the group members. The director and consultant have structured the groups

TABLE 8.1. Examples of Stimulus Activities

Grief and Loss Group	Reaching Adolescent Potential (RAP) Group
Journaling: Personal reflections on specific ideas	*Value-clarification activities*
Reviewing stages of mourning: Reading from age-appropriate books about loss	*Autobiography activities*
Viewing and discussing films (e.g., The Lion King, My Girl)	*Short stimulus videos* on teen self-esteem, peer pressure, and other teen adjustment issues
Talking about current events: Deaths of rap artists, neighborhood events, school issues	*Talking about current events*
Expressive games and activities	*Expressive games and activities*
Art activities appropriate to topic	*Art activities appropriate to topic*

in various ways. For example, initially the groups were not time-limited, nor were they as structured. Refreshments were tried but found to be too distracting. A small party with refreshments to be held at the end of each cycle has been much more successful. At times, groups have difficulty settling. The work of the groups at these times is to figure out why it is so hard to settle. In terms of professional use of self, the consultant realized she needs to be much more active in these groups. Often the consultant wondered whether her generally more reflective, low-key style was a good match for these emotionally over-burdened students. These worries decreased some with the following events.

One week, the grief and loss group had a particularly hard time settling. They were finally able to get to the idea that many feelings were getting stirred up by the content of the group. The facilitator framed what was happening as "laughing to keep from crying." She was surprised when several weeks later the director had the occasion to talk to a member of the group in reference to a separate peer conflict incident. The director said that it was initially hard work to get the involved students to focus. The director told the facilitator that the student from the grief and loss group said to her that maybe they were laughing to keep from crying, that she had learned that in the group.

During the final RAP group, the facilitator asked the students what they had learned from the group. She was surprised to hear one student from a particularly impulsive and violent environment say that she learned that "even though its gets bad sometimes, not to give up." In the same way, a member of the grief and loss group who was graduating said that he hoped his new high school would have a similar type of group. He had attended regularly and voluntarily for his three years in the school.

Psychotherapeutic Groups. Psychotherapy groups have the same purpose as individual psychotherapy, that is, providing insights into the behavior of individual participants. In group psychotherapy, the insights are gained through interaction with peers who may be managing issues and through interaction with the group leader and the authority issues that are involved in such relationships. The interaction with the group itself allows for growth of self-knowledge and the power, reinforcement, and support to change behavior. Pure psychotherapeutic groups are somewhat less common in social work practice than other types of groups. They tend to be small (five to seven people) and promote open sharing among the participants, while also discouraging relationships among members outside the group meeting time. Garvin and Reed (in Greene 1994) note that cultural diversity in these groups adds a layer of challenge that requires skillful facilitator intervention. Developing a group that feels a sense of sociocultural safety is imperative if the therapeutic use of the group is to be optimized. Power differentials may emerge that have more to do with minority/ majority status than with the interpersonal dynamics of the members involved. Group facilitators must therefore strive to create an environment that not only promotes open dialogue but also is open to discussion of diversity in safety, so that all may benefit and not reexperience oppressions found in the culture.

The following example describes the experience of one individual participating in a psychotherapeutic group.

Deedee Johnson, a tall 40-year-old white woman with long dark hair and fair skin, has been in individual counseling for several years. The mother of two young children, Ms. Johnson is in an exceptionally unsatisfying marriage in which she is verbally and emotionally abused. Because of work responsibilities and embarrassment about the chaos in her household, she has become increasingly isolated. Ms. Johnson blames herself for her lack of social opportunities, believing no one would want to be friendly with her even if she were less isolated. Low self-esteem has deeply affected her ability to manage her life tasks and has promoted a tendency toward depression with which she must cope as well. As part of her treatment, she joined a five-person women's psychotherapy group that meets weekly. The group is facilitated by social worker Ruth Simmel, who developed the group privately as a long-term closed group of women that met for the purposes of socialization, discussion, and support. Ms. Simmel's leadership style is relatively informal but professional. Group members provide the themes and foci for each session, and she intervenes when the group is "stuck" in order to keep it working. Ms. Simmel encourages the identification of common areas of experience but promotes respect for the differences in the group members. She supports group members' active problem solving and brainstorming with one another and eschews the role of expert.

Group members range in age from 35 to 55, and all the women have been married at some point in their lives. The group took several months before they felt safe enough to begin delving into each other's stories and providing feedback to one another. After that long beginning, the group members now share intimate details of their lives and are able to validate their experiences, help one another consider a range of options for handling problems, and give one another feedback about how a member's behavior affects them. Through this experience, Deedee Johnson has been able to view herself as likable for the first time in many years.

Within the last two months, another member of the group has confronted Ms. Johnson about how she uses her hopelessness to avoid trying to make changes in her life, and Ms. Johnson has thought deeply about this way of coping. With the ongoing support of the group, Ms. Johnson has been able to begin making small changes in her interaction style that allowed her to be more assertive. She has set goals for increasing her interactions in her community, while asserting boundaries with her husband, including no longer submitting to verbal or emotional abuse. She will continue to work toward providing more structure for and setting limits with her children, both of which will be of benefit to them and will bring some order to the household. Small successes in these areas have fostered an increased sense of efficacy and self-esteem for Ms. Johnson.

Support Groups. Support groups are used very successfully in helping those with chronic diseases to manage their illnesses (Foster 1997; Monahan and Hooker 1997). There are as many styles of group interaction as there are groups. For example, the Alcoholics Anonymous approach to helping those with drinking problems is a highly structured approach that relies on lay leadership, anonymity, the adherence to a strict meeting format, and the ultimate prescription of a list of rules. Other groups, such as those for people with diabetes, serious and persistent mental illness, or epilepsy, might meet along with a facilitator to discuss the day-to-day problems that result from living with an illness and its particular set of symptoms. In one example from a group with people who had experienced stroke, there was discussion of the problems that result when one has impairments that cannot be seen by others. In another example from a group of teenagers with diabetes, discussion focused often on food restrictions and how to deal with unaffected teenagers pressing teens with diabetes to "pig out" on pizza and beer.

Self-Help Support Groups. Self-help groups are generally led by someone who is affected by whatever issue, condition, or illness the group has set as its theme. There is no paid staff, and the costs of the group are defrayed through contributions. They are true mutual-aid groups; that is, there is no hierarchy, and the facilitator is a member of the group. Frequently these groups are open-ended in terms of time, meaning that they are ongoing with a regular meeting time and they are open to anyone who is affected. They tend to operate by providing support in the form of sharing the stories of their experience and gaining the support of the group as they make progress in their goals. Additionally, some groups allow members to provide feedback to one another about rationalizations and coping mechanisms and encourage "carefrontations" to promote progress in members' development (Morrison 1991; Riessman and Carroll 1995).

Many self-help groups follow the twelve-step model of Alcoholics Anonymous. This involves a fellowship of people who share their experience, strength, and hope with each other in order to solve their common problem and help others to recover from alcoholism. Although Alcoholics Anonymous (AA) was developed to address individuals' problems with alcoholism, the model has been effectively used for narcotics, stimulant, food, gambling, and sex addictions as well. The twelve steps involve moving through a progression of steps beginning with admitting that one is powerless over one's addiction, moving through acceptance of a power greater than oneself and a searching and fearless moral inventory of self, ultimately admitting past wrongs to others, and working to help others with similar addictions. The twelve traditions describe the nature of group interaction, acknowledging that personal recovery depends on the unity of AA, viewing "God as He may express Himself in our conscience" as the only authority, and viewing leaders as trusted servants, not as those with authority to govern the group. Alcoholics Anonymous eschews organization and endorsements, maintaining personal anonymity as a condition for providing the most helpful service. Although twelve-step programs do not appeal to everyone who shares the problems that are the focus of the work, when they can successfully embrace a troubled person, they can provide unmatched power and support. Such groups have sustained people and aided their recovery in ways that no professional or health facility can equal.

Professionally Led Support Groups. Social workers lead support groups that combine many of the facets of self-help groups with professional contributions of structure, focus, and insight (Foster 1997; Frank and Golden 1992; Getzel 1991). Reasons for viewing groups as an essential part of social work practice relate to the commonality of group members, the creative and problem-solving potential of groups, small-group forces, and convenience (Schopler and Galinsky 1995). Nevertheless, shared experiences of sexual abuse, genetic termination of pregnancy, or stigmatized illnesses promote a sense of shared knowledge only if members feel free to discuss differences as well. Although they may feel comfortable discussing how their particular health experience differs from the others' experiences, they may feel less comfortable discussing how their race, sexual orientation, religion, or other difference affects their experience.

In these groups, too, it is important to recognize the influence of diversity. Davis, Galinsky, and Schopler (1995) suggest an acronym—RAP— as a way to handle these situations: the facilitator is encouraged to (r)ecognize racial and other divisions and tensions, (a)nticipate potential effects of group makeup, environmental occurrences, and relationships among group members, and (p)roblem-solve when diversity issues arise and require resolution. They provide an instructive example of a cancer support group that was temporarily disabled owing to a community occurrence involving a white police officer shooting a black youth. The social worker was able to handle the tensions directly, having laid the ground-work for tolerance and mutual respect as part of the group norms at the very beginning of the group.

Often professionally led support groups are facilitated in order to di-minish a sense of tragically unique isolation and to allow people to begin to share strategies for coping. These groups are frequently used for situ-ations in which social stigma and shame are present. Knight (1990:203) comments on the value of the group experience for sexual abuse survi-vors: "It is only through a group experience that the survivor realizes she is neither as alone nor as different as she had believed, and that her feelings, beliefs, and actions are not unique or crazy." She notes that time-limited groups have the advantage of allowing members to know that they will have an end of treatment in sight and will therefore work more efficiently and less dependently toward making the most of the group experience.

The following is a practice example of a professionally led support group.

Mary and Bill Simpson became pregnant with their second child and were happily anticipating the baby's arrival until the obstetrician noted some de-formities during the ultrasound. After amniocentesis revealed trisomy 18, the Simpsons made the painful decision to interrupt the pregnancy. Because of the stigma of abortion and their uncertainty about social acquaintances' judg-ments, Mr. and Ms. Simpson felt they could not reveal to anyone the nature of how their pregnancy ended. They told people they had had a pregnancy loss, unable to call it a miscarriage because they were so far along in the pregnancy and unable to call it a stillbirth because it would have been untrue. The secrecy led to feelings of shame and also cut them off from the support of friends and family. Any support they did receive was under the auspices of the "pregnancy loss," and they did not feel entitled to it.

Ms. Simpson's grieving finally led her genetic counselor to refer her to a support group developed just for those who have had a genetic termination of pregnancy. After talking with the social worker who facilitated the group, Ms. Simpson was amazed to learn about the large number of people who had made similar decisions. When the next seven-week group started, the Simpsons at-tended. Ms. Simpson commented that the most helpful thing she experienced was walking into the group, finding that "no one was a purple, three-headed monster," and that she was "allowed to tell the whole story and to get support that was based on the full truth" of her loss. For the Simpsons, the mere expe-rience of knowing that they were not alone with their loss was helpful.

Task/Work Groups. Group skills for social workers in health and mental health systems are important in arenas other than direct client work. The ability to carry the social work role and play that role effectively in inter-disciplinary groups is vital in these settings. Such groups are used not only to address the problems of individual clients and groups of clients but also to resolve problems of the organizations and systems themselves.

> In collective entrepreneurship, individual skills are integrated into a group; this collective capacity to innovate becomes something greater than the sum of its parts. Over time, as group members work through various problems and approaches, they learn about each other's abilities. They learn how they can help one another perform better, what each can contribute to a particular project, how they can best take advantage of one another's experience. Each partici-pant is constantly on the lookout for small adjustments that will speed and smooth the evolution of the whole. The net result of many such small-scale adaptations, effected throughout the organization, is to propel the enterprise forward. (Reich 1998:213)

The history of social work is replete with examples of teamwork and interdisciplinary collaboration. Dramatic examples of this are part of social work's tradition with disaster work, war-related activity, and other work with the military (Kerson 1981; Martin 1997). Now, recent trends such as privatization, specialization, decentralization, and increasingly complex client problems demand collaborative efforts in order for all professionals to help their clients with experience (Abramson and Rosenthal 1995; Mer-ritt and Neugeboren 1990). Rather than come together in extraordinary circumstances, professionals of all types are finding that collaboration and teamwork are the norm in intra- and interorganizational work.

Although professionals agree that teamwork and collaboration are nec-essary for effective service delivery, they often see impediments to the process. Abramson and Mizrahi (1993, 1996) have studied social worker–physician collaboration (Abramson 1989; Mizrahi and Abramson 1994). One study regarding the collaboration of social workers and physicians compared the best and worst collaborative experiences of each. It was found that social workers valued interaction much more than physicians, whereas physicians viewed the competence of social workers as most im-portant (Abramson and Mizrachi 1996). The only dimension of collabo-ration about which there was absolute agreement was the importance of the communication of information. This is just one example of profes-sionals being socialized differently and often having different perspectives about goals and means (Cowles and Lefcowitz 1992; Sands 1989; Sands, Stafford, and McClelland 1990).

Like other kinds of groups, teams "can be powerful as well as versatile units of performance; but they can also be difficult to predict, control, and integrate into a balanced organizational system and leadership approach" (Katzenbach 1998:x). Teams are simple, natural units, and it is the simplicity of the team concept that makes it so powerful when it is used with resolve and discipline. Katzenbach (1998) suggests that there are four key guidelines for team creation:

1. Pay close attention to the fundamentals in identifying the opportunity and structuring the effort.
2. Provide for hard work, simplicity, and conflict.
3. Consider the range of small-group options.
4. Integrate the team with single-leader units.

Real team levels of performance require small size, complementary skills, common levels of member commitment to both a performance purpose and a set of performance goals, a clear working approach, and a strong sense of mutual accountability (Katzenbach and Smith 1998). Finally, a team's performance measurement system should help it in its work; therefore the team should adopt only a handful of measures to track its process (Meyer 1998).

Skills for collaborating and team building require a strategic or sociopolitical perspective in interprofessional relationships (Segal and Specht 1983). The process of collaboration includes negotiation, compromise, persuasion, and defense (Abramson and Mizrahi 1996). All team members and collaborators have to value the multidimensional knowledge base for assessment, strategizing, and problem solving that cross-professional work brings to the client (Abramson and Rosenthal 1995).

The following is a practice example of a social work–led interdisciplinary team.

An interdisciplinary team was formed at a hospital to increase the number of referred patients who kept their appointments at the hypertension clinic. The team was composed of the social worker who was the follow-up coordinator for the hospital, the follow-up clerk, the physician who was in charge of the medical clinic, an emergency medicine resident, and a representative from the business office. The team studied the records of patients who kept their appointments and those who did not. Next, the team decided on the percentage of increase they could hope to achieve, developed a set of inexpensive strategies for coping with the problem, and in six months had more than doubled the number of patients who kept their appointments. Since the team had met its goal by altering some of the structure of the clinic and the information provided to patients in the emergency room and the general medical clinic, the team was disbanded.

According to Heimer and Stevens (1997:158), "social workers are specialists in processing people in ways that preserve people's sense of their own humanness while enabling other organizational actors to stuff clients into routines." Social workers manage the dissonance between personhood and casehood on behalf of medical professionals and the hospital, and they are particularly likely to be routine players in medical spheres in which patient care is distributed among several different kinds of professionals. For some, social workers serve to prepare patients for doctors by turning human beings into medical cases so that physicians can treat "clearly defined technical problems" (Heimer and Stevens 1997:134). This is not to say that social workers function as the handmaidens of physicians or hospitals to turn human beings into cases. It is to say that social workers can provide the "human touch" while also explaining systems and protocols to clients so that they can make the most efficient and effective use of the health care system.

Occasionally, it may be useful to differentiate between teams and task or work groups. Although both ideally have similar dynamics, occasionally task or work groups do not function as teams as much as they function as a group of individuals doing circumscribed tasks. This differs from teams whose members may have different responsibilities but are designed to encourage cooperation and sharing of information and ideas. Several business consultants (Wetlaufer 1994) critiquing a dysfunctional team allude to this when they advocate for the ability of some groups to avoid the danger of "groupthink" by allowing a work group to avoid a strong sense of cohesiveness based on gaining consensus of ideas and focusing instead on the cohesiveness of the shared final goal of the work or task. This differs from the teamwork ideally found in health care settings, which ensures open communication and continuity of care. It may be that case management is more likely to entail work/task groups, whereas true team functioning happens more easily in health care settings where access to each member of the team is unimpaired.

Although every professional would agree that teamwork and collaboration are necessary for good work, there are many impediments to the process (Kulys and Davis 1987). Impediments to the work must be identified, some inevitable tensions must be managed, and social workers must work to identify and act on opportunities to improve collaboration. Professions compete for certain kinds of work, especially counseling and psychotherapy (Koeske, Koeske, and Mallinger 1993). This competition must be resolved in case management work groups to ensure nonduplicative service provision. On teams, the competition can be even more hazardous and must be resolved to ensure positive functioning of the team as a group. Professions are socialized differently and often have different perspectives about goals and means (Cowles and Lefcowitz 1992; Sands 1989; Sands et al. 1990). Social workers and other professionals have long had to deal with physician domination. As the authority of physicians is being altered through managed care, greater opportunities will arise for social workers and other professionals to collaborate in a more equal manner (Sheppard 1992; Walton, Jakobowski, and Barnsteiner 1993).

In many ways, managed care is transforming many services so that social workers and nurses are the frontline workers, doing triage and intake in a broad range of health and mental health systems. Good collaboration between nurses and social workers has grown in importance but has become more problematic as well. As roles and lines of authority are blurred, a great deal of competition may erupt between the disciplines. Open communication and team orientation are critical.

COMMUNITY ORGANIZATION

Community organization uses four methods of social change: service, advocacy, mobilizing, and organizing. Organizing, as a social process, conceives and nourishes an ongoing challenge to power relationships in society (Kahn 1994). One thinks of community organizing in relation to health and mental health issues especially in terms of public health concerns, that is, communicable illness, occupational illness, and environmental concerns. An interesting example is work done on behalf of Navajo uranium miners and millworkers who had been made sick through exposure to radiation and silica dust and on behalf of their families (Dawson 1993; Dawson, Charley, and Harrison 1997; Dawson and Madsen 1995). The goal was to obtain compensation (compassionate payment) for all underground uranium miners, civilian downwinders of the atomic testing program, and nuclear test site workers who are eligible through the Radiation Exposure Compensation Act. This example raises questions not only about social responsibility but also about mistreatment of underrepresented groups and about the effects of uranium exposure on Navajo cultural norms. Dawson et al. (1997:404) describe the social stress in a Navajo family that was caused by the death of a uranium worker:

> Wives were hit the hardest when a husband contracted the fatal lung disease. The wife had to assume a role she was taught belonged with the male. Many had very little education, no work experience, and consequently end up on welfare. This was a blow to their ego, their upbringing, and it was embarrassing. Navajos are taught never to

"beg" for handouts in order to feed and clothe their children. I recall one wife, rather than face this predicament, chose to divorce the miner. A constant battle to feed the family resulted in the oldest children dropping out of school and starting employment or to care for the father. The father was a strong central figure and when he was no longer available, family stress, disciplinary/emotional problems, and alcoholism developed among the children, and other problems resulted.

Just as in individual, family, and group interventions, a great deal of the variability of practice in community organization is determined by its organizational context. Need is defined more by the constitution and goals of the employing agency than by communication between the practitioner and community. Furthermore, the means selected to deal with community problems depend on organizational requirements, stances, and definitions. No matter what practitioners' activities are, they are guided, and to a great degree determined, by the structure, aims, and operating procedures of the organization under whose auspices they work. Thus, according to Zald (1995), four interrelated but not mutually exclusive concepts are necessary for community organizing activity. These concepts are very important for direct practitioners to understand. Frequently, when direct practitioners seek community support or action, they underestimate the degree to which they have to understand the community and its organizations. Just as the information about organizations in chapters 4 and 7 provide important information in this regard, this information on interventions is equally important. Not to understand other organizations in the community will lead to frustration and an inability to reach broader goals. *Organizations have constitutions;* that is, organizations have basic goals, activities, and norms of procedure and relationships that are more or less institutionalized and can be changed only with great effort and cost (Zald 1995:130). Constitutions are linked to the *constituency and resource base* of the organization. The constituency is not the clients but the people who control the organization and to whom the workers are most immediately responsible. These people include board members, legislators, grantors, and payers. Community organization agencies wish to affect target populations, organizations, or decision centers. No matter where they are located, they exist as one of many other agencies and institutions that can facilitate, impede, or be neutral to their goal attainment.

Certain conditions contribute to coordination, cooperation, and integration (Zald 1995:138–39). The greater the symbiotic relationship between agencies and institutions and the greater the likelihood that all parties will gain from the coordination, the more likely it is that the coordination will occur. The less constituencies overlap, the more likely it is that they either will be neutral toward each other or will distrust each other, and thus the longer it will take and the more difficult it will be to gain cooperation.

The following practice example describes the development of the Alliance of Genetic Support Groups.

The Alliance of Genetic Support Groups was formed when individual social workers who were engaged in direct practice became concerned that the individual genetic support groups they worked with could not keep current and were too small and specialized to have a voice in the public discourse. The community on which they had to focus was the country, and they had to become expert about many kinds of organizations and institutions in order to achieve their goal.

This example describes the development of a national coalition of individual genetic support groups formed for purposes such as sharing information and resources and advocacy. To form the coalition, social workers assessed gaps in resources and services, initiated changes in programs related to client concerns, and used linkage and advocacy strategies to accomplish their goals. Using individual, group, administration, and community organization strategies, social workers facilitated the formation of a powerful and continuing national coalition, and social workers continue as full partners in the alliance.

The attempt to form an alliance came about because the increasing numbers of genetic support groups, generally focused on specific disorders, were finding it difficult to keep current with rapid technological advancement in the prevention, diagnosis, and treatment of genetic disorders. The lack of a unified voice meant that the groups were not linked politically, scientifically, or educationally. An opportunity arose for social workers in genetic support groups and coalitions to develop partnerships in order to enhance services.

To assess need and capacity, questionnaires were mailed to executives of all support organizations included in the National Center for Education in Maternal and Child Health's directory of genetic organizations. Survey results showed that the organization needed an umbrella organization that could (1) be a conduit for sharing information about genetic disorders and their effects on individuals and families, (2) provide more visibility, and (3) address common problems in regard to fund-raising, the dissemination of information, and heightening legislatures' and social agencies' awareness of genetic disorders. Although some group objectives and issues diverged, three common goals emerged: (1) psychosocial support of affected individuals and families, (2) education of professionals and lay people about hereditary disorders, and (3) support of genetic research. Concerns had to be addressed in the initial formation that an alliance might result in the loss of individual genetic support group identity and too much focus on genetic research rather than on individuals.

A range of strategies was employed. A national symposium organized by a social worker at a hospital that is a center for treatment and research of genetic disorders and supported by the March of Dimes Birth Defects Foundation and the Division of Maternal and Child Health drew representatives of eighty voluntary genetic organizations. Afterward, a steering committee made up of nine members (the majority consumers, the organizing social worker, and a medical geneticist) structured the network, defined preliminary goals and objectives, and arranged start-up funding. The goals were (1) to raise the consciousness of the public and professions about the effect of genetic disorders on individuals and families, (2) to share organizational information, (3) to monitor and comment on pertinent legislation, (4) to address national issues when a consensus existed among constituent groups, (5) to encourage communication among its organizations, and (6) to enhance each group's awareness of cross-disability similarities. The priorities were to help groups increase efficiency and effectiveness and build on the conjoint potential of these groups.

The Alliance of Genetic Support Groups has become a recognized and respected coalition with full partnership between consumers and professionals. Coalition with other lay and professional organizations has influenced legislation and services in states, regional and community genetic facilities, and on the federal level. Also, it houses data banks and acts as a national clearinghouse for consumers and providers. Thus an effort begun because a small group of social workers were concerned about the ability to keep pace and the political voice of their small genetic support groups became the forging of a national alliance that involved many different constituencies.

CONCLUSION

According to Drucker (1974:217–25),

> The final step in making work productive is to fit the right tools to the work. Different kinds of work require different tools. . . . A tool is not necessarily better because it is bigger. A tool is best if it does the job required with a minimum of effort, with a minimum of complexity, and with a minimum of power. . . . The right question is not "Isn't there a bigger tool for the job?" It is always "What is the simplest, the smallest, the lightest, the easiest tool that will do the job?"

In choosing the means by which social workers intervene, a simple rule to follow is that the tool has to serve the work. The work does not exist for the sake of the tool; the tool exists for the sake of production. For social workers in health and mental health systems, the tools are the resources that we can help clients/consumers access, our understanding of the laws that protect and entitle our clients, the organizations and systems in which we work, and a range of intervention techniques. To be an effective social worker means that one has to be able to intervene using a combination of advocacy, solution-focused short-term work, group work, and case management. In addition, one has to be knowledgeable about and comfortable with the kinds of organizational and community interventions that one's client/consumer population might need in order to meets its goals and objectives. All these interventions require a fine social and psychological understanding of self and others in context.

Advocacy is the overarching intervention, and it can be argued that all social work intervention is advocacy. In addition, for social workers in health and mental health systems there are three primary tools for direct intervention: short solution-focused work, case management, and group work. Social workers most often use facets of all these techniques in their work. In fact, these techniques are helpful not only in direct work with clients/consumers but also in collaboration, work or task groups and teams, and in community outreach as well. Like all the other kinds of information and strategies discussed in this book, these are tools to be perfected over a professional lifetime.

The Evaluation of Social Work Practice in Health and Mental Health Systems

Evaluation refers to the act of appraising or valuing. It is a calculation or statement of value, a way to reckon up, ascertain the amount of, express in terms of something already known, make accountable, and require to answer for responsibilities and conduct. The process and its results are critical to many dimensions of health care and social work practice. The purposes of evaluation are to inform administrative and professional decision making, to improve current programs, to be accountable, to establish cause-and-effect relationships, and to build increased support inside and outside the organization (especially among those who fund the services) (Lewis, Lewis, Packard and Souflee 2001).

This chapter has five purposes: First, it makes both the place and process of evaluation for social work in health and mental health explicit. Second, it describes a range of evaluation techniques and examples on various levels of complexity and sophistication. Third, it reports that program evaluation is a requirement of state and federal programs and is designed and often conducted by professional evaluative consultants employing sophisticated qualitative and quantitative research techniques. Fourth, it demonstrates to social workers that it is possible to carry out simple forms of evaluation that allow for the examination of practice and programs. Fifth, it exhorts social workers to participate in all evaluative processes as fully as possible and assures them that these processes can be used to protect and strengthen clients, consumers, programs, and communities. Health and mental health care's increasing emphasis on outcomes-based evaluation at all levels of service is reflected in sections on evaluating programs and organizations particularly.

Because the process of evaluating programs is often carried out by consultants who are expert in the area, the chapter is written to inform readers about two different directions for evaluation. One is to think of processes of evaluation as discrete enterprises in which social workers measure and judge their own work and the work of small programs. The other is to think of processes of evaluation as large-scale operations carried out by consultant experts brought in from outside the organization. In the latter processes, social workers must contribute to the definition of what should be evaluated under what conditions, and then they should be competent to understand and use the results rather than carry out evaluations themselves. Both views of evaluation are not only correct but also need social workers' equal participation. The examples in this chapter describe a range of evaluation opportunities beginning with evaluating the structure of a relationship with an individual client/consumer to a project to a multiyear statewide program evaluation.

While it is beyond the scope of this book to discuss the evaluation of research, this is an important skill that all social workers must possess to the degree that they can evaluate what they read in scholarly journals and what they hear at professional conferences. Developing the ability to critically evaluate research studies and to understand their validity and reliability allows more competent practice. For example, many of the rapid-assessment instruments (RAIs) found in chapter 6 and referred to in this chapter are the outcomes of extensive reliability and validity testing; however, other RAIs are disseminated without adequate piloting and testing. In the present environment, measurement is often required without the additional time allocation to adequately conduct the testing process.

> When time and resources are limited, such as in managed mental health care today, practitioners tend to rely on uninterpreted or uninterpretable numbers. Caution must be used when accepting the veracity of a number as more efficient, such as to foster cost containment. This acceptance occurs when the number supports the clinicians' claim that treatment is necessary, that it was implemented correctly, or that reimbursement is warranted. It is also easy to dismiss a number that does not support one's position. (Corcoran 1997:141–42)

Thus it is imperative that social workers have the ability to evaluate the research techniques and findings in their fields.

Generally social workers are involved in evaluations of their own work, their clients' capacities, their clients performance, their clients' success in using social work services, and their programs, and occasionally they are involved in evaluations of entire organizations. Social workers evaluate clients, consumers, programs, and communities as the work begins because assessment is certainly one dimension of evaluation. "No discipline more acutely understands the importance of meeting the broad range of human needs than social work. It is important for the discipline to reassert itself as focusing on the whole person and to reinforce the importance of monitoring outcomes that encompass the full range of indicators addressing social, emotional, and physical well-being" (Shern and Trabin 1997:111).

As soon as one begins to assess, one also adds the dimension of judging the client, group, or project's capacity for and progress toward reaching goals. While assessment (the process of gathering information that allows social workers to understand problems and to assess capacity) is prospective, the process of evaluation is primarily retrospective. Generally, evaluation is the process of looking back at a set of interventions or a program or an organization in order to measure degrees of success. Evaluation uses specific techniques to measure the effectiveness of interventions or the outcomes of the work. Another dimension of evaluation is measuring the success of one's work, and since almost all contemporary health care involves teams and partnerships and work across organizations and systems, one evaluates the contributions of others as well.

EVALUATION AND ACCOUNTABILITY

Evaluation is closely related to needs assessment and the setting of goals and objectives. If social workers have been clear about objectives—that is, they have delineated operationalized and measurable objectives with the group or individual they are working with—the evaluation of social work practice should be apparent. Although the concept of delineating outcomes seems clear and simple, defining the measurable consequences of programs, actions, and interventions can be exceedingly problematic.

The tools of evaluation have become increasingly complex over time. Also, the reliance on quantitative measures, the rise of evaluation specialists, and the requirement that such specialists be "brought in" to make judgments about the work and the workers have made evaluation a frightening and overwhelming prospect for many social workers. Still, the demand for evaluation and particularly for outcome measures that can truly reflect the nature, depth, and impact of the work is increasing and must be met. To view this as a positive phenomenon can only help the enterprise. As Rossi (1997:20) says,

If the current emphasis on outcomes is nothing new, why is it worrying some of us? First, the trend appears threatening because we suspect that it is mean-spirited, carrying with it nightmarish visions of demonic policymakers shouting "Gotcha!" when our favorite policies and programs do not achieve their output production quotas. However, these nightmares are self-inflicted. Why can't we imagine the alternative, namely that our policies and programs will turn out to be effective and efficient?

Evaluation concerns political responses as much as it concerns facts. For example, an evaluation may yield recommendations about continuing service as it has been provided in the past, or making changes in service delivery. These recommendations obviously have political ramifications, particularly for the social worker wishing to continue to provide services in accustomed ways. Recommendations can be implemented effectively only if they are understood in the light of policy considerations, organizational politics, and future strategies (Royse and Thyer 1996:233). Evaluators, be they social workers or other professionals, from inside the system or acting as consultants to it, must manage this phase of the evaluation ethically (Applebaum and Austin 1990). In addition, evaluators must advocate combining evaluation (knowing the outcomes of a service) and quality assurance standards (knowing that the service is implemented in a consistent manner). Combining evaluation with quality assurance adds structural supports that help balance some of the political elements in evaluation. Additionally, as the goal of quality assurance is understood by social workers to protect clients (as well as themselves), it becomes a unifying point for evaluating the work and making any change recommendations.

To evaluate is to make accountable, and to be accountable also means to be reckoned or computed. At this point in time, measurement means numbers either in their simplest form (1, 2, 3, 4), in percentages, or in plain or fancy statistics that have to do with enhancing the meaning and power of the results by making them apply to larger numbers than their original population. These results are often used to predict future needs and outcomes. Social workers continually search for evaluative means that are focused on outcomes other than money expended or saved. In fact, the profession of social work would like to see the development of some other measures of success, some means of tracking value other than money. Social workers also despair over managers and accountants who are focused on the bottom line and on what transpires inside the organization, because those same social workers recognize that forces outside the system may drive almost everything that happens within the system. When evaluation focuses solely on the bottom line and organizational structures, the evaluation is shortsighted. Sometimes, too, payers wish to eliminate client/consumer goals that social workers know are important.

> Although the elimination of subjective discomfort might be extremely valuable to an individual's sense of well-being and overall-quality of life, it has been challenging for corporate and government purchasers of health care benefits to determine whether they should include coverage for such services in their health care benefits packages. These packages are particularly troublesome for purchasers when their criteria for value requires linkages between personal benefits and increased productivity—both a business and a social benefit. (Shern and Trabin 1997:102)

To honor social work's ethical codes, the profession must continue to work to have payers value the goals of clients and consumers.

EVALUATION AND ETHICS

To be valued, evaluation must explore factors of importance to clients, social workers, and administrators, and then it will be an integral part of service delivery and decision making. Its results must be disseminated to, and understood by, all stakeholders, including clients, consumers, programs, communities, administrators, and involved leaders. Thus social workers must contribute to decisions about what is to be evaluated and the processes and conditions of evaluation. To act otherwise means that evaluation, in its most restrictive and nonsupportive guises, may negatively affect social workers and their clients.

Social work's ethical codes require continuous improvement of practice. An additional ethical issue relates to informing clients about the usefulness and effectiveness of social work's methods and overall effort. Gambrill (1999:349) calls for more focus on "evidence-based practice," practice supported by empirical data, not just given authority by virtue of the fact that "that's the way we have always done it." She challenges social workers as follows:

> Honoring our own code of ethics to inform clients and to draw on practice-related research will help us to have courage and integrity to challenge puffery, avoid propagandistic appeals, and value truth over winning arguments. Embracing a justification approach to knowledge in which we seek support for our views rather than rigorously try to falsify them, encourages authority-based decision making. (Gambrill 1999:349)

The following example demonstrates the need for and use of an internal evaluation that could be carried out by a single social worker with the support and participation of everyone in her department. Because the clients/consumers in this particular example have serious mental illness, their capacity to live outside the institution is either enhanced or undermined by the social workers' discharge planning. To leave the hospital inadequately medicated, with inadequate prescriptions, health insurance, housing, and the like, means that these very vulnerable clients will soon be admitted to community hospitals on their way back to the state hospital, or be jailed for certain behaviors or worse. Thus this evaluation helps the department and satisfies various accrediting bodies and funding sources, but ultimately it helps the clients/consumers obtain the critical services they require.

Social worker Sophia Regal used the systematic planned practice framework to describe the process and outcomes of an outcome study she did of her social work department's discharge planning. For a full description of work with an individual client in this setting, see chapter 4. For a discussion of the systematic planned practice framework, see chapter 7.

The problem identified by the clients in the state mental hospital was help with discharge planning. Figure 9.1 is the mapping device for Ms. Regal's outcome study. The problem as formulated by the social workers and their rationale for intervention was that the patients were ready for discharge. In the problem disposition, the social worker began the discharge process. In relation to referral outside the state hospital system, Ms. Regal and the other social workers helped the clients to apply for benefits. They established the following order of priority for treatment: housing, income, intensive case management, insurance, and aftercare. Their ultimate outcome was excellent planned discharge. Their intermediate outcomes in terms of sequence and rationale were housing, income, intensive case management, and aftercare. Interventions were to submit appropriate applications and referrals. In relation to monitoring and evaluation, Ms. Regal instituted the Social Work Department Outcome Study. In relation to interventions employed and planned intermediate outcomes attained, she reported the following scores: housing (78 percent); income (54 percent); intensive case management (74 percent); insurance (61 percent); aftercare (51 percent). In relation to attainment of unplanned or undesirable outcomes, she reported percentages of incomplete records, unspecified prescription coverage, and some responsibilities delegated to others that would have been best executed by the social work department. The extent of attainment of the ultimate outcome was 91.7 percent excellent or very good planned discharges. The conclusions and implications for planning outcomes and interventions were to address training needs and

FIGURE 9.1. Systematic planned practice for outcome study of discharge planning.

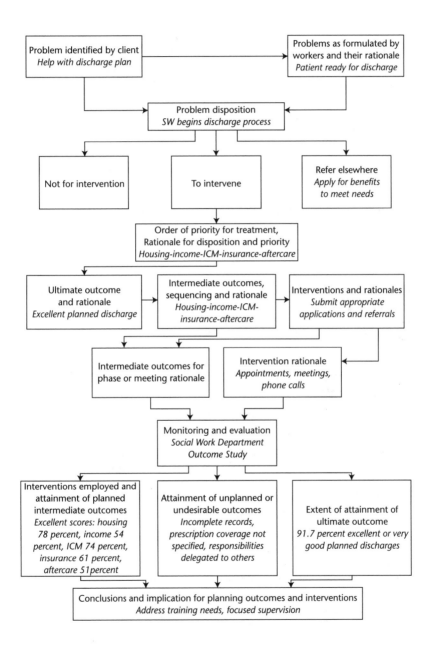

focus supervision on prescription coverage and other dimensions of the discharge process that required improvement.

Evaluations can be conducted at any level of practice, from the single case to national and even international programs. To function on the various practice levels, social workers have to be able to participate in some kinds of evaluation on the case and program or project levels. They should be able to understand and, it is hoped, to influence the factors considered in larger-scale evaluations, but these are highly specialized enterprises that are not within the practice realm.

This call to test the effectiveness of individual practice, programs, and organizations is one that must be heeded. It is repeated by Fortune (1999) in her editorial citing the work of Rosen, Proctor, and Staudt (1999), who reviewed social work journals from 1993 to 1997 and demonstrated that very little research is directed at evaluating interventions. Fortune decries this outcome and calls for more research to remedy this shortcoming. The demand for evaluation and particularly for outcome measures that can evaluate the work must be met. If the objectives are unclear, or if the objectives of social workers, clients, organizations, and funding sources (that is, various stakeholders) differ from each other, evaluation becomes much more difficult, but it is still manageable. In fact, it has been said that programs without goals in the form of identifiable outcomes cannot be assessed (Wholey 1979).

A BRIEF HISTORY OF EVALUATION IN SOCIAL WORK

Since the days of Richmond's *Social Diagnosis* (1917), the social work profession has utilized scientific methods to ensure accountability and to bolster its professional status. The early Charity Organization Societies were developed to ascertain what types of services were most effective in helping differing types of clientele (as well as to paternalistically monitor and modify client behavior and resource usage) (Leiby 1984). From these beginnings, evaluations of social workers' own practice skills, client goal accomplishment, program effectiveness, organizational efficiency, and community functioning have all been carried out for at least two reasons. First, they support social work accountability, and second, they further knowledge building for the most efficacious social work practice at every level of intervention.

Over the past twenty years, the concept of accountability, in the form of outcome evaluation, has been introduced intermittently in evaluation-literature in the human services (Martin and Kettner 1997). Outcomes monitoring requires the routine measurement and reporting of important indicators of outcome-oriented results (Affholter 1994). Set against the profession's long history of research evaluation, the new accountability model, with its use of effectiveness and efficiency measures, failed to gain great momentum. However, the concept found fertile ground in business and government circles. Eventually, the convergence of forces such as total quality management, managed care, and government performance reviews has served to increase the profession's interest and legitimized outcome-focused evaluation (Martin and Kettner 1997). Today, as payers, funding sources, and other stakeholders become increasingly more involved in program sustainability, the documentation and demonstration of effective program outcomes has become urgent. Thus accountability and outcome evaluation are critical components of many human service programs.

Although the social work profession has always attempted to evaluate its work, it has been suggested that formal evaluation of social programs has been required by the federal government only since the early 1960s. Evaluation was required in a juvenile delinquency program enacted by Congress in 1962 and in federal employment and training programs since the Manpower Development and Training Act of 1962 (Shadish, Cook, and Leviton 1993). As evaluation techniques have developed, it is clear that the process and results must correspond to the legislative mandates that create each program. For example, should a program be funded to accomplish full employment of a particular community, evaluation processes will demonstrate whether the goal has been accomplished. If evaluation shows that a program has not accomplished the goal, it may experience decreased funding, be closed, or be encouraged to make modifications designed to promote goal accomplishment. As such, in this simple example, the importance of evaluation for social work survival becomes quite evident.

Evaluation must reflect the goals and objectives of the organization, program, service, and/or clients that are its focus. If the evaluators have the desire to have their outcomes utilized, the evaluation must reflect the culture of the organization and have the involvement and the commitment of the staff members who are directly involved in the work. Certainly, evaluation of one's own work is less threatening than that of an outside evaluator, but it may also be viewed as less objective. In all circumstances, feedback about one's effectiveness should always be welcome, as it will ensure more helpful services to clients.

LEVELS OF EVALUATION: CASE, PROGRAM, AND COMMUNITY

Evaluations can be conducted at any level of practice, from the single case to local programs and projects, to organizations, to national and even international programs. Unless it can be classified as community outreach and needs assessment, much community evaluation referred to later in the chapter can also be seen as program evaluation. To participate on the multiple levels of practice suggested in this book, social workers in health and mental health care must be able to engage in some kinds of evaluation on multiple levels. They should be able to have some means of evaluating their own work and their levels of success in helping their clients/consumers/communities reach their goals, and they should be able to participate as fully as possible in evaluative processes that are conducted by professionals other than themselves. Participation should begin at the beginning; that is, social workers should be involved in deciding what factors should be the subjects of evaluation and under what conditions.

Following are descriptions of some applicable approaches to evaluation of direct practice, programs and projects, and community outreach. Most of the examples provided are very small in scale; one focuses on a statewide project.

Evaluating Cases and Direct Practice

There are many approaches to evaluating direct practice, including using some of the standardized assessment tools described in chapter 6 as before-and-after measures. An extensive literature concerns the evaluation of psychotherapy and a growing literature deals with the evaluation of case management, especially with regard to work with those who are seriously mentally ill.

The following is a practice example of an evaluation of an individual case in direct practice.

Social Worker Jodi Laufman works on the obstetrics floor in a community hospital and provides social work services to teen mothers at the community health district. A substantial portion of the population with whom she works are young women between the ages of 12 and 17 who have their pregnancies diagnosed at the health center and then go on to deliver at her hospital. Over the course of several years she has tried various methods for conveying information about contraception and abstinence to assist the young women in avoiding future pregnancies. Though the ideal situation involves planning evaluation of practice prospectively, Ms. Laufman realizes that she spent the first year of her job following her predecessor's pattern of describing contraceptive methods during the third trimester of pregnancy and then ensuring that the teen had selected a contraceptive method and received a prescription for it (if necessary) prior to her postpartum discharge from the hospital. In her second year, she began using the postpartum hospital visit (generally twenty-four to forty-eight hours after the birth) to again reiterate contraceptive information and talk with the young woman about the way various methods fit (or do not fit) her particular level and style of sexual activity. She maintained the goal of ensuring that the teen had made a selection and gotten any necessary prescriptions prior to the postpartum discharge.

By the third year, frustrated by teens returning with unplanned pregnancies, Ms. Laufman requested that time allowances be made so that she could also meet with each teen at the six-week postpartum visit. She justified the need for this with the administrators saying that the postpartum visit also entailed discussion of baby care and community resources and that teens often felt they would "never be sexually active again" so close to the time of delivery. These factors combined in ways that left Ms. Laufman feeling that discussion of contraception was less than optimal. The six-week postpartum social work interventions were implemented. After a year and a half, the administrators, interested in cost containment, stated that funding would no longer be available for the six-week social work follow-up. Ms. Laufman's detailed records were utilized to show the pregnancy recidivism rates for each of the different intervention strategies. Once graphed next to each other, the sharp reduction in second teen pregnancies following intervention including a six-week postpartum visit was very evident. This retrospective evaluation of practice allowed Ms. Laufman to identify the intervention strategy that appeared to be most effective with her clientele, while also providing evidence for maintaining funding for the six-week follow-up intervention.

Compton and Galaway (1998:457) state that "evaluation is the application of scientific methods to measure both change processes and their outcomes. At the level of individual-client relationships, evaluation research focuses on the nature of a particular intervention, its presumed results, and the evidence that it led to the results." Hepworth, Larson, and Rooney (1997) divide the work of evaluation into three parts: outcomes, process, and practitioner. They encourage outcome evaluation to occur by comparing baseline scores on RAIs or other measures of behavior/functioning to evaluate whether positive change has occurred. RAIs are standardized measures that reliably and validly assess the intensity, frequency, or duration of a client problem. An RAI can be a scale, a checklist, an index, or an inventory. It is easy to score and interpret and provides direct measures of attributes of interest to the client (ideally these correlate with the client's goals). RAIs require minimal training to score and interpret, and clients generally understand them (Corcoran 1997).

These are the types of evaluation most commonly requested by funders and those who pay for services. In addition, it is important that social workers solicit feedback from clients, consumers, and stakeholders about the process and structure of the work, as well as the social worker's style of interaction. In this way, social workers can determine which techniques

369

and approaches are most useful with a range of people. For example, a confrontational approach with a confident assertive client may have a very different effect with a depressed, passive client. Moreover, there may be something about one person's background that causes him or her to react in ways that would not be predicted based on personality, ethnicity, or other dimensions. A request for open and honest feedback can only enhance the relationship and the work.

Toward a Differential Discussion. One very simple self-evaluation task, referred to as differential discussion, asks that each time a case is closed or a project is completed, the social worker evaluate the work with that client or project to be able to generalize to a category of similar clients or programs (Kerson 1997). The purpose of this task is to build in an evaluative dimension to social workers' everyday practice. The facets of the differential discussion are fairly concrete and are primarily elements of the structure of the relationship between the social worker and the client/patient/consumer that the social worker can adjust in order to be more effective in helping clients reach their goals. Table 9.1 lists the dimensions in the structure of the social work relationship that social workers may wish to alter the next time they have a similar client or project. For example, the social worker may chose to see a client in a neutral place rather than in the social worker's office or the client's home, or a social worker may decide to be more direct and forceful the next time she has a client with

TABLE 9.1. Differential Discussion Chart

Client or Project _____ Similar Population _____

Practice Decisions	Retain	Alter	Specific Alterations
Definition of client or project			
Goals			
Contract			
Meeting place			
Use of time			
Approach or techniques			
Stance			
Outside resources			
Reassessment			
Termination			

TABLE 9.2. Differential Discussion Chart for Paul Cisco

Client or Project _Paul Cisco_ **Similar Population** _Burn patients with substance abuse issues_

Practice Decisions	Retain	Alter	Specific Alterations
Definition of client or project			
Goals	X		
Contract	X		
Meeting place	X		
Use of time	X		
Approach or techniques		X	Try a more structured approach
Stance	X		
Outside resources		X	Refer for alcohol counseling and to Alcoholics Anonymous/Al Anon
Reassessment/termination	X		

certain kinds of problems. The utility of this kind of exercise increases with experience.

"Paul [Cisco] was a 32-year-old heavy drinker admitted to the Burn Unit with a flame burn over 40 percent of his body surface. He was injured when his car caught fire and ignited his clothing. He suffered full- and partial-thickness burns on his head, face, chest, arms, and neck; very deep burns on his hands; and a severe injury to his lungs from the inhalation of smoke, superheated air, and toxic fumes from the burning car's upholstery" (Blades 1997:252).

In retrospect, Mr. Cisco's social worker thought she would have helped Mr. Cisco progress socially and psychologically more quickly if she had structured her work with him more tightly and had referred him to Alcoholics Anonymous as soon as he could have physically managed attending the groups, and she should have referred his wife to Al Anon as soon as the social worker became aware of Mr. Cisco's problem drinking. See Table 9.2.

Single-System Research. Compton and Galaway (1998:457) highlight the essentially exploratory single-system research technique used to explore the effect of an intervention (the independent variable, often in comparison with other interventions or with no intervention) on a chosen outcome (the dependent variable). They suggest the following process:

1. Describe the client's problem or its manifestation.
2. Specify the target behavior, attitude, or other factor (dependent variable) and how you propose to measure it.
3. Identify what pattern of the dependent variable exists (stable, falling, etc.).
4. Briefly specify the treatment or intervention to be used and how it will relate to other services the client will receive.
5. Conduct a literature review.
6. Select the single-system design most suitable for examining the relationship between variables (specify why it is best—time, ethics, other constraints).
7. Determine which pattern of the dependent variable would indicate that your intervention may be related to a desired effect.
8. Determine what pattern would suggest that your intervention may have promoted an unhealthy response such as dependency.
9. Conduct the research, carefully graphing the fluctuations in the dependent variable.
10. Carefully analyze the research results. If a desirable pattern is found in step 7, consider what types of clients may also find this intervention beneficial.
11. Replicate the research with other clients. While this process is ideal, retrospective application, as in earlier examples, is helpful and can be useful. It is important to avoid becoming so intimidated by the process that social workers desist from monitoring their work for the purposes of accountability to clients, employers, and one's professional development and integrity. Additionally, it is important to be clear that this is not controlled research in the standard scientific definition of that term. This does not require random, stratified samples and statistical significance. The patterns of improvement (or regression) are what are important in evaluating whether one's intervention is helpful and what aspects of the intervention can be modified for even more effective intervention.

Outcome Criteria. Fortune and Reid (1999) specify other issues in the selection of outcome criteria. They suggest that unintended consequences, the perspective of pertinent stakeholders, how short- or long-range the goals may be, the durability of the outcome, and cost-effectiveness must all be considered. Although many focus on the last criterion, more attention must be given to selecting criteria that allow social workers to assess outcomes in terms of any unintentional consequences that may arise as a result of interventions. For example, Fortune and Reid (1999:377–78) cite the impact on a mother's relationships with her other children when only one child is receiving behavior modification rewards. They and others also caution that if social workers consider outcomes only related to the long-term or "ultimate" goal, they may miss developing better short-term, partial-goal outcome indicators (Zeira and Rosen 1999). On the other side of temporal issues, it may be useful to develop an outcome indicator that allows one to evaluate the duration of the effect after intervention has stopped. All these issues are important in selection of outcome indicators, since they indicate the *process* and not just the bottom line. It is easier to undertake outcome evaluation now than it has been in the past, partly because research technology is now able to manage large-scale data collection and partly because the cost of computing has been greatly reduced even for small agencies.

Evaluating Programs

According to Shadish and colleagues (1993:37), "Program evaluation assumes that social problem solving can be improved by incremental improvements in existing programs, better design of new programs, or terminating bad programs and replacing them with better ones. If these conditions do not hold, evaluation cannot achieve its purpose. Theories of social programming, therefore, must show if and how these things can be done." Three elements must be included: (1) internal program structure and functioning, (2) external constraints that shape and limit programs, and (3) how social change occurs, how programs change, and how program change contributes to social change. There are two key types of program evaluation: in-depth/ad hoc and "regular" outcomes measurement (Hatry 1997:3–5). While in-depth/ad hoc evaluations, if designed properly, can clearly link necessary changes to future outcomes, such evaluations are very expensive and cover few agency programs. Regular outcomes measurement is the form that the government and many private agencies are currently considering. The regular outcomes measurement focuses on results, not just on activity. Regular outcomes measurement, on the other hand, can cover many agency programs at much lower cost, provide information that is collected on a regular basis, suggest ways to improve outcomes, and allow for greater ease of in-depth evaluations at a later date. The downside of regular outcomes program evaluation is that it does not add very much information on reasons for the outcomes, and it does not yield much information about ways to improve intervention.

One way to view program evaluation is in terms of scope. Lewis and colleagues (2001) describe three types of program evaluation: (1) process evaluation, (2) outcome evaluation, and (3) efficiency evaluation. Process evaluation involves an assessment of agency activities to determine whether programs are operating according to plans and expectations. This type is greatly simplified in organizations that have integrated management information systems. It depends on the active involvement of all staff in an organization because all are required to set objectives, meet those objectives, and gather data on a continual basis through observations, service records, and the like. Outcome evaluation, the second type, also depends on clearly specified objectives that are stated as expected results rather than projected activities. Efficiency evaluation, the third type, relates costs and outcomes. The simplest evaluation involves the determination of unit cost—that is, dividing the number of service units (outputs) into the dollar amount allocated (input) for that service. It also asks the question, Can the same program results be achieved either by reducing the amount of program effort or by choosing less costly alternatives (different kinds of efforts)? Lately, most attention is being paid to the second type, outcome evaluation.

In the following practice example, a small-scale outcome evaluation is carried out by a social worker with the participation of her entire department. This example relates to the fourth purpose of the chapter, to demonstrate that it is possible to carry out simple forms of evaluation that allow for the examination of practice and programs.

A small-scale outcome evaluation project was conducted by a social worker for a program called Well Babies/Well Mothers in a large and complex health system. The overall goal of the program is to lower the rate of infant mortality and morbidity in designated, economically depressed geographic areas through federally coordinated programs located within extant organizations. Well Babies/Well Mothers serves at-risk pregnant women and their babies who reside near the organization and come there for maternity care. The social work dimension of the program offers psychosocial assessment, crisis intervention, and follow-up case management. Social workers screen charts daily for new admissions in given zip code areas. If any of the following risk factors is present, the patient is seen by the social worker, who is funded through the government program. Nursing refers patients to social work when they notice risk factors as well. Risk factors include (1) drug or alcohol abuse, (2) teen pregnancy, (3) confirmed or suspected physical abuse or neglect, (4) involvement with the Department of Human Services, (5) inadequate prenatal care, (6) material need, (7) a baby in the intensive care nursery, (8) depression or mental illness, and (9) immigrant status. Family meetings are called by the social worker when deemed necessary for intervention.

A personal scorecard (table 9.3) is presented for an overall view of the program. (The use of the personal scorecard is explained in chapter 4, with

TABLE 9.3. Personal Scorecard for Well Babies/Well Mothers

Organizational Objectives
1. Provide the highest-quality patient and family care and service.
2. Care for patients and families with compassion and respect in a setting where parents benefit from the most advanced medical and scientific interventions, delivered with skill, integrity, and concern for their well-being and comfort.
3. Reduce infant mortality and morbidity.

Corporate Targets	*Scorecard Measures*
Health Care	
1. Achieve desired clinical outcomes in a cost-effective manner.	Serve 100 percent of patients within 85 percent of annual budget. Achieve 100 percent of scores in all quality assurance ratings.
2. Continually locate new forms of health promotion, screening, diagnosis, treatment, and rehabilitation for our patients.	Pilot three services annually; maintain 66 percent for five years.
Education	
1. Provide outstanding graduate educational programs and support undergraduate training at the highest level.	Enroll graduate programs to 100 percent of capacity yearly. Report 95 percent of placement of students upon graduation.
Research	
1. Support biomedical research and translate its use for medical care, health services research, and community-based care.	Fund 80 percent of anticipated research projects. Achieve 80 percent of publications from staff research efforts. Participate in eight health care coalitions to plan future.

Unit Targets	*Team/Individual Initiatives*
Well Babies/Well Mothers Program (WB/WM)	*Supports At-Risk Mothers and Their Infants*
1. Respond to risk factors for mothers and infants.	Provide psychosocial drug education (literature) to 100 percent of new clients. Refer 100 percent of eligible high-risk mothers and their infants to DHS for Services to Children in Their Own Homes.
2. Publicize the WB/WM program to clients, community residents, hospitals, etc.	Enroll 90 percent of projected target of 420 new clients. Maintain case management of sixty-five clients per month.
3. Provide emergency concrete needs as well as community resources to HB clients.	Provide minimum of three community referral resources per assessed client need.
Team/Individual Measures	*Targets*
1. Funding outreach.	Align with hospital executives.
2. Write shell proposal and cover letter about program.	Memo to hospital executives.
3. Network with other such programs in the area.	Contact other area health systems.

an additional example of its use in chapter 7.) Well Babies/Well Mothers has been funded by the federal government for nearly five years. In anticipation of the expiration of its funding, the program's director must demonstrate its importance to its host hospital so that the hospital will assume the responsibility for funding it or for locating outside funding.

The evaluation was conducted at a time that was critical for the future of this dimension of the program. The first five-year phase of the program, which was funded primarily by the federal government and administered by the state government, was ending. For the program to continue for the next five years, the organization would have to be willing to provide much more internal financial support or find that support from other sources. Concerned that the social work dimensions of the program might be reduced or eliminated when the organization looked for ways to reduce the costs of the program, the social worker and her colleagues knew they had to gather data to prove that they added value. Their worth would have to be demonstrated to the program administrator; the health system's Department of Social Work, Case Management, and Utilization Review; and to the organization itself.

Consistent with other such government-sponsored undertakings, the program had an outcome evaluation mechanism built into its design. Based on the contract it established with each program, the state chose outcome indicators for data collection and quarterly evaluation reports; however, the evaluation tool would not produce sufficient data to justify continued funding for the three major social work tasks: psychosocial assessment, crisis intervention, and follow-up. For the state, the program collected data on demographics and characteristics of those served, status of infant health and medical treatment, number of patients receiving each service, number and location of postpartum visits, and number of infant deaths. One purpose for part of the data collection in the first phase was the establishment of a baseline that would allow ongoing comparative analysis of client demographics, services provided, and the impact of services on infant health status.

The overall purpose of the evaluation was to gather information for the organization administrators and other potential sponsors, who could help secure program continuity. There were three objectives for the specific social work evaluation: (1) to provide data that would ensure funding for the social work components of the program over the next five-year phase, (2) to establish an outcome baseline for comparison in the future, and (3) to provide suggestions for improving service. Success was defined as yearly service improvement.

Structure of the evaluation process. Time was short. The project had to be designed, data gathered and analyzed, and a final report presented within three months. During that time, the social worker/evaluator received a small reduction in her usual workload. A stakeholders method was thought to be most efficacious, given all the constraints on the evaluation (Wholey 1979). It used rapid feedback, allowed the evaluator to take into account the developmental stage of the program, allowed for a focus on the informational needs of potential funders as important stakeholders, and was responded to positively by the staff.

The first step included a review of program documents, as well as possible approaches to evaluation and similar studies. To determine the content and structure of the evaluation, the social worker/evaluator met first with the chief social worker, the program administrator, and the head of the health system's social work department. The three concurred about necessary data. Questions were identified, and agreement was reached about outcome measures, size of the study group, and evaluation tools. The study group consisted of the five social workers' 150 closed client cases for the three-month period that had just ended. Data were collected from patient records, and a phone survey was conducted with all the clients seen in the three-month period. The phone survey helped to balance some of the subjectivity of the workers.

The following questions were asked:

1. What percentage of patients with risk factors were interviewed? What percentage of the clients received information about financial resources, or resources such as clothing, training, education, drug and alcohol counseling, and child welfare services (specifically Aid to Families of Dependent Children and Services to Children in Their Own Homes)?
2. What percentage of clients did the social workers counsel?
3. What percentage of clients were referred for follow-up social/financial or psychological services outside the organization? How does this compare to those who have received referrals for medical care outside the organization or medical care for their new babies?
4. What percentage of clients who were referred for services outside the system followed up?
5. How did this percentage relate to their medical follow-up?
6. What percentage of the clients viewed the referrals as helpful to them?
7. What percentage of the clients were satisfied with the services that were offered?
8. What suggestions do clients have to improve services?

The next step was to meet with the other program social workers to be sure that they were in agreement with content and structure. In these staff meetings, the evaluator realized that the social workers were defining terms differently from each other. For example, one social worker defined counseling only as cases in which a social worker referred the patient for formal weekly or biweekly sessions lasting at least forty-five minutes during which psychological issues were explored. Others defined counseling as sessions lasting at least fifteen minutes during which social workers and clients interacted about any topic that would assist the client. Also, although work with clients and their families in regard to Child Protective Services was not counted as counseling, this work was highly valued by everyone in the program.

In the same way, at first, follow-up on drug/alcohol treatment referrals was counted only by the patients' participation in formal programs. Sometimes staff learned about clients' drug and alcohol use as a result of routine blood work for clients and their babies. At other times, family members told social workers or other staff members about their concerns. In those instances, social workers counseled clients directly about the effects and possible effects of their drug and alcohol use. In fact, all these activities were examples of successful counseling. All these interventions had to be documented in addition to referrals to more formal programs. As a result of the staff meetings, key terms were defined and operationalized, and the definitions were included on the data collection forms. Without this kind of definitional agreement, the social worker/evaluator would not have been able to interpret the data in a meaningful way and the program might have appeared less successful than it was.

The second step was to gather the data. To do this, the social worker used two tools. For the first, she gained access to client demographics information, including the number and type of risk factors for the population. In addition, she modified a routine case closure form that had been used by the social workers so that the form would allow documentation of clients' follow-up on referrals after discharge from the hospital. She prepared a database key for entering the new data, drawing information from the standard database and the modified follow-up form (table 9.4). For the second tool, the patient sat-

TABLE 9.4. Some Results of Data Collection

	Goal (%)	Patient Response (%)
Clients interviewed for assessment	100	100
Clients receiving social services information	100	100
Clients receiving in-system counseling	90	85
Clients viewing outside referrals as helpful	90	55
Clients satisfied with social workers' services	90	80
Clients who kept medical appts. for infants	100	55
Clients who kept medical appt. for mothers	100	45

TABLE 9.5. Questions Regarding Client Follow-up for Referrals Made While Clients Were in the Hospital

	Goal (%)	Patient Response (%)
Clients who followed up referrals for material needs	75	55
Clients who followed up for Medical Assistance and other DHS services	100	70
Clients who followed up for drug and alcohol services	50	25
Clients who followed up for psychological counseling	50	20
Clients who followed up for parenting classes	50	10

isfaction phone survey, the social worker gathered data directly from clients, thus providing a balance for analysis. Clients were contacted by phone, their responses were documented, results were collated, and a preliminary evaluation was prepared. The phone survey results complemented the database study and contributed significantly to the recommendations that followed (table 9.5). Step three involved the preparation of a preliminary evaluation. The tasks consisted of computer queries performed on the database, the compilation of data, and an analysis of the information.

When those who had been referred for some form of counseling while in the hospital were asked about follow-up, 45 percent reported that they contacted the service they had been referred to, 15 percent said they had never received a referral, and 40 percent said they intended to follow up but various things had happened in their lives. Everyone who was surveyed said that she was hesitant to pick up the phone and make the appointment.

The study led to three action recommendations: First, the director should develop linkages with the drug and alcohol services located within the system so that a drug and alcohol counselor would come to the program and be introduced to the client by the social worker. This would also serve the interests of the system and might help reinforce management's engagement in the next phase of the program. Only the most highly motivated clients would be referred immediately to community resources. Second, the director would establish a stronger link with the Department of Child Welfare so that a parenting assessment could begin while the client was still involved with the health system. Third, 50 percent of the clients in the phone survey said that they would have liked parenting sessions while they were in the hospital. In response, the social workers would develop and implement educational programs. Program subjects would include (1) what to do the first week after the baby is discharged; (2) how to schedule the baby's care and activities, including feeding, bathing, changing, and dressing; (3) how to care for babies who have been in the intensive care nursery; (4) how to bond with the baby; and (5) how to parent infants. Such a program would probably be funded by a local foundation.

This small evaluation project was deemed a success by everyone involved. The system kept the social work dimensions of the program, and administrators thought that the new linkages and an additional educational component would strengthen the program. The stakeholder service theory gave direction to the dialogue, and the findings answered questions that were important to the program director—a middle manager stakeholder who is the chief agent in the program and the liaison between the state department and the hospital. Though the sample size was small, and validity was compromised by such issues as lack of term definition and limitation of cases to intern cases, the gains were visible. The social workers have decided to make this kind of evaluation a continuing part of their work and could use a modified version of the balanced scorecard (Kaplan and Norton 1996c).

Underutilized Results. Very often the results of evaluation studies are underutilized by agencies, and the majority of respondents in studies of evaluation research report that they do not use evaluation data in their decision making. Cherin and Meezan (1998) believe that one reason for this is that the external, nonparticipatory evaluations that are currently imposed on human service organizations create conflicts between the organization and the evaluator. If the evaluation process is not seen by the organization and those funding its programs as a practical learning opportunity, the evaluations will continue to be underutilized. For evaluation research to inform decision making, organizations have to have the ability and the capacity to understand and use the data. There must be a good fit between organizational needs and the available data, and the process itself must be conducted in ways that support the participation of agency personnel.

General Questions to Raise in Beginning Outcomes-Based Research. Research questions involve targeting outcome areas at the individual level and at the system or population level, determining their relative importance at each level, constructing measurement approaches for these areas, and developing norms or standards against which specific provider organizations can be compared. Specific questions include:

1. What do purchasers and consumers want to know to help them select providers?
2. What are good measures of access, utilization, appropriateness, quality, and outcomes?
3. What program, organizational, and system processes and characteristics are linked to outcomes?
4. What practice guidelines should be used?
5. What measures of health status are effective and how can they be measured?
6. What are appropriate performance standards for organizational benchmarking?

According to Rossi (1997:33), "To improve social welfare, programs must be devised that clearly produce significant increments in positively valued outcomes; these efforts can be guided by measuring the net outcomes of programs and revising them accordingly." Over time, assumptions and prescriptions about the issues that undergird practical program evaluation have changed in five areas: social programming, knowledge construction, valuing, knowledge use, and evaluation practice (Shadish et al. 1993). There is a different understanding of how social programs develop, improve, and change in relation to social problems, how evaluators study social action, how program descriptions are valued, how social science information is used for program and policy development, and what strategies evaluators use in their practice (Shadish et al. 1993).

As has been mentioned previously, goals are closely related to the purposes of a program. Examples might include improving the overall functioning of persons with chronic mental illness or providing medical, social, and psychological support for someone who is dying of cancer or AIDS. To measure goal achievement, goals must be related to specific measurable objectives, some of which will be outcome measures. Thus objectives for improving the overall functioning of a group of people who are seriously mentally ill might be that 90 percent of those who are in the program take medication as prescribed and 85 percent regularly attend a day program. While practitioners might agree about the goals of a program, they may have more difficulty agreeing to the outcomes—the measurable, practical indicators of their program's success or failure. Also, because goals are often very broad and far-reaching, some of the dimensions of goals may be lost or put aside when one is developing measurable objectives. Most programs have multiple goals and multiple outcome measures.

Generally, it is important to incorporate two broad areas of client/patient/consumer experience. The first is functional health and well-being, that is, the client/consumer's experience of the burden of disease, illness, or trauma and the benefit of treatment. The second is patient/ client/consumer satisfaction, that is, the experience with health care systems, services, and staff. In many situations, family functioning, well-being, and experience should be included as well.

The multiple preferences and perspectives of all stakeholders should be part of outcomes assessment. It is common in designing evaluations to pay attention to many stakeholders but to ignore consumer preferences (Booth and Smith 1997). This thinking is as faulty as ignoring the clients' goals in beginning the work. For example, a group of students who were on probation for drug offenses were coming regularly to open-attendance, highly structured "rap" sessions held by an attractive young black female social worker. The high school, rated as one of the worst in the greater metropolitan area for disciplinary problems, attendance, and graduation rate, decided it wanted the program evaluated. The probation officer, whose office was in the school because his entire caseload attended the school, decided that he must take attendance at the start of each session. It was not enough that the social worker report attendance to him later. Concerned that this formal role-taking would inhibit the students from coming to the sessions, the social worker implored the probation officer to accept her report of attendance. He refused, appeared twice to take attendance, and by the second time, all young men simply stopped coming.

Following is an excerpt of an evaluation of an ongoing, multicounty, multisystem program that addresses substance abuse in pregnant and postpartum women who are at risk for use of or are currently using drugs and alcohol. Although the population and goals of the program remain the same throughout, the purposes of and tools for evaluation continue to change as the program continues. Also, it is important to note at the outset that the first example was of a social work practitioner developing a simple system to evaluate the social work contribution to a small program that is part of a large health system and also part of a national effort. In the second example, the evaluation is being conducted by multiple professional evaluators and data manager/computer programmers working in nineteen different programs. Thus this example differs from the first in size, scope, and time period, in its multidisciplinary focus, and certainly in its goals and degree of sophistication. Thinking about the two examples together, as well as thinking about the range of evaluation possibilities discussed throughout the chapter, should help social workers in health and mental health care value the evaluation process and make it part of their work on any level with any population.

The New Dawn Program, serving a rural area that covers several counties, helps pregnant and postpartum women who are at risk for or are currently involved in abuse of drugs and alcohol. New Dawn is administered by the Medical School's Department of Obstetrics and Gynecology, is located at the University Hospital, and is accountable to and receives its funding from the area mental health center. New Dawn brings together three usually separate systems (public health, mental health, and medical care) to provide services to substance-using pregnant and postpartum women. There is close collaboration with public health departments and rural health clinics across the area of service. New Dawn has trained medical providers at the twelve public prenatal care sites in the region to screen every new obstetric patient for substance use. When there are concerns, medical providers consult with and/or refer the client to a New Dawn substance abuse counselor, who is either on site or available by telephone. New Dawn provides individual counseling and case management as well as substance abuse and parenting groups to women at their local health departments or at the New Dawn High-Risk Clinic at the Ambulatory Care Center.

A majority of New Dawn clients receive their prenatal care at the High-Risk Clinic from an interdisciplinary team composed of a perinatologist, a nurse midwife, clinical social workers/substance abuse counselors, a Maternal and Child Health nurse, and a psychiatrist. The underlying premise of this model of care is that this high-risk population is best engaged in both prenatal care and substance abuse treatment through a continuum of services provided at one site with consistent providers. Clients see the same staff, including the same medical provider each time they visit the clinic.

New Dawn is one of nineteen programs of the State Perinatal and Maternal Substance Abuse Initiative funded through the State Department of Human Resources, Division of Mental Health, Developmental Disabilities, and Substance Abuse Services. The overall goal of these projects is to increase the availability, accessibility, and coordination of comprehensive regional substance abuse programs for alcohol- and drug-abusing pregnant women and their children. These programs vary greatly in terms of treatment philosophy, auspices, and services provided. Some are outpatient settings providing intensive treatment and case management services, others are residential, and others primarily provide case management and information and referral services. Despite these differences, every program must participate in the State Perinatal Cross-Site Evaluation.

State perinatal cross-site evaluation: Background. Each of the eight perinatal substance abuse programs that were originally funded developed its own evaluation plan as part of its initial funding proposal. The wide variation among these evaluations reflected the differences in the programs. The State Division of Mental Health, Developmental Disabilities, and Substance Abuse Services recognized the importance of developing a statewide evaluation of the programs.

To sustain their funding base (a mix of federal and state funds) and to institutionalize the programs, it was essential that the division be able to demonstrate the need for these programs, how funding was being used, and program effectiveness. Approximately two years after the original funding was granted, program directors and evaluators began meeting with State Division of Mental Health, Developmental Disabilities, and Substance Abuse Services staff to develop a cross-site evaluation plan. While one evaluator was hired by the state to lead the effort, the process itself was highly interactive and collaborative, involving intense discussions about what should be evaluated and how to conduct such an evaluation. The primary objective of this evaluation was to provide a periodic profile on recipients of service and a description of their service needs and the type, intensity, and amount of services they were receiving from the programs. Program outcomes were not included in the early years of the cross-site evaluation.

To develop an evaluation that was useful to funding sources as well as to programs, it was necessary to address of the following issues:

1. Developing consensus regarding what data need to be and can be collected from all programs, given that the programs vary considerably in terms of auspices, program philosophy, and services provided.
2. Developing reliable and valid definitions for types of services and ways to measure service delivery (intensity, amount, frequency).
3. Developing reliable and valid definitions of what it means to be a client.
4. Defining and measuring concepts and issues such as whether the client has dependent children and has or is seeking custody of the children; substance use in terms of frequency, primary drug of choice, amount, and so on; engagement or involvement with treatment; support from or involvement with nonusers; and involvement with the criminal justice system.
5. Developing data collection instruments that are clinically useful as well as useful to cross-site evaluation.
6. Making data collection part of everyday practice. In most of these programs clinicians are involved in data collection. Thus a central issue is how to make the data collection part of their practice, not overly burdensome, and useful, as well as to train clinicians in the importance of accurate data collection.

This collaborative process of meeting on a regular basis over a period of several years was useful and provided important opportunities for shared learning and cooperative linkages among the programs. The cross-site evaluation evolved over time as the programs became fully operational and the data demands of the state, legislators, and individual program auspices changed. These changes put enormous demands on evaluators and data managers/computer programmers, and program directors and staff as data collection tools and data management programs had to be modified on a regular basis while still being able to generate annual reports.

Two years ago, outcomes were included in the Perinatal Cross-Site Evaluation. Unfortunately, these were originally introduced in a manner that was not consistent with the collaborative process that had been established by the programs to work on the evaluation. The programs were asked to collect outcomes data using an instrument that had been developed for all substance abuse programs in the state and thus did not take into account the unique goals and objectives and evaluation needs of the perinatal substance abuse programs. The programs met, developed modified outcome measures, and with the assistance of the individual in the division who worked with these programs, were able to develop a more useful outcomes measurement instrument. However, once programs began to use the instrument, they discovered many problems with reliability, which are still being addressed.

Specific Approaches to Program Evaluations. The following descriptions of applicable approaches to program or project evaluation may be used for the evaluation of individual cases as well.

The Stakeholder Service Model. Stakeholder service theory is one practical and widely adopted approach that is especially appealing to social workers for several reasons. First, recognizing that all stakeholders are critical to the evaluation process, stakeholder service theory links the interests of the three kinds of people who have the greatest stake in any program: policymakers, providers, and consumers. Including consumers, providers, and policy makers tailors the evaluation process to the critical information needs of those who have the most control over the program. Second, the model's emphasis on results for immediate application uses methods that are rapid and provide helpful, if approximate, answers to a range of questions rather than slow, precise responses to a few questions. Thus the process supplies critical, timely information that can effect change in a specific context. Other dimensions of traditional evaluation methods are subordinated.

The stakeholder model describes evaluation as "the measurement of program performance, the making of comparisons based on those measurements, and the use of the resulting information in policy-making and program management" (Shadish et al. 1993:253). Stakeholders make major decisions about the definition of problems, the identification of questions, and the determination of interventions and methods, while the evaluator is described as a "consciousness-raising educator" (Shadish et al. 1993:474).

Even among those who support the stakeholder model, there is some difference in particular group focus and method. Wholey (1993) uses a management-focused, results-oriented evaluation process because the goal of his type of evaluation is to affect program management. "As we are using the term here, results-oriented management is the purposeful use of resources and information to achieve measurable progress toward program outcome objectives related to program goals" (Wholey 1983:11). While Wholey is primarily geared to program evaluation for federal evaluators, he also works at state and local levels and means his work to be applicable to all levels. In this approach, the evaluators work with managers throughout the process to negotiate changes in the process as needs change. Wholey is a pragmatist who strives for instrumental use. His work is about action and change, about incremental program improvements that can be implemented immediately.

Wholey (1986:6) himself defines evaluation as "the comparison of actual program performance with some standard of expected program performance, and the drawing of conclusions about program effectiveness and value." He outlines a comprehensive outcome evaluation model flowing from stakeholder theory that consists of distinct components to be used separately or sequentially, given the stage of the program development and the constraints of the project (Wholey 1979). The first component is evaluability assessment. The first task of the preassessment evaluation phase is to determine with high-level management the desired results of the evaluation. It is critical that both the intent and reality of the program be clearly defined. Then, the evaluator and management agree on the performance indicators to be studied, the feasibility of managing the findings, and their commitment to acting on the possible evaluation findings. The second component is rapid feedback evaluation and/or outcome monitoring, and the third is intensive experimental or quasi-experimental evaluation. Depending on the sophistication of the evaluation, the components can range from purchased services to in-house practice. Wholey stresses that evaluation be done only when results will be used. In light of the important place that the understanding of organizations and business management play in this book, it is also interesting to note that Wholey's recent work is as much a theory of management as a theory of evaluation (Shadish et al. 1993:234).

Program Evaluation for Psychosocial Rehabilitation Centers. Linhorst (1988) describes a process of evaluation for psychosocial rehabilitation centers that uses seven data collection instruments to evaluate a program: (1) a database information sheet, (2) a rehabilitation plan review that measures individual goal attainment but also describes patient goals and helps the organization identify common, unattained goals, (3) a referral questionnaire, (4) a member survey, (5) a member life satisfaction survey, (6) a member social contact survey, and (7) a discharge summary form. The evaluation is carried out every three years. This approach is all-encompassing in that it covers marketing, client satisfaction, goal attainment, assurance that members are fully involved in the evaluation process, ways to measure the importance of the center to its members, and what categories of people were discharged from the centers and why.

Developmental Social Administration. Grasso (1993) has devised a developmental approach to social administration that works well in program evaluation. He says that the developmental approach believes that the improvement of a human service organization depends on the development of each staff member in the organization. The approach is rational and information-based, helps address organizational conflict caused by varying role obligations and informational and reporting needs across all primary organizational levels, and helps in clinical decision making. Grasso (1993:29) delineates four states:

1. Recognition of the current state and the problems that exist. Grasso points out that the system will initially resist intervention.
2. Understanding the function or dysfunction of the current state or the nature of the problem. Here one assists in developing an understanding of the sequencing of events and helps individuals identify issues that support the performance of current behaviors so that they can be understood in selecting alternatives.
3. Teaching or developing alternatives to the current state or problem. The goal is to state the stage of organizational performance. This is the stage of outcome assessment and goal attainment that the organization must report on for externally established requirements.
4. Teaching the individuals and the system to use the approach. Here the target of change is empowered to sustain development and apply the approach to self-determined problems. The desired end is not the achievement of goal behavior but "the teaching of the system to apply the four stages for changing future states."

This approach is closely related to the organizational learning approaches of Argyris and Schon (1978; Argyris 1982, 1993) and Cherin and Meezan (1998).

Evaluation as Organizational Learning. In the mode of organizational learning associated with Argyris and Schon (1978; Argyris 1993) and others described in chapter 4, Cherin and Meezan (1998) present a model for evaluation as a means of organizational learning. According to Argyris (1982), organizational learning is a process of detecting and correcting error. "The more the organization is capable of self-reflection, self-study, and rigorous examination of the consequences of its past actions, the more likely it is to be able to discover and correct deficiencies, adjust to new priorities, and alter existing operational tasks to ensure effective and efficient goal attainment" (Bastoe 1999:126). Evaluation is one of the processes that can enhance such learning. Many of those writing about evaluation as organizational learning are working at national levels. For instance, Per Oyvind Bastoe (1999:126), senior evaluation officer in the Operations Evaluation Department in the World Bank's Washington, D.C., headquarters, says that "evaluation can nurture and enhance organizational learning in governance systems—this leading to improved performance and successful adaptation to changing environments." Leeuw and Sonnichsen (1994) indicate that the proper design of evaluations precipitates debate on core organizational issues by asking the questions, How well are we doing? and Does it make sense to do it, even if it is being done well? Well-designed evaluations will stimulate such debates when they are managed well by the organization.

Cherin and Meezan (1998) apply similar principles to smaller-scale evaluations in much smaller organizations. Their framework ensures that organizations not only will use the results of the evaluations in which they participate but also will use these experiences to generalize to the next levels of learning. The model employs all available organizational information regarding what makes it possible for organizations to change. It is important to involve all possible participants in the evaluation process so that everyone will understand and be committed to the process and be willing to institute suggested changes. Thus, in many ways, the members of the evaluation team who come from within the organization are more important to the process and the utilization of results than the external members.

The model has five interacting phases: discovering, refining, launching the evaluation, utilizing, and archiving. In this model, a team from within the organization acts as coinvestigators and engages others in the organization in the discovery process and in testing ways of gathering information (Patton 1997). The first three phases are designed to enable the organization to use the results of the evaluation. In the discovering phase, information about the program and process of service delivery is gathered. Refining, employing research questions that have been agreed on by all team members, and sharing a draft of the evaluation process throughout the organization are the outcomes of the next phase. In launching the evaluation, the strategy is discussed, explained, and mutually determined. Interestingly, during this phase the evaluator teaches or reviews basic research principles to all those who are involved so they can make informed decisions. In the utilizing phase, the organization is provided with new information drawn from the evaluation that can enrich the performance repertoire of the organization. Here, results are quantified, meaningful reports are written, feedback sessions are held by the evaluation team throughout the organization, and recommendations for action are explained. The external evaluator is available to the team to ensure that information is meaningful and useful. In archiving, the last phase, double-loop learning is enabled by documenting the process so that the entire present and future organization can learn from it.

Planning, developing strategies for, and implementing social service programs are worth the use of resources only if the programs prove useful. Evaluations are carried out to assess whether services were provided as expected and whether they accomplished what they set out to. Thus program evaluation is a way of making judgments about effort, effectiveness, efficiency, and adequacy based on systematic data collection and analysis. It is designed to be used in program management, external accountability, and planning, and it is focused on accessibility, acceptability, awareness, availability, comprehensiveness, continuity, integration, and cost (Attkisson and Broskowski 1978:24). "Evaluation of service outcomes means that results can be compared with measured community needs, leading to an assessment of the program's adequacy. With systematically collected data on hand, agency personnel can make improvements either in the nature of the services or in the ways they are delivered" (Lewis et al. 2001:236).

In every approach to program evaluation that has been described and in every example provided here, evaluators first had to decide which dimensions of a program to study. Programs can be evaluated through needs assessments, program monitoring, impact assessment, or efficiency. Barriers can exist for any of these dimensions, and the barriers may be so considerable that it is not worth proceeding. According to Weiss (1972), an evaluation is not worth doing if (1) no decisions will be based on the evaluation results, that is, decisions about the evaluation's future are not extant or have already been made, (2) the program has no clear orientation, (3) people who are invested in the program disagree about what its purpose is, or (4) there are not sufficient money or qualified staff to conduct the evaluation.

By the same token, three questions must be answered in considering whether a program should be monitored or evaluated:

1. Can the results of the evaluation influence decisions about the program?
2. Can the evaluation be done in time to be useful,
3. Is the program significant enough to merit evaluation? (Wholey, Hatry, and Newcomer 1994)

Designing a project means choosing methods of data collection and analysis to meet the informational needs of the program.

The Growing Emphasis on Outcomes. As can be noted throughout this chapter there is a growing emphasis on outcomes evaluation in all health and social services. Although social work has known that outcomes were important, for many reasons, over the years, it has tended to focus on process measures rather than outcomes. Choices of this kind are less and less possible for several reasons. One is that managed care companies, which directly or indirectly control payment for social work in health and mental health, increasingly demand evidence of positive outcomes for payment. "A focus on outcome performance measurement is an inherent characteristic of managed care regardless of the status (public or private) of the payer" (Martin and Kettner 1997:20). Second, the Government Performance and Results Act of 1993 requires each major program in the federal government to (1) identify its mission and general goals, (2) determine performance indicators, that is, how progress is to be measured, (3) establish targets for each performance indicator, and (4) report at the end of each fiscal year on the actual results for each performance indicator (Government Performance and Results Act 1993). The National Performance Review, the federal government's approach to reinventing government, extends these initiatives. The "service efforts and accomplishment" (SEA) reporting initiatives of the Governmental Accounting Standards Board further support this effort. "By most accounts today, purchase of service contracting is the major mode of human services delivery in this country. Consequently, the only way for state and local government human service agencies to report SEA data on their human service programs is by requiring their nonprofit and for-profit contractors to collect and report performance data" (Martin and Kettner 1997:21). Martin and Kettner argue that SEA reporting is the most important of the five forces promoting increased accountability and the use of performance measures.

The SEA reporting procedure is built on inputs, outputs, and outcomes. Inputs are the service efforts or resources that make up a program. They can be measured as total program costs, total program full-time work positions, and total employee hours worked. Service accomplishments are outputs—meaning efficiency plus quality—and outcomes—meaning measures that identify the accomplishments the program can take credit for. Finally, a service efforts/accomplishment ratio relates efforts to accomplishments. The SEA reporting system is highly useful for social service programs of all types because it provides a common language, helps identify and monitor points of intervention, promotes client/consumer centeredness, improves worker morale, and assists managers in ensuring effectiveness, quality, and efficiency. Finally, because social service programs generally have stakeholders representing different points of view, this system allows the stakeholders to see the systems from several perspectives (Martin and Kettner 1997).

Quality Assurance and Total Quality Management. Just as outcomes evaluation is now a critical issue for social work in health and mental health care, quality assurance has become part of the language of every evaluative function. Currently the approach most discussed by business, health, and social service managers is Total Quality Management (TQM) (Berman 1995), which is based on the concept of quality. It has been defined as "the application of quantitative methods and human resources to improve the material and services supplied to an organization, all the processes within an organization, and the degree to which the needs of the customer are met, now and in the future" (Mossard 1991:223). The five key elements central to TQM demonstrate its relationship to evaluation:

1. Quality is the primary organizational goal.
2. Customers define quality.
3. Variation in processes must be understood and reduced.
4. Change is continuous and comes as a result of teamwork.
5. Top management is committed to the process.

To this list, Martin (1993) adds a sixth element that is relevant to contracted human services: contractors must be included in any TQM program.

Some states preceded the federal government in addressing this topic of outcomes measurement and outcome-focused reporting. Now some state, federal, and local agencies are reporting the use of performance contracting that builds indicators of outcomes into contracts. In addition, agencies are working together to contribute to the definition of outcomes and outcome indicators. "It takes many agencies, preferably working together, to produce favorable results on many, if not most, human services outcomes indicators" (Mullen and Magnabosco 1997:9).

Nonpublic funding sources such as the United Way (UWA) are also beginning to require outcomes data from service agencies. The UWA includes training for low-cost data collection, though the aim is specific programs instead of across sectors. Community foundations, on the other hand, are interested in studies that cross many organizations in a community—for example, state, federal, and local government agencies, schools, as well as informal information from residents. These performance partnerships choose joint selection of performance indicators and time-based targets for those indicators "to give lower-level governments more flexibility in exchange for results-based accountability." (Mullen and Magnabosco 1997:14)

Mullen and Magnabosco (1997) suggest that thus far, public health and vocational rehabilitation are the leaders in identifying outcomes indicators and developing data, perhaps because their outcomes are more measurable. Social services have lagged in these same areas. Information regarding outcomes data is meant to help professional groups and teams to focus. Regularly available data can be used to structure sessions to gauge progress. In such sessions, teams discuss successes, intermediate successes, unplanned outcomes, and failures. As a result, they anticipate improvements that will be evaluated next. At the end of a previously established time period, the groups look at the data together to evaluate outcomes and then decide whether to alter their courses of action and what new directions to take.

To begin to identify outcomes, agencies have to answer the following questions:

1. When should follow-up occur?
2. How does the agency obtain an adequate response rate?
3. How does the agency assess prevention practically? (Mullen and Magnabosco 1997)

Studying program outcomes involves a number of conceptual and measurement issues. The concept of outcomes is deceptively simple, considering the life changes that social workers often wish to come to pass. Other definitions and concepts are also unclear. Many are part of an ecological perspective. Examples of such concepts are "at-risk populations," "community," and "boundaries." Questions are also raised regarding the definition of clients/consumers, communities, and programs and how these definitions reflect relationships and culture.

Dimensions of Outcome Evaluations. Four dimensions of outcome evaluations are services, cost, satisfaction, and clinical outcomes. Here, services refers to access, continuity, comprehensiveness. In regard to cost, cost for the last generation has meant cost containment rather than quality service for cost. Satisfaction refers to the degree to which consumers are satisfied. Consumer satisfaction measures are standard practice for many health insurance, health maintenance, and health management companies. Such information is easy to collect but may have little relationship to clinical change or clinical effectiveness (Berman and Hurt 1997).

The design of an outcomes system should include client definition (who is the client), domains, necessary data, sources for data, time frames, predictors, and processes to be studied. It is suggested that social workers measure only what they will use; anticipate time and costs; emphasize data completion rates; make the study simple and flexible; make the study customizable for varied populations, sites, and goals; use appropriate measurements; include some common assessments; and make the study usable across systems (Berman and Hurt 1997).

Rapid Feedback Evaluation. Rapid feedback evaluation, one component of Wholey's stakeholder approach, is a quick assessment of a program's accomplishments in regard to agreed-upon indicators and objectives. This can also yield plans for more encompassing evaluations. Service delivery assessment is a goal-free method of rapid feedback that documents program outcomes without predetermined indicators or objectives. Rapid feedback evaluation is suggested as an intermediate step between evaluability assessment and further intensive evaluation. The method draws on existing data relevant to the identified outcome measures and gathers new data by various practical and quick methods, such as surveys, interviews, and documentation. The belief is that information gained in the evaluation is sufficient for managers to effect incremental change in the program. The management may then assess the need to move to the next level, a large-scale evaluation.

The rapid feedback method presents a number of advantages:

1. It affords quick access to outcome data.
2. Outcomes are directly related to goals and objectives.
3. Outcomes test what is needed for further evaluation designs.
4. The method is inexpensive.
5. It is often sufficient for policy purposes.

The five steps of rapid feedback evaluation are as follows: (1) collection of existing data on program outcomes identified for study, (2) collection of new data on program outcomes, (3) preliminary evaluation, (4) development and analysis of alternative designs for full-scale evaluation, and (5) assistance with policy and management decisions. The approach is logical, practical, and sensible.

Outcome Measures Specifically Related to the Medicaid Population. Egnew (1997) describes the development of relevant public sector outcome measures related to specific needs of the Medicaid population. Four different categories of outcome measures have special relevance for public sector managed care: (1) access indicators, to review the penetration roster by categories such as age, gender, distinct levels of care, and specific ethnic population; (2) utilization indicators, to review by category, including expenditures by category and recidivism; (3) systems indicators, to monitor utilization and costs in areas where mental health organizations share responsibility for care with other public sector programs, such as juvenile justice and the school system; and (4) consumer satisfaction indicators, with the understanding that these consumers are often continual users of service and are thus reluctant to offer criticism (also see Ware 1997). In addition, a set of basic performance standards should be put into place for all capitated public sector mental health services, including twenty-four-hour toll-free telephone lines to access services, language-assisted telephone service, geographically accessible inpatient and outpatient services, sufficient numbers of geographically accessible bilingual providers, an appropriate array of community-based and rehabilitation services, and an educational outreach program to educate consumers regarding the availability of services (Egnew 1997:79–80).

Evaluation in Case Management Programs. As can be seen in several of the examples in this chapter, case management services are increasingly evaluated for quality. Such evaluations are conducted to monitor compliance with agency regulators, to demonstrate program effectiveness and accomplishments to payers and other funding sources, and to improve practice. Applebaum and Austin (1990:73–74) report that evaluation and quality assurance are separate functions.

> Evaluation poses the basic question of whether the services that are delivered have had their intended effects. Do the individuals that receive a particular service(s) do better than those not receiving such care? ... Quality assurance asks the question: How can this beneficial outcome be assured across time and across a variety of settings and case managers? Quality assurance involves two major components. First, the product must be operationally defined, and second, precise standards must be developed.

While previous outcomes strategies in quality assurance had been limited and focused on the individual or client group without the benefit of experimental design, the presence of experimental design is more common now, although it is still most often used in demonstration projects. Applebaum and Austin (1990) say that to design a useful evaluation and monitoring system, an organization should link planning, administration, and evaluation functions; an individual or a team from within the organization should have the primary responsibility for planning and evaluation; and there should be broad participation. Many of the themes in these approaches to evaluation are quite similar. They include broad participation, clear definitions, client/consumer input, and strong emphases on quality and accountability.

Programs, Outcomes, and Legislation. If programs are mandated, it is essential that outcomes be directly related to the legislation that has mandated and/or funded the program. All programs must be designed in ways that produce results in the form of useful outcomes that can prove worth to those who are responsible for funding or otherwise supporting them. Related to this is the question of inflated outcomes, of promising outcomes that social workers know are impossible to achieve in order to procure or secure funding, or of exaggerating results in order to satisfy those who fund or evaluate programs or interventions. Inflating outcomes is courting failure, and exaggerating results is unethical. Rossi provides a fine example of "cooking" data when he reports on a study by Chen (1995) of the counting of drug-abusing students by high school principals in Taiwan (Rossi 1997). When the principals learned that those who showed a decline in figures were rewarded while those who showed a rise were punished, their figures converged and everyone reported similar low numbers of drug users. This is an example of why "the observations on which outcomes measures should be based should not be made the responsibility of organizations or people who can be affected by the outcomes" (Rossi 1997:32).

Social work is increasingly asked to evaluate its work. Although little research is available at this time, research, documentation, and reliable data are necessary to prove effective service delivery. Valid intended outcomes are those that people who are knowledgeable agree should be accomplished. Valid outcomes measures will ultimately yield additional resources and recognition for social work (Mullen and Magnabosco 1997). Gross outcomes are the effects of the program plus the effects of all other processes that led to outcomes. Net outcomes are changes that would not have occurred without the program.

Cost-Benefit Ratio. One way to evaluate the success of programs and interventions is to examine the benefits they produce. A problem for social work is finding ways to value behavioral health interventions that others will understand. The great personal and social costs to untreated behavioral problems have been documented. However, "because mental health and substance abuse problems are stigmatized and because the symptoms of mental illness are often subjective experiences, the effectiveness of treatment for these problems has been particularly suspect" (Shern and Trabin 1997:102). Another approach to costs is to see whether these effects save society or the taxpayers or some other entity more than they cost. In that way costs, benefits, and savings are measured, if possible. It is hoped that this would not be the sole basis on which the government would decide whether to fund a program, but positive net savings would help allay the fears of those who worry about the burden created by social programs (Karoly et al. 1998). However, it is very important that social workers be able to understand and be able to participate in these kinds of analyses because this kind of estimate of worth is most common for those who fund programs and draft and vote on legislation.

The connection between cost and value and its critical examination will continue to be the driving force behind outcomes-oriented accountability strategies in mental and behavioral health care. "Current measurement tools represent a 'Tower of Babel' approach with no standard language or ability to compare value of services and attached costs" (Abramovitz, Ivanoff, Mosseri, and O'Sullivan 1997:296).

RAND, a nonprofit corporation that helps improve policy and decision making through research and analysis, evaluated two early intervention programs according to costs and benefits. It chose the programs according to five criteria:

1. The evaluation had to have an experimental design and, therefore, include a treatment group and a control group.
2. The sample size had to be sufficiently large for statistical methods to highlight differences between the two groups.
3. Sample attrition had to be small over time.
4. The outcomes or potential benefits that could save money (such as a lessening of welfare use) had to be measured as part of the evaluation.
5. A full accounting of savings required long-term follow-up.

One home visits program provided parent education, social support for the mother, and social services referrals beginning with the prenatal period and continuing until the child became 2 years old. The results of the cost/savings/benefit analysis first carried out for that program showed that government savings did not exceed costs, and the majority of government savings were derived from reductions in the mothers' use of Aid to Families with Dependent Children (AFDC) and other social services (Karoly et al. 1998:80). The other program offered preschool classes to 3- and 4-year-olds. Program costs were about $12,000 per child. According to the previous study of this program, savings to the government exceeded costs by more than seven to one, with the largest portion of savings from reductions in crime, a large percentage of which is the estimated reductions in intangible loss to crime victims during the lifetimes of the participants in the programs (Barnett 1993). RAND reevaluated both programs comparing program costs to the government savings the programs generate and found at least four types of savings: (1) increased tax revenues owing to employment and earnings of the program participants, (2) decreased outlays, including Medicaid, Food Stamps, and AFDC, (3) reduced expenditures for education, health, and other services, and (4) lower criminal justice system costs. Additional monetary benefits to society are the greater income of program participants as opposed to nonparticipants and savings to people who might have been crime victims if the programs had not been available. RAND did not calculate the intangible costs calculated by the previous evaluator. These studies also point to the importance of distal in addition to proximal outcomes. We generally think in terms of what can be accomplished immediately by a program or intervention. Obviously, distal outcomes are extremely important, and it is critical to be able to use data to project long-term outcomes, even while designing programs:

> If it were possible to include and monetize all the benefits of a program, one could generate a complete cost-benefit ratio. However, monitizing many of the benefits of early childhood interventions is difficult or impossible. It is difficult, for example, to monetize the benefits of improved behavior or IQ, either for the child or for other members of the child's family or classroom. We cannot attach a monetary value to a mother's greater satisfaction with her relationship with her child. Neither can we determine at this time the monetary value to society of greater academic achievement on the part of children participating in early interventions. The same goes for many of the health benefits realized. Furthermore, benefits that can be monetized may result in future benefits that cannot. For example, if early intervention means that a child will be more economically successful as an adult (a monetizable benefit) that adult's children may not be exposed to the same stressors he or she was (a benefit that is difficult to monetize). (Karoly et al. 1998)

Issues of Debate Concerning Outcome Measures. Booth and Smith (1997:37–39) present several issues of scientific debate about outcome measures:

1. Should measures be disorder-specific or use a common general assessment?
2. Should a sample be drawn and studied or should entire populations be assessed?
3. Should assessments be brief or should they be more comprehensive?
4. Should tracer conditions be followed or should the assessment include all disorders seen in an organization? A tracer condition is one that is followed in an organization and is thought to be generalizable throughout the system. It allows the focus on a particular disorder or disease over time.
5. What are the advantages and disadvantages of various data collection methods?

Booth and Smith answer these questions as follows:

1. They believe that a combination of disease-specific and general assessments is most helpful.
2. Sampling is the only realistic and practical way to assess outcomes, but samples must be true probability samples and not convenience samples.
3. A tracer condition facilitates the evaluation of a disorder over time, but the condition has to be chosen carefully to reflect the nature and goals of the organization being assessed.

According to Booth and Smith (1997:42), "The ability to conduct case-mix adjustment is important for the development of national, state, or local benchmarks or report cards to which clinical programs can aspire." Brief assessments are most practical and less costly, but multidimensional studies are more precise and yield more information. As Booth and Smith (1997:39) suggest, it is generalizable and statistically powerful to "collect brief, well-validated measures on a large number of people compared with longer assessments of just a few individuals."

Assessment Tools as Outcome Measures. In part, assessment tools can be used as outcome measures in social work:

> A measurement tool can be used for assessment as well as to examine outcomes, but first and most important a measurement tool is little more than a device that captures (hopefully accurately) information about some attribute that is used to describe something (for example, a client). A measurement tool must not be confused with an assessment tool, an outcomes measure, or a measure of effectiveness. It is important to remember that a measurement tool has no value orientation whatsoever: it just measures. (Mullen and Magnabosco 1997:69)

Outcome often has two different meanings: (1) results of help sought for a problem, and (2) the kind and level of professional help offered to address a problem. Assessment scales can be used to measure the former but not the latter (Hudson 1997). Measures of effectiveness mean measures of change. To demonstrate that a service or intervention was responsible for "change," the procedures that make up the service have to be carefully defined, and even then, because the service is only one dimension in a client or consumer's life, the most that can be claimed is that it contributed to positive changes for the client or consumer.

Intended and Unintended Consequences. Rossi (1997:21) defines program outcomes as changes, intended or not, in the program's target that accompany exposure to the program. In human service programs, targets can be people, families, neighborhoods, schools, agencies and firms to which the program is directed. Programs can cover a variety of activities designed to achieve intended outcomes, including the providing of information, counseling, material support, training, laws and legal sanctions, medical therapy, and so forth.

Distinctions need to be drawn between intended and unintended outcomes:

> It is essential that social workers anticipate the unintended as well as the intended consequences, that they maintain a healthy skepticism about the relationship between data and meaningful information, and that they insist that use of outcomes measures be linked to demonstrated enhancement of more effective and appropriate practice. (Nurius and Vourlekis 1997:146)

Even more than understanding intended outcomes, interpreting unintended outcomes depends on understanding the organization and other dimensions of context in which the outcomes have occurred. Rosen (1993) places the notion of unintended outcomes in the context in his framework for systematic planned practice, an example of which can be found in chapter 7. This is even more imperative when evaluating entire organizations.

Evaluating Organizations

A particularly helpful classic example can be found in Lauffer (1982). The author describes an agency that was losing funding, getting few referrals, and was not able to refer out effectively. To help evaluate the situation, the new director called a meeting and created a large map with the agency at the center. Linkages to other agencies were identified and then described in relation to recent history. It became clear that the agency was poorly connected to other agencies. Agencies with whom linkages had been helpful in the past had changed and were no longer as helpful; those with whom the relationships had been less useful had evolved into agencies that might be helpful. This concrete map provided direction for understanding the context of the organization and for understanding why a seemingly effective agency was not functioning well within the greater community context.

Organizations also benefit from evaluating their mission on a regular basis. This includes evaluating objectives and goals and evaluating how close the organization has been able to come to accomplishment of goals previously identified as important to the organization's mission. While this seems so basic as to be almost nonsensical, it is anything but that. "Organizations with a clear mission from which they can derive a set of specifiable goals should be in the best position to set boundaries on their service delivery and to assess outcomes. Such a mission enables the program to specify where it is going and how it might get there" (Segal 1997:157). Often, organizations continue to operate the way they always have, without reevaluation of the new social context surrounding the organization or with little awareness of a changed mandate from the community for their services. Evaluation of objectives, goals, and mission can clarify these situations and allow organizations to stay efficient and effective within changing community contexts.

Evaluation of Community Outreach

Especially in relation to public health, social work has a long, distinguished record in community outreach. One early example was social workers canvassing neighborhoods during the 1918 influenza epidemic. One such plan in New York City set up a police canvass plus forty social centers from which social service staff would go to homes of those whose names were given to them by police (Kerson 1978a). In this way, the City Health Department hoped to "identify motherless and fatherless children, those who needed medical attention, and to provide emergency aid" (Kerson 1981:96). This was evaluation of need that could easily be counted and measured. Another such historical example was the evaluation of need of crippled children through a program of the Children's Bureau. In 1935, Edith Baker, director of the Medical Social Unit of the Children's Bureau's Division of Health Services wrote, "Preceding the admitting process, some public programs, notably the crippled children's programs, are obligated to locate the persons for whom the services are designed" (Baker 1939:13).

Baker placed Theodate Soule in charge of one study of crippled children that she managed with three additional social workers. She recounted,

We did Alabama, Kentucky, Virginia, Minnesota, Michigan, and New Jersey. . . . We had very good access to places. That was very revealing to me because it showed me a fact that was dreadfully disturbing, that you could get care if you had been born in one part of the country, but not if you were born in another. Some of the other states were just dreadful. These children had gotten some kind of care, but, in many instances it hadn't done them much good because there wasn't any follow-up that made it possible for them to live a decent life still handicapped. Particularly in the southern states, a great deal of the problem was due to burns because so many of them were cooking on open fires. (Kerson 1978a:123)

Again, social workers were sent out to gather information to evaluate need.

Contemporary examples include partnering between social work departments in health systems and community residents to accomplish the following:

- Understand the community's social-health status
- Identify health and social needs, the gaps in service, and the programs essential to meet them
- Optimize availability of and accessibility to services
- Draw on social-epidemiological methods to screen for vulnerable populations and provide primary prevention
- Contribute to social-health planning efforts
- Further the understanding of public policy as it affects funding and service delivery
- Create a network of social-health services to allow for comprehensive care, including information and referral services for the local populace (Peake, Brenner, and Rosenberg 1998:112)

Young, Gardner, Coley, Schorr, and Bruner (1994) suggest a six-level developmental approach to evaluation that is designed to take into account the developmental nature of collaborative relationships. Since this book strongly supports collaborative work between systems at all levels, this approach to evaluation is salient. The six levels are as follows:

1. *Service penetration* is the needs assessment phase that explores the capacities, needs, and service penetration of those who might benefit from a program.
2. *Engagement* is the phase for determining to what extent those who are targeted are willing to participate in a partnership with an organization.
3. *Growth* is the phase in which those involved try to understand the nature and extent of growth in participants and to determine the degree to which the growth can be attributed to program initiatives.
4. In *community embeddedness,* the scope of the evaluation is broadened to include more of the community that was outside of the original partnership.
5. In *system response, climate for reform, and change,* the goal is to measure the extent of community response outside the partnership.
6. In *community-wide well-being,* outcomes are addressed by looking at

the originally addressed population to evaluate changes attributed to all the interventions. (Young et al. 1994)

Rohrer (1996:83) argues that "at first glance, it might appear that the same information used to identify community needs (for example, morbidity, mortality, consumer perceptions) can serve to document performance. However, this is not uniformly the case, because most indicators of community health status are not sensitive to changes in the service delivery system." Thus while deaths from Alzheimer's disease cannot be eliminated by improving access to primary care, low birth weights and infant mortality rates can be influenced by prenatal care. In the latter case, increased access can be measured in terms of visits per capita, thus documenting that the system has directed its resources properly (Rohrer 1996:83). Social workers in health and mental health are often involved in those indicators of community health status that are sensitive to changes in the service delivery system. Examples include AIDS outreach services, services to the frail elderly, Early Periodic Screening Diagnosis and Treatment services, as well as a range of other maternal and child health services, outreach services to the homeless, and case management services for the people with serious mental illnesses.

CONCLUSION

This chapter has discussed the process of evaluation, the place of evaluation in the work of social workers in health and mental health care, and several kinds of evaluation related to direct practice, program evaluation, and community outreach. All forms of evaluation and particularly outcome measures should be part of the formulation of any kind of social work, from designing programs to assessing clients, consumers, and communities in terms of need and capacity. The ability to prove that it pays to have social workers intervene with clients and consumers in health and mental health settings is critical to the future of the profession. Social workers must be able to evaluate their own work, their clients' and their own successes and failures, as they work toward their goals, the effectiveness of their programs, and the needs and capacities of the communities in which their clients reside. Thus, for social workers, evaluation is in part a process of participation with evaluative consultants who come into their workplaces to measure various dimensions of the work, and it is in part a continual self-evaluation of work, clients, and programs. Evaluation is critical to every part of the work. In fact, the future of social work in health and mental health care depends on it.

Germain (1984:197) said that the social worker and client evaluating "the work together reinforces the client's sense of accomplishment, the acceptance of a new self-image and new life goals if those were issues, and the courage to face and carry out continuing tasks." The sense of accomplishment and courage to face the future supported by the process of evaluation is just as true for the evaluation of programs, community outreach, organizations, and health-related social work itself. To evaluate is to appraise or value, the final phase of social work practice from an ecological perspective . . . before we begin again.

References

A narrative discussion of the Bipartisan Consensus Managed Care Improvement Act of 1999. (2001). http://www.house.gov/commerce_democrats/pbor/bipartisanbill.narrative.htm.

A right to sue. (1999). *The Economist, 353*(8), 30–31.

Aaron, H. (2000). Medicare choice. In A. J. Rettenheimer and T. R. Saving (Eds.), *Medicare reform: Issues and answers* (pp. 37–64). Chicago: University of Chicago Press.

Abramovitz, R., Ivanoff, A., Mosseri, R., and O'Sullivan, A. (1997). Comments on outcomes measurement in mental and behavioral health. In E. J. Mullen, and J. L. Magnabosco (Eds.), *Outcome measurement in the human services: Cross-cutting issues and methods* (pp. 293–96). Washington, DC: NASW Press.

Abramson, J. S. (1993). Orienting social work employees in interdisciplinary settings: Shaping professional and organizational perspectives. *Social Work, 38*(2), 152–157.

Abramson, J. S., and Mizrahi, T. (1993). Examining social work/physician collaboration: An application of grounded theory methodology. In C. Riessman (Ed.), *Qualitative studies in social work research* (pp. 28–48). Newbury Park, CA: Sage.

Abramson, J. S., and Rosenthal, B. B. (1995). Interdisciplinary and interorganizational collaboration. In R. L. Edwards (Ed.), *Encyclopedia of social work* (19th ed.) (pp. 1479–89). Washington, DC: NASW Press.

Abramson, J. S. (1989). Making teams work. *Social Work with Groups, 12*(4), 45–63.

Abramson, J. S., and Mizrahi, T. (1996). When social workers and physicians collaborate: Positive and negative interdisciplinary experiences. *Social Work, 41*(3), 270–81.

Abramson, M., and Black, R. B. (1985). Extending the boundaries of life: Implications for practice. *Health and Social Work, 10*(3), 165–73.

Abramson, M. (1989). Autonomy vs. paternalistic beneficence: Practice strategies. *Social Casework, 70,* 101–5.

Abramson, M. (1990). Keeping secrets: Social workers and AIDS. *Social Work, 35,* 169–73.

Abramson, M. (1991). Ethical and technological advances: Contribution of social work practice. *Social Work in Health Care, 15*(2), 5–17.

Achenbaum, W. A. (1983). Towards the next watershed in aging America. In W. A. Achenbaum (Ed.), *Shades of gray: Old age, American values, and federal politics since 1920* (pp. 137–67). Boston: Little, Brown.

Affholter, D. P. (1994). Outcome monitoring. In J. S. Wholey, H. P. Hatry, and K. E. Newcomer (Eds.), *Handbook of practical program evaluation* (pp. 96–118). San Francisco: Jossey-Bass.

Akiskal, H. S., and Cassano, G. B. (1997). *Dysthymia and the spectrum of mental disorders.* New York: Guilford.

Alcoholics Anonymous, Grapevine, Inc. (1984). *The twelve traditions/the twelve steps.* New York: Author.

Allen-Meares, P., and Lane, B. (1987). Grounding social work practice in theory: Eco-systems. *Social Casework, 68*(9), 515–21.

Alpert, J. L. (1990). An analyst views the case. In D. W. Cantor (Ed.), *Women as therapists* (pp. 63–74). Northvale, NJ: Springer.

Alpert, S. (1993). Smart cards, smarter policy: Medical records, privacy, and health care reform. *Hastings Center Report, 23*(6), 13–23.

Alter, C. and Hage, J. (1993). *Organizations working together.* Newbury Park, CA: Sage.

Amason, R. (1996) Functional conflict vs. dysfunctional conflict. *Academy of Management Journal,* 39(1), 123–48.

American Psychiatric Association (APA). (1980). *Diagnostic and statistical manual of mental disorders* (3rd ed.). Washington, DC: American Psychiatric Association.

American Psychiatric Association (APA). (1987). *Diagnostic and statistical manual of mental disorders* (3rd ed., rev.). Washington, DC: American Psychiatric Association.

American Psychiatric Association (APA). (1994). *Diagnostic and statistical manual of mental disorders* (4th ed.). Washington, DC: American Psychiatric Association.

Americans with Disabilities Act of 1990, P. L. 101–336, 104 Stat. 327, 42 U.S.C.S. 12101.

Anderson, P. L., Kazmierski, S., and Cronin, M. E. (1995). Learning disabilities, employment discrimination, and the ADA. *Journal of Learning Disabilities, 28*(4), 196–204.

Anderson, S. C., and Mandell, D. L. (1989). The use of self-disclosure by professional social workers. *Journal of Contemporary Social Work, 70,* (May), 259–67.

Andrulis, D. P., and Carrier, B. (1999). *Managed care and the inner city: The uncertain promise for providers, plans, and communities.* San Francisco: Jossey-Bass.

Annas, G. (1989). *The rights of patients*. Tutowa, NJ: Humana Press.

Applebaum, R., and Austin, C. (1990). *Long-term case management: Design and evaluation*. New York: Springer.

Arana, G. W. (2000). An overview of side effects caused by typical antipsychotics. *Journal of Clinical Psychiatry, 61*(Supp. 8), 5–11.

Argamaso, R. (1999). Pharyngeal flap surgery for velopharyngeal insufficiency. http://www.crosslink.net/marchett/vcfs/argflap.htm.

Argyris, C., and Schon, D. (1978). *Organizational learning*. Boston: Addison-Wesley.

Argyris, C. (1982). *Reasoning, learning, and action*. San Francisco: Jossey-Bass.

Argyris, C. (1990a). *Knowledge for action*. San Francisco: Jossey-Bass.

Argyris, C. (1990b). *Overcoming organizational defenses: Facilitating organizing learning*. Boston: Allyn & Bacon.

Argyris, C. (1991). Teaching smart people how to learn. *Harvard Business Review*, (May–June), 99–109.

Argyris, C. (1993). *Knowledge for action*. San Francisco: Jossey-Bass.

Argyris, C. (1994). Good communication that blocks learning. *Harvard Business Review*, (July-August), 77–85.

Asamoah, Y. (Ed.). (1996). *Innovations in delivering culturally sensitive social work services: Challenges for practice and education*. New York: Haworth.

ASAP! Update. (July 2001.) *Whither the Patients' Bill of Rights*? http://www.familiesusa.org.

Attkisson, C. C., and Broskowski, A. (1978). Evaluation and the emerging human service concept. In C. C. Attkisson, W. A. Hargreaves, M. J. Horowitz, and J. E. Sorensen (Eds.), *Evaluation of human services programs* (pp. 24–38). New York: Academic Press.

Auerswald, E. (1968). Interdisciplinary versus ecological approach. *Family Process, 7*(2), 202–15.

Austin, C. D., and McClelland, R. W. (Eds.). (1996). *Perspectives on case management practice*. Milwaukee: Families International.

Bailey, D., and Grochau, K. E., (1993). Aligning leadership needs to the organizational state of development: Applying management theory to organizations. *Administration in Social Work, 17*(1), 23–28.

Baker, E. M. (1939). The administration of the Social Security Act as it affects crippled children: From the standpoint of the Federal Government. California District of American Association of Medical Social Workers, Oakland, CA (May 16, 1939).

Balanced Budget Act of 1997, 42 U.S.C. 4001 et seq.

Ballew, J. R., and Mink, G. (1996). *Case management in social work: Developing the professional skills needed for work with multiproblem clients* (2nd ed.). Springfield, IL: Thomas.

Bare, M. (1997). Confronting a life-threatening disease: Renal dialysis and transplant programs. In T. S. Kerson (Ed.), *Social work in health settings: Practice in context* (2nd ed.) (pp. 269–90). New York: Haworth.

Barnett, W. S. (1993). Benefit-cost analysis of preschool education: Findings from a 25-year follow-up. *American Journal of Orthopsychiatry, 63*(4), 500–508.

Bartlett, C. A., and Ghoshal, S. (1992). Matrix management: Not a structure but a frame of mind. In J. Gabarro (Ed.), *On management* (pp. 370–81). Boston: HBS Publications.

Bartlett, H. M. (1958). Toward clarification and improvement of social work practice. *Social Work,* 3(3), 3–9.

Bartlett, H. M. (1970). *The common base of social work practice.* New York: National Association of Social Workers.

Bartlett, H. M. (1976). Interview. In T. S. Kerson, *Eleven medical social work interviews.* Boston: Archives, Simmons College School of Social Work.

Bastoe, P. O. (1999). Linking evaluation utilization and governance. In R. Boyle, and D. Lemaire (Eds.), *Building effective evaluation capacity: Lessons from practice* (pp. 93–131). New Brunswick, NJ: Transaction.

Bayles, M. (1981). *Professional ethics.* Albany, NY: Wadsworth.

Beatty, J. (1998). *The world according to Peter Drucker.* New York: Free Press.

Bechtel, S. (1993). *The Practical Encyclopedia of Sex and Health.* Emmaus, PA: Rodale.

Beder, J. (1998). The home visit, revisited. *Families in Society,* (September–October), 514–21.

Behroozi, C. S. (1992). A model of social work practice with involuntary applicants in groups. *Social Work with Groups,* 15(2/3): 223–38.

Belcher, J. R. (1988). Rights vs. needs of homeless mentally ill. *Social Work,* 33(4), 398–402.

Belcher, J. R., and Toomey, B. G. (1988). Relationship between the deinstitutionalization model, psychiatric disability, and homelessness. *Health and Social Work,* 13(2), 145–53.

Bellah, R. N., Madsen, R., Sullivan, W. M., Swidler, A., and Tipton, S. M. (1985). *Habits of the heart: Individualism and commitment in American life.* Berkeley: University of California Press.

Berkman, B., Chauncey, S., Holmes, W., Daniels, A., Bonander, E., Sampson, S., and Robinson, M. (1999). Standardized screening of elderly patients' needs for social work assessment in primary care: Use of the SF-36. *Health and Social Work,* 24(1), 9–16.

Berman, E. M. (1995). Implementing TQM in State welfare agencies. *Administration in Social Work,* 19(1), 55–72.

Berman, W., and Hurt, S. (1997). Developing clinical outcomes systems: Conceptual and practical issues. In E. J. Mullen, and J. L. Magnabosco (Eds.), *Outcome measurement in the human services: Cross-cutting issues and methods* (pp. 81–97). Washington, DC: NASW Press.

Berman-Rossi, T. (Ed.). (1994). *Social work: The collected writings of William Schwartz.* Itasca, IL: Peacock.

Bertalanffy, L. (1974). General system theory and psychiatry. In S. Arieti (Ed.), *American handbook of psychiatry* (pp. 1095–117). New York: Basic Books.

Bertelli, A. (1998). Should social workers engage in the unauthorized practice of law? *Boston Public Interest Law Journal,* 8(15), 1–28.

Bielefeld, W., and Corbin, J. J. (1996). The institutionalization of nonprofit human service delivery: The role of political culture. *Administration and Society,* 28(3), 362–89.

Biestek, F. P. (1957). *The casework relationship.* Chicago: Loyola University Press.

Binder, R. L., and McNeil, D. E. (1996). Application of the Tarasoff ruling and its effect on the victim and the therapeutic relationship. *Psychiatric Services, 47*(11), 1212–15.

Birdwhistell, R. L. (1970). *Kinesics and context: Essays on body motion and communication.* Philadelphia: University of Pennsylvania Press.

Birenbaum, A. (1997). *Managed care: Made in America.* New York: Praeger.

Bishop, K. K., Taylor, M. S., and Arango, P. (1997). *Partnerships at work: Lessons learned from programs and practices of families, professionals, and communities.* Burlington, VT: Partnerships for Change.

Blades, B. C. (1997). Psychological recovery from burn injury: Regional burn center. In T. S. Kerson (Ed.), *Social work in health settings: Practice in context* (2nd ed.) (pp. 243–68). New York: Haworth.

Bloom, M., Fischer, J., and Orme, J. (1994). *Evaluating practice: Guidelines for the accountable professional* (2nd ed.). Boston: Allyn & Bacon.

Booth, B. M., and Smith, G. R. (1997). Outcomes measurement: Where we are. In E. J. Mullen and J. L. Magnabosco (Eds.), *Outcome measurement in the human services: Cross-cutting issues and methods* (pp. 35–43). Washington, DC: NASW Press.

Bowling, A. (2001). *Measuring disease: A review of disease-specific quality of life measurement scales.* Buckingham, England: Open University Press.

Bowman, C. G., and Mertz, E. (1996). A dangerous direction: Legal intervention in sexual abuse survivor therapy. *Harvard Law Review, 109,* 551–639.

Bracht, N., and Kingsbury, L., and Rissel, C. (1990). A five-stage community organization model for health promotion. In N. Bracht (Ed.), *Health promotion at the community level* (pp. 83–118). Newbury Park, CA: Sage.

Bracht, N. (Ed.). (1990). *Health promotion at the community level.* Newbury Park, CA: Sage.

Brager, G., and Holloway, S. (1978). *Changing human service organizations: Politics and practice.* New York: Free Press.

Brager, G., Specht, H., and Torcayner, J. L. (1987). *Community organizing.* New York: Harper & Row.

Brannigan, V. M. (1992). Protecting the privacy of patient information in clinical networks: Regulatory effectiveness analysis. *Annals of the New York Academy of Sciences, 670,* 190–201.

Briar, S., and Miller, H. (1971). *Problems and issues in social casework.* New York: Columbia University Press.

Briar, S. (1977). Social work practice: Contemporary issues. In R. L. Edwards (Ed.), *Encyclopedia of social work* (19th ed.) (pp. 1529–34). Washington, DC: NASW Press.

Bronfenbrenner, U. (1979). *The ecology of human development.* Cambridge, MA: Harvard University Press.

Bronfenbrenner, U. (1989). Ecological systems theory. *Annals of Child Development, 6,* 187–249.

Budman, S. H., and Gurman, A. S. (1996). Theory and practice of brief therapy. In J. E. Groves (Ed.), *Essential papers on short-term dynamic therapy* (pp. 43–65). New York: New York University Press.

Budman, S. H., and Gurman, A. S. (1988). *Theory and practice of brief psychotherapy.* New York: Guilford.

Burgelman, R. A., and Grove, A. S. (1996). Strategic dissonance. *California Management Review, 38*(2), 8–28.

Burkhart, P. J., and Reuss, S. (1993). *Successful strategic planning: A guide for nonprofit agencies and organizations.* Newbury Park, CA: Sage.

Burson, J. A. (1998). AIDS, sexuality, and African American adolescent females. *Child and Adolescent Social Work Journal, 15*(5), 357–65.

Campbell, A., and Alexander, M. (1997). What's wrong with strategy? *Harvard Business Review,* (November–December), 42–51.

Cannon. I. M. (1913). *Social Work in Hospitals.* New York: Russell Sage Foundation.

Cantor, D. W. (1990). Women as therapists: What we already know. In D. W. Cantor (Ed.), *Women as therapists* (pp. 3–19). Northvale, NJ: Springer.

Carlton, T. (1984). *Clinical social work in health settings.* New York: Springer.

Cascio, T. (1998). Incorporating spirituality into social work practice: A review of what to do. *Families in Society,* (September–October), 525–31.

Castex, G. (1996). Providing services to Hispanic/Latino populations: Profiles in diversity. In P. Ewalt, E. Freeman, S. Kirk, and D. Poole (Eds.), *Multicultural issues in social work* (pp. 523–38). Washington, DC: NASW Press.

Center for families coping with addiction opens in former lower east side bodega. (October 20, 1996). Press release, New York.

Chapin, H. D. (1918). The work of the babies' wards of the New York Post-Graduate Hospital for convalescent children. *Archives of Pediatrics,* April 1905, reprinted in *Hospital Social Service Quarterly, 1,* 114–21.

Chen, H. (1995). *The effectiveness of a drug abuse education program in Taiwan.* Unpublished manuscript, University of Toledo, Ohio.

Cherin, D., and Meezan, W. (1998). Evaluation as a means of organizational learning. *Administration in Social Work, 22*(2), 1–21.

Child Abuse Prevention and Treatment Act of 1974, 42 U.S.C. 5101–7.

Chirikos, T. N. (1991). The economics of employment. *Milbank Quarterly, 69* (supp. 1–2), 150–79.

Christensen, C. M. (1997). Making strategy: Learning by doing. *Harvard Business Review,* (November–December), 141–56.

Clapp, J. D. (1995). Organizing inner city neighborhoods to reduce alcohol and drug problems. *Journal of Community Practice, 2*(1), 43–54.

Clemens, E. L. (1995). Multiple perceptions of discharge planning in one urban hospital. *Health and Social Work, 20*(4), 254–61.

Cohen, B. J. (1999). Fostering innovation in a large human services bureaucracy. *Administration in Social Work, 23*(2), 47–59.

Colenda, C. C., Banazak, D., and Mickus, M. (1998). Mental health services in managed care: Quality questions remain. *Geriatrics, 53*(8), 49–50, 56.

Collins, J. C., and Porras, J. I. (1996). Building your company's vision. *Harvard Business Review,* (September–October), 65–77.

Comparison of House and Senate patient protection legislation. (1999). http://www.house.gov/commerce_democrats/pbor/27231344sbs.htm.

Compher, J. V. (1987). The dance beyond the family system. *Social Work, 32*(2), 105–8.

Compton, B. R., and Galaway, B. (1998). *Social work processes* (6th ed.). Pacific Grove, CA: Brooks/Cole.

Contract with America Advancement Act of 1996, 42 U.S.C. 1382.

Congress, E. (1994). The use of culturagrams to assess and empower culturally diverse families. *Families in Society, 75,* 531–38.

Cooper, J. F. (1995). *A primer of brief psychotherapy.* New York: Norton.

Corcoran, K., and Vandiver, V. (1996). *Maneuvering the maze of managed care.* New York: Free Press.

Corcoran, K. (1997). Use of rapid assessment instruments as outcomes measures. In E. J. Mullen and J. L. Magnabosco (Eds.),. *Outcome measurement in the human services: Cross-cutting issues and methods* (pp. 137–43). Washington, DC: NASW Press.

Corcoran, K. (2000). *Measures for clinical practice: A sourcebook* (3rd ed.). New York: Simon & Schuster.

Corwin, M. D., and Read, E. (1997). Brief treatment: Community mental health. In T. S. Kerson (Ed.), *Social work in health settings: Practice in context* (2nd ed.) (pp. 427–44). New York: Haworth.

Cournoyer, B. (1996). *The social work skills workbook* (2nd ed.). Pacific Grove, CA: Brooks/ Cole

Cowin, R. (1970). Some dimensions of social work practice in a health setting. *American Journal of Public Health, 60*(5), 860–69.

Cowles, L., and Lefcowitz, M. (1992). Interdisciplinary expectations of the medical social work in the hospital setting. *Health and Social Work, 17,* 57–65.

Cox, E. O., and Parsons, R. J. (1994). *Empowerment-oriented social work practice with the elderly.* Pacific Grove, CA: Brooks/Cole.

Cressman, E. (Ed.). (1944). *Functional casework in a medical setting.* Philadelphia: Pennsylvania School of Social Work.

Crow, R. (1995). Planning and management professions. In R. L. Edwards (Ed.), *Encyclopedia of social work* (19th ed.) (pp. 1837–43). Washington, DC: NASW Press.

Croze, C. (1995). Medicaid waivers: The shape of things to come. *Proceedings of the Fifth Annual National Conference on State Mental Health Agency Services Research and Program Evaluation* (pp. 334–38). Alexandria, VA: NASMHPD.

Culver, C. M. (1995). Commitment to mental institutions. In W. T. Reich (Ed.), *Encyclopedia of bioethics* (Rev. ed.) (pp. 418–23). New York: Macmillan.

Dane, B., and Simon, B. (1991). Resident guests: Social workers in host settings. *Social Work, 36*(3), 208–13.

Davidson, T., Davidson, J. R., and Keigher, S. M. (1999). Managed care: Satisfaction guaranteed . . . not! *Health and Social Work. 24*(3), 161–68.

Davis, L. E., Galinsky, M. J., and Schopler, J. H. (1995). RAP: A framework for leadership of multiracial groups. *Social Work, 40*(2), 155–65.

Davis, T. R. V. (1996). Developing an employee balanced scorecard: Linking frontline performance to corporate objectives. *Management Decision, 34*(1), 14–18.

Dawson, S. E., and Madsen, G. E. (1995). American Indian uranium millworkers: The perceived effects of chronic occupational exposure. *Journal of Health and Social Policy, 7*(2), 19–31.

Dawson, S. E. (1993). Social work practice and technological disasters: The Navajo uranium experience. *Journal of Sociology and Social Welfare, 20*(2), 5–20.

Dawson, S. E., Charley, P. H., and Harrison, P. (1997). Advocacy and social action among Navajo uranium workers. In T. S. Kerson (Ed.), *Social work in health settings: Practice in context* (2nd ed.) (pp. 391–407). New York: Haworth.

Deal, L. W., and Shiono, P. H. (1998). Medicaid managed care and children: An overview. *Future of Children, 8*(2), 93–104.

Denton, D. K. (1999). How a team can grow. *Quality Progress, 32*(6), 53–58.

Des Jarlais, D. C., and Stepherson, B. (1991). History, ethics, and politics in AIDS prevention research. *American Journal of Public Health, 81,* 1393–94.

Developmental Disabilities Assistance and Bill of Rights of 1990, 42 U.S.C. 6000 et seq.

Dewar, D. (1999). Thirteen keys to successful teamwork. *Workforce, 78*(2–3) supp.

Dickson, D. T. (1995). *Law in the health and human services: A guide for social workers, psychologists, psychiatrists, and related professionals.* New York: Free Press.

Dobrof, J. (1991). DRG's and the social worker's role in discharge planning. *Social Work in Health Care, 16*(2), 37–54.

Donovan, C., Blanchard, E., and Kerson, T. S. (1997). A transitional residence for the mentally ill: To achieve independent living. In T. S. Kerson (Ed.), *Social work in health settings: Practice in context* (2nd ed.) (pp. 481–504). New York: Haworth.

Doolan, E. (1997). Beyond survival by machine: Reflections of a spouse. In T. S. Kerson (Ed.), *Social work in health settings: Practice in context* (2nd ed.) (pp. 291–308). New York: Haworth.

Dore, M. M. (1990). Functional theory: Its history and influence on contemporary social work practice. *Social Service Review, 64,* (September), 358–74.

Drucker, P. (1954). *The practice of management.* New York: Harper & Row.

Drucker, P. (1959). *Landmarks of tomorrow: A report on the post-modern world.* New York: Harper.

Drucker, P. (1974). *Management: Tasks, responsibilities, practices.* New York: Harper & Row.

Drucker, P. (1990). *Managing the non-profit organization: Practices and principles.* New York: HarperCollins.

Drucker, P. (1994). The theory of the business. *Harvard Business Review,* (September–October), 95–104.

Drucker, P. (1998). Management's new paradigms. *Forbes,* (October 5), 152–77.

Drucker, P. (1999). *Management challenges for the 21st century.* New York: Harper Business.

Duncan, W. J., Ginter, P. M., and Kreidel, W. K. (1994). A sense of direction in public organizations: An analysis of mission statements in state health departments. *Administration and Society, 26*(1), 11–27.

Dunkle, R. E. (1984). An historical perspective on social services delivery to the elderly. *Journal of Gerontological Social Work, 7*(3), 5–18.

Early and Periodic Screening, Diagrams, and Treatment Program of 1967, 42 U.S.C. 501 et seq.

Editorial comment. (1952). *Medical Social Work, 2*(2), 121–22.

Edmondson, A. (1999). Psychological safety and learning behavior in work teams. *Administrative Science Quarterly, 44*, 350–83.

Education for All Handicapped Children Act of 1975, 20 U.S.C. 1400 et seq.

Edward, J. (1999). Is managed mental health treatment psychotherapy? *Clinical Social Work Journal, 27*(1), 87–102.

Egnew, R. C. (1997). Developing relevant public sector outcome measures. *Administration in Social Work, 21*(2), 77–80.

Ell, K., and Northen, H. (1990). *Families and health care: Psychosocial practice.* New York: Aldine de Gruyter.

Emerson, C. P. (1910). Social service department of general hospital. *National Hospital Record.*

Employee Retirement Income Security Act of 1974, 29 U.S.C. 1001 et seq.

Enthoven, A. (1993). The history and principles of managed competition. *Health Affairs,* (Supp.), 24–48.

Epstein, M. W., and Aldredge, P. (2000). *Good but not perfect: A case study of managed care.* Boston: Allyn & Bacon.

Erickson, A. G., Moynihan, F. M., and Williams, B. L. (1991). A family practice model for the 1990s. *Families in Society, 75*, 36–46.

Etzioni, A. (1964). *Modern organizations.* Englewood Cliffs, NJ: Prentice Hall.

Ezell, M. (1994). Advocacy practice of social workers. *Families in Society, 75*(1), 36–46.

Fair Housing Amendment of 1988, 42 U.S.C. 3601 et seq.

Farley, J. E. (1994). Transitions in psychiatric inpatient clinical social work. *Social Work, 29*(2), 207–12.

Fein, R. (1986). *Medical care: Medical costs.* Cambridge, MA: Harvard University Press.

Feldblum, C. R. (1991). Employment protections. *Milbank Quarterly, 69* (supp. 1–2), 81–110.

Fellin, P. (1995). Emergency of social class and ethnic minority neighborhoods. In *The community and the social worker* (pp. 96–113). Itasca, IL: Peacock.

Fine, S., and Glasser, P. (1996). *The first helping interview.* Thousand Oaks, CA: Sage.

First Annual Report of Social Work Permitted at the Massachusetts General Hospital: October 1, 1905, to October 1, 1906. (1906). Boston: Fort Hill Press.

Flexner, A. (1915). Is social work a profession? *National Conference of Charities and Correctional Proceedings* (pp. 576–90). Chicago: Hildemann.

Flynn, J. (1992). *Social agency policy: Analysis and presentation for community practice.* Chicago: Nelson-Hall.

Fortune, A., and Reid, W. J. (1999). *Research in social work* (3rd ed.). New York: Columbia University Press.

Fortune, A. (1995). Termination in direct practice. In R. L. Edwards (Ed.), *Encyclopedia of social work* (19th ed.) (pp. 2398–403). Washington, DC: NASW Press.

Fortune, A. (1999). Editorial: Intervention research. *Social Work Research, 23*(1), 2–3.

Foster, Z. (1997). Mutual help for emphysema patients: Veterans Administration Medical Center. In T. S. Kerson (Ed.), *Social work in health settings: Practice in context* (2nd ed.) (pp. 375–90). New York: Haworth.

Frank, P. B., and Golden, G. K. (1992). Blaming by naming: Battered women and the epidemic of codependence. *Social Work, 37*(1), 5–14.

Frankel, D., Harmon, L. I., and Kerson, T. S. (1997). Children's intensive case management in an urban community mental health center. In T. S. Kerson (Ed.), *Social work in health settings: Practice in context* (2nd ed.) (pp. 539–60). New York: Haworth.

Frankena, W. (1973). *Ethics.* New York: Prentice-Hall.

Freud, A. (1946). *Ego and the mechanisms of defense.* New York: International Universities Press.

Fritz, R. (1989). *Path of least resistance.* New York: Fawcett-Columbine.

Gage, B. (1998). The history and growth of Medicare managed care. *Generations, 22*(2), 11–18.

Galambos, C. (1999). Resolving ethical conflicts in a managed health care environment. *Health and Social Work, 24*(3), 191–97.

Gambrill, E. (1999a). Evidence-based practice: An alternative to authority-based practice. *Families in Society, 80*(6), 341–50.

Gambrill, E. (1999b). *Social work practice: A critical thinker's guide.* New York: Oxford University Press.

Garrett, L. (2000). *Betrayal of trust: The collapse of global public health.* New York: Hyperion.

Garvin, D. A. (1993). Building a learning organization. *Harvard Business Review,* (July-August), 78–91.

Gary, L. (1996). Foreword. In Y. Asamoah (Ed.), *Innovations in delivering culturally sensitive social work services: Challenges for practice and education* (pp. i–xii). New York: Haworth.

Gaudin, J. M. (1988). Treatment of families who neglect their children. In E. W. Nunnally, C. S. Chilman, and F. M. Cox (Eds.). *Mental Illness, Delinquency, Addictions, and Neglect* (pp. 167–88). Newbury Park, CA: Sage.

Gazmararian, J. (1999). Health literacy among Medicare enrollees in a managed care organization. *Journal of the American Medical Association, 281*(6), 545–51.

Gelfand, D., and Bechill, W. (1991). The evolution of the Older Americans Act: A 25-year review of the legislative changes. *Generations, 15*(3), 19–22.

Geller, J. L. (1996). Mental health services of the future: Managed care, unmanaged care, mismanaged care. *Smith College Studies in Social Work, 66*(3), 223–39.

Germain, C. B. (1979). Introduction: Ecology and social work. In C. B. Germain (Ed.), *Social work practice: People and environments* (pp. 1–22). New York: Columbia University Press.

Germain, C. B., and Gitterman, A. (1995). Ecological perspective. In R. L. Edwards (Ed.), *Encyclopedia of social work* (19th ed.) (pp. 816–24). Washington, DC: NASW Press.

Germain, C. B., and Gitterman, A. (1996). *The life model of social work practice: Advances in theory and practice* (2nd ed.). New York: Columbia University Press.

Germain, C. B. (1984). *Social work practice in health care: An ecological perspective.* New York: Free Press.

Getzel, G. S. (1991). Survival modes for people with AIDS in groups. *Social Work, 36*(1), 7–11.

Gibelman, M., and Whiting, L. (1999). Negotiating and contracting in a managed care environment: Considerations for practitioners. *Health and Social Work, 24*(3), 180–90.

Gilbert, D. (1937). The dilemma of medical social work. *Journal of Social Work Process, 1*(1), 127–47.

Gilbert, N., Specht, H., and Terrell, P. (1993). *Dimensions of social welfare policy* (3rd ed.). Englewood Cliffs, NJ: Prentice Hall.

Gilgun, J. F. (1994). An ecosystems approach to assessment. In B. R. Compton and B. Galaway, *Social work processes* (6th ed.)(pp. 380–94). Pacific Grove, CA: Brooks/Cole.

Gitterman, A., and Shulman, L. (1994). *Mutual aid groups, vulnerable populations, and the life cycle* (2nd ed.). New York: Columbia University Press.

Gitterman, A. (1991). Introduction to social work practice with vulnerable populations. In A. Gitterman (Ed.), *Handbook of social work practice with vulnerable populations* (pp. 1–34). New York: Columbia University Press.

Goffee, R., and Jones, G. (1996). What holds the modern company together? *Harvard Business Review,* (November–December), 133–45.

Goffman, E. (1972). *Relations in Public.* New York: Harper & Row.

Goldstein, E. G. (1995). *Ego psychology and social work practice* (2nd ed.). New York: Free Press.

Goldstein, H. (1983). Starting where the client is. *Social Casework, 64* (May), 267–75.

Gomez, J. S., and Michaelis, R. C. (1995). An assessment of burnout in human services providers. *Journal of Rehabilitation, 61,* 23–26.

Gordon, W. (1969). Basic constructs for an integrative and generative conception/social work. In G. Hearn (Ed.), *The general systems approach: Contributions toward an holistic conception of social work* (pp. 5–12). New York: Council on Social Work Education.

Gostin, L. O., and Looney, B. L. (1995). Disability: Legal issues. In W. T. Reich (Ed.), *Encyclopedia of bioethics* (Rev. ed.) (pp. 622–26). New York: Macmillan.

Gostin, L. O., Turek-Brezina, J., Powers, M., Kozloff, R., Faden, R., and Steinauer, D. (1993). Privacy and security of personal information in a new health care system. *Journal of the American Medical Association, 270*(20), 2487–93.

Government Performance and Results Act of 1993, P. L. 103–62, August 3, 1993.

Grant, D., and Haynes, D. (1996). A developmental framework for cultural competence training with children. In P. Ewalt, E. Freeman, S. Kirk, and D. Poole (Eds.), *Multicultural issues in social work* (pp. 382–99). Washington, DC: NASW Press.

Grasso, A. J. (1993). Developmental social administration. *Administration in Social Work, 17*(2), 17–29.

Green, J. W. (1998). *Cultural awareness in the human services: A multi-ethnic approach* (3rd ed.). Needham Heights, MA: Allyn & Bacon.

Greene, R. R., and Watkins, M. (1998). Ecological perspective: Meeting the challenge of practice with diverse populations. In R. R. Greene and M. Watkins (Eds.), *Serving diverse constituencies: Applying the ecological perspective* (pp. 1–28). New York: Aldine de Gruyter.

Griffiths, L. (1997). Accomplishing team: Teamwork and categorization in two community mental health teams. *Sociological Review, 45*(2), 59–78.

Gripton, J., and Valentich, M. (1983). Assessing sexual concerns of clients with health problems. In L. Lister and D. A. Shore (Eds.), *Human sexuality in medical social work* (pp. 53–66). New York: Haworth.

Grumbach, K. (1999). Primary care in the United States: The best of times, the worst of times. *New England Journal of Medicine, 341*(26), 2008–10.

Gummer, B., and McCallion, P. (1995). *Total quality management in the social services: Theory and practice.* Albany: State University of New York Press.

Gur, R. E., Cowell, P. E, Latshaw, A., Turetsky, B. I., Grossman, R. I., Arnold, S. E., Bilker, W. B., and Gur, R. G. (2000). Reduced dorsal and orbital prefrontal gray matter volumes in schizophrenia. *Archives of General Psychiatry 57*(8), 761–68.

Guterman, N. B., and Bragal, D. (1996). Social workers' perceptions of their power and service outcomes. *Administration in Social Work, 20*(3), 1–20.

Gutierrez, L. (1990). Working with women of color: An empowerment perspective. *Social Work 35*(2), 149–53.

Hamel, G. (1996). Strategy as revolution. *Harvard Business Review,* (July–August), 69–82.

Hamel, G. (1998). Strategic innovation and the quest for value. *Sloan Management Review, 39* (Winter), 7–14.

Hamel, G., and Prahalad, C. (1989). Strategic intent. *Harvard Business Review,* (May–June), 63–76.

Hammer, D. L., and Kerson, T. S. (1998). Reducing the number of days for which insurers deny payment to the hospital: One primary objective for a newly configured department of case management. *Social Work in Health Care, 28*(2), 31–49.

Hammer, D. L., and Kerson, T. S. (1997). Discharge planning in a community hospital: A patient whose symptoms the system could not manage. In T. S. Kerson (Ed.), *Social work in health settings: Practice in context* (2nd ed.) (pp. 227–41). New York: Haworth.

Hancock, M. R. (1997). *Principles of social work practice.* New York: Haworth.

Hartman, A., and Laird, J. (1983). *Family-centered social work practice.* New York: Free Press.

Hartman, A. (1978). Diagrammatic assessment of family relationships. *Social Casework, 59*(8), 465–76.

Hartz, G. W., and Splain, D. M. (1997). *Psychosocial intervention in long-term care: An advanced guide.* New York: Haworth.

Hasenfeld, Y., and Patti, R. (1992). Management activities and information utilization. In A. Grasso and I. Epstein (Eds.), *Research utilization in the social services.* New York: Haworth.

Hasenfeld, Y. (1992). (Ed.). *Human services in complex organizations.* Newbury Park, CA: Sage.

Hatry, H. P. (1997). Outcomes measurement and social services: Public and private sector perspectives. In E. J. Mullen and J. L. Magnabosco (Eds.), *Outcome measurement in the human services: Cross-cutting issues and methods* (pp. 3–19). Washington, DC: NASW Press.

Heifetz, R. A., and Laurie, D. L. (1997). The work of leadership. *Harvard Business Review*, (January–February), 124–34.

Heilbrun, C. (1988). *Writing a woman's life*. New York: Norton.

Heimer, C., and Stevens, M. (1997). Caring for the organization: Social workers as frontline risk managers in neonatal intensive care units. *Work and Occupations, 24*(2), 133–63.

Henry, R. M. (1996). Psychodynamic group therapy with adolescents: Exploration of HIV-related risk taking. *International Journal of Group Psychotherapy, 46*(2), 229–53.

Hepworth, D. H., and Larson, J. A. (1986). Negotiating goals and formulating a contract. In *Direct social work practice: Theories and skills* (pp. 300–35). Homewood, IL: Dorsey Press.

Hepworth, D., Larsen, J., and Rooney, R. (1997). *Direct social work practice*. Pacific Grove, CA: Brooks/Cole.

Hodgkin, D., Horgan, C. M., and Garnick, D. W. (1997). Make or buy: HMOs' contracting arrangements for mental health care. *Administration and Policy in Mental Health Care, 24*(4), 359–74.

Hollis, F. (1970). The psychosocial approach to the practice of casework. In R. W. Roberts and R. H. Nee (Eds.), *Theories of social casework* (pp. 33–76). Chicago: University of Chicago Press.

Hollis, F., and Woods, M. E. (1981). *Casework: A psychosocial therapy* (3rd ed.). New York: Random House.

Hooyman, N. R., and Kiyak, H. A. (1993). *Social gerontology: A multidisciplinary perspective*. Boston: Allyn & Bacon.

Hoyt, M. F. (1994). Characteristics of psychotherapy under managed behavioral health care. *Behavioral Healthcare Tomorrow, 3*(5), 59–62.

Hudson, W. W., and McMurtry, S. L. (1997). Comprehensive assessment in social work practice: The multi-problem screening inventory. *Research on Social Work Practice, 7*, 79–98.

Hudson, W. W. (1997). Assessment tools as outcome measures in social work. In E. J. Mullen and J. L. Magnabosco (Eds.). *Outcome measurement in the human services: Cross-cutting issues and methods* (pp. 68–80). Washington, DC: NASW Press.

Hudson, W. W. (1997). Assessment tools as outcomes measures in social work. In E. J. Mullen and J. L. Magnabosco (Eds.), *Outcomes measurement in the human services* (pp. 68–80). Washington, DC: NASW Press.

Hudson, W. W., Nurius, P., and Reisman, S. (1988). Computerized assessment instruments: Their promise and problems. *Computers in Human Services, 3*, 51–70.

Hughes, W. C. (1999). Managed care, meet community support: Ten reasons to include direct support services in every behavioral health plan. *Health and Social Work, 24*(2), 103–11.

Icard, L. D., Schilling, R. F., and El-Bassel, N. (1995). Reducing HIV infection among African Americans by targeting the African American family. *Social Work Research, 19*(3), 153–63.

Idle, J. R. (2000). The heart of psychotropic drug therapy. *Lancet 355*(9217), 1824–25.

Iglehart, J. K. (1999a). The American health care system: Medicaid. *New England Journal of Medicine, 340*(5), 403–8.

Iglehart, J. K. (1999b). The American health care system: Medicare. *New England Journal of Medicine, 340*(4), 327–32.

Individuals with Disabilities Education Act of 1992, 20 U.S.C. 1400 et seq.

Indyk, D., Belville, R., Lachapelle, S., Gordon, G., and Dewart, T. (1993). Community-based approach to HIV case management: Systematizing the unmanageable. *Social Work, 38*(4), 380–87.

Ingersoll, V. H., and Adams, G. B. (1992). *The tacit organization.* Greenwich, CT: JAI Press.

Ivey, A. (1994). *Intentional interviewing and counseling: Facilitating client development in a multicultural society.* Pacific Grove, CA: Brooks/Cole.

Jackson, V. H. (Ed.). (1995). *Managed care resource guide for social workers in agency settings.* Washington, DC: National Association of Social Workers.

Jansson, B., and Simmons, J. (1986). The survival of social work units in host organizations. *Social Work, 31*(5), 339–43.

Jarrett, M. (1919). *The psychiatric thread running through all social casework.* National Conference of Social Work. Atlantic City, New Jersey.

Jehn, K. A. (1997). A qualitative analysis of conflict types and dimensions in organizational groups. *Administrative Science Quarterly, 42,* 530–57.

Johnstone, E. C. (Ed.). (1999). *Schizophrenia: Concepts and clinical management.* New York: Cambridge University Press.

Kagle, J. D., and Kopels, S. (1994). Confidentiality after Tarasoff. *Health and Social Work, 19*(3), 217–22.

Kahn, S. (1995). Community organization. In R. L. Edwards (Ed.), *Encyclopedia of social work* (19th ed.) (pp. 569–76). Washington, DC: NASW Press.

Kaluzny, A., and Hernandez, S. (1988). Organizational change and innovation. In S. Shortell and A. Kaluzny (Eds.), *Healthcare management: A text in organizational theory and behavior* (pp. 379–417). New York: Wiley.

Kane, R. L., and Kane, R. A. (2000). *Assessing older persons: Measures, meaning, and practical applications.* New York: Oxford University Press.

Kanter, J. (1996). Depression, diabetes, and despair: Clinical case management in a managed care context. *Smith College Studies in Social Work, 66*(3), 358–69.

Kao, R. S., and Lam, M. L. (1997). Asian American elderly. In E. Lee (Ed.), *Working with Asian Americans: A guide for practitioners* (pp. 208–23). New York: Guilford.

Kaplan, H. I., and Sadock, B. J. (1995). *Comprehsive textbook of psychiatry.* Philadephia: Williams & Wilkins.

Kaplan, H. S. (1995). *The sexual desire disorders.* New York: Brunner/Mazel.

Kaplan, R. S., and Norton, D. P. (1992). The balanced scorecard: Measures that drive performance. *Harvard Business Review,* (January–February), 71–79.

Kaplan, R. S., and Norton, D. P. (1996a). Linking the balanced scorecard to strategy. *California Management Review, 39*(1), 53–79.

Kaplan, R. S., and Norton, D. P. (1996b). Using the balanced scorecard as a strategic management system. *Harvard Business Review*, (January–February), 75–85.

Kaplan, R. S., and Norton, D. P. (1996c). *The balanced scorecard: Translating strategy into action.* Boston: Harvard Business School Press.

Karls, J. M., and Wandrei, K. E. (Eds.). (1994a). *Person-in-environment system: The PIE classification system for social functioning problems.* Washington, DC: NASW Press.

Karls, J. M., and Wandrei, K. E. (Eds.). (1994b). *PIE Manual: Person-in-environment system.* Washington, DC: NASW Press.

Karoly, L. A., Greenwood, P. W., Everingham, S. S., Hoube, J., Kilburn, M. E., Rydell, C. P., Sanders, M., and Chiesa, J. (1998). *Investing in our children: What we know and don't know about the costs and benefits of early childhood interventions.* Santa Monica, CA: RAND.

Karp, N., and Wood, E. (1998). Resolving managed care disputes: Where do we stand? *Generations, 22*(2), 79–81.

Karp, N. (1996). Individualizing wrap-around services for children with emotional, behavioral and mental disorders. In G. H. S. Singer, L. E. Powers, and A. L. Olson (Eds.), *Redefining family support: Innovations in public-private partnerships* (pp. 291–310). Baltimore: Brookes.

Katzenbach, J. R., and Smith, D. K. (1998). The discipline of teams. In J. R. Katzenbach (Ed.), *The work of teams* (pp. 205–17). Boston: Harvard Business School Press.

Katzenbach, J. R. (Ed.). (1998). *The work of teams.* Boston: Harvard Business School Press.

Keefe, R. S., and Harvey, P. D. (1994). *Understanding schizophrenia: A guide to the new research on causes and treatment.* New York: Free Press.

Keks, N., Mazumdar, P., and Steele, K. (2000). The new antipsychotics: How much better are they? *Australian Family Physician, 29*(5), 445–50.

Kelley, M. L., and Stokes, T. F. (1984). Student-teachers contracting with goal setting for maintenance. *Behavior Modification, 8*(2), 223–44.

Kenney, J. J. (1990). Social work management in emerging health care systems. *Health and Social Work, 15*(1), 22–31.

Kerson, T. S. (1978a). Sixty years ago: Hospital social work in 1918. *Social Work in Health Care, 4*(3), 331–43.

Kerson, T. S. (1978b). The social work relationship: A form of gift exchange. *Social Work, 23*, 326–27.

Kerson, T. S. (1978c). *Eleven medical social work interviews: A contribution to the oral history of social work in health care.* Boston: Archives, Simmons College School of Social Work.

Kerson, T. S. (1981). *Medical social work: The pre-professional paradox.* New York: Irvington.

Kerson, T. S. (Ed.). (1997). *Social work in health settings: Practice in context* (2nd ed.). New York: Haworth.

Kerson, T. S., and Kerson, L. A. (1985). *Understanding chronic illness: The medical and psychosocial dimensions of nine diseases.* New York: Free Press.

Kettner, P. M., Maroney, R. M., and Martin, L. L. (1999). *Designing and managing programs: An effectiveness-based approach* (2nd ed.). Thousand Oaks, CA: Sage.

Kirk, S., and Kutchins, H. (1992). *The selling of DSM: The rhetoric of science in psychiatry*. New York: Aldine de Gruyter.

Knight, C. (1990). Use of support groups with adult female survivors of child sexual abuse. *Social Work, 35*(3), 202–6.

Koeske, G., Koeske, R., and Mallinger, J. (1993). Perceptions of professional competence: Cross-disciplinary ratings of psychologists, social workers, and psychiatrists. *American Journal of Orthopsychiatry, 63*, 45–54.

Kohl v. Woodhaven Learning Center, 865 F. 2d 930 (8th Cir. 1989).

Koop, C. E. (1993). Will the crisis in health care deprive us of its opportunities? *Transactions and Studies of the College of Physicians, Series 5,* (15), 57–66.

Kopels, S. (1995). The Americans with Disabilities Act: A tool to combat poverty. *Journal of Socal Work Education, 31*(3), 337–46.

Kopels, S., and Kagle, J. D. (1993). Do social workers have a duty to warn? *Social Service Review, 67*(1), 101–26.

Kopp, R. R. (1995). *Metaphor therapy: Using client-generated metaphors in psychotherapy*. New York: Brunner/Mazel.

Kotter, J. (1979). *Power in management*. New York: American Management Association.

Kotter, J. (1996). *Leading change*. Cambridge, MA: Harvard Business School Press.

Kugelman, W. (1992). Social work ethics in the practice arena: A qualitative study. *Social Work in Health Care, 17*(4), 59–77.

Kuhn, T. (1970). *The structure of scientific revolutions*. Chicago: University of Chicago Press.

Kulys, R., and Davis, M. (1987). Nurses and social workers: Rivals in the provision of social services? *Health and Social Work, 12*, 101–12.

Kurtz, P. D. (1998). A case study of a network as a learning organization. *Administration in Social Work, 22*(2), 57–74.

Kutchins, H., and Kirk, S. (1987). DSM-III and social work malpractice. *Social Work, 32*(3), 205–11.

Kutchins, H., and Kirk, S. (1997). *Making us crazy DSM: The psychiatric bible and the creation of mental disorders*. New York: Free Press.

Kutchins, H. (1991). The fiduciary relationship: The legal basis for social workers' responsibilities to clients. *Social Work, 36*(2), 106–14.

Kuttner, R. (1999). The American health care system: Health insurance coverage. *New England Journal of Medicine, 340*(2), 163–68.

Lamanna, M. A. (1999). Living the postmodern dream: Adolescent women's discourse on relationships, sexuality, and reproduction. *Journal of Family Issues, 20*(2), 181–217.

Landers, S. (1997a). Leaving agency to go solo calls for caution. *NASW News, 42*(9), 3.

Landers, S. (1997b). Standing up to a managed care goliath. *NASW News, 42*(6), 3.

Langwell, K., and Menke, T. (1991). *Rising health care costs: Causes, implications and strategies*. Washington, DC: Congressional Budget Office.

Lauffer, A (1982). *Assessment tools for practitioners, managers, and trainers.* Beverly Hills, CA: Sage.

Lee, E. (1997). Chinese American families. In E. Lee (Ed.), *Working with Asian Americans: A guide for practitioners* (pp. 46–78). New York: Guilford.

Lee, P. (1929). Presidential address. *National Conference of Charities and Corrections Proceedings* (pp. 2–20). Chicago: University of Chicago Press.

Leeuw, F., and Sonnichsen, R. (1994). Evaluation and organizational learning: International perspectives. In F. Leeuw, R. Rist, and R. Sonnichsen (Eds.), *Can governments learn?* New Brunswick, NJ: Transaction.

Leiby, J. (1984). Charity organization reconsidered. *Social Service Review, 58,* 523–38.

Leveille, S., Guralnik, J., Ferrucci, L., Corti, M., Kaspar, J., and Fried, L. (1998). Black/white differences in the relationship between MMSE scores and disability: The women's health and aging study. *Journals of Gerontology, Series B: Psychological and Social Sciences, 53B*(3), 201–8.

Levine, C. (Ed.). (1989). *Cases in bioethics: Selections from the Hastings Center Report.* New York: St. Martin's Press.

Levinson, H. (1992). Fads, fantasies, and psychological management. *Psychology Journal,* (Winter), 1–12.

Levinson, H. (1996). When executives burn out. *Harvard Business Review,* (July–August), 152–63.

Levit, K. R., Lazenby, H. C., Braden, B. R., and the National Health Accounts Team. (1998). National health spending trends in 1996. *Health Affairs, 17*(1), 35–51.

Levitt, J. L., and Reid, W. J. (1981). Rapid assessment instruments for practice. *Social Work Research and Abstracts, 17*(1), 13–19.

Lewis, J. A., Lewis, M. B., Packard, T. and Souflee, F., Jr. (2001). *Management of human services programs* (3rd ed.). Monterey, CA: Brooks/Cole.

Lewis, O. M. (1944). Social care of syphilis. In E. M. Cresswell (Ed.), *Functional casework in a medical setting.* Philadelphia: Pennsylvania School of Social Work.

Libby, A. M. (1997). Contracting between public and private providers: A survey of metal health services in California. *Administration and Policy in Mental Health, 24*(4), 323–38.

Lieberman, F. (1982). The triangle: The worker, the client, and the agency. *Clinical Social Work Journal, 10,* 77–90.

Linhorst, D. (1988). The development of a program evaluation system for psychosocial rehabilitation centers. *Psychosocial Rehabilitation Journal, 12*(2), 35–43

Lister, L., and Shore, D. A. (Eds.). (1983). *Human sexuality in medical social work.* New York: Haworth.

Litzelfelner, P., and Petr, C. (1997). Case advocacy in child welfare. *Social Work, 42*(4), 392–402.

Livingston, G., Manela, M., and Katona, C. (1997). Depression and other psychiatric morbidity in cases of elderly people living at home. *British Medical Journal, 312*(7024), 153–57.

Lockery, S. A., Dunkle, R. E., Kart, C. S., and Coulton, C. J. (1994). Factors contributing to the early rehospitalization of elderly people. *Health and Social Work, 19*(3), 182–91.

Loeb, M. B. (1960). The backdrop for social research: Theory-making and model-building. In L. S. Kogan (Ed.), *Social science theory and social work research*. New York: NASW.

Lubove, R. (1975). *The Professional Altruist*. New York: Atheneum.

Ludmerer, K. (1999). *Time to heal: American medical education from the turn of the century to the era of managed care*. New York: Oxford University Press.

Mackelprang, R. W., and Salsgiver, R. O. (1996). People with disabilities and social work: Historical and contemporary issues. *Social Work, 41*(1), 7–14.

MacNair, R, H. (1996). Theory for community practice in social work: The example of ecological community practice. *Journal of Community Practice, 3*(3/4), 181–202.

Magney, J. (1996). Teamwork and the need for cooperative learning. *Labor Law Journal, 47*(8), 564–70.

Maher, C. A. (1987). Involving behaviorally disordered adolescents in instructional planning: Effectiveness of the goal procedure. *Child and Adolescent Psychotherapy, 4*(3), 185–89.

Makar, K., Cumming, C. E., Lees, A. W., Hundleby, M., Nabholtz, J. M., Kieren, D. K., Jenkins, H., Wentzel, C., Handman, M., and Cumming, D. C. (1997). Sexuality, body image, and quality of life after high dose or conventional chemotherapy for metastatic breast cancer. *Canadian Journal of Human Sexuality, 6*(1), 1–8.

Mama, R. S., and Kerson, T. S. (1994). Area project on occupational health and safety. In T. S. Kerson (Ed.), *Field instruction in social work settings* (pp. 123–38). New York: Haworth.

Managed care and patient protection: Major issues addressed by pending legislation. (1999). *Congressional Digest, 78*(10).

Mangalmurti, V. S. (1994). Psychotherapists' fear of Tarasoff: All in the mind? *Journal of Psychiatry and Law, 22*(3), 379–409.

Manning, S. S. (1997). The social worker as moral citizen: Ethics in action. *Social Work, 32*(3), 223–30.

Manning, W., Wells, K., Duan, H., Newhouse, J., and Ware, J. (1986). How cost sharing affects the use of ambulatory mental health services. *Journal of the American Medical Association, 256*, 1930–34.

Marchett, D. (1999). Velo-cardio-facial syndrome: Parent and family information booklet. http://www.crosslink.net/marchett/vcfs/auspar.htm.

Marmor, T., and Oberlander, J. (1998). Rethinking Medicare reform. *Health Affairs, 17*(1), 52–68.

Marquis, M. S., and Long, S. H. (1999). Trends in managed care and managed competition, 1993–1997. *Health Affairs, 18*(6), 78–83.

Marti-Costa, S., and Serrano-Gracia, I. (1995). Needs assessment and community development: An ideological perspective. In J. Rothman, J. L. Erlich, and J. E. Trotman (Eds.), *Strategies of community intervention* (5th ed.) (pp. 256–74). Itasca, IL: Peacock.

Martin, D. A., Conley, R. W., and Noble, J. H. (1995). The ADA and disability benefits policy. *Journal of Disability Policy Studies, 6*(2), 1–15.

Martin, J. (1992). *Cultures in organizations: Three perspectives*. New York: Oxford University Press.

Martin, J. A. (1997). Mental health care in a combat environment: The application of small unit stress debriefings. In T. S. Kerson (Ed.), *Social work in health settings: Practice in context* (2nd ed.) (pp. 561–80). New York: Haworth.

Martin, L., and Kettner, P. (1997). Performance measurement: The new accountability. *Administration in Social Work, 21*(1), 17–29.

Martin, L. I. (1993). Total Quality Management. *Administration in Social Work, 17*(2), 1–16.

Mattaini, M., and Kirk, S. (1991). Assessing assessment in social work. *Social Work, 36*(3), 260–66.

Mattaini, M. (1993). *More than a thousand words: Graphics for clinical practice.* Washington, DC: NASW Press.

Mattaini, M. A. (1997*). Clinical practice with individuals.* Washington, DC: NASW Press.

Matthews, W. J. (1997–1998). *Current thinking and research in brief therapy solutions, strategies, narratives* (2 vols.). Philadelphia: Bruner/Mazel.

Maynard-Moody, S., and McClintock, C. (1987). Weeding an old garden: Toward a new understanding of organizational goals. *Administration and Society, 19*(1), 123–42.

McGoldrick, M., and Gerson, R. (1985). *Genograms in family assessment.* New York: Norton.

McGowan, B. G. (1996). Values and ethics. In C. H. Meyer and M. A. Mattaini (Eds.), *The foundation of social work practice: A graduate text* (pp. 28–41). Washington, DC: NASW Press.

McKusick, V. A. (1999). Velocardiofacial syndrome. http://www3.ncbi.nlm.nih.gov:80/htbin-post/Omim/dispmiml192430.

McMurtry, S. L., Kettner, P. M., and Netting, F. E. (1992). Strategic choices made by nonprofit agencies serving low-paying clients. In T. Mizrahi (Ed.), *Community organization and social administration: Advances, trends, emerging principles* (pp. 107–25). New York: Haworth.

Medicaid, 42 U.S.C. 1396a.

Medicare, 42 U.S.C. 1395cc.

Menefee, D. (1997). Strategic administration of nonprofit human service organizations: A model for executive success in turbulent times. *Administration in Social Work, 21*(2), 1–19.

Mental Health Parity Act of 1996, 42 U.S.C. 300gg-5. http://www.hcfa.gov/hipaa/mhpsum1.htm.

Mercer, S. O. (1996). Navajo elderly people in a reservation nursing home: Admission predictors and culture care practices. *Social Work, 41*(2), 181–89.

Mercer, S. O., Robinson, B., and Kerson, T. S. (1997). Alzheimer's disease: Intervention in a nursing home environment. In T. S. Kerson (Ed.), *Social work in health settings: Practice in context* (2nd ed.) (pp. 651–68). New York: Haworth.

Merriam-Webster's collegiate dictionary (10th ed.). (1993). Springfield, MA: Merriam-Webster.

Merritt, J., and Neugeboren, B. (1990). Factors affecting agency capacity for interorganizational coordination. *Administration in Social Work, 14*(4), 73–88.

Meyer, C. (1988). The eco-systems perspective. In R. Dorfman (Ed.), *Paradigms of clinical social work* (pp. 275–94). New York: Brunner/Mazel.

Meyer, C. (1998). How the right measures help teams excel. In J. R. Katzenbach (Ed.), *The work of teams* (pp. 51–64). Boston: Harvard Business School Press.

Meyer, C. (1993). *Assessment in Social Work*. New York: Columbia University Press.

Meyer, C. (Ed.). (1983). *Clinical social work in the eco-systems perspective*. New York: Columbia University Press.

Meyer, S., and Nash, S. C. (1994). *Prostate cancer: Making survival decisions*. Chicago: University of Chicago Press.

Meyers, M. K. (1993). Organizational factors in the integration of services for children. *Social Service Review, 67*(4), 547–75.

Mezzich, J. E., Kleinman, A., Fabrega, H., and Parron, D. (1996*). Culture and psychiatric diagnosis*. Washington, DC: American Psychiatric Press.

Michelsen, R. W. (1994). Social work practice with the elderly: A multifaceted placement experience, In T. S. Kerson (Ed.), *Field instruction in social work settings* (pp. 181–88). New York: Haworth.

Michelsen, R. W., and Kerson, T. S. (1997). Hospital-based case management for the frail elderly. In T. S. Kerson (Ed.), *Social work in health settings: Practice in context* (2nd ed.) (pp. 597–618). New York: Haworth.

Miller, D. C. (1991). *Handbook of research design and social movement* (5th ed.) Thousand Oaks, CA: Sage.

Miller, D. D. (2000). Review and management of clozapine side effects. *Journal of Clinical Psychiatry, 61*(Supp. 8), 14–17.

Milstein, R., and Slowinski, S. (1999). *The sexual male: Problems and solutions*. New York: Norton.

Minahan, A. (Ed.). (1981). Special issue: Conceptual frameworks II. *Social Work, 26*(1).

Minahan, A., and Briar, S. (Eds.). (1977). Special issue: Conceptual frameworks I. *Social Work, 22*(4).

Mintzberg, H., and Lampel, J. (1999). Reflecting on the strategy process. *Sloan Management Review, 40*(3), 21–30.

Mintzberg, H., and Quinn, J. B. (1991). *The strategy process: Concepts, contexts, cases* (2nd ed.). Englewood Cliffs, NJ: Prentice Hall.

Mintzberg, H., and Van der Heyden, L. (1999). Organigraphs: Drawing how companies really work. *Harvard Business Review,* (September–October), 87–94.

Mintzberg, H. (1994). *The rise and fall of strategic planning*. New York: Free Press.

Minuchin, S. (1974). *Families and family therapy*. Cambridge, MA: Harvard University Press.

Mizrahi, T., and Abramson, J. (1994). Collaboration between social workers and physicians: An emerging typology. In E. Sherman and W. J. Reid (Eds.). *Qualitative methods in social work practice* (pp. 135–51). New York: Columbia University Press.

Monahan, D. J., and Hooker, K. (1997). Caregiving and social support in two illness groups. *Social Work, 42*(3), 278–87.

Monkman, M. M. (1991). Outcome objectives in social work practice: Person and environment. *Social Work, 36*(3), 253–58.

Mordacci, R., and Sobel, R. (1998). Health: A comprehensive concept. *Hastings Center Report, 28*(January–February), 34–37.

Morrison, J. (1997). *When psychological problems mask medical disorders: A guide for psychotherapists.* New York: Guilford.

Morrison, J. D. (1991). The black church as a support system for black elderly. *Journal of Gerontological Social Work, 17*(2), 105–20.

Mossard, G. (1991). A TQM technical skills framework. *Journal of Management Science and Policy Analysis, 8*(3/4), 222–46.

Mullen, E. J., and Magnabosco, J. L. (1997). (Eds.). *Outcome measurement in the human services: Cross-cutting issues and methods.* Washington, DC: NASW Press.

Mulroy, E. A., and Shay, S. (1997). Nonprofit organizations and innovation: A model of neighborhood-based collaboration to prevent child maltreatment. *Social Work, 42*(5), 515–24.

Munson, C. E. (2000). *The mental health diagnostic desk reference: Visual guide and more for learning to use the diagnostic and statistical manual (DSM-IV).* New York: Haworth.

Murdach, A. D. (1995). Decision-making situations in health care. *Health and Social Work, 20*(3), 187–91.

National Association of Social Workers (NASW). (1996). *Code of Ethics.* Washington, DC: NASW Press.

National Association of Social Workers (NASW). (1999). *Are ethics and contemporary social work compatible?* [videotape]. Washington, DC: NASW Press.

National Conference of Commissioners on Uniform State Laws. (1999). Uniform Anatomical Gift Act of 1987. http://www.nccusl.org/summary/uaga87.html.

National Mental Health Association. (2001). http://www.nmha.org.

Netting, F. E., Kettner, P. M., and McMurtry, S. L. (1998). Understanding and analyzing community strengths and problems. In *Social work macro practice* (2nd ed.) (pp. 126–58). New York: Addison Wesley Longman.

Netting, F. E., Williams, F. G., Jones-McClintic, S., and Warrick, L. (1990). Policies to enhance coordination in hospital-based case management programs. *Health and Social Work, 15*(1), 15–21.

Neugeboren, B. (1996). Environmental practice in the human services: Integration of micro and macro roles, skills, and contexts. New York: Haworth.

Nicholi, A. M. (1999). *The Harvard guide to psychiatry* (3rd ed.). Cambridge, MA: Belknap.

Northen, H. (1995). *Clinical social work knowledge and skills* (2nd ed.). New York: Columbia University Press.

Nurius, P., and Hudson, W. (1993a). *Computer assisted practice: Theory, methods, and software.* Belmont, CA: Wadsworth.

Nurius, P., and Hudson, W. (1993b). *Human services practice, evaluation, and computers.* Pacific Grove, CA: Brooks/Cole.

Nurius, P. S., and Vourlekis, B. S. (1997). Comments and questions for outcome measurement in mental health and social work. In E. J. Mullen and J. L. Magnabosco (Eds.), *Outcome measurement in the human services: Cross-cutting issues and methods* (pp. 144–48). Washington, DC: NASW Press.

Nurius, P. S., Kemp, S. P., and Gibson, J. W. (1999). Practitioners' perspectives on sound reasoning: Adding a worker-in-context component. *Administration in Social Work, 23*(1), 1–27.

O'Brien, J. E. (1991). Merger problems for human service agencies: A case study. *Administration in Social Work, 15*(3), 19–28.

Occupational Safety and Health Act of 1970, 29 U.S.C. 651 et seq.

Occupational Safety and Health Administration. (2001). http://www.osha.gov.

Ogden, J. R., and Ogden, D. T. (1992). Perceptions of the community on the pricing of community mental health services. *Health Marketing Quarterly, 9*(3–4), 37–40.

O'Hare, T. (1996). Court-ordered versus voluntary clients: Problem differences and readiness for change. *Social Work, 41*(4), 417–22.

Olmstead v. *L. C.,* 119 S. Ct. 2176 (1999).

Omnibus Budget Reconciliation Act of 1990, 5 U.S.C. 7701(b)(2); sec. 831.204.

Oncken, W. J., and Wass, D. L. (1992). Management and time: Who's got the monkey? In J. J. Gabarro (Ed.), *Managing people and organizations* (pp. 501–56). Boston: Harvard Business School Press.

O'Neill, M. (1997). Residential care facility: Treatment of a child with severe disabilities. In T. S. Kerson (Ed.), *Social work in health settings: Practice in context* (2nd ed.) (pp. 207–24). New York: Haworth.

One hundred years of health-related social work. British Association of Social Workers, 1995.

Orlin, M. (1995). The Americans with Disabilities Act: Implications for social services. *Social Work, 40*(2), 233–39.

Overholser, L. C. (1994). *Ericksonian hypnosis: A handbook of clinical practice.* New York: Irvington.

Oxford English dictionary (compact edition). (1971). Oxford: Oxford University Press.

Panos, P. T., and Panos, A. J. (2000). A model for a culture-sensitive assessment of patients in health care settings. *Social Work in Health Care, 31*(1), 49–62.

Parad, H., and Parad, L. (1990). *Crisis intervention, book 2: The practitioner's source book for brief therapy.* Milwaukee: Family Service Association.

Parker, J. (1997). *Brief solution-focused therapy in health care settings* (videotape). Houston: University of Houston Graduate School of Social Work.

Patient Self-Determination Act (Omnibus Budget Reconciliation Act of 1990), 42 U.S.C. 1395cc (f)(l), 1396a (w)(l).

Patti, R. J. (1985). *Social work administration: Managing social programs in a developmental context.* Englewood Cliffs, NJ: Prentice Hall.

Patton, M. D. (1997). *Utilization-focused evaluation: The new century text.* Thousand Oaks, CA: Sage.

Peake, K., Brenner, B., and Rosenberg, G. (1998). Community development and lay participation. In H. Rehr, G. Rosenberg, and S. Blumenfield (Eds.), *Cre-*

ative social work in health care: Clients, the community, and your organization (pp. 103–15). New York: Springer.

Pearce, J. A., II, and David, F. R. (1987). Corporate mission statements and the bottom line. *Academy of Management Executive, 1*(2), 109–16.

Pekarik, G. (1996). *Psychotherapy abbreviation: A practical guide.* New York: Haworth.

Perlin, M. (1994). Law and the delivery of mental health services in the community. *American Journal of Orthopsychiatry, 64*(2), 194–208.

Perlman, H. H. (1979). *Relationship: The heart of helping people.* Chicago: University of Chicago Press.

Perlman, H. H. (1976). Believing and doing: Values in social work education. *Social Casework, 57,* 381–90.

Personal Responsibility and Work Opportunity Reconciliation Act of 1996, 42 U.S.C. 615 et seq.

Peters, T. J., and Waterman, T. (1982). How the best-run companies turn so-so performances into big winners. *Management Review, 71* (November–December), 8–16.

Pinderhughes, E. (1995). Empowering diverse populations. Family practice in the 21st century. *Families in Society, 76*(2), 131–40.

Plan for Achieving Self-Support, 42 U.S.C. 1202 et seq.

Posavac, E. and Carey, P. G. (1996). *Program evaluation methods and case studies* (5th ed.). Upper Saddle River, NJ: Prentice Hall.

Poulin, J. E., Walter, C. A., and Walker, J. L. (1994). Interdisciplinary team membership: A survey of gerontological social workers. *Journal of Gerontological Social Work, 22*(1/2), 93–107.

President's Commission for the Study of Ethical Problems in Medicine and Biomedical and Behavioral Research. (1982). *Making health care decisions: A report on the ethical and legal implications of informed consent in the patient-practitioner relationship.* Washington, DC: Government Printing Office.

Proctor, E. K., and Davis, L. E. (1994). The challenge of racial difference: Skills for clinical practice. *Social Work, 39*(13), 314–23.

Proctor, E. K., and Rosen, A. (1983). Problem formulation and its relation to treatment planning. *Social Work Research and Abstracts, 19*(3), 22–28.

Proctor, E. K., and Morrow-Howell, N. (1990). Complications in discharge planning with Medicare patients. *Health and Social Work, 15*(1), 45–54.

Proctor, E. K., Rosen, A., and Livne, S. (1985). Planning and direct practice. *Social Service Review, 59*(2), 161–77.

Pumphrey, M. W. (1986). Mary Ellen Richmond. In W. I. Trattner, (Ed.), *Biographical dictionary of social welfare in America* (pp. 622–25). New York: Greenwood.

Quam, J. K., and Abramson, M. S. (1991). The use of time lines and lifelines in work with chronically mentally ill people. *Health and Social Work, 16*(1), 27–33.

Raiff, N. R. (1993). *Advanced case management.* Newbury Park, CA: Sage.

Random House dictionary of the English language. (1973). New York: Random House.

Reamer, F. G. (1987). Informed consent in social work. *Social Work, 32*(5), 425–29.

Reamer, F. G. (1990). *Ethical dilemmas in social service* (2nd ed.). New York: Columbia University Press.

Reamer, F. G. (1991). AIDS, social work, and the "Duty to Warn." *Social Work, 36*(1), 56–60.

Reamer, F. G. (1995). *Social work values and ethics.* New York: Columbia University Press.

Reamer, F. G. (1998). The evolution of social work ethics. *Social Work, 43*(6), 488–500.

Rehabilitation Act of 1973, 29 U.S.C. 701 et seq.

Reich, R. (1998). Entrepreneurship reconsidered: The team as hero. In J. R. Katzenbach (Ed.), *The work of teams* (pp. 205–17). Boston: Harvard Business School Press.

Reich, W. T. (1995). Introduction. In W. T. Reich (Ed.), *Encyclopedia of bioethics* (Rev. ed.) (pp. xix–xxxii). New York: Macmillan.

Reid, K. E. (1991). Worker interventions. In *Social work practice with groups: A clinical approach* (pp. 147–72). Pacific Grove, CA: Brooks/Cole.

Reid, W. (1989). *Research in social work.* New York: Columbia. University Press.

Reid, W. J., and Shyne, A. W. (1969). *Brief and extended casework.* New York: Columbia University Press.

Reid, W. J. (1997). Long-term trends in clinical social work. *Social Service Review, 71* (June), 200–213.

Resnick, H., and Patti, R. J. (1980). *Change from within: Humanizing social welfare organizations.* Philadelphia: Temple University Press.

Retiring the Pacemaker. (1997). *Hastings Center Report, 27*(January–February), 24–26.

Rhodes, M. (1986). *Ethical dilemmas in social work practice.* Boston: Routledge and Kegan Paul.

Rhodes, M. (1992). Social work challenges: The boundaries of ethics. *Families in Society, 73*(1), 40–47.

Richmond, M. (1901). Charitable cooperation. In *Proceedings of the national conference of charities and corrections.* Boston: Elles.

Richmond, M. E. (1907). *The good neighbor in the modern city.* Philadelphia: Lippincott.

Richmond, M. E. (1917). *Social diagnosis.* New York: Russell Sage Foundation.

Richmond, M. E. (1922). *What is social casework?* New York: Russell Sage Foundation.

Riessman, F., and Carroll, D. (1995). *Redefining self-help in the human services: Policy and practice.* San Francisco: Jossey-Bass.

Roberts, R. W., and Nee, R. H. (Eds.). (1970). *Theories of social casework.* Chicago: University of Chicago Press.

Robinson, V. P. (1930). *The changing psychology of social casework.* Chapel Hill: University of North Carolina Press.

Robinson, V. P. (1978). *The development of a professional self: Teaching and learning in professional helping processes: Selected writings, 1930–1968.* New York: AMS Press.

Rocha, C. J., and Kabalka, L. E. (1999). A comparison study of access to health care under a Medicaid managed care program. *Health and Social Work, 24*(3), 169–79.

Rogers, C. R., and Roethlisberger, F. J. (1991). Barriers and gateways to communication. *HBR Classic,* 105–11.

Rohrer, J. E. (1996). *Planning for community-oriented health systems.* New York: American Public Health Association.

Rose, S. D. (1995). *Advocacy and empowerment: Mental health care in the community.* Paper presented at the annual meeting of the Council on Social Work Education, San Diego, CA.

Rose, S. D. (1981). Assessment in groups. *Social Work Research and Abstracts, 17*(1): 29–37.

Rosen, A. (1993). Systematic planned practice. *Social Service Review, 67*(1), 84–100.

Rosen, A., Proctor, E. K., and Staudt, M. M. (1999). Social work research and the quest for effective practice. *Social Work Research, 23*(1), 4–14.

Rosen, W. B. (1999). Moments of truth: Notes from a lesbian therapist. *Smith College Studies in Social Work, 69*(2), 293–308.

Rosenbaum, S., Serrano, R., Magar, M., and Stern, G. (1997). Civil rights in a changing health care system. *Health Affairs, 16*(1), 90–105.

Ross, J. W. (1992). Are social work ethics compromised? *Health and Social Work,* (3), 163–65.

Rossi, P. H. (1997). Program outcomes: Conceptual and measurement issues. In E. J. Mullen and J. L. Magnabosco (Eds.), *Outcome measurement in the human services: Cross-cutting issues and methods* (pp. 20–34). Washington, DC: NASW Press.

Rothbard, A. B., Kuno, E., Schinnar, A. P., Hadley, T. R., and Turk, R. (1999). Service utilization and cost of community care for discharged state hospital patients: A three-year follow-up study. *American Journal of Psychiatry, 156*(16), 20–28.

Rounds, K. A., Zipper, I. N., and Green, T. P. (1997). Social work practice in early intervention: Child service coordination in a rural health department. In T. S. Kerson (Ed.), *Social work in health settings: Practice in context* (2nd ed.) (pp. 111–29). New York: Haworth.

Rovner, J. (1999). The politics of patients' rights. *Business and Health, 17*(6a), 121–26.

Rowland, D., and Lyons, B. (1996). Medicare, Medicaid, and the elderly poor. *Health Care Financing Review, 18*(2), 61–69.

Royse, D., and Thyer, B. (1996). *Program evaluation: An introduction.* Chicago: Nelson-Hall.

Rozovsky, F. A. (1984). *Consent to treatment: A practical guide.* Boston: Little, Brown.

Ruderman, E. B. (1986). Gender-related themes of women psychotherapists in their treatment of women patients: The creative and reparative use of countertransference as a mutual growth experience. *Clinical Social Work Journal, 14*(2), 103–26.

Safran, D., Tarlov, A., and Rogers, W. (1994). Primary care performance in fee for service and prepaid health care systems. *Journal of the American Medical Association, 271,* 1579–86.

Saleeby, D. (Ed.). (1997). *The strengths perspective in social work practice* (2nd ed.). New York: Longman.

Saleeby, D. (1998). The strengths perspective: Principles and practices. In B. Compton and B. Galaway (Eds.), *Social work processes* (6th ed.) (pp. 14–27). Pacific Grove, CA: Brooks/Cole.

Salgo v. *Leland Stanford Jr. University Board of Trustees,* 154 Cal. App. 2d 560, 317 F. 2d 170, 1957.

Saltz, C. C., and Schaefer, T. (1996).Interdisciplinary teams in health care: Integration of family caregivers. *Social Work in Health Care, 22*(3), 59–70.

Sands, R. (1989). The social worker joins the team: A look at the socialization process. *Social Work in Health Care, 14*(2), 1–14.

Sands, R., Stafford, J., and McClelland, M. (1990). "I beg to differ": Conflict in the interdisciplinary team. *Social Work in Health Care, 14*(3), 55–72.

Scharfstein, B. A. (1989). *The dilemma of context.* New York: New York University Press.

Schatz, M. S., Jenkins, L. E., and Shaefor, B. W. (1990). Milford redefined: A model of generalist and advanced generalist social work. *Journal of Social Work Education, 26,* 217–31.

Schlesinger, B. (1996). The sexless years or sex rediscovered. *Journal of Gerontological Social Work, 26*(1/2), 117–31.

Schloendorff v. Society of New York Hospital, 105 N. E. 92 (1914).

Schlossberg, S. B., and Kagan, R. M. (1988). Prevention strategies for engaging chronic multiproblem families. *Social Casework, 69*(1), 3–9.

Schlossberger, E., and Hecker, L. (1996). HIV and family therapists' duty to warn: A legal and ethical analysis. *Journal of Marital and Family Therapy, 22*(1), 27–40.

Schmid, H. (1992). Strategic and structural change in human service organizations: The role of the environment. *Administration in Social Work, 16*(3/4), 167–86.

Schmid, W. (1997). Family-centered care: Life span issues in a spina bifida specialty care program. In T. S. Kerson (Ed.), *Social work in health settings: Practice in context* (2nd ed.) (pp. 165–88). New York: Haworth.

Schmidt-Posner, J., and Jerrell, J. M. (1998). Qualitative analysis of three case management programs. *Community Mental Health Journal, 34*(4), 381–93.

Scholes, R. (1998). *The rise and fall of English: Reconstructing English as a discipline.* New Haven, CT: Yale University Press.

Schopler, J. H., and Galinsky, M. J. (1995). Group practice overview. In R. L. Edwards (Ed.), *Encyclopedia of social work* (19th ed.) (pp. 1129–42). Washington, DC: NASW Press.

Schroeder, L. O. (1995). *The legal environment of social work.* Washington, DC: NASW Press.

Schwartz, W., and Zalba, S. (Eds.). (1971). *The practice of group work.* New York: Columbia University Press.

Schwartz, W. (1962). Toward a strategy of group work practice. *Social Service Review, 36*(3), 268–79.

Schwartz, W. (1971). On the use of groups in social work practice. In W. Schwartz and S. Zalba (Eds.), *The practice of group work* (pp. 22–34). New York: Columbia University Press.

Schwartz, W. (1994). Between client and system: The mediating function. In T. Berman-Rossi (Ed.), *Social work: The collected writings of William Schwartz* (pp. 324–46). Itasca, IL: Peacock.

Scialli, A. R. (Ed.). (1999). *Book of Women's Health*. New York: Morrow.

Scott, D. (1989). Meaning construction and social work practice. *Social Service Review, 63*(1), 39–51.

Segal, S. (1997). Outcome measurement systems in mental health: A program perspective. In E. J. Mullen and J. L. Magnabosco (Eds.), *Outcome measurement in the human services: Cross-cutting issues and methods* (pp. 149–59). Washington, DC: NASW Press.

Segal, S. P., and Specht, H. (1983). A Poor House in California, 1983: Oddity or Prelude? *Social Work, 28* (July–August), 319–23.

Segal, S. P. (1995). Deinstitutionalization. In R. L. Edwards (Ed.), *Encyclopedia of social work* (19th ed.) (pp. 704–12). Washington, DC: NASW Press.

Senge, P. (1990). *The fifth discipline: The art and practice of the learning organization*. New York: Currency Doubleday.

Senge, P. M., Roberts, C., Ross, R. B., Smith, B. J., and Kleiner, A. (1994). *The fifth discipline field book*. New York: Doubleday.

Shadish, W., Cook, T., and Leviton, L. (1993). *Foundations of program evaluation: Theories of practice*. Newbury Park, CA: Sage.

Shalala, D. (2000). Letter to Governors.

Shapiro, B. P. (1992). Functional integration: Getting all the troops to work together. In J. Gabarro (Ed.), *Managing people and organizations* (pp. 353–69). Boston: Harvard Business School Press.

Sheafor, B. W., Horesji, C. R., and Horejsi, G. A. (1991). *Techniques and guidelines for social work practice* (2nd ed.). Boston: Allyn & Bacon.

Sheafor, B., Horesji, C., and Horesji, G. (1988). *Techniques and guidelines for social work practice*. Newton, MA: Allyn & Bacon.

Sheppard, M. (1992). Contact and collaboration with general practitioners: A comparison of local workers and community psychiatric nurses. *British Journal of Social Work, 22,* 419–36.

Shern, D., and Trabin, T. (1997). System changes and accountability for behavioral health care/services: Lessons from the private and public sectors. In E. J. Mullen and J. L. Magnabosco (Eds.), *Outcome measurement in the human services: Cross-cutting issues and methods* (pp. 101–12). Washington, DC: NASW Press

Shortell, S., and Kaluzny, A. (1988). Organization theory and health care management. In S. Shortell and A. Kaluzny (Eds.), *Healthcare management: A text in organization theory and behavior* (pp. 5–37). New York: Wiley.

Silverman, P. R., and Worden, J. W. (1992). Children's reactions in the early months after the death of a parent. *American Journal of Orthopsychiatry, 62*(1), 93–104.

Simon, B. (1960). *Relationship between theory and practice in social casework*. New York: National Association of Social Workers.

Simon, B. (1990). Rethinking empowerment. *Journal of Progressive Human Services, 1,* 27–37.

Siporin, M. (1980). Ecological systems theory in social work. *Journal of Sociology and Social Welfare, 7*(4), 507–32.

Sledge, W. H., Moras, K., Hartley, D., and Levine, M. (1990). Effect of time-limited psychotherapy on patient dropout rates. *American Journal of Psychiatry, 147*(10), 1341–47.

Smalley, R. E. (1970). The functional approach to casework practice. In R. W. Roberts and R. H. Nee (Eds.), *Theories of social casework* (pp. 77–128). Chicago: University of Chicago Press.

Smyrnios, K. X., and Kirby, R. J. (1993). Long-term comparison of brief versus unlimited psychodynamic treatments with children and their parents. *Journal of Consulting and Clinical Psychology, 61*(6), 1020–27.

Social casework: Generic and specific. (1929). New York: American Association of Social Workers.

Social Security Act of 1935, 42 U.S.C. 1305.

Social Security Act Amendments of 1965, 42 U.S.C. sec. 1396 et seq.

Social Security Administration Publications. (2001). http://gopher.ssa.gov/work/self-referral.htm

Social Security Administration Publications. (2001). http://www.ssa.gov/pubs/englist.html.

Soskis, C., and Kerson, T. S. (1992). The Patient Self-Determination Act: Opportunity knocks again. *Social Work in Health Care, 16*(4), 1–18.

Spampneto, A. M., and Wadsworth, R. O. (1996). Addressing sexual issues in the treatment of alcoholic women. *Alcoholism Treatment Quarterly, 14*(1), 1–9.

Sparer, M. S. (1996). *Medicaid and the limits of state health reform.* Philadelphia: Temple University Press.

Specht, H., and Specht, R. (1986). Social work assessment: Route to clienthood (Part I) *Social Casework, 67,* 525–32.

Spickard, P., Fong, R., and Ewalt, P. (1996). Undermining the very basis of racism—its categories. *In* P. Ewalt, E. Freeman, S. Kirk, and D. Poole (Eds.), *Multicultural issues in social work.* (pp. 14–20). Washington, DC: NASW Press.

Spiegel, D. (1999). *Efficacy and cost-effectiveness of psychotherapy.* Washington, DC: American Psychiatric Press.

Spike, J. (1997). Commentary. *Hastings Center Report, 27*(January–February), 25–26.

State Children's Health Program of 1997, 42 U.S.C. 1397 et seq.

Steiner, J. R., Gross, G. M., Ruffolo, M. C., and Murray, J. J. (1994). Strategic planning in non-profits: Profit from it. *Administration in Social Work, 18*(2), 87–106.

Stern, S., Smith, C. A., and Jang, S. J. (1999). Urban families and adolescent mental health. *Social Work Research, 23*(1), 15–27.

Stewart, A. L., Hays, R., and Ware, J. (1988). Communication: The MOS short-form general health survey: Reliability and validity in a patient population. *Medical Care, 26,* 724–35.

Stiller, J. M., Won, D. K., Donham, C. S., Long, A. M., and Stewart, M. W. (1996). National health expenditures, 1995. *Health Care Financing Review, 18*(1), 175–98.

Strebel, P. (1996). Why do employees resist change? *Harvard Business Review,* (May–June), 86–92.

Strom, K. (1992). Reimbursement demands and treatment decisions: A growing dilemma for social workers. *Social Work, 37*(5), 398–403.

Strom-Gottfried, K. (1998). Is ethical managed care an oxymoron? *Families-in-Society, 79*(3), 297–307.

Stroul, B. A., Pires, S. A., Armstrong, M. I., and Meyers, J. C. (1998). The impact of managed care on mental health services for children and their families. *The Future of Children, 8*(2), 119–33.

Studdert, D. M., and Brennan, T. A. (1997). HIV infection and the Americans with Disabilities Act: An evolving interaction. *Annals of the American Academy of Political and Social Science, 549* (January), 84–100.

Sunley, R. (1997). Advocacy in the new world of managed care. *Families in Society, 78*(1), 84–94.

Supplemental Security Income, 42 U.S.C., 1320 et seq.

Taft, J. (1937). The relation of function to process in social casework. *Journal of Social Work Process, 1*(1), 1–18.

Tarasoff v. *Regents of the University of California,* 17 Cal. 3d425, 55 P. 2d334 (1976).

Temporary Assistance for Needy Families 1996, 42 U.S.C. 605 et seq.

Thomas, H., and Caplan, T. (1999). Spinning the group process wheel: Effective facilitation techniques for motivating involuntary client groups. *Social Work with Groups, 21*(4), 3–21.

Thyer, B. A., and Hudson, W. W. (1987). Progress in behavioral social work: An introduction. *Journal of Social Service Research, 10*(2/3/4): 1–6.

Tolson, E. R. (1988). *The metamodel and clinical social work.* New York: Columbia University Press.

Tolson, E. R., Reid, W., and Garvin, C. D. (1994). *Generalist practice: A task-centered approach.* New York: Columbia University Press.

Towle, C. (1969). Social work: Cause and function. In H. Perlman (Ed.), *Helping: Charlotte Towle on social work and social casework* (pp. 277–99). Chicago: University of Chicago Press.

Tracy, E. (1995). Family preservation and home-based services. In R. L. Edwards (Ed.), *Encyclopedia of social work* (19th ed.) (pp. 973–83). Washington, DC: NASW Press.

Tracy, E. M., and Whittaker, J. K. (1990). The social support network map: Assessing social support in clinical practice. *Families in Society, 71*, 461–70.

Trolander, J. A. (1973). The response of settlements to the Great Depression. *Social Work, 18*(5), 92–102.

Tufte, E. R. (1997). *Visual explanations: Images and quantities, evidence and narrative.* Cheshire, CT: Graphics Press.

Turner, F. J. (Ed.). (1979). *Social work treatment: Interlocking approaches* (2nd ed.). New York: Free Press.

U.S. Bureau of the Census. (1990). Statistical abstract of the United States (110th ed.). Washington, DC: Government Printing Office.

Vitberg, A. K. (1996). *Marketing health care into the twenty-first century: The changing dynamic.* New York: Haworth.

Wakefield, J. (1996a). Does social work need the eco-systems perspective? Part 1: Is the perspective clinically useful? *Social Service Review, 70*(1), 1–32.

Wakefield, J. (1996b). Does social work need the eco-systems perspective? Part 2: Does the perspective save social work from incoherence? *Social Service Review, 70*(2), 183–219.

Wallace, A. F. C. (1985). Rethinking technology "and" culture: or What is the nature of "fit"? *Mellon Seminar on Technology and Culture*. Philadelphia: University of Pennsylvania.

Walsh, P. C., and Worthington, J. F. (1995). *The Prostate*. Baltimore: Johns Hopkins University Press.

Walther, V., Mason, J., and Preisinger, J. (1997). Social work in a perinatal AIDS program. In T. S. Kerson (Ed.), *Social work in health settings: Practice in context* (2nd ed.) (pp. 69–88). New York: Haworth.

Walton, M., Jakobowski, D., and Barnsteiner, J. (1993). A collaborative practice model for the clinical nurse specialist. *Journal of Nursing Administration, 23*(2), 55–59.

Wardell, P. J. (1988). The implications of changing organizational relationships and resource constraints for human services survival: A case study. *Administration in Social Work, 12*(1), 89–105.

Ware, J. E., and Sherbourne, C. D. (1992). The MOS 36-item short form health survey (SF-36): Conceptual framework and item selection, Part I. *Medical Care, 30*, 473–81.

Ware, J. E. (1997). Health care outcomes from the patient's point of view. In E. J. Mullen and J. L. Magnabosco (Eds.), *Outcome measurement in the human services: Cross-cutting issues and methods* (pp. 44–67). Washington, DC: NASW Press.

Ware, J. E., Snow, K. K., Kosinski, M., and Gandek, B. (1993). *SF36 health survey manual and interpretation guide*. Boston: New England Medical Center Health Institute.

Warren, R. B., and Warren, D. I. (1977). *The neighborhood organizer's handbook*. Notre Dame, IN: University of Notre Dame Press.

Warren, R. B., and Warren, D. I. (1984). How to diagnose a neighborhood. In F. M. Cox, J. Rothman, and J. L. Erlich (Eds.), *Tactics and techniques of community practice* (pp. 27–40). Itasca, IL: Peacock.

Wasow, M. (1997). He's schizophrenic and the system is not helping: Reflections of a troubled parent and professional. In T. S. Kerson (Ed.), *Social work in health settings: Practice in context* (2nd ed.) (pp. 523–38). New York: Haworth.

Weaver, H. N. (1999). Indigenous people and the social work profession: Defining culturally competent services. *Social Work, 44*(3), 217–25.

Weick, K. (1996). Prepare your organization to fight fires. *Harvard Business Review*, (May–June), 143–48.

Weinberg, L. (1996). Seeing through organization: Exploring the constitutive quality of social relations. *Administration and Society, 28*(2), 177–204.

Weiner, B. A., and Wettstein, R. M. (1993). *Legal issues in mental health care*. New York: Plenum.

Weisman, A. D., and Worden, J. W. (1976–77). The existential plight in cancer: Significance of the first 100 days. *International Journal of Psychiatry in Medicine, 7*(1), 1–15.

Weiss, C., and Kerson, T. S. (1997). Intensive case management for people with serious and persistent mental illness. In T. S. Kerson (Ed.), *Social work in health settings: Practice in context* (2nd ed.) (pp. 505–22). New York: Haworth.

Weiss, C. (1972). *Evaluation research: Methods of assessing program effectiveness.* Englewood Cliffs, NJ: Prentice Hall.

Wells, C. C., and Masch, M. K. (1991). Social work ethics day to day: Guidelines for professional practice. New York: Waveland.

Wells, R. (1994). *Planned short-term treatment.* New York: Free Press.

Wernet, S. P. (Ed.). (1999). *Managed care in human services.* Chicago: Lyceum Books.

Werrbach, G. (1996). Family strengths-based intensive child case management. *Families in Society, 77*(4), 216–26.

West, J. (1991). The social and policy context of the act. *Milbank Quarterly, 69* (supp. 1–2), 3–24.

Westmoreland, T. M., and Perez, T. (2000). Letter to State Medicaid Directors (January 14).

Wetlaufer, S. (1994). The team that wasn't. *Harvard Business Review,* (November–December), 22–37.

Wettstein, R. M. (1995). Competence. In W. T. Reich (Ed.), *Encyclopedia of bioethics* (Rev. ed.) (pp. 445–51). New York: Macmillan.

Wholey, J. S. (1979). *Evaluation: Promise and performance.* Washington, DC: Urban Institute.

Wholey, J. S. (1983). *Evaluation and effective public management.* Boston: Little, Brown.

Wholey, J. S. (1986). Using evaluation to improve government performance. *Evaluation Practice, 7,* 5–13.

Wholey, J. S. (1991). Evaluation for program improvement. In W. Shadish, T. Cook, and L. Leviton (Eds.), *Foundations of program evaluation: Theories of practice* (pp. 225–69). Newbury Park, CA: Sage.

Wholey, J. S., Hatry, H. P., and Newcomer, K. E. (Eds.). (1994). *Handbook of practical program evaluation.* San Francisco, CA: Jossey-Bass.

Williams, J. B. W. (1995). Diagnostic and Statistical Manual of Mental Disorders. In R. L. Edwards (Ed.), *Encyclopedia of social work* (19th ed.) (pp. 729–39). Washington, DC: NASW Press.

Williams, J. B. W., Goldman, H., Gruenberg, A., Mezzich, J. E., and Skodol, A. E. (1990). DSM-IV in progress: The multi-axial system. *Hospital and Community Psychiatry, 40,* 1125–27.

Williamson, S., Stevens, R. E., Loudon, D. L., and Migliore, R. H. (1997). *Fundamentals of strategic planning for health care organizations.* New York: Haworth.

Wilson, S. (1978). *Confidentiality in social work.* New York: Free Press.

Wineburgh, M. (1998). Ethics, managed care, and outpatient psychotherapy. *Clinical Social Work Journal, 26*(4), 433–43.

Winslade, W. J. (1995). Confidentiality. In W. T. Reich (Ed.), *Encyclopedia of bioethics* (rev. ed.) (pp. 455–59). New York: Macmillan.

Witkin, S. L. (1999). Identities and contexts. *Social Work, 44*(4), 293–97.

Wolk, J. L., Sullivan, W. P., and Hartman, D. J. (1994). The managerial nature of case management. *Social Work, 39*(2), 152–66.

Woods, M. E., and Hollis, F. (2000). *Casework: A psychosocial therapy* (5th ed.). New York: McGraw-Hill.

World Health Organization. (2001). www.who.int/aboutwho/en/definition.html.

Wulkop, E. (1926). *The social worker in a hospital ward.* Boston: Houghton Mifflin.

Yalom, I. (1985). *The theory and practice of group psychotherapy.* New York: Basic Books.

Yankey, J. A. (1995). Strategic planning. In R. L. Edwards (Ed.), *Encyclopedia of social work* (19th ed.) (pp. 2321–28). Washington, DC: NASW Press.

Yellow Bird, M., Fong, R., Galindo, P., Nowicki, J., and Freeman, E. (1996). The multicultural mosaic. In P. L. Ewalt, E. M. Freeman, S. A. Kirk, and D. L. Poole (Eds.), *Multicultural issues in social work.* Washington, DC: NASW Press.

Young, N., Gardner, S., Coley, S., Schorr, L., and Bruner, C. (1994). *Making a difference: Moving to outcome-based accountability for comprehensive service reforms.* Falls Church, VA: National Center for Service Integration.

Zajicek-Farber, M. L. (1998). Promoting good health in adolescents with disabilities. *Health and Social Work, 23*(3), 203–13.

Zald, M. N. (1995). Organizations as polities: An analysis of community organization agencies. In J. Rothman, J. L. Erlich, and J. E. Trotman (Eds.), *Strategies of community intervention* (5th ed.) (pp. 129–39). Itasca, IL: Peacock.

Zayas, L. H. (1997). Cultural competency training for staff serving Hispanic families with a child in psychiatric crisis. *Families in Society, 78*(July–August), 405–12.

Zeira, A., and Rosen, A. (1999). Intermediate outcomes pursued by practitioners: A qualitative analysis. *Social Work Research, 23*(2), 79–87.

Zuniga, M. E. (1995). Aging: Social work practice. In R. L. Edwards (Ed.), *Encyclopedia of social work* (19th ed.) (pp. 173–83). Washington, DC: NASW Press.

Zweben, A., and Fleming, M. F. (1999). Brief interventions for alcohol and drug problems. In J. A. Tucker, D. M. Donovan, and G. A. Marlatt (Eds.), *Changing addictive behavior: Bridging clinical and public health strategies* (pp. 252–81). New York: Guilford.

Name Index

Subject Index